Galusha A. Grow

Engraved by Emily Sartain, Phil^a.

Galusha A. Grow

SPEAKER 37TH CONGRESS

Galusha A. Grow

The People's Candidate

Robert D. Ilisevich

University of Pittsburgh Press

Published by the University of Pittsburgh Press, Pittsburgh, Pa., 15260
Copyright © 1988, University of Pittsburgh Press
All rights reserved
Feffer and Simons, Inc., London
Manufactured in the United States of America

Library of Congress Cataloging-in-Publication Data

Ilisevich, Robert D.
    Galusha A. Grow : the people's candidate / Robert D. Ilisevich.
        p.   cm.
    Bibliography: p. 309.
    Includes index.
    ISBN 0-8229-3606-2
    1. Grow, Galusha A. (Galusha Aaron), 1823–1907.   2. Legislators—
United States—Biography.   3. United States. Congress. House—
Biography.   I. Title.
E415.9.G89I45   1989
328.73′092′4—dc19
[B]   88-27927
                                                                      CIP

The 9 June 1848 entry from the diary of Charles Francis Adams (microfilm edition), and a letter from Galusha Grow to Elihu B. Washburne, 17 May 1884, from the Alexander C. Washburn Autograph Collection, are quoted by permission of the Massachusetts Historical Society. The William Bigler Papers and the Simon Gratz Collection are quoted by permission of the Historical Society of Pennsylvania. The John Covode Papers are quoted by permission of the Library and Archives, Historical Society of Western Pennsylvania. The Joshua R. Giddings Papers (microfilm edition) are quoted by permission of the Ohio Historical Society. Materials pertaining to Galusha Grow are quoted by permission of the Historical Manuscripts Collection, Amherst College Library. The Charles Robinson Papers (microfilm edition) are quoted by permission of the Manuscripts Department, Kansas State Historical Society. The Ida M. Tarbell Papers are quoted by permission of the Special Collections Department, Pelletier Library, Allegheny College. The letters of David Wilmot are quoted by permission of the Bradford County (Pennsylvania) Historical Society; Grow Papers, Susquehanna County Historical Society.

To Agnes, Debbie, and Dan, my devoted family

Contents

Preface

OF ALL THE illustrious Pennsylvanians of the nineteenth century, recorded history has perhaps dealt most unjustly with Galusha A. Grow. Though his political career spanned more than a half-century, no scholarly biography has been published until now. In 1917, his executor, James T. DuBois, drawing almost exclusively from Grow's reminiscences and autobiographical notes, authored *Galusha A. Grow, Father of the Homestead Act*. This eulogistic book contains a number of interesting quotations and letters, which are not available elsewhere, but it ignores most of Grow's post–Civil War career and, particularly, his role in Pennsylvania politics.

Historians have stayed away from Grow because his personal papers were destroyed in a house fire many years ago. Fortunately, the public record remains, and it is upon this record that the present biography is based. Grow's numerous addresses and position papers complement congressional sources and his correspondence with leading statesmen of the day adds to the understanding of his political views and activities. Then there are the many newspapers whose editors wrote about the highs and lows of a career that never lacked excitement.

Missing from this wide assortment of sources, however, is sufficient material that could tell us what Grow did when he was neither in Congress nor running for elective office. Did he exhibit the same enthusiasm and righteousness in nonpolitical activities as he did in Congress or on the campaign circuit? Because of the dearth of documentary information on his business career and private life, no complete answer can be given. As expected, people remembered him differently. Some believed him to be a highly honorable, decent, patriotic citizen who was devoted to his family and friends. Others, seeing more negative qualities, characterized him as a shrewd and heartless businessman who did not hesitate to foreclose mortgages on unfortunate widows and who easily sulked in defeat. Neither group denied that Grow's political ambitions exceeded his other expectations.

His political career up to the Civil War was admirable, although it was tainted by his ardent dislike of those who defended slavery. Yet this course is understandable, for he believed slavery to be the Achilles' heel of the Democratic party and a natural impediment to the economic development of the nation. He was not one of those moderate northerners of his generation who could rise above sectional influences. Had he done so, he could not have remained in Congress because his constituents, noted for their antislavery bias, would not have supported him. The reasons why many men in the 1850s switched from the Democratic to the Republican party can be found in Grow's congressional performance. The Union and the old party of Jefferson and Jackson, in his opinion, had been manipulated, perverted, and then destroyed by the reckless exploits of selfish "slavocrats."

Grow's meteoric rise to power in the national House of Representatives, and his becoming its Speaker in 1861, were testament to his skills as a partisan combatant and parliamentarian. The stresses and strains of the Kansas controversy propelled him to the foreground of that great debate. No one in the House was better identified than Grow with the extremism generated by the territorial question. As chairman of the Committee on Territories, and then as Speaker, he personified the highhandedness and arrogance of that coterie of lawmakers who comprised the first radical Republicans.

Just as he had championed the cause of the radicals, so he championed the cause of the common man. Grow prided himself on having the respect and support of the working classes. His genuine concern for their rights and welfare was rewarded by their general endorsement of him as a favorite candidate. He defended the protective tariff, hard money, and homestead legislation because he believed they were beneficial to the masses who labored hard for a living, whether they were farmers, miners, or factory workers. He hated slavery, not simply because it was morally wrong, but also because it violated the democratic work ethic based on free labor.

His radicalism sprang from the new liberalism of the nineteenth century. Liberals had always looked with suspicion on the state and demanded that its activities be contained within narrow limits, either by constitutional guarantees or by the assumption that legislation is apt to interfere with freedom. Grow's liberalism, on the contrary, was a frank acceptance of the necessity of the government's interfering in a positive manner to contribute to freedom and the general welfare without creating evils worse than those it removed. Thus, he was convinced that the government must go further than it had in land reform. Grow's struggle for homestead legislation, a genuinely liberal federal policy of free land to actual settlers, was the most important goal of his legislative career. Granting equal, free, inalienable tracts of the public domain to settlers was only honoring man's natural right to the soil, he argued, for it allowed man to exercise his basic freedoms and, at the same time, promote the common good.

To many of his friends, Grow was the conscience of the Republican party. They saw in him everything that was ideally sound in Republicanism at a time when party leaders seemed more and more content with the notion that politics must be regarded as amoral. He never pretended to be an organization man within the state party system. Identifying himself more with the ideas and principles of the Republican party than with its workings, he naturally became a nuisance to oligarchs such as Simon Cameron and Matt Quay. Their displeasure was both his gain and his loss. While his independent course made him very popular with voters and editors who deplored the ugliness of party patronage and corruption, his differences with party bosses denied him the opportunity to achieve high elective office. They refused to endorse his candidacy for the governorship, the U.S. Senate, and the vice-presidency of the United States. Not until he was too old to be a threat did they support him for congressman-at-large, a position he held for four consecutive terms.

In his last years in Congress, Grow represented a half century of Republican leadership and thought. Playing the role of the redoubtable sage, he defended traditional party positions on issues like the tariff and generally followed the party line on current issues. For a man of eighty, he demonstrated remarkable stamina and wit. Full of the grandeur of old age, he provided a keener insight into the problems of the day than many of his younger colleagues.

Both in Congress and in Pennsylvania, Grow was as prominent and important as most of his political contemporaries in the state, including Simon Cameron, David Wilmot, and Thaddeus Stevens, all of whom have been immortalized by their biographers. It is hoped that this political study of his impact will fill a gap in knowledge about a long line of notable Pennsylvanians who are important to the student of history and government.

Acknowledgments

MANY PEOPLE assisted me in the preparation of this study. I received courtesy and cooperation from the staffs of Allegheny College Library, the Manuscript Division of the Library of Congress, the Susquehanna County Historical Society, the Historical Society of Pennsylvania, the Historical Society of Western Pennsylvania, the Kansas State Historical Society, the University of Rochester Library, the Ohio Historical Society, the Pennsylvania State University Library, the Bradford County Historical Society, the Massachusetts Historical Society, and the Pennsylvania Historical and Museum Commission in Harrisburg.

I am also grateful to Philip S. Klein, Emeritus Professor of the Pennsylvania State University, and Professor Van Beck Hall of the University of Pittsburgh for reading the entire manuscript and offering helpful suggestions. My editors at the University of Pittsburgh Press, especially Jane Flanders, did a splendid job of guiding the work through its final stages of production.

My greatest debt of gratitude is owed to Professor James A. Kehl of the University of Pittsburgh. He suggested the study many years ago, encouraged me in its progress, and gave every chapter a careful and critical reading.

Galusha A. Grow

1

The First Hurrah

TWO IMMODERATE desires obsessed Galusha A. Grow on that August morning in 1844. The first was to involve himself in what would become one of the bitterest presidential campaigns in the nation's history; the other was to get home. He had just graduated from Amherst College, where he had spent four years compiling a distinguished, if not brilliant, record. Now it was time to return to the hills of Pennsylvania that he missed so much.

On that particularly warm day he was in Springfield, Massachusetts, saying goodbye to friends and taking in a massive Whig rally. Daniel Webster, Horace Greeley, R. C. Winthrop, and Rufus Choate debated the Texas annexation question and slavery before a crowd estimated at 15,000 to 20,000. The two issues were foremost in the minds of many Americans and were destined to influence the course of Grow's political career. In an age when oratory and debate flourished, he was witnessing the very best. Capable of creating a magnificent illusion that what they were saying was exactly what their listeners believed, these speakers personalized the issues and enthralled audiences with allegory and wit. Many in the crowd had come to hear Webster, the greatest of all northern Whigs. He probed into the real motivation behind the annexation of Texas and warned the crowd that, whatever the disguise, the intent among southerners was to extend slave power.[1]

Still, Grow was less impressed with what Webster and others had to say than with how they said it. As a keen student of debate, he was interested in their style and techniques. Grow was not unaware of his own abilities as an orator. For a young man approaching his twenty-first birthday, he had already attained a reputation as a fine extemporaneous speaker. A fellow classmate and Psi Upsilon brother of his, writing shortly after Grow's first election to Congress, con-

3

firmed this talent.[2] He was never without words, the friend remarked, and his skills as a speaker won him audiences on campus as well as in the village coffeehouses and lyceums. He participated in the "exhibitions" put on at the college, which consisted of orations, disquisitions, and disputations. In the spring exhibition of 1843, for instance, Grow is credited with a disputation: "Is Credulity Unfavorable to the Discovery of Truth?" On the same program he took part in a colloquy, "The Thaumaturgic Therapeutikon," written by a classmate.[3]

.At his commencement he delivered a short address entitled "Moral Mobocracy." It was an ornate essay with a simple theme: the pursuit of truth despite all adversity. Commenting about a progressive society in which institutions must adapt to the new discoveries of science, Grow said, "He who would cling blindly to all the notions of other times is suicidal to the best interest of the present. For while truth and society are progressive, he who would seek the one with an honest heart and fearless mind cannot entertain all the opinions of his predecessors."[4]

As a college freshman, Grow gained instant notoriety for his inability to adapt to New England propriety. His gestures were crude and his expressions naive; indicative of the simple life on the Susquehanna and in the forests of north-central Pennsylvania, they excited his more sophisticated classmates to uncontrollable laughter. He knew more of the sublimities of the Alleghenies and the agonies of frontier survival than of Homer, Virgil, or Tacitus. But Amherst marked the intersection of these two seemingly incompatible cultures in Grow's life and provided the anvil on which a forceful character was forged. With forbearance and patience he overcame his apparent shortcomings. Awkwardness soon gave way to a polished demeanor that earned him the respect of students and teachers. As his speech and eloquence improved, he became more of an activist, with democracy, popular rights, and Jeffersonian idealism his constant texts. He showed no reverence for moss-covered systems, monopolies, and aristocracies. Before Grow had completed his studies, his classmates were predicting that with his talents and compassion for humanity he would someday sit in Congress.

Life in New England may have been strange to Grow, but the countryside was not. He had spent the first ten years of his life in his native state of Connecticut. His birthplace was Ashford, Windham County, and his date of birth is generally accepted as August 31, 1823.[5] He was slightly more than four when his father, Joseph, died, leaving a widow and six children; Galusha was the second youngest. After the father's death the family temporarily scattered, and Galusha went to live with his grandfather, Samuel Robbins, a Revolutionary War veteran. Robbins kept a hotel at Voluntown, some twenty-five miles away, where the boy earned his keep by doing general household chores. What influence his grandfather may have had on him is unknown, but it is reasonable to presume that the old man filled his grandson's head with tales and legends of the great war with Britain, the raising of liberty poles, and the battles between New England Federalists and Republicans.

In 1834, when he was nearly eleven, Galusha left Connecticut with his mother, Elizabeth Grow, brother Edwin, sisters Julia and Elizabeth, and several other families to go "up country" to northern Pennsylvania. Elizabeth Grow purchased the old homestead of Solomon Millard, one of the early settlers of Lenox township, Susquehanna County. The farm of some four hundred acres sat in the valley of Tunkhannock Creek near the village of Glenwood, about fifteen miles from the junction of the creek with the Susquehanna River, in a peaceful glen surrounded by high green hills. Whether the land was sufficiently fertile to support a large family remained to be seen.

Subsistence farming and poverty were universal in the valley. In Connecticut the Grows had observed farm families of some means, but in Susquehanna they witnessed many settlers grubbing out a living on land that at best was marginal in quality. Different levels of rural poverty existed — the poor and the very poor. Often the hardworking pioneer lived in destitute humility. While plowing his land with a yoke of oxen borrowed from a more prosperous neighbor, he was most likely trying to pay off some land shark. Young Grow could not help but pity those who were worse off than his own family. In a society dominated by money, power, and privilege, he soon nourished a deep regard for the downtrodden and harbored an unrelenting prejudice against the speculator who invidiously used an inequitable land system against the settler. These were probably the first signs Grow detected that a new testament of land development was needed; its exact nature gradually took form in his mind over the succeeding decades.

Grow had great admiration for his mother. She called him "Boy Galusha," a name mockingly used later by his political opponents. Psychologists might accuse Elizabeth Grow of being an overbearing and possessive mother, and she probably was. She made the major decisions in the household and became a businesswoman. But what were the alternatives for a pioneer widow with six children to raise by herself? Galusha was normally responsive to his mother's advice. When she insisted that he seriously pursue his studies, first at Franklin Academy and then at Amherst, to become an attorney, he obeyed. Perhaps it was due to her meddling that Grow never married. Her standards for a suitable wife were so high that no local girl could qualify. But he remembered his mother as a lovable, fun-loving woman who also possessed a good business mind. Later in life Grow admitted that he was indebted to his mother for whatever success he had.

Since farming was insufficient to meet the family's needs, Elizabeth Grow opened a general store in the farmhouse. One of her older sons, Frederick, who had been left at Voluntown to clear up family affairs, came to Glenwood and soon thereafter was put in charge of the store. With Galusha as his chief clerk, they traded groceries and finished goods for dairy products, bark, and hides. With business flourishing, the Grows erected a three-room building to handle the increased volume. In time the family decided to try their fortune in the lumber industry. It was not long before Galusha and his brothers were rafting boards down the Tunkhannock to markets along the Susquehanna and out into Chesapeake Bay, reaching such distant points as Port Deposit and Annapolis.

Galusha was fourteen when he made his first trip down the river. The depression caused in 1837 by the financial panic hurt the lumber industry. Lumbermen faced with a dull market reached far to find new customers. Frederick instructed young Galusha to go as far south as Richmond or Norfolk, if necessary, to sell the lumber and then to meet him in Baltimore with the cash. Galusha started on a journey that would take him into strange lands. Outside Annapolis he found a customer who owned a plantation. It was the first time he had seen slaves working in the field. When he was asked what the people up north thought of slavery, the young raftsman replied that they did not like it and that someday they would end it. In the nation's capital he witnessed with apprehension, as did many other visitors, the horrors of the slave trade that so disturbed John Q. Adams as he sat in Congress.

In the autumn of 1840 Grow entered Amherst and began an education that would cost about $400 per year. The fact that his family and friends believed college to be too expensive probably troubled him and therefore prompted him to do his very best. The choice of Amherst may have been the result of the influence of William S. Tyler, a friend who had been associated with Franklin Academy and was now a professor of Greek and Latin at the college. Although Grow was eager to prepare himself for the law, he took his mother's advice and studied surveying as a practical alternative career. In a country bursting with new settlements, there was a growing need for surveyors.

Grow may have thought about some of these experiences as he journeyed home after graduation from Amherst, but his attention turned more to the current presidential campaign, which seemed to be generating greater enthusiasm than the hard-cider crusade of four years earlier. Everywhere there were reminders of the upcoming elections: party broadsides and banners were freely displayed on wagons, storefronts, and farm buildings. In addition to speeches and position papers of national leaders, newspapers carried accounts of the latest regional and local political happenings. Their editorials, long and short, either lashed out at the candidates or supported them with vigor. The cigar-smoking, tobacco-chewing politicos in their fancy garb strutted down the streets of every town and village, appearing as obvious as a Santa Claus in a toy department and promising as much.

Not far from the Susquehanna County line, a Democratic rally was in progress. About two hundred men, women, and children were jammed in wagons and carriages, some decorated with hickory. (Hickory was a term associated with the Democratic party.) Even the teams of oxen and horses wore colorful ribbons. A brassy band of pretentiously dressed amateur musicians trudged ahead of the cavalcade, blaring out tunes, which helped electrify the crowd but terrified the already weary animals. Suddenly everything stopped at a predetermined site and everyone disembarked. Thunderous cheers of "Polk and Dallas" filled the surrounding fields. Several banners with Democratic mottos were unfurled: "No National Bank" and "Tariff for the Support of Government." Amid more cheers, a hundred-foot hickory pole displaying the stars and stripes was hoisted overhead. After the demonstrators ate and drank from a neatly dressed table, they settled back in small groups in a shady grove, fanning themselves with newspapers and bonnets as they listened to speeches by party spokesmen. Despite its spontaneity, the entire scene seemed so remarkably planned that it was unreal.

What was real was the hope of the participants. This fanfare on a hot August afternoon reflected the party's optimism in the election year. None denied that the party faced organizational problems, but the issue of national expansion in 1844 gave the Democrats an issue that appeared less divisive than domestic questions. To them the issue was much better than the log-cabin, coonskin humbug that the Whigs were handing out to the voters. The thought of the nation moving further westward appealed to the uninhibited imagination of the typical American. It was a timely topic as well. Both Texas and Oregon were waiting to enter the Union, while California or, for that matter, all of Mexico seemed available for the taking. A New York journalist, John L. O'Sullivan, later used the phrase "manifest destiny" to replace the traditional arguments for territorial acquisition. Catchwords and catch phrases such as "faith," "inevitability," and "spiritual exaltation" seemed to derive their force from teleological laws of immutability. How could anyone deny them?

But expansion contained hidden dangers and was therefore a source of irritation and embarrassment to the party's stalwarts. Certainly they did not wish to see party unity broken on the wheel of sectionalism. But when John C. Calhoun, as secretary of state, opened treaty negotiations with Texas and officially admitted that the preservation of slavery was the controlling motive in his annexation diplomacy, the antislavery Democrats became enraged because many of them were supporters of Martin Van Buren, who opposed the annexation.[6] When their leader failed to receive the nomination at the Democratic National Convention in May, they sought revenge. To make the break between themselves and the Calhoun forces complete, the Van Burenites helped defeat the Texas bill in the Senate.

The antislavery faction as an antidote to the present danger of expansion was neutralized almost immediately. Instead, a realignment of Democratic leaders and bosses, representing each section of the country, was nationalizing the Texas and Oregon questions within the framework of manifest destiny. This new political cadre moved toward the control center of the party and included such prominent names as James Buchanan, Lewis Cass, Robert J. Walker, William Marcy, Stephen A. Douglas, John C. Calhoun, and James K. Polk. By the time of the national convention in Baltimore it had become clear that Van Buren was being seriously challenged as the titular head of the party.

The Van Burenites approached the quadrennial convention confident of another nomination for their man, since more than half the delegates were committed to him. But long before the delegates arrived in Baltimore, the support base for Van Buren had already cracked and many of his backers were defecting. Party brass in hotels, boardinghouses, and taverns lamented the fact that the New Yorker had spoken out too loudly against the annexation of Texas. The convention planners were betting that Texas would prove an unbeatable issue. Whatever their ultimate designs on party and campaign, members of this group were convinced that Van Buren was not their man in 1844. When his opponents proposed the infamous two-thirds rule of 1832 for the selection of a presidential nominee, cries of protest were heard among his supporters. But the motion easily carried because of the strong endorsements from the Illinois, Michigan, and Pennsylvania delegations. Van Buren could command a majority perhaps, but never two-thirds. The same rule that blocked his candidacy, however, was now used by his supporters to manipulate the balloting. Their wrath was not to be denied.

So the battle of ballots among the titans, particularly Buchanan and Cass, was on. When it became apparent that none of the favorites could win the convention shifted its attention to Polk of Tennessee, who is usually considered a dark-horse candidate. Because this unpretentious, humorless, shy man had received the personal blessing of Andrew Jackson, the delegates bestowed upon him the name "Young Hickory." What was good for the old sage at the Hermitage was also good for them. Like his mentor, Polk was a staunch expansionist and he swayed the majority of the delegates. The second position on the ticket was offered to Sen. Silas Wright of New York, a supporter of Van Buren; he used the new electric telegraph to decline. The delegates then picked George M. Dallas of Pennsylvania as their vice-presidential nominee. As another conciliatory gesture to the northerners the "reoccupation of Oregon" was given equal treatment on the platform with the "reannexation of Texas."

With their work done, the Democratic delegates went home. Struck by the strange course of events, they prepared to make adjustments in their campaign game plan. What months earlier had promised to be a campaign headed by Van Buren, Buchanan, or Cass, and waged over issues like the tariff and the bank, now demanded new strategies. On the surface, expansionism looked popular enough and promised sufficient catalytic strength to pull together the factions that had asserted themselves in Baltimore. But the potential for disruption manifested itself in one word: Texas. With the candidacy of Polk, a southern expansionist, and the likelihood that southern influence would increase in Washington, the issue of slavery loomed greater than ever. Before these fears and hopes could be tested, however, the ticket of Polk and Dallas had to triumph over Henry Clay and the Whigs.

The Whigs greeted the Democratic ticket with wit and song:

> Come, Log Cabin boys, come one and come all,
> This Polk stalk we surely will bury next fall,
> Our country its seeds ne'er again will infest,
> While we merrily shout for Clay of the West,
> > For Clay of the West,
> > For Clay of the West,
> While we merrily shout for Clay of the West.

Optimism ran high. Delegates to the Whig National Convention nominated Clay, now sixty-seven, by acclamation; they were confident that the Kentuckian's notoriety would pull the party bandwagon up and down and across the country to ultimate victory. The Whig platform did not equivocate on matters of economic policy, but it lacked something, perhaps emotionalism and commitment, in foreign affairs.

Conservative bosses from the North and the South were deeply concerned that the Texas matter threatened the peace with Mexico, and they pursued a moderate and safe course. Antislavery Whigs, like their Democratic counterparts, did not trust southern intentions with regard to Texas. But it was Henry Clay's vacillation on the annexation issue that caused the most embarrassment for the party. Every time he wrote a letter to explain exactly where he stood on the issue, he sank deeper and deeper into the quagmire. Whig newspapers, on the defensive, wasted editorial space trying to spell out what their candidate really meant. The Democratic press enjoyed the constant switch in positions immensely. Clay was lampooned not only for wavering on the Texas question, but also for being a poorer tariff man than his reputation suggested. Optimistic Whigs, however, concluded that the election pivoted more on personalities than on issues. How could any voter, they asked, reject the legendary Clay for the unknown Polk? It was a salient point, but such confidence failed to soften the blow of defeat when it came.

That Taste of Victory

Grow returned home in time to share in the campaign hullabaloo. Susquehanna County, along with Bradford and Tioga, made up Pennsylvania's Twelfth Congressional District, an area that would soon be known as the Wilmot district. Commonly referred to as the northern tier of counties, it had a rich Democratic tradition. As those Democrats reeled from the disasters of the Baltimore convention, attitudes ranged from contemptuous disgust to benign apathy. Many had worked hard for Van Buren and had lost; others were disappointed Buchanan supporters. Neither Polk nor Dallas was palatable to the dominant Buchanan wing of the party, and the antislavery element was aghast over the prospect of a southern administration in Washington. But throughout the district and the state, for the most part, the party faithful, with the Democratic press leading the way, pleaded for unity and wasted little time in making a moderately graceful adjustment to the political realities of the situation.

Grow joined the majority of Democrats who were not seeking revenge but wanted only sweet victory at the polls. As a neophyte in politics, he had little choice if he intended to progress in the party. Political apprenticeships are usually well structured and built upon party tradition, discipline, and protocol; Grow's was no exception. He busily performed his assigned tasks and ran errands for the bosses and candidates. And though he traveled extensively in the district, he spent a large amount of time in his own county, where he became best known. He assisted the special and correspondence committees in circulating party literature, but speechmaking became his greatest asset. He delivered his first address at the south end of the bridge that crossed the Susquehanna at Hallstead, then called Great Bend Village, not far from the New York state line. Long before the campaign ended, he became noted for his eloquence, a reputation which had carried over from his college days and would continue throughout his career. One of Grow's attributes and a contributing factor to his success was his ability to move a crowd, even a hostile one.

Selling the Baltimore package to the district voters was not the easiest part of the campaign. Aside from the Texas question and the Polk-Dallas combination, the gubernatorial candidate, Francis R. Shunk, also presented a problem for local Democrats. They viewed him as too close an ally to Buchanan and the crafty Simon Cameron, a particular anathema to the Van Burenites. Cameron had opposed Van Buren at the convention, allegedly for his free-trade views, and had pushed for Buchanan's candidacy.[7]

Perhaps the only bright spot on the ticket was the party's unanimous choice for Congress, David Wilmot. He was running for the first of three successive terms he would serve before being replaced by Grow. The affable candidate from Towanda in Bradford County had supported Van Buren and seemed to show little enthusiasm for the national ticket. But, being a good Democrat, Wilmot did not reject it. His opponent was Col. David M. Bull, who ran on a protective tariff issue as an independent. The opposition press labeled Bull a Whig even though that party showed little interest in his candidacy, but he did manage to get a number of Whigs to vote for him. They were joined by high-tariff Democrats who assaulted Wilmot for his repeated remonstrances and public condemnation of the tariff of 1842. Wilmot's pledge to modify that measure was unpopular; most Pennsylvanians supported the protectionist movement. In some parts of the commonwealth the tariff was not looked upon as a key issue in the campaign, but in Wilmot's district it became just that because of his position.[8] Despite the tariff controversy, Wilmot carried his district by nearly 3,000 votes — a better victory margin than was earned by the state electoral ticket or by Polk.

The victory cemented a friendship between Grow and Wilmot that lasted until the latter's death in 1868. The influence of one career on the other was significant. Evidence of this relationship can be gleaned from passages in Grow's reminiscences, but the compatibility of their public statements provides the most convincing proof, especially with regard to their views on the tariff, labor, hard money, special interest groups, and slavery in the territories. Grow's views were neither the mirror of his friend's, nor were they in fundamental conflict. The differences between them lay more in procedure and method than in concept.

The two men had a great deal in common, though they were different in physical appearance.[9] Both traced their political roots back to Jackson and Jefferson, but what Democrat didn't? Neither had to bear the drudgery of sitting in the state legislature before being elected to Congress. Both were gifted orators and masters in debate. Late in life Grow remarked that he knew of no one who could debate issues better while sitting down than Wilmot. As youngsters, each had suffered the loss of a parent and had watched the remaining one scramble to provide security for the family. Like many young men in the first half of the century, both pursued the study of law, which they considered tedious and uninteresting, largely because it was a respectable profession. Of the two Wilmot was probably the better attorney. Politically, they maintained the tradition of being "radical" in a district noted for its Democratic radicalism. Believing that principles and issues were more important than party organization, both men found it exceedingly difficult to understand or cope with the machinations of political bosses and hacks. Col. Alexander K. McClure wrote of Grow a few years before his death: "He was not a political manager in the narrow and meaner sense of the term. No man could better master a broad wise policy for the party in State or Nation, but he was a stranger to the arts of modern politics, and for many years was not in favor with the dominant power of the Republican party in Pennsylvania."[10]

When both men believed that enough Jeffersonianism had been stripped from the Democratic party and sacrificed for expediency in the Kansas-Nebraska debacle, they broke from the party and took an active lead in the formation of the Republican party. Grow and

Wilmot were purists at a time when great causes and issues were dominant. Finally, both achieved immortality by associating themselves
with measures that played a major part in the development of the
West: the proviso to prevent the spread of slavery in the territories
and the homestead bill.

The warm relationship between Grow and Wilmot prepared them
for the disharmony in the aftermath of the 1844 victory. President Polk's
prosperity did not include a united party. His election had presaged
both a policy of nationalizing slavery extension and a modification
of the tariff of 1842. In the Democratic canvass the first issue had been
candy-coated with the romantic lure of expansionism, and the latter
had been subdued by the usual gesture of campaign promises. Polariza-
tion over these two issues intensified in the first year of Polk's administration. Nowhere was this fact clearer than in Wilmot's district
where the intraparty imbroglio over the selection of a U.S. senator
preceded the trauma over the tariff and proviso. The rift was to have
a lasting effect upon Grow's career.

When Sen. James Buchanan resigned the day after Polk's inauguration, Cameron decided to run for the vacancy. The obvious choice
of the Democratic party was Judge George W. Woodward of Luzerne.
The Whigs did not caucus to nominate anyone because they knew
their candidate would stand little chance in a Democratic-controlled
legislature. As a would-be lawyer Wilmot had studied in Woodward's
Wilkes-Barre law office. The two were not only old friends, but also
disciples of Polk, who endorsed a tariff for revenue — with protection
secondary. This alignment was not adequate to subdue Cameron.
With a firm grip on patronage through the Canal Board, coupled with
his advocacy of protection and his support for the distribution of the
proceeds from the sale of public lands, Cameron connived with Whigs,
Native Americans, and enough protection Democrats in the legislature to secure the election on the fifth ballot. Most Democrats were
shocked, but their appeal to Buchanan and Vice-President Dallas to
do something about Cameron's effrontery failed to result in any censure. Buchanan urged that the election of Cameron be accepted in
the spirit of party harmony.[11]

Wilmot considered the request unsatisfactory. He was sure that
Buchanan had been at least partially responsible for Woodward's defeat. His suspicions were later confirmed when the U.S. Senate rejected Woodward's nomination for a seat to the Supreme Court. Polk
believed that Cameron had manipulated the vote against Woodward
and that Buchanan also had conspired to defeat the nomination so
that he might secure the office himself.[12] This exposed the rift be-

tween Wilmot and Buchanan to public view and produced a permanent fissure in the Democratic party of Pennsylvania. The ensuing battle indubitably disrupted the party and punctured the political careers of both men and their associates, including Grow.

Wilmot and Buchanan were as deeply involved in the tariff controversy as were Cameron and Polk. The maelstrom which engulfed the four of them equaled the intensity of the Woodward incidents. During the campaign Polk could not avoid addressing himself to the tariff, the issue of foremost importance to Pennsylvanians. He may have mollified their apprehensions with his famous letter to John K. Kane of Philadelphia, which implied the possibility that the protective policy might not be abandoned.[13] Surprisingly, the letter satisfied both the free traders and the protectionists, but Polk's inaugural, in which he declared himself against a tariff for protection, rekindled protectionist anxieties. In his message to Congress in December 1845, he insisted that "making suitable modifications and reductions of the rates of duty imposed by our present tariff laws" would permit the government "to raise revenue to pay the necessary expenses of government."[14] His position was supported by the accompanying report of his treasury secretary, Robert J. Walker of Mississippi, who was becoming a defender of the policy of free and unrestricted trade among nations. Earlier, when Walker's report had been read to the cabinet, Buchanan attacked it as a "strong free trade document." After the documents had been presented to Congress, both Wilmot and Cameron congratulated the president; the wily senator commented "We Pennsylvanians may scratch a little about the tariff but we will not quarrel about it."[15]

Cameron and other Pennsylvanians must have scratched a great deal in the months that followed. Whether they liked it or not, the tariff was up for another review. In June the House of Representatives resolved itself into a Committee of the Whole to consider the tariff of 1842 and its proposed substitutes. With the exception of Wilmot, the entire Pennsylvania delegation voted consistently against every move to change the current law; its Democratic members even refused to attend the party caucus when the tariff was discussed. Their supporters in Harrisburg adopted resolutions instructing the Pennsylvania senators and representatives in Washington to resist any tariff revision, but opposition to these resolutions came from Bradford and Tioga counties. Wilmot prepared to attack the present tariff system as he had promised he would. On July 1, 1846, he addressed the House, repeating many of the points he and Grow had stressed during the campaign.[16] He rejected the argument of the protectionists that high restrictive and prohibitory duties benefit the whole nation and all its industries. As he saw it, protection as it was generally understood benefited the manufacturer, not the farmer and the mechanic. In his perception, it contributed to the creation of a privileged class and reduced the free laborer to a degrading and disgusting condition worse than slavery. In addition, he reasoned that maritime and commercial interests would suffer when international trade was stifled. Denying that he was a free-trade exponent, he simply advocated a tariff for revenue and protection for labor.

If Wilmot annoyed the Democratic protectionists of Pennsylvania, then another Pennsylvanian, Vice-President Dallas, surely must have infuriated them. When the Walker measure reached the Senate in late July, after having been adopted by the House, Dallas found himself entrapped. His problem was one of conscience. How could he not support an administration measure even though he was known as a protectionist? When he saw that the senators were evenly divided on the House bill, he probably wished he were anywhere but in the Senate chamber. Realizing that he would have to cast the tie breaker, he explained his reasons for the position he was about to take. Though there were provisions in the bill he did not like, he believed it to be on the whole a better piece of legislation than the 1842 act.

His approval and the president's signature on July 30, 1846, set off an avalanche of editorial opinion, most of it negative, across the commonwealth and catapulted the tariff into the 1846 campaign. One Whig paper in Pittsburgh was quick to see a possible relationship between the new tariff and the war with Mexico. Since the act was a revenue measure, and since it was framed *after* Polk had involved the country in the war, the editor asked whether it was not logical to assume that the administration's intention was to increase the government's income to wage hostilities.[17] And while the president was celebrating this hard-fought victory, dissidents in Pennsylvania were burning Dallas in effigy. No one bothered to distinguish between Democratic and Whig torchbearers; the anger was universal. Despite the demonstrations and the many threats against him, the vice-president managed to remain remarkably cool.

Many observers were surprised by Pennsylvania's behavior. Polk had not anticipated such negativism, and many southerners could not understand the state's grievances. The *Charleston Mercury* remarked that just because Pennsylvania was "too ignorant and stupid" to realize what the real issues in the last election were, it was pretentious of her to blame Congress for passing this bill.[18] Most Pennsylvania voters probably attributed the ignorance and stupidity less to a misunderstanding of the issues than to the selection of representatives who had misrepresented the issues, or had failed to defend the state's vested interests, or both. In any event, the campaign was used to flush out the guilty.

Law or Politics?

During all this political turmoil, Grow perfunctorily prepared for a career in law, much to the satisfaction of his mother. After the 1844 elections he had returned to New England, not far from his birthplace, to the Hampton, Connecticut, office of Chauncey E. Cleveland, a man who was to compile a distinguished record as state legislator, governor, and congressman. Noted as a progressive Democrat, Cleveland dedicated himself to those principles of human justice commonly associated with Jeffersonian egalitarianism. Grow read law in Cleveland's office for only a few months before returning home; what influence the attorney may have had upon Grow's budding career is unknown. One might think that some of Cleveland's crusading zeal was passed on to the young man from Susquehanna. If anything, Grow's short sojourn in Connecticut probably enabled him to define better the crucial issues of the day. The burning of schools for black children in Connecticut and New Hampshire and the persecution of abolitionists in Massachusetts stirred him deeply and broadened the scope of his social philosophy. Most likely he moved closer toward an antislavery stance because violence often strengthens one's convictions. Later in life he remarked that incidents like those in New England "drove [him] into the anti-expansionist Democratic party of the North."[19] When he left Connecticut, little did he imagine that someday he would be fighting the evils of slavery alongside Cleveland as the two served together in the Thirty-second Congress. A few years later, they bolted the Democratic party with other free-soilers and joined the new Republican party.

In early 1845 Grow was reading law in the office of Ralph B. Little and Farris B. Streeter of Montrose, Susquehanna County. These two young men later distinguished themselves as attorneys in northeast Pennsylvania. Here Grow remained until April 1847 when he was finally admitted to the bar on the motion of Little. He opened his office on Turnpike Street in Montrose and immediately ran an advertisement in the local paper:[20]

G. A. Grow
Attorney at Law — office on Turnpike St.,
two doors East of Bentley and Read's Drug Store.

Just how good an attorney was Grow? Certainly he was not re-membered as a brilliant one. There is no evidence to suggest that he was ever seriously considered for a judgeship or that he ever craved a position on the bench. His close friends seemed to believe that he was quite able; his political opponents, however, claimed he was so mediocre that he drifted from partner to partner until he concluded that law was not to be his purpose in life. For most of his biographers the only bright feature in Grow's legal career was his partnership with Wilmot, which lasted only a year. According to Grow, he dissolved the partnership because of ill health, and he abandoned his practice so that he might return home and regain his failing health by pur-suing a vigorous outdoor life.

His record as an attorney was a balance of wins and losses. In *Commonwealth v. Sprout,* Grow and Little represented the common-wealth and Sprout was found not guilty on a charge of assault and battery. With partners Dimock and Mulford, Grow defended James Gayner on charges of conspiracy to raise wages; Gayner was found guilty. Later he teamed with his former teacher, Streeter, to represent the commonwealth against John O'Brien and this time the defendant was found guilty. So ran the log of Grow's efforts before the bar.[21]

While preparing himself for what seemingly became an undistin-guished career in law, Grow kept a close watch over political happen-ings. Obviously politics had more glitter than did the dusty law books in Streeter's office. Ernest Hempstead, who was born in Dimock, Sus-quehanna County, and later became a successful newspaperman in Meadville, Pennsylvania, came to know Grow intimately in the post–Civil War period. Active in Republican politics, Hempstead was one of Grow's consistent and reliable boosters. He wrote that his father, Orlando G. Hempstead, who was editor of the *Montrose Democrat,* once told him that Grow spent more time reading political dispatches in the newspaper room than he did reading law with Little and Streeter.[22]

What Grow learned in Hempstead's newsroom perpared him for the shock wave that followed. Strong rumblings from Washington were felt throughout Wilmot's district. Wilmot's vote for the admin-istration tariff had attracted national attention. Although opposed to the rest of the Pennsylvania delegation in Congress, his action was in line with general Democratic politics. This fact put his opponents, especially among the party old guard in his state and district, at a disadvantage. But it also made his position with some of the Van Burenites tenuous at best. Not only had Wilmot satisfied the admin-istration on the tariff, but also he had supported Polk's veto of the river and harbor bill. Yet Wilmot did not believe he was making any progress toward getting concessions from the administration; for example, he wanted to have his good friend Col. Victor E. Piollet nominated for a paymastership in the army, but he failed to secure the nomination. This rejection was enough evidence for his political enemies that he was simply being used by the prosouthern administration. Therefore, they were preparing a not-too-happy reception for him upon his return from Washington.

No sooner had Congress adjourned in early August than the movement to block Wilmot's bid for another term intensified. Although he still retained considerable backing in his county of Bradford, protectionist Democrats led by C. M. Bull took the field against him. In Tioga and Susquehanna counties the anti-Wilmot threat surpassed that in Bradford, with the bad press Wilmot had received throughout the state after his vote on the tariff providing the necessary ammunition for his adversaries. Still, the major papers in his district, the *Bradford Reporter,* the *Tioga Eagle,* and the *Northern Democrat,* defended him for the courageous course he had taken. His supporters argued that he was only carrying out the wishes of his constituents. The antiprotectionist viewpoint certainly was nothing new in the district. Long before the 1844 candidacy of Wilmot, the *Reporter* had attacked protectionism as something that helped the capitalist against the poor consumer.[23]

Grow did not wait for Wilmot's nomination for reelection before he took the stump for him. The opposition forces were gaining momentum, probably not without the encouragement of certain state Democratic leaders.[24] On August 24, 1846, the county Democrats held their ratification convention in Montrose and quickly took up the tariff. They were confronting an emotionally charged issue capable of swaying large numbers of people. Immediately the anti-Wilmot men attempted to have the group register its disapproval of the new tariff and to urge its repeal. Grow and his brother, Frederick, listened to C. L. Ward extol the 1842 tariff as a most democratic act which had been good for Pennsylvania. Amid confusion, the Grow brothers, along with J. H. Dimock and Daniel Brewster, reorganized the meeting and turned its direction toward the full endorsement of the new tariff, Wilmot, and the Polk administration. From the back of the crowded room clouded with thick layers of cigar smoke, Galusha Grow followed the proceedings with the eye of a seasoned politician. In time, chants of "Grow — Grow — Grow!" summoned him to the podium. Making his way to the front of the room, he met with more cheers and back slaps. As far as he was concerned, the campaign had started.

In a speech characterized as "able, lucid, and eloquent," Grow lashed at the protectionist argument and insisted that tariff revision had been long overdue.[25] The new law of 1846 restored the economic well-being of the nation and strengthened the quality of life for the poor masses. Although he was equipped with a copy of Wilmot's recent tariff address to the House of Representatives, Grow nonetheless used standard antiprotectionist ideas, which were of long standing in the district. These observations undergirded a consistency of thought on the subject, which asserted itself when he spoke on the tariff during the Thirty-second Congress.[26] Like Wilmot, he stood neither with the drum-beating protectionists nor with the liberal free traders. Any system of protection, he believed, must be for the benefit of the laboring classes and against the cruel demands of capital. His agrarianism singled out the manufacturer who sought restrictive and prohibitory duties for selfish ends, and he argued that government must not assist in that purpose. The only protection that the farmer or the workingman wanted from his government was that which safeguarded his interests from the rapacity and malice of those who represented capital. Serving special interests, in Grow's opinion, was not the Democratic party's idea of how government should perform.

Grow's remarks proved strong enough to persuade the majority of those in attendance to adopt resolutions approving the 1846 tariff as an act that would best serve the interests of all Americans. It was a progressive step for free labor against the "unjust exactions of moneyed power." The Polk-Dallas team received a vote of confidence, while Wilmot got the nod for a second term in Congress.

Along with John Blanding, Grow was appointed to meet with Democratic conferees from Tioga and Bradford to support Wilmot for renomination. At the district conference at Towanda on September 8, Wilmot received that honor with "unparalleled unanimity." But his opponents did not give up; in all three counties they called for protest conventions, which produced another set of conferees and the endorsement at Towanda on September 16 of Robert G. White, a protectionist.[27] Politically White suffered from the disadvantage of being rich and was therefore looked upon as a representative of the large landholding class. Wilmot's defense of the bona fide settler against the greedy land grabbers endeared him to the district's poor voters. He and Grow made the theme of the maldistribution of wealth because of an inequitable land system commonplace in their campaign rhetoric. It became basic to Grow's later bid for homestead legislation.

Wilmot also had disadvantages, but they proved less a handicap than White's affluence. In addition to his controversial stand on the "odious British tariff," the congressman returned with a questionable legacy on two other legislative items: his vote against a bill providing for the graduation of prices for public lands and the infamous Wilmot Proviso forbidding slavery in any territory acquired from Mexico. Neither of these proved important in the campaign. The Bradford County Democrats did adopt a resolution to "exclude slavery from the territory to be acquired," but no one seemed to take notice. The proviso would have to wait for another day to be fully aired.

The October election results stunned Democrats throughout Pennsylvania, but Wilmot's majority of almost 800 votes was a tribute to him and his dedicated supporters.[28] Belated efforts by the Democratic press and leadership to give at least a qualified approval to the Walker tariff helped little. The Whig sweep of offices approached the proportions of a landslide and signaled possible disaster for the Democrats in the presidential race two years hence. There were also unexpected losses in the other states. Most Democratic observers admitted that the stigma of the tariff had eroded the party base in the Northeast. But if the tariff was such a negative factor in the election, then so was the war with Mexico. Whigs capitalized on the charge made by the Liberty party that the Polk administration was deliberately prosecuting the war in order to give the South more slave territory. Many northerners agreed, especially those who did not care for the administration. In Washington the president must have wondered what was happening. The grand alliance arranged at Baltimore two years before now appeared to be crumbling; scattered reports of party losses rocked any illusion of party unity that Polk still retained. The next two years produced further disintegration.

For Grow, these two years after his graduation from Amherst had to be gratifying. Political apprenticeship must begin somewhere, and the experience he acquired in grassroots politics of the Twelfth Congressional District was more than any neophyte could hope for. This was a time for his political development. He studied assiduously the machinery of electioneering and became fascinated with the maneuvers of office-seekers, bosses, and party hacks. The successes he enjoyed with Wilmot were more than mere victories; they strengthened his ideas of party teamwork, discipline, and responsibility. They also promoted an egocentrism that swells in the heart of every budding politician. It meant a great deal to be asked to speak before groups, to enjoy the trust and confidence of party leaders, and to receive favorable voter response. This was the beginning of a glorious political career — a time when Grow learned the rules of the game and tried to apply them as an old pro.

2

A Compromise Candidate Goes to Washington

CHRISTMAS DAY, 1846. For many Americans it was not a joyous occasion. High in the Sierra, fourteen survivors of a party that had left Donner Lake a week earlier drifted aimlessly through deepening snow. Hoping their Indian guides would help them find landmarks that would lead them to Bear Valley and safety, they had somehow wandered off the trail and become lost. Cold, without food, and drained of strength and hope, some resorted to the most primitive of all survival instincts, cannibalism, in a last desperate effort to remain alive. Meanwhile, hundreds of miles to the south, a crisis of a different nature existed. Gen. Stephen Kearney was trying to fight a war. Ailing and frustrated with command difficulties, he was organizing an expedition to retake Los Angeles from the Californians. Americans and Mexicans were killing each other daily as their leaders pondered the next moves and the overall objectives of this ridiculous struggle. The purpose of the war, or the lack of it, did not bother the Irishman, James Kirker. He and his gang of cutthroats were getting several dollars for every Apache scalp they brought in; they did not particularly care who won the damn war. To these adventurers, Christmas was just another day of agonizing pain, a grim reminder of the other side of manifest destiny.

In Washington, President Polk did not bother to attend church on this holy day. Maybe he believed that divine guidance would more likely come to him at his desk in the White House. He needed help, whatever the source. The problems he faced were not as awesome as those of the Donner party or the servicemen under fire, but they were bad enough. Both the war and the plight of the Democratic party exhausted him. He seemed confused and unable to satisfy critics who demanded remedial action. Polk grew paranoid, suspecting plots by his outspoken subordinates and members of Congress. The heavy

21

burdens of the office, slavery, and the war exhausted his endurance, and he gradually lost the qualities of effective popular leadership.

The election defeats in 1846 were symptomatic of a party malignancy that even Polk must have suspected. Party veterans did not hesitate to blame the war and the Walker tariff for cutting into Democratic pluralities. Though admitting he opposed the new tariff, Buchanan refused to say that it would make Pennsylvania permanently Whig.[1] Yet Polk's handling, or mishandling, of other issues pointed to a deep-rooted sectionalism that was about to erupt. Principles combined with emotionalism to erode what Polk valued as one of the party's time-honored virtues—compromise. Certain northwestern groups were unhappy with him on two counts: his veto of the river and harbor bill, and his acceptance of the 49th parallel in Oregon after having declared in his inaugural address the American title to "the whole of Oregon"—the entire region between the 42nd parallel and 54°40'. Some northerners interpreted the former as a southern victory and irrefutable proof that the president was at the mercy of Calhoun and his clique of arrogant slavocrats. New Englanders were unhappy with the war and the way Polk was using it to acquire additional territory for slavery, and the Van Burenites expressed disdain for the president and his henchmen over their unfair distribution of patronage. Finally, the Barnburners of New York attributed the defeat of Silas Wright in the gubernatorial race to the perfidy of the Hunkers, spokesmen for administration policy.[2] These two factions were engaged in a vicious struggle for control of the Democratic party in that state.

Then there was the Wilmot Proviso. Limited to the simple question of whether slavery should be extended into territory acquired from Mexico, it became a rallying cry for all who opposed the Polk administration and the strong arm of slavocracy. The proviso was more than an attempt to contain slavery; it was a declaration of political war against southern leadership. Its dramatic effect upon the rift within the party ranks was most noticeable in New York and Pennsylvania's northern tier counties. There some vengeful Democrats backed the proviso only to embarrass the administration, although others subscribed to its underlying principle. For the latter group it was time to decide whether the federal government should become slavery's chief promoter by implanting it upon Mexican soil. The two factions were far less disparate in their interests than the alliance formed by the northern Hunkers or "machine" Democrats with the southern proslavery elements to control the power and spoils of office. The southerners clearly saw the threat to their dominance of the party from the proviso advocates. A few, including Calhoun, were less pessimistic and relied upon moderate Democrats in the North and West to apply the necessary braking action to the party's cowboys.

The moderates tried, but the more they discredited the proviso and its supporters, the more they intensified the dissension over slavery. Most attention turned to the presidential hopefuls, James Buchanan and Michigan Sen. Lewis Cass, both of whom were considered by the ardent free-soilers as lackeys of southern spokesmen. Obviously neither man liked the proviso; both feared it would disrupt the party and the nation, and both proposed alternative solutions. Buchanan suggested that the line of the 1820 Missouri Compromise be extended into any new territory that might be acquired from Mexico.[3] The expansionist Cass argued that the people of a territory had the right to regulate their own institutions, including slavery. In Congress he warned that a continuation of the proviso controversy might impede a united war effort and prevent the nation from acquiring a single square foot of territory.[4] Like Buchanan, he seriously questioned whether slavery would extend into the far Southwest because of climatic conditions.

Many Americans found the proposals of Buchanan and Cass to be a refreshing relief from the divisive consequences of the proviso. Cass's popular sovereignty idea seemed especially acceptable to moderates of both parties, North and South. Western editors were also pleased with it, and even northern cynics could not deny that Cass had made a strong case for freedom by offering a safeguard against the further extension of slavery. But not all northerners were cynics; some were downright disbelievers. The Barnburners accused the exponents of popular sovereignty of violating the Ordinance of 1787, which had prohibited slavery in the Northwest Territory. They no more trusted Cass and his humbug or, for that matter, Buchanan and his, with regard to slavery and the territories than they had trusted Polk on Texas. The plans of both candidates may have comforted the party's sachems by offering political equilibrium on slavery, but the proviso touched the northern conscience. It emotionalized more than intellectualized the slavery issue, and alerted the parties that their greatest struggle still lay ahead. As Bernard DeVoto remarked, "Slavery was out of the closet, and it was going to stay out."[5]

Where Does Grow Stand?

In 1847, the proviso dramatically replaced the tariff as the most critical issue before the public, not only in Wilmot's district, but also throughout Pennsylvania and the nation. It was discussed in Congress, in the press, in courthouses, on the stump, and any place where men sought controversy. Proviso leagues sprang up in the free states, while mass meetings of protest were held through the South. David Wilmot's name became as familiar as that of the president.

Grow never hesitated to identify Wilmot as the proviso's true author although he admitted that the idea could be traced back at least to Jefferson and the Ordinance of 1787: "I do not recall Wilmot ever mentioning the question of authorship, although we discussed the words and spirit of the Proviso many times. As these perfectly harmonize with the views he often expressed and emphasized to me, I am convinced that he is responsible for the Proviso both in text and spirit and that he merits all the fame that came to him by its existence."[6]

When Wilmot recommended Grow as the congressional nominee in 1850, he assured his friends that his former law partner had been a "charter" supporter of the proviso.[7] Actually this was not saying much. Most antislavery men in 1847, especially those in the Twelfth Congressional District, claimed they stood behind the proviso. Even Calhoun recognized its widespread acceptance and reported to his daughter, "The North is united on Wilmot's proposition."[8] During the first three months of that year nine northern states, including Pennsylvania, requested their representatives in Washington to vote in favor of the proviso.[9] By every standard it had become a sectional issue.

Grow agreed with Wilmot that free territory should remain free. In 1847 neither man was an abolitionist. They simply argued that the government should remain neutral on the question of slavery because it had the responsibility to protect freedom in any free territory under its jurisdiction, just as it stood ready to defend slavery in an annexed territory, such as Texas, where slavery was already established. Once states were formed and admitted to the Union, the people of those states were free to adopt or reject slavery, they realized.

Both Grow and Wilmot believed that slavery encompassed more than political and moral issues, and was inextricably tied to the nation's economy. It was a curse on the natural development of the territories because only free labor had a right to settle in these new lands, they believed. Wilmot tended to treat slavery with greater detachment than Grow, who dwelled upon the proviso's economic side. Grow believed the slavery question should be approached through allied economic issues; the disposition of the public domain was among the more important. The federal government had failed to provide a policy that would open the public lands to actual settlers. The acquisition of new lands and their settlement by free men would unite rather than sectionalize the nation and serve as a foil to slavery. As a source of wealth, land was like a raw diamond; free labor transformed and shaped it, giving it the sole source of value. During his first term in Congress, Grow applied his idea that man had a fundamental right to the soil in defense of the homestead principle.

Grow's position on the proviso in the 1848 campaign raised questions about his convictions. Years later a local editor remarked that in that campaign Grow had acted inconsistently on the territorial issue.[10] He had stumped in nearly every township of Susquehanna County in favor of Cass, said the editorial, urging people to vote for the national Democratic ticket and for popular sovereignty, which was in conflict with his endorsement of the proviso. Apparently, what Grow had to say about slavery in the territories depended upon who was listening. When he ran his own campaign in 1850, his critics rummaged through the countryside to find copies of speeches he had delivered two years earlier to prove that he was less a free-soil candidate than his opponent. By then, however, the political winds had shifted. In the year of the great compromise measures, free-soilism had lost much appeal.

Cass received the support of most Democrats in Grow's district, but elsewhere in Pennsylvania and nationally, the Michigan senator faced a hostile party. The free-soilers could not stand beside the "Benedict Arnold" who had once accepted the proviso in principle and was now against it.[11] Neither did many southerners trust him and his popular sovereignty; they demanded a repudiation of the proviso spirit. But no northerner in good conscience could do this. Actually the Democrats did not yet have a candidate who was strong enough to reconcile the extreme factions of the party. The moderates — Cass, Buchanan, or Dallas — lacked adequate appeal to compensate for their languid positions on slavery, and seemed to be shadowboxing on that issue while many leaders of both parties were demanding that this election be fought for "free" principles.[12]

In Pennsylvania the Democrats faced serious problems. Central to all their difficulties was the breakdown of party harmony, which had followed the inauguration of Polk. Rivalry over patronage, the struggle for control of the state Democratic machinery, and the run for the presidency converted members' enthusiasm for unity to antagonistic barbs. Clashes of opinion on substantive issues, such as the tariff and the proviso, only added to the confusion. Although Buchanan had the credentials to rank as the foremost Democrat in the state and as a prime candidate for the presidential nomination, he had his enemies. The editor of the *Lancastrian,* Reah Frazer, broke publicly with him and joined the Dallas camp. Accusations of tax evasion by Buchanan were drummed up and passed on by Frazer to opponents like Wilmot to be used in their assaults against the secretary of state. Some supporters of Dallas who never regarded their man as having a chance at nomination joined the Cass people to discredit Buchanan and to help establish a power base in Pennsylvania for the Michigan senator. All this jockeying spelled grief for Buchanan and woe for the party. He did remain in good graces with Cameron and Governor Shunk, neither of whom blocked his candidacy. Yet Cameron's independent actions and his delay in endorsing Buchanan were frustrating.

The supporters of Buchanan experienced the most frustration in the northern tier counties, where free-soilism remained a dominant issue, and Buchanan had only managed to enrage proviso backers with his recommendation to extend the 1820 line. Both his compromised position on slavery and his stand against the 1846 tariff hurt him. In addition to the difficulty Buchanan faced on the issues, the charge still persisted that he had conspired with Cameron against the popular Woodward. All these concerns made him persona non grata with Wilmot and many Democrats. Wilmot strengthened his case when he informed his friends that the vicious attacks made against him by the *Pennsylvanian* and the *Washington Union* resulted from his open promotion of the proviso and his opposition to Buchanan's pretensions to the presidency.[13] He was pleased to see his friends stand by him. At the Susquehanna County Democratic convention in January 1848, for example, Grow blocked a resolution by local anti-Wilmot Buchaneers that praised Buchanan for his "integrity, ability and patriotism."[14] The resolution died on the table, and Grow went on to commend the Polk administration and to vindicate the country in its "war of defense" against Mexico. Grow articulated his views of the war and helped frame the resolutions, which were prototypical of those to be adopted in early March by the Democratic state convention in Harrisburg.

At that convention the majority of delegates anticipated that Buchanan would receive the state party's endorsement, but they also suspected that his nomination would not necessarily enhance his national candidacy.[15] The convention refused to approve his solution to the territorial question; at the same time, it adopted resolutions praising Van Buren and Cass. These actions may have damaged his image outside Pennsylvania and ruined his chances nationally. Furthermore, the supporters of Cass, Dallas, and the proviso had carried their opposition to Buchanan to the national convention in Baltimore. There

Buchanan managed to receive consistently the unanimous support of Pennsylvania's twenty-six delegates, but this was not good enough. On the fourth ballot Lewis Cass received the nomination.

The confusion among the Democrats encouraged the Whigs, although they could not put their act together nationally. Henry Clay was the sentimental favorite for president, especially among those who were sensitive to the tariff, but a war hero, Zachary Taylor, was most appealing to the masses even among Democrats.[16] Other Whig possibilities included Winfield Scott, Judge John McLean, and Daniel Webster. Neither Clay nor Webster could excite the proviso Whigs, and Taylor was anathema to them. The free-soilers were quite visible, outspoken, and not averse to bolting the party should the wrong candidate be chosen. Greeley was blunt: "Our candidate must be unequivocally in favor of the Proviso."[17] Salmon Chase of Ohio suggested a quick call for a national convention of antislavery men.[18] Candidates were measured against the issues and against each other. The dialogue seemed endless. By the time the national Whigs gathered in Philadelphia in June, the Pennsylvania delegates still had not agreed on a presidential nominee. They divided their votes among Clay, Taylor, and Scott, and many returned home wondering if they had made the right choice in Taylor.

As far as the free-soilers were concerned, it was a horrible choice. The nominee was everything the proviso men had rebuked: a southern slaveholder, a militarist, and an expansionist. To Whig intellectuals and purists, Taylor's selection was a mockery of the entire political system, a sham perpetrated by southerners in collusion with northern weaklings who had shouted down antislavery resolutions to win votes in the South. When he heard the news, Charles F. Adams declared war on the party and threw himself wholeheartedly into the free-soil movement.[19]

Since both parties had avoided taking a clear position on the question that most concerned the future of the nation, an independent movement of party bolters became a reality. With both Barnburners of New York, and free-soil Democrats of the northern counties of Pennsylvania, the proviso Whigs shared a common battlefield. At the Utica convention in June the free-soil movement crystallized. Proviso men held meetings throughout the North to assail the candidates and platforms of the two parties and to organize a third one. The result was the Free-Soil party, which in August called its first national convention in Buffalo. With Martin Van Buren as its presidential hopeful and a banner of "Free Soil, Free Speech, Free Labor, and Free Men," the open revolt by the men of principles was under way.

Wilmot was one of the early advocates of the movement that led to Buffalo. His decision to join, because he believed in the triumph of free-soilism as a national issue, was at "peril to his own political future and fortunes."[20] Combining national and local issues, he continued to work for Van Buren and the Buffalo platform after his own campaign for Congress was over. Observers had assumed that he would seek a third term, but Tioga Democrats claimed that his renomination would violate an established party tradition of rotating the district's congressional seat from county to county, and it was Tioga's turn to have the nominee. This manufactured campaign issue was obviously a weak gesture on the part of the Hunkers. When Susquehanna and Bradford declined to yield to the Tioga dissenters, they withdrew from the congressional conference with a few of their Bradford allies and nominated Jonah Brewster, a Hunker; their resolutions criticized Wilmot and the proviso. The Whigs, ecstatic over this Democratic disturbance, nominated Henry W. Tracy and entered the contest confident of victory. But Wilmot easily smashed his opponents to win by a comfortable majority.

Eagerly Grow took the stump for Wilmot, but he refrained from joining the free-soil bolt. His canvass for Cass and the Baltimore platform left the Van Burenites dismayed. Grow's seemingly contradictory actions stemmed from his almost blind faith in the ability of the Democratic party to resolve the nation's problems, whatever they were, through effective leadership. He interpreted this as the rare genius of the party since the days of Jefferson, and he was ready to stand by the party of unity. He never doubted that the northern Democrats better represented the principles of Jefferson and Jackson than did the southern wing of the party. And certainly he had no delusions about southern power and its insistence on the assent to slavery extension as a test of party loyalty. Yet Grow saw no need for a third party to cope with the problem of slavery. His strongest statement on the subject came during a heated House debate in the Thirty-second Congress over the finality question. "The country needs no new party," he cautioned his colleagues, "especially to save the Union. If ever political parties of the country shall be organized solely with reference to men's views of the institution of human slavery, it will be the most fearful day the Republic ever saw."[21] His inveterate hostility toward slavery naturally led him into the camp of radical or free-soil Democrats, but he was a Democrat first, then a free-soiler. Though he was devoted to the proviso, there is no evidence to suggest that Grow aggressively campaigned for its adoption.

Other considerations may have prompted Grow to support Cass

instead of Van Buren. After the Utica convention, the *Northern Democrat* warned its readers not to throw their votes away on the Free-Soil candidate, thus assuring a Whig victory.[22] "Barnburning" had cut into the ranks of both of the district's parties, but Democratic leaders believed that more Democrats than Whigs would bolt in favor of Van Buren. After all, he was an old Jacksonian, a man Wilmot had endorsed.

Grow had to be happy with his own efforts in the campaign, although only one out of three of his candidates won. Wilmot's victory was overshadowed by the losses of Cass and Morris Longstreth, the gubernatorial candidate from Montgomery County. Grow had been elected representative delegate to the Harrisburg convention that nominated Longstreth, had voted for him at that convention, and then supported him as did most Democrats. The regular and free-soil Democrats may have divided on the presidency, but they stood united behind Longstreth. Grow's joy came from seeing all three Democratic contenders triumph in his district. The results in Susquehanna, where Grow had canvassed the most, were particularly impressive. Wilmot had a better victory percentage in that county than in his own Bradford, while the vote total for Cass in Susquehanna was greater than the combined votes for Taylor and Van Buren. (See table 1.)

Had Grow joined the Van Burenites in 1848, the switch would have been easily understood, in light of this apprenticeship under such

TABLE 1

1848 Election Returns in the Twelfth Congressional District

	Bradford	*Tioga*	*Susquehanna*
For president			
Taylor	3,272	1,264	1,853
Cass	1,889	1,344	2,563
Van Buren	1,779	1,039	301
For governor			
Johnston	3,241	1,219	1,597
Longstreth	3,741	2,077	2,416
For Congress			
Wilmot	4,175	1,714	2,708
Tracy	2,580	1,023	1,192
Brewster	215	640	67

Source: *Bradford Reporter*, October 18, November 22, 1848.

notable free-soilers as Cleveland and Wilmot. Because he remained loyal to the party and its platform even at the expense of appearing opportunistic, Grow's early career was not derailed. His pragmatism was forged by the harsh realities of party survival. After the militant cries of party extremists for a return to principles, Grow and the great mass of Democrats devoted themselves to the preservation of their party above all else.

In the Footsteps of a Legend

After an analysis of the 1848 election returns, Grow had to feel some remorse and pangs of disappointment. His own rhetoric had contributed to the victories of Cass and Wilmot in his district and thus helped sharpen the edge of dissent between hunkerism and free-soilism. Perhaps his grief was sufficient to force his retirement from politics. His own explanation was that his health had worsened so that he could no longer pursue political life or maintain his law practice.[23] Whatever the reason, he retreated from the public scene, refused to run for the legislature, and sought solace in the tranquility of the family farm.

What frustrated Grow may have frustrated other Pennsylvanians as well, Democrats and Whigs. His party never fully recovered from the shocks of 1848: the free-soil bolt, the rejection of Buchanan by the national convention, and the failure of both Cass and Longstreth to carry the state. At the same time, the Whigs could not relax with their victory laurels. Many of them were still embarrassed by the ticket of General Taylor, a slaveholder, for president and William P. Johnston, a free-soiler, for governor. The open clash between the free-soil supporters of the governor and the compromise Whigs weakened the party's credibility. Furthermore, differences over patronage were now crumbling the coalition with the Native Americans, which had been put together in time for the 1848 elections. So it came as no surprise to many observers when, in the off-year elections of 1849, the Democrats secured a majority in both houses of the legislature and elected John A. Gamble as canal commissioner.[24]

In 1849, most Pennsylvanians, like most Americans, looked to Washington with deep concern. The responsibility for settling the question of slavery in the Mexican cession belonged to the new president and the Whig leadership in Congress. What would they do? the nation asked. California's territorial government demanded action too. By December the population soared to 100,000, far more than the minimum required for statehood. Three months earlier, with the blessing of Taylor, a convention of Californians had adopted a constitution that excluded slavery, and then overwhelmingly ratified it in a popular referendum.

The news came as a terrible shock to the South. If California were to be admitted as a free state, the equilibrium between free and slave states would be destroyed. Worried southerners envisaged this as an aggressive policy of the North and developed an attitude of insecurity and apprehension. They began to cultivate the theory that the admission of California without slavery was tantamount to the adoption of the proviso. Evidence of their deepening anxiety appeared in the House in the Thirty-first Congress, when three weeks and sixty-three ballots were required to elect a moderate, Howell Cobb of Georgia, to the speakership.

The growing despair called for qualities of statesmanship, and no institution of government was more responsive to this need than the U.S. Senate. Clay, Webster and Calhoun, their megalomania riveted by past successes, realized that the Union itself was at stake. To younger men the challenge seemed as great as that facing the delegates at the Constitutional Convention. Clay offered a set of proposals that were undergirded by the hope that moderation of opinion might hold back extremism in both parties and restore sectional sanity through compromise. Though the final product, known as the Compromise of 1850, differed in detail from Clay's proposals, the spirit was the same. Regardless of its merits or shortcomings, the compromise was acceptable to most northerners and southerners. Some grasped it as a final settlement; the less naive accepted it as a tenuous truce.

In Grow's district, as in other parts of the North, the compromise tended to shove the proviso into a corner of oblivion. The free-soilers were no more thrilled by this development than they were with the organization of the House under Cobb. In their obstinacy in supporting Wilmot for Speaker, they had allowed the Georgian to win by a margin of two votes. Backing the Whig nominee, Robert C. Winthrop of Massachusetts, would have been far better than tying up a block of votes for a man who had no chance of winning; Wilmot's opponents held him responsible for this impolitic behavior of his backers. Suddenly, the proviso men saw that they were less popular with their northern colleagues and constituents than in 1848.

To Wilmot it was remarkable how quickly the mood of the district voters had changed. In Susquehanna County, the *Montrose Democrat's* editor, O. G. Hempstead, began to question Wilmot's wisdom in deliberately forcing the proviso to the forefront in the House. While the free-soilers were doing everything possible to keep the proviso alive, the major parties were addressing themselves to other matters of national importance. Some cynics doubted Wilmot's sanity. Not only was he blamed for the speakership debacle, but he was also accused of using his group of recalcitrants to block the appointment of John W. Forney, a Democrat and friend of Buchanan, to be the Clerk of the House. This asinine action proved too much for the Hunkers; Wilmot had to go.

Long before the Thirty-first Congress had adjourned, Wilmot's enemies, with support from Buchanan, were busy plotting his political demise. Buchanan befriended Colonel Piollet, a Democratic leader from Bradford County and initially one of Wilmot's strong supporters, as well as C. L. Ward, another of Wilmot's fellow townsman. Both these men turned against their former friend. It was Ward who helped set up the *North Pennsylvanian* at Towanda with Wien Forney, cousin of J. W. Forney of the *Pennsylvanian*. The Towanda paper lasted less than a year, just long enough to help remove Wilmot from the congressional race.

Wilmot knew that he and his proviso were in serious trouble.[25] He was sure he could be reelected if he were nominated. But many district leaders believed that the charge of party treason hurled at Wilmot by the Buchaneers would hold sway with the Democratic voters. Secondly, the proviso no longer had the attraction it once possessed. The Democratic state convention at Williamsport in late May had rejected it and called for Congress to provide governments for the new territories without delay on the principle of *nonintervention*—"thus disposing forever, in a just and equitable manner, of the embarrassing subject of domestic servitude." Wilmot now feared that a coalition of Hunkers in his district might prompt the selection of a candidate who would not support the principles he had battled to establish.

Whatever party discipline may have existed in Wilmot's district broke down by September. The Bradford Democrats dutifully stood by Wilmot and his proviso, but the Hunkers of Susquehanna and Tioga moved to endorse James Lowrey of Tioga and to reject the proviso. The only way out seemed to be a compromise that would find either Wilmot or the proviso, or both, removed from the congressional campaign. Seeing that it was futile to press for their favorite son, the Bradford Democrats drew up a list of declarations that included the principle of the proviso and the choice of John W. Guernsey, a prominent attorney from Tioga. But the Susquehanna people announced that they would reject any man who committed himself to the proviso. Now more angry than frustrated, the Bradford Democrats pivoted and apologetically reaffirmed their trust in Wilmot. With the election only weeks away, the party seemed hopelessly divided.

In mid-September, some of the Bradford Democrats accompanied Wilmot to Montrose to challenge the Lowrey forces. The Susquehanna Hunkers were ready. In a wild meeting at the courthouse, Democrats of every creed and curious onlookers packed the assembly room to watch Wilmot and his antagonists tear into each other in a donnybrook that had been in the making since 1846. Col. Piollet harangued for two hours, throwing invectives at his former friend and professing that since "public men are public property" they should be exposed openly for their aberrations and failures. Amid cheers and jeers, Wilmot ably defended himself. There is no record of his words, but it can be surmised that he urged party unity and the continued support of the proviso. The editor of the *Bradford Reporter,* E. O. Goodrich, argued that the entire attack staged against Wilmot by "guppies" like Piollet was inspired by maneuvers at Wheatland, Washington, and Philadelphia. It was an obvious move to split the district's Democrats and subvert the issues of tariff adjustment and free-soilism.[26]

The strategy proved successful. The wings of the party in Wilmot's district were as far apart now as ever, and it seemed probable that the Whig nominee for Congress, John C. Adams of Bradford, would easily win. One reasonable option remained: Wilmot and Lowrey could both withdraw from the race in favor of a compromise candidate. Whether the decision to compromise originated with one of the candidates or with their managers is not clear, but both men were aware that neither could secure the nomination. Wilmot announced his willingness to pull out provided Lowrey did the same; a candidate whom Wilmot regarded as sound on the issues would then be named. Lowrey, also willing to decline for the sake of party unity, submitted to Wilmot a list of names, any of whom he and the regular Democrats could support. Galusha Grow's name was on that list, and Wilmot promptly accepted Grow as the candidate.

The committee sent to discuss the candidacy with Grow found him busy at work on the family farm. In some ways this period in the young man's life had to be a psychological low. Not only was his legal career sputtering, but also his physical ailments were still gnawing him. What relaxation and enjoyment he received came from outdoor labor, which he believed was necessary to restore his health. He worked as a surveyor, peeled hemlock bark for a tannery, and helped his brothers put up a hotel in Glenwood. Certainly none of these activities proved intellectually rewarding, but they did have therapeutic value. Grow needed time to assess his talents, ambitions, and goals and to resharpen his attitudes and philosophy. While exercise strengthened him physically, the love, devotion, and understanding of his family revitalized him spiritually.

Still a young man, Grow was close to his family. With his mother and brothers, he helped operate the country store, the farm, and the mills. He was seen often in the company of his brother Frederick, attending political rallies and social gatherings. Together they combined their carpentry skills on construction projects such as the hotel in Glenwood, a fine structure with several stories and verandas. With its recreational facilities and spacious ballroom, it became the social hub of the community; Grow spent many happy moments here with family members and friends. Writing years afterwards, Mrs. W. D. Green recalled the fairyland atmosphere of the hotel with its bright lights and fine music. She also remembered how Grow had carried her as a child upstairs to the ballroom so that she could watch the dancers.[27]

Grow loved to socialize with those close to him. Even after he had been elected to Congress, he continued to enjoy camping and hunting with his friends. Though he was not particularly known as a ladies' man, he liked to be in the company of charming women. His youthful pleasures were simple ones typical of rustic life in the nineteenth century; there is no evidence suggesting that he caroused or gambled. He avoided scandal and anything else that might bring shame to himself or his family. He seemed to seek the life of a country squire whose devotion to family, country, and career was all that was necessary for personal fulfillment.

Grow was prepared for the committeemen, who did not have to remind him that his friend Wilmot, the proviso, and the Democratic party were retreating to a defenseless position. Newspapers and friends kept him abreast of events in Washington, Harrisburg, and his district. At first glance the party's problems seemed insoluble; the compromise measures represented, at best, a reprieve or a temporary respite. Upon his return from Washington, Wilmot had indicated to Grow that he did not believe the 1850 truce would last long. "There can be one real and lasting settlement of the slavery question," the congressman had prophetically warned, "and that will come only with the abolition of slavery."[28]

Until now Grow had viewed the political situation in his district with a degree of detachment. Watching Democratic leaders shred the bonds of party unity annoyed him greatly. But the opportunity to sit in Congress does not come often to a young man in his twenties. After discussing the offer with his mother and Frederick, Grow agreed to the nomination, provided that it was a genuine offer from both wings of the party. He stated his conditions of acceptance in a letter to the representatives of the congressional conference:[29]

Millardsville, Sept. 20, 1850.

Dear Sirs:

Your favor of this date is before me and in reply have only to say, if my name can be of any service in uniting and ensuring success to the Democratic party, I have no objections to its being used, but in this case only on the following conditions:

First, that Mr. Lowrey and the people of Tioga County agree fully to the propositions you make.

Second, that Mr. Wilmot willingly withdraws as a candidate and will yield his support to the arrangement.

Third, that your proposition is satisfactory to the district and to save the Democracy from a defeat; but these assurances, gentlemen, I have in your letter, and am not, therefore, at liberty to doubt their correctness, and upon that base my reply. Were I to consult my own feelings alone, I should most earnestly desire my name not to be used as a candidate for any office at this time, for reasons of which you are already informed, and I now yield to your solicitation, only on the assurance, that my name will contribute to the harmony of the Democratic party and the success of its principles.

Accept, gentlemen, the assurances of my regard,

Yours truly,

G. A. Grow

To F. B. Streeter, M. C. Tyler and C. L. Brown, Esqrs.

On September 25 a powwow of congressional conferees from the three counties took place at Wellsboro and received Grow's letter and those from Wilmot and Lowrey announcing their withdrawal. It did not take the conferees long to endorse Grow and to adopt a free-soil plank: "That we are unalterably opposed to the extension of slavery into territory now free, and that we hold it to be the duty of Congress to prohibit by positive law its introduction therein." Undoubtedly Wilmot had much to do with the free-soil resolution and the selection of Grow. But the regular Democrats did not object strenuously because they achieved their primary intention of preventing Wilmot from returning to Congress.

It was a brief campaign but not without some fanfare. The outcome promised to be close. Worried Democrats speculated on the resiliency of their party; could the factions unite behind Grow? The editor of the *Susquehanna Register,* a Whig organ, asked cynically if a "mere youth" should even be asked to carry on both shoulders free-soilism and hunkerism.[30] A political rally in Montrose three days after the nomination suggested how the campaign might go. Speakers included party bigwigs David Wilmot, Ulysses Mercur, and Martin Grover, but many came just to hear the guest of honor, John Van Buren. "Prince John," the son of the former president, arrived from New York to help Wilmot get reelected, only to discover his friend was not a candidate. Disappointed, he nonetheless agreed to speak in Grow's behalf. To the embarrassment and ire of the Hunkers present, Van Buren instead praised Wilmot for his fine work in behalf of the free-soil movement. Wilmot's enemies had hoped that this meeting would not be an occasion to resurrect a fallen hero. Later Van Buren took the stump for Grow, but without enthusiasm. Wilmot's withdrawal produced a letdown among the district's free-soil Democrats as it did among proviso backers everywhere. The lack of any editorial comment with respect to Grow's candidacy by the *Bradford Democrat* indicated the general apathy.

With Wilmot out of the running, the district Whigs naturally became more optimistic; they were convinced their opponents were still divided despite the desperate eleventh-hour compromise. They saw the ratification rally for Grow as a sham, and could not believe that the bonds between the free-soil Democrats and the Hunkers were genuine. A strong rumor circulated among the Whigs that Wilmot had sold out to his adversaries in return for a future judgeship.[31] In addition, the Whigs charged that Grow's selection by a privileged group of five conferees was a clear violation of both republican principles and the caucus system; at no time, in any primary meeting or convention, had the Democratic party seriously considered Grow. Motivated more by expediency than tradition, the party bosses had ignored the rank and file. When the Bradford Democrats met in Towanda to ratify Grow, the Hunker chairman refused to entertain a motion to ascertain by vote of those present whether Grow's nomination emanated from the people.[32]

For Grow the bid for elective office was a baptism in public ridicule. His opponents managed to manufacture a political past for him. In a day when editorial abuse and slander were commonplace in a campaign, the politician had to fight back with equal amounts of venom and nerve if he hoped to survive until election day. Many of the invectives tossed at Grow, especially those relating to his youth, lack of seasoning, and experience, he fielded without overt resentment.

Some of the epithets were actually catchy — "the school-boy Grow," the "Lenox Greenhorn," and the "Tunkhannock Creek Parrot."

More obnoxious comments questioned his integrity regarding the issues, specifically his record on the tariff and the proviso. The *Susquehanna Register* reminded him of his support for the 1846 tariff and quipped that this was the only time he and Wilmot had agreed on anything.[33] When he was labeled a friend of the Manchester School of British free traders, a traitor who would put foreign interests above those of the American workingman, Grow struck back. He challenged his critics to explain how protection for American industry could help eliminate poverty among dirt farmers. The quality of life for the agricultural masses, he argued, was poor enough; higher prices for American finished goods would not ease the pain.

Local Whigs attacked Grow's stand on free-soilism, assigning him the dubious distinction of being at best a Cass free-soiler in 1848. They also dared him to deny that he had opposed a free-soil resolution by George Keeler at the last Democratic nominating convention in his own county. In their most serious charge, the Whigs chided him for his failure to express his position on the proviso when he had accepted the nomination. If Grow was as strong a free-soil Democrat as Wilmot, the *Register* demanded to know, why then did the Hunkers object to Wilmot's candidacy? To Grow's claim that he had introduced free-soil resolutions in a county meeting some years before, the Whigs countered that every northerner probably did so when such action was fashionable. Cass and Piollet had once been supporters of the proviso; now Cass was encouraging popular sovereignty while Piollet was promoting Buchanan and chastising Wilmot and the free-soilers. The Whigs saw their candidate, John C. Adams, as a more consistent advocate of free-soilism, but they weakened their attack against Grow with an undue emphasis on the proviso, which was no longer a viable issue.

Grow polled nearly two thousand votes less than Wilmot had received in 1848 (see table 2). A good part of the difference lay in his failure to carry Wilmot's Bradford County. There the Democrats demonstrated stronger support for their party's nominees for canal commissioner, auditor-general, and the surveyor-general than for Grow. Many Democrats in Bradford believed that Grow was an unsatisfactory substitute for Wilmot and that they would do better to vote for the popular Adams; even though he was a Whig, he was a Bradford resident.

Grow's victory could hardly be called a personal triumph. The lackluster campaign of Adams, plus the traditionally Democratic majori-

TABLE 2

1850 Congressional Election Returns in the Twelfth Congressional District

	Bradford	Tioga	Susquehanna
Grow	2,826	1,696	2,356
Adams	3,168	1,189	1,373

Source: *Bradford Reporter,* October 26, 1850.

ties in the district, returned Grow as the winner. He achieved this success without having had time to develop a campaign strategy or to address the issues philosophically. There was only time to respond smartly to the Whig charges as they had appeared. In reality it would have been difficult for a compromise candidate to devise a game plan suitable to all strata of the Democratic party's hierarchy. Grow spoke carefully to avoid further division within the ranks. And though many Democrats were not particularly impressed with Grow's candidacy, they were gratified with the apparent solidarity it promised. His biggest advantage lay in his innocence of any involvement in his selection as the party's choice. He did not seek the nomination; the party came to him. On the other hand, he faced the disadvantage of having to follow the legendary Wilmot to Washington.

ℬ 3

The Youngest Radical on the Floor

W HEN THE House of Representatives of the Thirty-second Congress convened on December 1, 1851, Galusha Grow took his seat as its youngest member. Just twenty-eight, he typified the youthfulness of the new Congress. Joining him were such future giants John C. Breckinridge, Alexander Stephens, Robert Toombs, and Andrew Johnson, while in the upper chamber sat a dazzling array of talented lawmakers that included Salmon Chase, Hannibal Hamlin, Charles Sumner, Jefferson Davis, John P. Hale, and Stephen A. Douglas. These men in their thirties and forties were prematurely and painfully seasoned by the political vicissitudes and anxieties of the day. They were honorable men, confident of their abilities, and bullish on the future of the country.

The "old triumvirate" of Clay, Webster, and Calhoun, along with Jackson, Van Buren, Adams, and Benton, either were dead or had stepped aside for a new generation of political leaders. The mantle of responsibility demanded that the younger men adroitly maneuver through the legislative process with minimal impact upon sectional tension. Soon after the newly elected Sumner took his seat in the Senate, Benton said to him: "You have come upon the stage too late, sir. Not only have our great men passed away, but the great issues have been settled also. . . . Nothing is left you, sir, but puny sectional questions and petty strifes about slavery and fugitive slave laws, involving no national interests."[1] It is not clear that this was sarcasm; possibly Benton saw things this way.

But Sumner and his colleagues viewed these "puny" and "petty" problems as involving crucial national interests. They disagreed with Benton that the great issues had been settled; national survival was still at stake. They sensed that most Americans in 1851 divided themselves not so much as liberals and conservatives, or Democrats and

Whigs, but more as optimists and apocalyptic alarmists. Could the
Union endure the slavery paranoia? they asked. The Senate's gallant
efforts toward a solution to the 1850 crisis relieved those who agreed
that a real catastrophe had been narrowly averted. Yet the great Compromise of 1850 was only a mirage to those congressional realists who
instinctively understood the destructive capability of slavery. Unlike
Don Quixote, who mistook a flock of sheep for advancing soldiers,
these men refused to see something that was not there.

No one felt this way more strongly than Grow and his fellow Democrats. Their party, with a majority in Congress, faced the second half
of the nineteenth century with cautious reserve and trepidation. Aware
of the particularistic forces within their ranks and the effect this situation might have upon legislative deliberations, the Democrats came to
lean heavily on the compromise measures for unity. Their unity assured
national unity. These measures had focused upon the issues, especially
territorialism and the fugitive slave law, but behind the great issues
were their protagonists, critics, and watchdogs. Were the old fires of
dissent to be rekindled, these men stood ready by the bellows. Sacrifice of principle was not to come easy, and Grow recalled how Congress in the 1850s was the combat zone for many "personal uprisings."[2]

Assessing Grow's performance in the Thirty-second Congress, the
Bradford Reporter believed the young lawmaker had been "always sound
and radical" in his remarks.[3] Its publisher, E. O. Goodrich, had been
an ardent supporter of Wilmot. As protectors of the district's radical
reputation, the two men were anxious to see Grow perform in that
tradition. His first term in office apparently had not disappointed
them; his unorthodox conduct in Washington had betrayed neither
their trust nor that of his constituents. Even his opponents conceded
that he gained instant notoriety and acclaim with his comments on
Kossuth, finality, the tariff, and the homestead bill.[4] Some Van Burenites, free traders, and abolitionists still believed that Grow was too
timorous a liberal, an opportunist who only flirted with ideals other
men had grafted upon their souls. But his brand of radicalism was
good enough to satisfy free-soilers without alienating the Hunkers.
His election in 1850 and again in 1852 proved this.

The traditional radicalism of Grow's district was based on a combination of institutionalized grievances and dates back to early frontier
days. Most of the pioneers who settled in northeastern Pennsylvania
had come from New England in search of independence, freedom,
and a better quality of life. For the most part, however, they found
only frustration and misery. Proud and imbued with the spirit of the

Revolution, they fought back, and they and their descendants were soon noted for their "anti" attitudes. They deplored the greed and exploits of land speculators, some of whom operated through the Susquehanna and Delaware companies. At the same time, they protested against irresponsible politicians who were prolonging the agony over disputed land claims between Connecticut and Pennsylvania while failing to halt Indian ravages. Later, these simple settlers, perhaps because of their New England heritage, were among the first Pennsylvanians to organize against slavery. Montrose became an early center for abolitionism and a station on the Underground Railroad. The Liberty party flourished there from 1840 to 1856, when it was absorbed by the Republicans. Many of Grow's friends, including Ralph B. Little, in whose office he read law, supported the antislavery crusade. In addition, the Laborers' party in Bradford — the "Workies" as they were called — were antigovernment and antilawyers, while the temperance movement in the county was one of the more active in the state. Not to be overlooked, finally, was their general rejection of a tariff that protected not the worker or farmer, but special interests. To take a hard stand against land speculators, incompetent government, slavery, liquor, and special interests was a must for anyone who cared to represent the district in Congress.

As a freshman congressman, Grow strengthened his political philosophy by subjecting his beliefs to the rigors of legislative debate. He demonstrated an ability to weld a coalition of conflicting ideas in a political party whose philosophy was flexible enough to attract antagonistic groups without insisting they abandon their principles. He sifted through ideas and programs of land reformers and foreign policy makers of varied proclivities. Trying this and that scheme, he embraced some and rejected others, an eclectic method based significantly on what he believed the democratic myth to be. In the end he retained his Jeffersonian purity and Jacksonian zeal by making sacred the cause for human rights everywhere. He was an interventionist who did not want to see his government turn its back on the oppressed in foreign lands; a legalist who viewed the Compromise of 1850 not as the final solution but as the law in temporary defense against militant extremists; a reformer who called for the overhaul of the nation's land policies to help the actual settler; and a free-soiler who saw slavery in the territories as a deterrent to liberty and the natural development of the country. He believed he could play all those roles and remain a good Democrat. He continued to believe this until the disaster of the Kansas-Nebraska bill.

Intervention for Nonintervention

"Washington, in 1851," said Grow fifty years later,

was a promise of the noble city of today. Though it then had a population
of 40,000 it presented much of the appearance of an overgrown village.
Its homes, as a rule, were built of wood and destitute of architectural pretensions. Many of its avenues and walks were unpaved and ill kept, and
there were few squares or shades, or places of public resort. Not a street
was lighted except Pennsylvania Avenue. Southeastern Washington was
cut off from the rest of the city by a wide, shallow canal, which extended
from the Potomac nearly to Capitol Hill, and was a receptacle for the city's
filth and refuse. There was not a sewer in the city; weeds grew in the
parks and commons; the present Departments and the Capitol were unfinished, and stables, wooden fences and patches of bare earth surrounded
the White House.[5]

While the city was physically desolate and unfinished, its social
life, according to Grow, "had never been more animated and delightful" than it was during his first years in Congress. At frequent danc-
ing and dinner parties, and a constant round of house gatherings,
conversation flowed easily, filled with anecdotes and barbs aimed at
opposition politicians. Many toasts were drunk, many visionary plans
unveiled, and many failures confessed. Elegant food, fine Madeira,
and excellent cigars usually topped the evening. The excesses of this
side of political life never appealed to an abstainer like Grow. But
he long remembered how well the receptions of President Millard
Fillmore were attended, as were the occasional functions of Queen
Victoria's minister, Sir John Crampton. Perhaps the most popular
house for Washington society was that of Sen. Daniel Dickinson of
New York, whose gracious wife was acknowledged as a peerless hostess, the Perle Mesta of the time.

Washingtonians also craved visiting artists, and Jenny Lind's concert appearance in the winter of 1851 did not disappoint them. It seemed
that all America wanted to see this charming and gifted singer from
Sweden. Grow told a delightful story of her performance before a
Washington audience. After the concert had begun, several members of the Senate and cabinet, including Daniel Webster, arrived
at the hall and took their seats. After the applause that greeted them
had subsided, Miss Lind burst forth with "Hail! Columbia." His patriotism deeply moved by this national air, Webster arose and added
his rich, sonorous voice to the chorus. His embarrassed wife, who
sat behind him, pulled at his coattail to make him sit down or stop

singing, but to no avail. The volunteer basso joined in at the close of each verse, and everyone, including Miss Lind, seemed delighted. As the last notes of the song died away, Webster made a profound bow to the singer. The blushing artist curtsied and the audience applauded. Webster, not to be outdone in politeness, bowed again; Miss Lind recurtsied. This was repeated nine times with audience laughter and applause louder each time.[6]

After Jenny Lind came Louis Kossuth, undoubtedly the most famous political personality to visit this country since Lafayette. This Hungarian patriot and hero to millions stirred compassion and controversy everywhere he went. Moving events in Hungary had captured this country's concern two years earlier when the Magyar nationalist rallied his people against their Hapsburg rulers. Few observers, if any, associated Kossuth with the new doctrines of Karl Marx and Friedrich Engels, which had been outlined in their *Manifest der Kommunisten.* Instead, to most Americans, his heroism typified the audacity of a revolutionary crusading for liberty and republicanism.[7] By late August 1849 the ragged rebel forces in Hungary fell before the combined crush of Austrian and Russian armies. Kossuth fled to Turkey where he was seized by the authorities.

News of the Hungarian defeat shocked the American people. The press and political leaders expressed their outrage at Austria and her ally, Czar Nicholas of Russia. Yet, what was to be done? A group known as the Young Americans insisted that the government should at least seriously consider suspending relations with Austria. Others warned of entanglements that would undermine the nation's neutrality stance. Meanwhile, in an open letter from Turkey to the American people, Kossuth begged for their support. In early 1851 Washington took delicate steps to secure his release and safe journey to America, as the country anxiously awaited his arrival.

Kossuth came to America too soon to please the administration in Washington. His mission unavoidably became confused with the Cuban crisis, much to the embarrassment of President Fillmore. In August 1851 a military expedition from New Orleans, comprised of some four hundred American adventurers and aliens, including Cubans, had failed to seize the island from the Spanish authorities. Some of the invaders had been killed, and others who had been captured were either executed or left in prison. In his December message to Congress, President Fillmore had denounced this "illegal and ill-fated" expedition and chastised those responsible for it.[8] Now his administration had the burden of patching matters with the Madrid government to obtain the release of the Americans.

While the president warned against future filibusters, some members of Congress boldly but logically spoke of parallels between the Cuban and Hungarian situations. Was not the struggle for freedom on the island identical to that in eastern Europe? they asked. Maybe it was; then again, maybe the revolutions were dissimilar. The Cuban insurrection did relate to possible American annexation which, if encouraged by a southerner, implied the expansion of slavery. On December 3 Sen. John P. Hale of New Hampshire offered a resolution that expressed sympathy for "victims of oppression everywhere" — an obvious catchall to include the American slaves.[9] Coming from this candid free-soiler, the resolution's intent was obvious, and southerners were furious. Suddenly the issues of Cuba, Hungary, and slavery became intertwined. Kossuth was disillusioned by the issue of freedom for his people being politicized and deliberately corrupted by events in Cuba and slavery in the American South. He tactfully avoided taking sides on slavery, which only alienated the abolitionists and many of the free-soilers and Young Americans.[10]

Despite the politics, Washington was a gracious host when Kossuth arrived on December 30, just in time to toast the New Year. A delegation of congressmen and cabinet members greeted him in his rooms at Brown's Hotel. Joshua Giddings, one of Kossuth's staunchest supporters in the House of Representatives, observed how dashingly splendid the visitor had looked in his rich green velvet suit.[11] On January 7, Congress honored Kossuth with a public dinner at the National Hotel. It was a festive and plush affair, with tickets selling for five dollars apiece. Sen. William King of Alabama, soon to become the vice-president under Franklin Pierce, presided. A good cross section of the government and Washington society were among the 200 guests, who gawked at the visitor and longed to meet him. His dress, elegant manners, and lucid comments may have shocked some who had expected to see a swashbuckling, uncouth revolutionary, not a polished gentleman with the bearing of an aristocrat.

Grow sat at the head table with the honored guest, Speaker of the House Linn Boyd, Daniel Webster, and other dignitaries, having earned his seat among them for his many public and private endorsements of Kossuth. Like countless Americans he was mesmerized by the dynamism of this foreign hero, but his convictions ran deeper. Inspired by the sincerity with which Kossuth espoused the principles of freedom, Grow believed in the man and his mission. Although he realized that the latter could never be achieved, he knew that the memory of the rebel would remain forever. "Kossuth was worthy of all the honor that was heaped upon him," Grow believed. "His handsome presence, the marblelike paleness of his complexion, caused by hardship while in prison, and the picturesqueness of his foreign dress, captivated the popular fancy; while, more than all, his wonderful eloquence and the fervor with which he pleaded his country's cause, left an influence upon the hearts of those who heard him that nothing could destroy."[12]

Grow had planned to make his maiden address as a congressman in behalf of the homestead bill, but the disparaging remarks against Kossuth by Fayette McMullen of Virginia changed his mind and brought him to his feet. The Virginian opposed the U.S. government's helping Hungary with either men or money and charged Kossuth with "impudence" for attempting to subvert the teachings of George Washington. On December 11 Kossuth had told a New York audience that Americans should not be foolishly guided altogether by the principles laid down by their founding fathers; Washington had only recommended neutrality, not nonintervention or indifference to the fate of other nations. Kossuth's interpretation led him to conclude that the United States must intervene to insist upon Russian nonintervention in Hungary. It was more than a request; it was a sober reminder of this nation's fundamental dedication to the pursuit of freedom everywhere. But Kossuth's challenge to Washington's farewell address subjected him to a vicious counterattack by opponents of intervention.

Grow's concurrence with Kossuth's views put him to the political left of those in Congress who supported the Hungarian cause but shied away from any intervention, especially military. "How is he impudent?" Grow asked McMullen, demanding to know how this apostle of liberty should appeal for sympathy and support.[13] "Is it impudent for a man to stand up and advocate the conscious rights of man?" In answering the Virginian he inserted some of Kossuth's own language and admonished his colleagues that the time had come to examine the doctrine of nonintervention and to decide whether it was an inveterate rule from which departure was unthinkable. "It becomes not the American to bow with blind reverence to opinions or institutions because of their grey age," Grow asserted. To him truth and society were progressive; one who acts in the best interest of society by looking ahead with renewed hope cannot entertain all the notions of his predecessors. "I follow no standard hung with the moss-coated and exploded theories of a by-gone age."

While Grow and McMullen were engaged in polemics, Kossuth's crusade showed signs of deteriorating nationally and intensifying along party and sectional lines. Simultaneously with his repeated request for financial and military assistance came a chorus of cries from citizens, many from Grow's district, to deny that request.[14] The administration Whigs and southerners especially grew cool. The attorney general, John Crittenden of Kentucky, warned against the "foreign influence"; Benton of Missouri expressed concern that the Magyar might arouse younger Americans toward intervention; and Gen. Winfield Scott, waiting in the wings for a presidential candidacy, considered the foreign visitor a "gigantic humbug." Realizing that he could do little else in Washington, Kossuth set out to plead his case before the American people. As he toured the states, interest in his mission continued to wane back in the capital. By the time he returned to the East, the mystique surrounding his every move had nearly disappeared. The number of his critics increased as he pressed for more contributions; money stopped rolling in and his debts accumulated. It was rumored that when he left the United States he had less money than when he arrived. His frenzied American journey had generated widespread sympathy, but few dollars and confirmation of the policy of nonintervention.

For Grow the Kossuth affair revealed one dominant fact: that beyond all the ceremonial glitter and hullabaloo, sectionalism continued to pose a threat, like the hollowness beneath the surface of a gigantic sinkhole. The tranquilizing quality of the compromise measures had been insufficient to put tensions to rest. The hard reality was that new issues only revived old attitudes. Instead of redirecting Americans to a wonderful policy of helping an oppressed people, Kossuth had unconsciously refocused their attention upon an issue that annoyed them most — slavery. That the issue of American intervention for Hungary touched upon American slavery and the Cuban question, Grow did not doubt. But what a pity and gross injustice to a noble cause! If the question of American intervention to settle a quarrel among East European powers could be so warped by slavery, he thought, what issue was absolutely free of similar manipulation? Perhaps none. A steady confluence of slavery with issues before Congress made Grow acutely aware of the fate awaiting his favorite program of homestead legislation. Like many of his colleagues, when he addressed these issues, he was confronted with the apprehensions of southerners, who became his sharpest adversaries.

The Compromise — A Final Settlement

During Kossuth's American visit references to slavery turned members of Congress into querulous adversaries and only confirmed the symptoms of a lingering malady. Unionists were worried; instead of settling the slavery question, the 1850 Compromise had given it fresh importance. The amended Fugitive Slave Law, which renewed the license of an abominable and anachronistic institution, was greeted with widespread indignation by abolitionists, free-soilers, and even some moderates. The Underground Railroad increased its activities, and the lecture circuit expanded to include political evangelists who either praised or damned the act. Not wishing to be slave catchers, federal officers and citizens in the North proved insensitive to the demands of plantation owners that the law be upheld. Throughout the North, wave after wave of public sentiment lashed out against the ubiquitous law. And in the South frustrated party leaders devised new strategies to safeguard the only real concession made to them in the 1850 agreements. Having failed was one thing; being content with that failure was something else.

Everywhere unionists pushed their parties to adopt the 1850 measures as an official plank in the 1852 platforms. Clay Whigs and Hunkers who had passed those measures over the objections of party extremists were now determined to see the law carried out. There was even talk of a coalition or "Union" party to see this through, but nothing came of it.[15] Just the thought of losing voters to some absurd solidarity movement midwifed by self-anointed prophets of salvation horrified party bosses. They sorted their options and concluded that they had little choice but to rally their parties behind the Compromise of 1850 with supportive platforms and candidates.

In Washington, congressional leaders took the initiative for their respective parties. Before the opening of the Thirty-second Congress, members of the House attempted by caucus to exact a pledge of unequivocal support for the 1850 measures. William H. Polk of Tennessee asked his fellow Democrats to adopt his resolution that called for the compromise to be regarded as a permanent settlement of the slavery question. Free-soilers and states'-rights advocates joined to table the resolution by a 59–30 vote.[16] Disappointed backers had to console themselves with the selection of Linn Boyd of Kentucky, a compromise man, as the party's choice for Speaker. In their caucus the Whigs did manage to approve a notion similar to the one defeated by the Democrats, but with no more unanimity than there had been among the opposition. Only twenty-seven of the forty-one assembled Whigs voted for "finality" of the compromise.[17] It was a poor showing, since there were ninety-two Whigs in the lower house. Chagrined, some walked out of the caucus, including Thad Stevens of Pennsylvania and Orin Fowler of Massachusetts; Edward Stanly of North Carolina remarked that there had been a "secession from [the] ranks."[18]

Finality festered like an ulcerous lesion in both houses of Congress, as debate dragged for months. To an outside observer it had to look like a replay of the performance two years earlier. Sen. Henry S. Foote of Mississippi introduced a resolution of finality on December 8, but no vote was taken. In the House, even before Boyd was elected Speaker, Stanly had requested to know just "how far the Compromise measures have been repudiated." Thompson Campbell of Illinois admonished his colleagues not to bring up the question, for he feared "another revolution" might erupt; it was just too early in the session for this to happen![19]

Campbell may have been right, for no other issue in the Thirty-second Congress contained as many destructive ingredients as did finality. House members sparred with one another until early spring when all niceties were lifted and serious debate began. By then each party had successfully lambasted the other for its nefarious handling of the fugitive slave law, the only remaining measure of the 1850 settlement still in serious dispute. In April, Junius Hillyer, a Union Democrat from Georgia, amended the Fitch-Jackson resolution by resurrecting the Polk resolution, which had been killed in the Democratic caucus:

Resolved, That the series of acts passed during the first session of the Thirty-first Congress, known as the compromise, are regarded as a final adjustment and permanent settlement of the questions therein embraced, and should be maintained and executed as such.

After a futile attempt by the opposition to table, both the Fitch-Jackson resolution and Hillyer's amendment passed.[20] For various reasons, more than a quarter of the representatives absented themselves when the balloting started. One Harrisburg newspaper lamented the fact that so many Pennsylvanians had helped thin the party ranks at such an important time.[21]

Only three from the Pennsylvania delegation voted against the measures: John Allison of Beaver and Thomas M. Howe of Pittsburgh, both Whigs, and Democrat Grow. Dutifully the Susquehanna lawmaker attended the sessions, listened to the endless wrangling, and then voted his conscience. Although he gave most effort to the discussion over the homestead bill, he could not avoid stating his position on finality, with a little cutting sarcasm, arrogance, and deeply felt repugnance. He spoke at length on May 27, two weeks after the homestead bill had cleared the floor and seven weeks after the adoption of the Hillyer amendment.[22] Finality was still a live issue, because the unionists were hoping to include finality planks in the platforms of their national conventions.

With the results of sectionalism becoming discernibly broader, Grow lashed out against those responsible for keeping slavery and finality in the foreground. For six months he had watched the latter linger in the legislative chamber like a toxic gas from some earthly fissure. Now he was going to tell his colleagues how annoyed he was. He scolded the southerners for being unjustifiably suspicious of their fellow lawmakers from the North and fearful of deliberate and continued violations of the fugitive slave law. He ridiculed the "noble" efforts of Senator Foote, governor-elect from Mississippi, who left his home and pending duties as governor to go to Washington at the government's expense for twenty days to help save the Union. "Save it from what?" asked Grow. Certainly he was not aware of any danger.

He also singled out Alexander Stephens and Thomas Bayly for making the most noise about northern disloyalty to the Constitution. The utterly groundless accusation was made because all the provisions of the fugitive slave law did not happen to please everyone in the North. There may have been instances of nonenforcement and disagreement over detail and the implementation of the law. But this could be said of any legislation. With an exception here and there, Grow assured the southerners, officials in the North were law-abiding. Differences of opinion did not mean disloyalty. Grow may have deliberately picked on Stephens for the treatment his friend John Goodrich of Massachusetts had received as a result of the Georgian's whip cracking over fellow Whigs. When Goodrich had intimated that he would not be opposed to a modification of the fugitive slave law, he had been unceremoniously kicked out of the party within a half hour of taking his seat![23] Like Grow, the New Englander went on to vote against Hillyer's amendment.

Grow recognized no doctrine of finality in the legislative process. "By declaring any law final, you are freeing it from any possible amending," thus putting an act of Congress above the people and their Constitution. Laws must adapt to the needs of every new generation, Grow said; he saw little point in having Congress approve something the previous Congress had done. If a law does not have enough merit to earn the support of the people and the courts, then no reenactment can give it greater vigor and virtue. Probably what angered Grow most was that the Democratic party was being asked to make this doctrine of finality an integral part of the platform as the "touchstone of truth, the test of party fidelity, and political orthodoxy." He urged that party tests, party platforms, and president making be left to the people, who alone are competent to dispose of them. His speech shows that he was reacting to the extensive electioneering in this session of Congress.

His closing advice to his southern colleagues: "End forever this slavery agitation without any sacrifice of principle or interest. Cease proscribing Northern men on account of their opinions of slavery and cease your attempts to silence the thoughts of men." He told them what they did not wish to hear: that the South had committed its initial mistake when it tried to silence the early abolitionists, who were exercising their freedom of thought. Garrison and those like him only came back stronger and more determined than ever.

With these actions Grow crossed the Rubicon. His constituency may have applauded his radical position, but the Democratic hierarchy was not impressed. The young man from Susquehanna had gone too far. His vote against finality and his flamboyant discourse on the subject seriously undermined the party's election strategy. At their state convention in Harrisburg, Pennsylvania Democrats expressed their joy in those who, despite their dissatisfaction with the compromise measures, were willing for the sake of union "to acquiesce in them as a final settlement."[24] This sentiment was strong enough to find its way into the state party's platform a month before the passage of Hillyer's amendment.

Contrary to his intent, Grow's assault against the southerners widened the breach between the sections. He did not wish to see any fresh dust kicked up by slavery, an issue which, if left alone, "would soon have gathered cinders enough to cover [itself]." But this was not to be. Grow carried into the House many effervescent, boyish traits which pleased, perhaps amused, all his associates, including southerners, until they discovered how deep his convictions ran and how powerful were his cogent arguments. Now Grow's ideological posture was readily identified. To the South his youthful impertinence and his utterances, so frank and cynical, qualified him as one of those "freedom shriekers" bent on the destruction of southern rights and interests. The southerners' assessment of him did not change.

Who Is Frank Pierce?

As Grow pleaded for a relaxation of slavery tension, some lawmakers already had gone home to mend their own political fences, as well as those of their parties. For most of them it was a moment of truth. As convention time neared, they had to tell their constituents whether or not they would support the fugitive slave law. Many Whigs and Democrats in the North said they would not; their refusal to accept the compromise measures as a final settlement worried party bosses. Determined Hunkers and unionists, free of ideological commitment, spread the word: only the party that endorsed those measures and only a presidential candidate who supported them could look forward to victory. This was more than preconvention rhetoric; it was a flat warning that no wise party man could ignore. The alternatives were defeat and a return to the crisis politics of 1850. But the recalcitrant ideologues of both parties, North and South, did weigh the alternatives. Sharing a spiritual bond with so many Americans regarding either slavery or states' rights, they pondered seriously the choice between principles and "appropriate" candidates with their platforms of expediency.

Yet the contest between principles and party expediency could not equal the battle among presidential hopefuls. It took fifty-three ballots before the majority of Whig delegates in Baltimore agreed that Gen. Winfield Scott was a better candidate than either Fillmore or Webster. He seemed "neutral, colorless, and safe, with a good war record."[25] Several weeks earlier, meeting in the same city, the Democrats literally sweated through the oppressive heat and forty-nine roll calls before they selected the dark-horse choice, Franklin Pierce of New Hampshire. Upon hearing the news, Pierce uttered to a friend, "Impossible!" Also shocked was Mrs. Pierce, who dreaded the thought of returning to Washington.[26] Neither candidate possessed strong credentials for the nation's highest office. What edge in political experience Pierce enjoyed was offset by Scott's superior military record. And for a nation that trusts its battlefield commanders to become the chief executive, the comparison was not so unreasonable.

What about the platforms and the compromise measures? Both parties perfunctorily adopted similar resolutions. The Democrats promised they would "abide by and adhere to" the measures, but there was no mention of finality. For this reason the resolution allowed for greater interpretation and wider acceptance by men like Grow, who recognized that this concession was a token designed to keep the free-soilers from deserting. Still, some of the party dissenters complained that the resolution had not been debated and that the entire platform, for that matter, had been passed at a time when many of the delegates were off the floor. The Whigs had their problems too. A southern caucus at the convention had attempted but failed to add the word *final* to the compromise plank. The delegates then agreed that the 1850 measures, including the fugitive slave law, were to be "received and acquiesced in by the Whig party." This position was "essential to the nationality" of the party. For many the resolution was a bitter disappointment — too weak for the states'-rights people and too strong for the antislavery men. To critics, this "compromised" position was further proof that the party had declared a moratorium on traditional principles in this election year.

In Pennsylvania the news from Baltimore met with both jubilation and disgust. Since Scott had been the choice at their state convention, most Whigs expressed joy over his nomination. But maverick John W. Howe, congressman from Franklin, addressing a Scott rally in Venango County, voiced bitterness. With undisguised wrath, he accused the Whigs of having abandoned principles for an abominable set of resolutions "not fit for a dog to lie on" — a platform essentially identical to the one adopted by the opposition party.[27] Obviously the Democrats agreed that the Whig platform was a sham, but they had a crisis of their own. The Wilmot people were upset with the party's endorsement of the compromise measures, and the Buchaneers were stunned by the defeat of their man in Baltimore. Both groups were now looking at Pierce to see how he measured up to his opponent. Many had serious reservations about his chances.

Among the presidential hopefuls Buchanan was probably the most attractive to the South. He seemed the most capable of uniting that section with the party organizations in the North. His doctrine of the extension of the Missouri Compromise was still preferable to anything other northerners had to offer; the popular sovereignty ideas of Cass and Douglas were not good enough. It remained for the elder statesman from Pennsylvania to show how it was possible and necessary to put slavery to rest without jeopardizing southern interests. Notwithstanding his support bases in some of the southern states, Buchanan was just one of several leading candidates who cancelled each other out. Observers noted that his enemies outside the convention "warred against him most bitterly."[28] Frustrated, he confided to a friend his intention to retire from politics.[29]

Yet he could gain nothing by denouncing the convention system or deploring the diffusion of his support and his subsequent loss. Buchanan was too good a party man for that. After the convention he wrote a letter to a number of Bradford Democrats who had advocated his candidacy and told them in an eloquent and dignified manner how he liked Pierce and King.[30] A week later he wrote a congratulatory note to the presidential nominee, calling him a states'-rights Democrat of the old Jeffersonian school.[31] Then he went on to campaign for the ticket and platform, with no apparent qualms about either.

For that matter, Grow also lacked reservations about the ticket. His canvass won him general praise by the Democratic press and helped him receive support for a second term in Congress. Unity of purpose among the district's Democrats in this presidential election wiped away the bad feelings generated two years before. On September 8 at Towanda, conferees of the three counties unanimously endorsed Grow for his "uniform support of Democratic Jeffersonian principles."[32] No other nomination was made. Affectionately called the "Bark-Spudder," he enjoyed complimentary and encouraging remarks wherever he went. His constituents remembered him for his able defense of Kossuth, his right-to-soil address on the homestead bill, and his scathing attack against the southerners in his speech on finality. They admired his courage for not always voting with the majority of his party. Plainly, his independent course marked his beginnings as a nonorganizational leader. No longer did the charge that Grow was "tainted with hunkerism" hold up before the evidence.

Even the opposition press tended to soften its criticism of him in a campaign characterized by plenty of hard shouting and drinking. Grow did not mind the shouting, but he was never a good mixer and often drank iced water at political gatherings. The loudest noise in the district came from the *Susquehanna Register,* which accused him of becoming testy at the county "loco-foco" meeting. There he chastised several county postmasters who, according to the paper's editor, were bold enough to disagree with the lawmaker regarding the best mail routes for the county. Grow interpreted their flak as a deliberate ploy to play up the fact that his family business interests would not suffer as a result of his proposed mail service. The editor predicted that Grow's flare-up before fellow Democrats would hurt his chances of reelection.[33]

The editor could not have been more wrong. Grow's margin of victory was an unprecedented 7,500 votes — a mandate that prompted the accolade, "Great Majority Grow." His defeated opponent was neither a Whig nor a politician, but Dr. George F. Horton of Bradford, a respectable physician who was more at ease reading a paper on childhood diseases before the county medical association than addressing a brassy crowd of voters. He ran against Grow as a Free Democrat. His party rejected the Democratic and Whig platforms and insisted that the fugitive slave law must go. Although there had been wide sentiment against this law throughout the northern tier counties, many free-soilers among the Democrats urged voters to support Pierce and the Baltimore platform. A number of them, including Horton, refused. As a consequence, both he and the presidential nominee of the Free Democrats, John P. Hale, fared poorly in the district. Hale polled only 575 votes — far short of the more than 3,000 that Van

Buren, running on a Free-Soil ticket, had received four years earlier. At the same time Horton lost to Grow by a 3,090 to 458 vote in his own county, where the influence of Wilmot was felt. In Susquehanna Grow received 2,710 votes to Horton's 37.[34]

Pierce carried Pennsylvania by nearly 11,000 votes and the nation by more than 200,000 over Scott. Part of the success story belonged to campaign managers who, through propaganda and promotional organizations, took a relatively unknown but "available" New Englander and transformed him into a viable contender. Despite charges of being a bigot, a drunk, and a coward, Pierce triumphed behind a phalanx of Democrats who were unionists, Young Americans, free-soilers and states'-rights ideologues. On the surface at least, his victory was a great example of party harmony and union, a truly national effort.

In contrast, the Whigs appeared doomed from the start. Many northerners supported Scott halfheartedly because of the platform, while southerners in large numbers turned their backs on him. After the convention in Baltimore a group of southern congressmen, which included Alexander Stephens and Robert Toombs, bolted. Although he had assented to what was considered a prosouthern resolution on the compromise measures, Scott naively believed that he could win in the South as long as Horace Greeley and William Seward were stumping for him. He could not have misjudged popular attitudes in the South more completely. As a result, "weakened by personal strife, hopelessly divided on questions of principle, the Whig party was led to the slaughter."[35]

The fact that Democrats of various proclivities had momentarily muzzled their differences to pull together at the polls had to please Grow. The spontaneity reinforced what he always believed the true genius of the party to be: the ability to synthesize divergent and often conflicting philosophies within the context of Jeffersonian-Jacksonian democracy. His own political philosophy by this time had become a seemingly paradoxical effort to link the past to the future. He clung tenaciously to the Constitution, and just as tenaciously to party traditions and practices. He remained wedded to the virtues and value systems of the small farmers, the mechanics, and the laborers — all those whose livelihood was based on honest industry. Yet his liberalism accepted evolution as natural to social development long before social Darwinism became popular in America. This acceptance was implicit in his Amherst commencement address and explicit in his remarks on Kossuth and finality. His rejection of stationary ideas and standards, even when sanctified by time, implied a logical tour de force that demanded that public policies adapt to the needs of the people. He asked that the Constitution and the institutions and laws that support it be interpreted against inevitable social change. Whether in society or the world of physics, the principle of change is constant; in society it entails the spirit of the democratic process that promotes progress. Still, without harmony, the entire social system is disjointed, awkward, and devoid of fulfillment.

Looking beyond the victories of 1852, Grow and the Democrats wondered if their party might maintain the harmony that had given them success. Grow's own intentions were clear: he planned to return to Washington and work for those interests he believed were best for the party and nation. And there was nothing more inspiring, more challenging, than the continued development of the American West. He hoped to test party unity and resolve in his struggle for homestead legislation.

🦋 4

Man's Right to the Soil

G ROW, SURVEYING his political options in 1852, had a clear
choice between two platforms; he unhesitatingly took the weaker
and more traditional. The Democratic party's set of resolutions re-
hashed the historic principles of the party, pledged resistance to any
revival of the slavery agitation, couched the compromise measures
in conciliatory language, and ignored the homestead bill. The alternative was the platform of the Free Democrats who, in Pittsburgh,
declared their independence from the two regular parties, denounced
the compromise measures, opposed any additional slave states or territories, and demanded free homesteads. "The right of all men to
the soil is as sacred as their right to life itself," the platform stated.[1]

For a free-soiler like Grow, whose depth of conviction regarding
the homestead principle was well known, the Pittsburgh platform had
to be both attractive and enticing. Many of his friends, including Giddings, Chase, and Hale, gave it their blessings and campaigned for
its success.[2] Yet Grow stayed with his party as he had four years earlier when the free-soilers attempted to put their strength behind Van
Buren. Now, as then, he rejected the third party movement. But he
was disappointed with his party's failure to add a homestead plank
to its Baltimore platform. With others he had tried unsuccessfully to
get the convention to adopt one.[3] Instead the Democratic delegates
accepted the following: "That the proceeds of the public lands ought
to be sacredly applied to the national objects specified in the Constitution; and that we are opposed to any law for the distribution of
such proceeds among the States, as alike inexpedient in policy and
repugnant to the Constitution." As one Whig paper cynically remarked,
"Is that all?" The freedom of the public lands was now a pressing
issue, the editor went on, and the Democrats had managed to ignore
it.[4] For that matter, so did the Whigs.

Both parties spurned a homestead plank on practical grounds. They did not want their chances of victory at the polls to be endangered by some whimsical scheme to dispose of the public domain. The fear that a homestead bill would increase immigration, along with a probable drain of eastern labor, generated enough surface hostility to the bill to block its passage in the Senate. Capitalistic interests in both the Northeast and Southeast expressed concern over what might happen to wages and land prices in the older states should the bill be enacted. Then again, the Free Democrats' endorsement of the bill stirred fears among those who candidly observed that the issue of free land was being tied to the chariot of free soil, thus giving a new thrust to the already overworked question of slavery expansion. Whatever the reasons, by election time enthusiasm for the bill had waned.

To Grow the setback came as no surprise. In Congress the bill was entwined with competitive land schemes and the important issue of national expansion. It had not yet elbowed its way into political respectability. Southern nationalists wondered why it was even discussed at a time when the fugitive slave law was being violated. Not until it had become a sectional issue did the homestead bill free itself from the entanglements and advance to a position of legislative prominence. Grow never doubted the validity of the ties between the homestead idea and other issues. As a single face on the many-sided public domain question, the homestead bill was on a collision course with territorialism and sectionalism. The clash did not occur in the Thirty-second Congress, but Grow sensed its inevitability.

The Public Domain

The movement to grant free tracts of land to bona fide settlers by the government, for which the Homestead Act of 1862 is principally noted, climaxed in the decade prior to the Civil War. But it was a deep-rooted pioneer idea that had found expression in the colonial and revolutionary eras. Andrew Johnson of Tennessee, a leading advocate of homestead legislation, traced the concept back to the time of Moses. He followed its turbulent course in American history and declared before the Senate in 1858 that the idea had been recognized, appreciated, and sanctioned by such leaders as Washington and Jefferson. As far as he was concerned, it was "well-nigh as old as the government itself."[5] Despite this assertion, the idea had remained dormant for many years while Congress experimented with other land schemes.

Unoccupied public lands were of little value to anyone. Newer states of the West did not want them, for they could neither be taxed nor put to good use. Of the many plans entertained in and out of Congress, two alternatives stood out: cession of the lands to the states in which they were situated, or lowering the price of the lands with an ultimate distribution of the proceeds among the states in proportion to population. In their quest for cheaper lands, these newer states turned for support to the South, increasingly alienated from the Northeast over slavery and the protective tariff. If the South agreed to liberal land laws, the West might reverse its support of protective tariffs. Thus, the West-Northeast alliance on the tariff would be broken and replaced by a West-South partnership that promised a workable land policy. Architects of this new alignment included Calhoun, Jackson, and Benton. Of the three, Thomas Hart Benton of Missouri emerged as the most dedicated champion of land reform. His comprehensive program embodied preemption, graduation, and donation.[6]

The first of these, like the homestead idea, enjoyed a colonial background. Unlike homestead, however, preemption did not imply a free grant of land; it simply gave the actual settler the right of first purchase at the government price. Residence on and improvement of the land were required. Far from lessening the revenue derived from the public lands, preemption was calculated to increase that revenue by providing a fair inducement to the poor settler and his family. The country would be filled with farms as more and more settlers purchased the land. A natural expansion of industry had to follow; all this development meant annual increases in revenue. Enthusiasts supported preemption as a merited right because of the government's delay in opening new lands for sale. Settlers who "squatted" on unseated land contended that they should not be penalized by a government whose commissioners were dilatory in settling claims, since they would have gladly purchased the land had it been for sale. Benton and friends of preemption kept the idea before Congress until it was firmly established by the Preemption Act of 1841.

By no means did the new law remove all the inadequacies of the land system. Two acute problems still persisted. Under preemption the settlers naturally selected the most fertile and best-located tracts, thus leaving public-land states with large unwanted areas upon which the government had to maintain idle land offices. Secondly, while the 1841 law did protect the settler from the speculator, it did not go far enough. Speculators could still acquire as much land as their greed allowed, provided they did not infringe upon a settler's preemption rights. By hiring lackeys to locate and squat upon the choicest tracts, the cunning land shark frequently got the best of the system. His agents selected lands with the greatest potential value due to their location, quality of soil, water sources, and possible mineral deposits. At the public sale the speculator, through his agents, reaped the benefits of his cupidity. What the West wanted was a liberal law that would vitiate speculation by reserving the public domain for actual settlers.

Obviously preemption had its shortcomings, but the attractiveness of Benton's total land scheme was that one policy generally compensated for the weaknesses of another. His plan for selling land on a graduated scale was an excellent case in point. For years he objected to the practice of offering both good and bad lands at the same price. Newer states opposed this system because it deprived them of population, and the federal government had to admit that the poorest lands failed to generate sufficient sales. Benton asked the government to adjust prices to the quality of the land.[7] In this way, he predicted, the habit of settlers deliberately passing through states to get to better lands further west would be arrested. Year after year Benton kept his graduation bill before Congress, supporting it with the same vigor as he did preemption.

His bill must be viewed along with still a third idea: donation. Duly anticipating that some public lands would not sell at any price, Benton urged that they be given away: "Pass the public lands cheaply . . . sell, for a reasonable price, to those who are able to pay; and give, without price, to those who are not."[8] He recommended that the undesirable "refuse" lands be given to poor settlers. He attached the idea of donation to his graduation bill, but it received scant attention. Giving away land to every destitute soul who came along was not popular with settlers who were mortgaged to the hilt. Similar to homestead and preemption, donation was not new. It had been used by the colonies and by the states after the Revolutionary War to compensate veterans. Yet the practice of issuing bounties in the form of assignable land warrants had only contributed to the entrepreneurial avarice of land barons, whose agents were always ready to accommodate the veteran who wanted to dispose of his entitlement. Very often the veteran, not wishing to venture into a frontier wilderness, sold his warrant to a land agent at a small cost.

From each new administration in Washington the West demanded instant action to resolve the public domain problem, and numerous proposals were advanced. By the 1840s everyone seemed in favor of land reform, and everyone appeared to have a program in mind. Surprisingly, a strong impulse for liberal land legislation emanated from the older states, where the miseries, evils, and frustrations of industrial depressions made many easterners promoters of land reform. With his *New York Tribune,* Horace Greeley provided great stimulus to the movement.[9] Trade unions and workers' parties explored the potential of the public domain as an outlet for thousands of impoverished people who overcrowded the cities; many land-reform petitions sent to Congress were influenced by these groups. The idea of labor associating itself with the land issue intrigued a number of eastern radicals, some of whom cared little for the West. Their primary concern rested with the depressed worker. One prominent agitator was George Henry Evans, editor of the *Working Man's Advocate.*

Evans belonged to a brassy breed of literary and social activists who believed in the freedom of the public lands as an "entering wedge" to effect the regeneration of society. A number of things disturbed him: the increased influence and power that capital exerted upon government and the social inequities this produced; the widening cleavage between rich and poor; and the great influx of immigrants into the labor market. An obvious remedy to relieve the glut of unemployed newcomers was to encourage them, with government assistance, to take a farm in the nation's hinterlands. Along with other reformers, Evans supported an educational campaign through an organization called the National Reform Association, which dedicated itself to the task of reserving the public lands to actual settlers. Evans and his friends helped forge a new coalition, this one between the Northeast and the West. Its participants faulted traditional land policies and advanced the homestead idea as the best solution for most Americans. Neither major political party went along. The Whigs favored Clay's distribution plan while the Democrats found territorial expansion a more popular issue with the voters.[10] The only real land question in the campaign of 1844 was the acquisition of Texas and Oregon, not the disposition of the public domain. Unfortunately for most land reformers, the issues of territorialism and the public lands became almost synonymous.

The Homestead Bill

After the election of Polk the agitation for homestead legislation intensified. Although the new president and his administration supported graduation, resolutions demanding free land poured into Congress. An early one received on January 3, 1845, two months prior to Polk's inauguration, asked for a law by which "every citizen, who may be desirous of cultivating the earth for a living, shall be enabled to enter upon the public lands and occupy a reasonable sized farm thereon, free of cost."[11] A month later, Congressman William P. Thomasson of Kentucky offered an amendment to a graduation bill that included a donation of forty acres to every settler who was the head of a family.[12] His proposal was rejected.

Advocates of a homestead bill persisted. The honor of being called the "father of the homestead bill" belongs to a number of men, including Grow.[13] Among the first in Congress were Felix Grundy McConnell of Alabama and Andrew Johnson of Tennessee. In the first session of the Twenty-ninth Congress both representatives submitted independent bills. McConnell offered his on March 9, 1845; three days later Johnson asked leave to introduce his bill authorizing every poor head of a family to enter 160 acres of the public domain "without money and without price." With little chance of either bill passing, Johnson joined Cornelius Darragh of Pennsylvania to amend a graduation bill with a homestead provision for actual settlers. Johnson's proposal called for the granting of 160 acres of vacant and unappropriated public land to any destitute head of family who would cultivate the land for four years. On the other hand, Darragh's amendment provided for the donation of lands that had been in the market for ten years or more to actual settlers after a three-year occupancy. Neither Johnson's proposal nor Darragh's amendment received the assent of the House.[14]

Despite these early defeats, the homestead idea continued to win friends. As more and more immigrants swelled the ranks of the unemployed, eastern reformers redoubled efforts to pressure political candidates to pledge themselves to the homestead bill and many did. For all of them the year 1848 was a pivotal time. With the old parties frustrated over slavery, thus making the prospects of a third party encouraging, the common ground between those who opposed the extension of slavery and those in favor of parceling out small tracts to actual settlers was the public domain. The slogan "Free soil and Free farms" fascinated those who wanted to fill the West with settlers who were hostile toward slavery.

Land reformers looked to the free-soilers in their convention that year but they were soon disappointed. While one faction grappled with the idea of free lands, a larger group expressed deeper concern over the matter of slavery in the territories. The free-soilers and their candidate, Martin Van Buren, nodded toward the homestead idea, but gave no promise of pushing for its enactment. Without a firm commitment to the bill, the party probably ruined whatever chance it might have had with the western voters. The West showed reluctance to back a candidate from New York who seemed vague or negative on the homestead bill and supported instead a fellow westerner, Lewis Cass, who remained mum on the issue. But Van Buren's managers realized the hidden dangers of the homestead bill. Had their candidate supported the measure, he would have alienated many conservative easterners.

With none of the parties endorsing the homestead bill, its future was uncertain. Interest in Congress lagged as bills introduced by Johnson and Greeley in the Thirtieth Congress had no chance and those presented in the next Congress did no better. Public land committees in both houses displayed little enthusiasm while special interest groups urged better use of the public domain than to squander it on the poor settlers. Other issues more important to national survival, therefore, dominated the sessions. Whirlpools of dissent over the Wilmot Proviso and the Compromise of 1850 raised doubt that the federal government could ease the agitation over slavery. That prospect conjured up so many fears that southern nationalists became defensive and believed that any legislation that encouraged immigration and, at the same time, populated the Northwest with antislavery settlers had to be defeated. In the same vein, rabid free-soilers legitimated the homestead bill as a bulwark for freedom in the territories. Considering the fragmentation of the national parties and the unfolding cohesiveness of sectional sentiments, the bill at this time was politicized by groups that exploited the public domain in their political bargaining.[15] As Sen. William Dawson of Georgia phrased it, "The truth about it is that the public lands are made a mere battle-door for political purposes."[16]

The bill had a poor track record before Grow took his seat in the House. Homestead friends knew their bill faced a long, uphill battle. Southern opposition was not the only obstacle; challenges also came from competitive measures designed to divide the public lands among grants to veterans, or the building of canals, railroads, lunatic asylums, and other projects that had powerful lobbies.[17] Johnson admitted in 1851 that, although the homestead bill had stumbled in previous sessions, the need for such a bill was steadily and surely being impressed on the public mind.[18] He was right.

Fully aware of the bill's poor performance, Grow still hoped to swing support for it by appealing not to the intractable opportunists, but to those who liked its intrinsic qualities. More completely than most land reformers, he treated the bill as an instrument for dealing with the public domain as part of national economic development. Within this broad context he planned to silence the cries of the crit-

ics. He envisaged a network of alliances with Congress, the poor laborer and farmer, the immigrant, the reformer, and the parties — all
directed toward advancing the happiness and prosperity of thousands of unnamed pioneers. His quarrel with the southerners on the
land issue was not that they defended their rights but that those rights
single-mindedly encouraged localism and regionalism. He simultaneously questioned the strategy of the antislavery forces that reduced
the public land question to simply extending or restricting slavery.
The ends he sought with the bill were national, not state and regional.
With respect to the bill's constitutionality, Grow argued that the basis
of the government's authority to give away public land was the provision that gives Congress the power "to dispose of and make all need-
ful Rules and Regulations respecting the Territory or other Property
belonging to the United States" (Art. 4, Sec. 3).

Soon after the House had organized in December 1851, Johnson,
by unanimous consent, reintroduced his homestead measure, which
was referred to the Committee on Agriculture.[19] Supporters were
hopeful. When the bill finally reached the floor the discussion soon
revealed indeterminate levels of party and sectional commitment.
Friends and enemies of the measure avoided arbitrary grouping. As
Democrats and Whigs they reacted to its flush of popularity with a
resolve not to make it an issue in the coming elections. It was a political gadfly on their backs.

The homestead bill in 1852 had friends and enemies in every party
and section of the country. In the newer states sentiment leaned
most heavily toward its adoption. No true westerner who hoped to
remain long in politics could deprecate something that meant so much
to that section. Free land to actual settlers was only sound economic
policy. Whatever unified opposition existed in the West quickly melted.
Stubborn conservatives like Alpheus Felch of Michigan and John
Welch of Ohio persevered in their belief that the settlement of the
public lands had advanced enough for the public good and that the
homestead bill would only stimulate growth that was unhealthy and
grotesque.[20]

The South also exhibited contrasting attitudes. Citizens of New
Orleans did not mind seeing the rapid development of western lands
vitalize regional economy with an increase in the flow of goods on
the Mississippi. Neither did the very poor wish to pass up an opportunity to acquire free land under federal sponsorship. Then there were
the expansionists who were not opposed to southern institutions extending westward. Yet those in favor of the bill generally found
themselves in the shadows of an imperious oligarchy. Some of the

bill's staunchest opponents in Congress obsequiously served the interests of the slavocracy. At first, the thrust of their arguments was economic, with little reference to slavery. By 1860 the *Charleston Mercury* denounced the homestead bill as the "most dangerous abolition bill which has ever indirectly been pressed in Congress."[21] But in 1852 southerners argued that with the passage of Johnson's bill at least one-twenty-fifth of federal revenue would be lost. Diminishing receipts in the treasury, they feared, were the only excuse the devious North needed to jack up the tariff. The South moved closer to the position of one of its leading propagandists, George Fitzhugh, who believed that free land, like free love, tended to "depress civilization."[22]

In the Northeast, attitudes toward the bill covered every possible argument, for and against. Many liked it because it committed the government to a more paternal role, thus affording the largest exercise of liberty and opportunity consistent with the public safety. Labor leaders valued it as a practical means to resolve a distressing situation in the overcrowded cities. With the removal of surplus labor, both wages and the quality of life had to improve. On the other hand, New York Democrats Timothy Jenkins and Josiah Sutherland grumbled that the bill would "take labor from the manufacturing states to the land states . . . and thereby increase the cost of labor and the cost of manufacturing."[23] Certainly the industrialist had to agree. Price increases meant hardships for those who remained and for farmers dependent upon city goods. Other critics espoused the judgment of the sagacious free trader, George Opdyke, that the homestead bill rested upon the fake notion that society owes its members a stake. Maine's Thomas Fuller objected to the bill because it favored one class of citizens over another; a fellow congressman from the same state, Israel Washburn, just did not like the bill. And in Pennsylvania, Whig Thaddeus Stevens, not yet committed to the idea of free land and free soil, contested the right of the government to grant aid to settlers in this manner. "It would be a very unhappy condition in society," he remarked, "if that country [the West] was to be settled altogether by paupers—by men who had no means."[24]

Grow disagreed with his fellow Pennsylvanian. Why must society discriminate against a man because he is poor? It was the deprived individual who needed the most help. Before the House on March 30, 1852, Grow presented a progressive scheme of land administration that embraced the precept of man's inherent right to the soil.[25] This first major address on the homestead bill stood out not so much for its originality as for the clarity and frankness of its arguments. "What right has government," he asked, "to monopolize any of the gifts of

God to man and to make them the subject of merchandise and traffic?" If man has the right to live, he has the right to the free use of whatever nature has provided for his sustenance: air to breathe, water to drink, and land to cultivate. These are necessary and indispensable means for enjoyment of his unalienable rights of life, liberty, and the pursuit of happiness. The gist of this argument underscored the homestead plank in the platform of the Free Democrats.

The argument's forte was its reasonable alternative to the sad record the government had compiled in selling the land. Citing reports from the secretary of treasury, Grow showed how the government could not really expect any real revenue from its sale of lands for years to come, if then. "And while the receipts from the lands are thus diminishing," he added, "the expenses of legislation relative to them are increasing." Since projections for the next twenty years looked bleak, why not throw open the land, instead, and make it truly productive? "From every person that you induce by this grant [the homestead bill] to settle upon the lands, you derive more revenue than you would by a sale without settlement to a speculator." This idea was of special interest to the states; it would allow them to increase their tax bases and develop their resources.

Grow lashed out at his old enemy, the speculator. For generations this sycophant had slavishly curried favor with the government and had received millions of acres. How long must this go on? Grow asked. And why must Congress continue to be part of this diabolic scheme to strip the nation of its most abundant and precious commodity? He reminded his colleagues of their obligation to dispose of the public domain in the best interest of all Americans. The struggle between capital and labor was unequal enough; why should Congress assist the capitalist who invested in public lands only for avarice and power? What chance was there that this manipulator would ever sell his land to settlers for anything less than a handsome profit? The usual pattern was simple: The government surveys its lands, unloads the tracts in large number at ridiculously low prices to those who have ready cash, and then withdraws from the scene. This approach leaves the prospective settler at the mercy of the land barons, the land companies, and their agents or jobbers. Grow proclaimed this a cruel, unconscionable, and antidemocratic system.

The best argument against Johnson's bill seemed to be, Grow admitted, that the public lands were purchased by the common treasury and now were being offered only to a single class of individuals—the poor, would-be settlers. To critics, the bill was unequal, unjust, and discriminatory. What was wrong with a person's exercising his fundamental right to speculate in any venture of his choice, including land? Was this bill another of those socialist devices to destroy the free enterprise system? Not at all, Grow responded. If circumstances prevented a man from availing himself of the advantages of the bill, then "it is his misfortune, and no fault of the law!" The law was there to help those who wished to become actual settlers. The choice was left to the individual.

Grow's uncompromisingly agrarian approach to land reform and his skepticism toward the economic platitides that supported capitalism were rooted in his background. Having been reared in an area where poverty was no stranger, and having limited associations with the prosperous elements of American society, he was not to be bought off with a set of euphemisms contrived as a defense of the free enterprise system. Either this system was naturally incapable of beneficent ends, he maintained, or irresponsible elements were preventing it from working for the common good. As a youngster he saw the poor farmer languish on land that was not his and the speculator maneuver under the watchful but approving eye of the government. It was fitting that he closed his address as he had begun, with a hearty concern for the actual settler:

All he asks of his country and his Government is to protect him against the cupidity of soulless capital, and the iron grasp of the speculator. Upon his wild battle-field these are the only foes that his own stern heart and right arm cannot vanquish. While, then, the shield of this Government is thrown over the moneyed interests of the country, fostering, by your protective laws, its associated capital, withhold not justice from the men who go forth, single-handed and alone, to subdue the forest, tame the savage and the wild beast, and prepare, in the wilderness, a home for science and a pathway for civilization.

Grow invoked not only a new compassion for the settler, but also a harder defense of the homestead principle. It had been his intention to take no active part in congressional debate until the land policy was brought up. On this matter he had a "well settled opinion formed by observation in boyhood and confirmed by the thoughts and studies of maturer years."[26] Inscrutable and aggressive, he stood aloof from most of the currents of conventional thought that swirled about him on the public domain question. He cherished his independent course. In his first Congress none of his views pertaining to the homestead idea were new, but when he expressed them collectively, they put him ahead of the pack as the most liberal among homestead advocates in the lower house.

What made him so liberal — or "radical" to his opponents — was his promise of free land to the immigrant at a time when nativism was a national phenomenon.[27] Most representatives hesitated to enact any legislation that would encourage an influx of foreigners. Even the majority of those who favored the homestead concept abhorred the prospect of their bill being used as bait to attract hordes of homeless Europeans. A critical *Mississippi Palladium* exemplified southern opposition to immigration when it scorned the "impudence of foreigners," obviously in reference to Kossuth, and expressed grave concern that continued immigrant influence was destined to unite with abolitionism.[28] In Grow's own state, the obvious link between the homestead bill and immigration was not overlooked. After the bill had passed the lower house, a Whig paper in Pittsburgh cynically remarked that the first effect of the bill, should it become law, would be to give a "vast impetus to immigration."[29]

This wave of antiforeignism did not derail Grow in his determination to help the future immigrant. On May 10, two days before the bill's adoption, he offered to amend its Section 6, which extended the provisions only to those who were residents of the states or territories at the time the bill would go into effect. His amendment would have enabled those who entered the country after the bill's enactment to avail themselves of its provisions. Conceding that the government should require foreigners to become naturalized before they could receive any benefits under the law, he shunned the idea of making a distinction between those already in the country and those future citizens who were still in their foreign homelands. "Why should any difference be made between men," he asked, "forced by oppression and wrong from the land of their birth, to seek a home in the western wilderness, whether they come in one year or another?"[30]

Grow knew his amendment stood little chance. The House rejected it and, for a moment, the hostility and moodiness that had characterized the discussion on the bill returned and hovered above the final deliberations like a thick, ominous cloud. When Grow introduced his amendment, the friends and opponents of the bill were fairly visible. But there remained a large bloc of representatives, Democrats and Whigs, who had not participated in the debates. No one knew what was going through their minds or how they intended to vote. Their silence worried those who entertained strong feelings for or against the bill. McMullen of Virginia, who had crossed swords with Grow over Kossuth, went after his colleagues who spoke about the bill only to make it a "political scape-goat" in their harangues bearing upon the presidential election.[31]

Victory and Defeat

On May 12, 1852, the House passed Johnson's bill by nearly a two-to-one margin, 107–56.[32] Last-minute efforts to amend or defeat the bill failed; several attempts to adjourn were shouted down. More than half of the negative votes came from southerners, with most of these from the Atlantic states. But more southerners were for the bill than not. Most northerners who voted against the bill also came from the Atlantic states. Five from Ohio, all Whigs, also voted in the negative. In the end, the voting reflected not so much an interparty skirmish, or a division between slave and free states, as a contest between westerners and those from the Atlantic states. Interestingly, nearly a third of the House members did not bother to vote, among them, a number of prominent Whigs, including Stephens and Toombs of Georgia and Stevens of Pennsylvania. The abstentions suggested that the controversial nature of the bill, as in the case of finality, frightened many timid lawmakers on the eve of the national conventions.

Although his amendment had been defeated, Grow voted in the affirmative. He was responding to the need to provide the nation with the most acceptable homestead measure; amendments would come later. Johnson's bill enabled heads of families to enter 160 acres of unreserved lands of the public domain without the payment of any fee. After five years of continuous habitation and cultivation, the settler qualified to obtain a patent for the land. The bill applied only to heads of families who were either citizens or residents of a state or territory prior to January 1, 1852. Noncitizens at the time of their claims had to become naturalized before they could receive their patents.

In the Senate the prospects for the bill appeared dim. The Committee on Public Lands sat on the measure for months before reporting it back to the floor. In July, Chase of Ohio demanded an explanation for the delay. Chairman Alpheus Felch of Michigan replied that additional data had to be collected and that the absence from committee sessions of Joseph Underwood of Kentucky, who had special interest in the bill, prevented other members from taking final action.[33] When the bill finally reached the floor on August 6, its opponents expressed annoyance over the way it was being pushed for consideration before other bills on the floor. "It must wait its turn!" they shouted. Hale, Chase, and Dodge were doing most of the pushing, but they failed to penetrate the inner defenses of the antagonists.

Southern opposition to the bill centered in the pompous, but able senator from Virginia, James Mason. Annoyingly arrogant to northern supporters, he preferred not to take up the bill—at any time. It had come from a "very suspicious quarter," he sneered, and it was being forced by a senator who had been recently nominated for the presidency by an abolitionist party. After this obvious reference to Hale and the Free Democrats, Mason added that he could not in good conscience support a measure endorsed by a party whose victory could destroy the Union. In retaliation, Hale corrected his Virginia colleague by saying that the bill's source was a state a little south of Virginia; his reference was to Johnson of Tennessee. Hale's remarks brought laughter to the Senate floor, but levity was not going to help the homestead bill. With southerners spearheading the opposition, the votes on discussion of the bill were overwhelmingly negative. At the close of the first session of the Thirty-second Congress, prospects for the bill's adoption were not bright.

When Grow returned to Washington for the second session, which began on December 6, 1852, he found the Democrats still celebrating their recent victories and looking forward to the incoming administration. Their party's confidence exuded from the taverns, hotels, and government offices. In contrast, the Whigs appeared to be a depressed group of losers who had been maligned, dispossessed of everything spiritual, and routed out of town. Many of Grow's friends were back, including Benton, Giddings, Chase, and Wade, with the comfortable knowledge that they would be sitting in the next Congress. He liked Giddings for his vitality, praised Chase as a great stimulus, and admired Wade for his frankness, honesty, and sarcasm, although admitting that he could never resign himself to the senator's profanity.[34]

Of the returnees, however, none was closer to Grow than the gritty Missourian, whom he described as: "a born fighter, [with] the figure and face of one. He was a trifle under six feet in height, broadshouldered, deep-chested and large of limb, and his massive head ran up to a peak like the island of Teneriffe, while his features reminded one both of the eagle and the lion."[35]

Benton was not reelected to the Senate in 1852 but returned as a Compromise Democrat to the lower house. "He was a great friend of young men," Grow said of him, "and my acquaintance with him was as intimate as that of any public man I have ever known."[36] It was a lasting friendship rooted in a common loyalty to democratic principles and the welfare of the common man. Both despised moral cowardice in public men. They did not always see eye to eye on issues, but the influence of the elder statesman was enduring. Grow's concern for the immigrant's right to public land may have come in part from Benton. And there is little doubt that Benton's strong position on the Kansas-Nebraska bill helped convinced Grow of the validity of his own stance.

The Missourian took an immediate liking to the young congressman from Pennsylvania who was a stranger in town without many friends. Grow lived in a bachelor's flat in an obscure boardinghouse. He later admitted that during his first years in Washington he lived like a monk. He attributed his reclusive existence to recurring health problems and the fact that he did not care to socialize. "This led some to believe I was odd and in a way affected," he told his biographers. "But, after all, my absence from society was not a great deprivation, for I never liked those social functions which seemed to lack real sincerity."[37]

Grow lived near Benton and made it a practice to stop often to visit with the senior statesman. The two men discussed legislation, the ups and downs of the Democratic party, and the general affairs of state. The crusty old Jeffersonian Democrat probably enjoyed airing his views on states' rights and the Union with a much younger man who wanted to listen. Grow looked upon him as a formidable teacher and came to lean heavily upon Benton's seasoned understanding of men and their motives. Benton liked Grow for his simplicity and frankness as well as his sincere concern for the actual settler. When he began to prepare his memoirs of thirty years in Washington, he asked Grow to keep him informed on what was happening on Capitol Hill. Grow always spoke admiringly of the man from Missouri. His early years in Congress were the most enjoyable, and Benton's companionship was one of the reasons why.

Both men agreed that not much could be expected from the lame-duck session of the Thirty-second Congress. Although unfinished business remained, a languid Congress clearly indicated that there were few important issues, if any, that could not wait until the new administration took office. No bill demanded urgent attention. Still, special-interest groups persisted in their claims for the tariff and the homestead bill. Pierce and most of the other candidates had managed to maintain a "discreet silence" on both issues.

Indeed, the tariff had been conspicuously downplayed in the campaign. But now that the elections were over some House members, including Grow, resurrected the issue with nearly the same intensity that had characterized the debate over the Walker tariff. John Freeman of Mississippi sought a 1 to 2 percent reduction for railroad iron, but Tom Howe pointed to the sluggishness of the iron industry in western Pennsylvania. He received support from Grow, who argued that the taxpayer wanted railroad iron taxed since it was not an article of necessary and universal consumption. "Repeal the duties on railroad iron," he warned, "and you strike a deadly blow at the iron industry of this country."[38] Chagrined, Freeman accused Grow of dealing more of a death blow to the farmers, who benefit the most from railroad expansion, than to the iron manufacturers — a strange position for a representative from an agricultural district in Pennsylvania to take. But Grow was not trying to hurt any economic class, especially the farmers. Carefully he added that he was not speaking out for protection as a protectionist, nor was he blindly committed to the policy of free trade, as were some Democrats. What he wanted was what every taxpayer wanted — fairness and what was good for the country.

While he debated the tariff, Grow kept a close watch over the progress of the homestead bill in the upper house, where it found the going no easier in the second session than in the first. Chase and Dodge made a concerted effort to have the bill considered before adjournment but, as before, too many senators insisted that other bills had precedence. Dodge tried to set a specific date for the bill's consideration, but failed. On February 21, 1853, a week before adjournment, the Senate defeated a motion to take up the bill by an impressive vote, 23–33. Again, the contest essentially was one between the East and West, although more than half of the negative votes came from slaveholding states. Three days after the vote, R. M. Carlton of Georgia seemed to summarize the South's opposition with the provocative charge that the bill would lend a helping hand to "idleness, profligacy and vice."[39]

Despite its defeat in the Senate, the homestead bill of 1852 was not without significance. The attitudes of the federal lawmakers established the bill as neither a sectional nor a party issue. For supporters, its popularity was clothed in a majestic purity that promised eventual triumph; for opponents, its radicalness only assured self-destruction. Between these views, many Democrats and Whigs blunted their public utterances on the bill so as not to sever ties with either extreme. A timid posture seemed politically more judicious than either a firm acceptance or flat rejection. But through all this, slavocracy was beginning to coalesce into opposition. With its adoption by the Free Democrats, the homestead bill suddenly became tainted with free-soilism and abolitionism, those twin sisters of northern fanaticism. With tension over slavery on the rise, the future of the bill in the South appeared dim. Just as the South and West once had allied themselves in common intent on the public domain, so a covenant between an industrial Northeast and an agrarian West loomed as a necessary maneuver if a homestead bill were to be enacted. Slavocracy and the conservative interests of the north Atlantic states, for the moment, halted the legislative crusade for free land. Grow, Johnson, and other friends of the bill took the defeat in stride; at least the measure had passed the lower house. With this half victory, they predicted with confidence that the momentum for free land was building and that in the next Congress it would break down all barriers.

For a congressman in his first term, Grow had shown considerable ability as an independent thinker and leader. He had to be pleased with his performance. His remarks on Kossuth, the homestead bill, and the finality question created a lasting impression and left little doubt in the minds of his colleagues that he was on his way to a distinguished career. His voting record was not unlike that of other representatives: he did not always vote with the majority of his party. In fact, there was a remarkable absence of party-line voting in the first session of the Thirty-second Congress; party cohesion was evident on only two-fifths of selected roll calls.[40] Yet Grow was consistent on several issues. In particular, he supported land legislation that favored the settler, opposed railroad land-grant bills, and refused to back resolutions that compromised slavery. He was the only Pennsylvania Democrat to vote against the resolution declaring the 1850 measures to have been a final settlement. He was among some twenty northern Democrats not willing to denounce agitation against slavery. This development indicated that in the days ahead the slavery issue would be further sectionalized and intensified. Grow was soon to see the homestead bill become one of its innocent victims.

✨ 5

Free Soil and Free Land

I NAUGURATION DAY, March 4, 1853. The morning was portentous of unfavorable weather, with snow slightly falling, but near
noon the skies began to clear and the sun became visible. The frozen
vapor presented no problem to the thousands of people who thronged
Pennsylvania Avenue and gathered around the rotunda of the Capitol. An estimated crowd of 100,000 jammed the area where Franklin
Pierce was to be sworn in as the nation's fourteenth president. Hundreds had spent the chilly night sleeping in the rotunda and warm
passageways of the Capitol while thousands just walked the streets.
As the clock struck twelve, the grand procession began from City Hall
with artillery units from Fort McHenry and Virginia. National guard,
fire companies, political organizations, all marched to the spontaneous sounds of marching bands, church bells, and cannon. Many eyes
caught the flag of the Senate being run down, then raised again, to
mark the beginning of the new Senate.

At half past one, Pierce stepped before the cheering crowd and,
without notes, delivered his address. What he had to say surprised
no one.[1] He spoke of economy in government departments and
warned of the dangers of concentrated power in the national government. Both the states and the federal government were expected to
stay within their constitutional spheres. He affirmed the legality of
the 1850 Compromise measures and promised to carry them out.
Slavery was an admitted right recognized by the Constitution and,
like other southern rights, had to be safeguarded. In foreign affairs
the new president suggested an aggressive program: "Certain possessions" may have to be acquired, Americans abroad would be protected, and new lines of trade were to be opened. The Monroe Doctrine was reaffirmed; a strong military defense assured. There seemed

73

to be something for nearly everyone. Pierce looked like the right man for the job.

But his cabinet appointments excited few and angered many. Free-soilers, states'-rightists, and the friends of Stephen A. Douglas and James Buchanan felt slighted. Many muttered to themselves about the president's choices for department heads. Even the backers of the administration kept asking "Who?" when informed of some of the appointees. Men like Robert McClelland (secretary of the interior), James Campbell (postmaster-general), James Dobbin (secretary of the navy), and James Guthrie (secretary of the treasury) were virtually unknown beyond their own states. On the other hand, the new secretary of state, William L. Marcy, a New Yorker who knew little of foreign affairs, and the secretary of war, Jefferson Davis, a Mississippian who knew what was best for the South, were better known nationally but represented viewpoints that often clashed. Democratic critics wondered if these men were the best available to bring the party factions together. Could they do it? A great deal would depend upon the crises that challenged them.

Nothing proved more traumatic to the political mind at midcentury than the issue of Kansas. Before it lost its driving force, the Pierce administration would be gone, the Democratic party would be in a shambles, and the Union would stand on the precipice of disaster. Yet Kansas was not the real culprit. Whether it or any territory was to allow slavery seemed less important than the limits an industrial and expansionist North might place upon an oligarchic South, and vice versa. Was the North to acquiesce in the possibility of slavery in Kansas or was the South to submit to the pressures of a northern majority? That was the real question.

While it is true that slavery influenced most issues, Grow believed the opening of the western lands was a more positive matter. It linked such powerful questions as immigration, railroad expansion, industrial growth, and the public lands. Land programs therefore were basic. Whatever policy the government adopted toward the public domain was crucial to both the future of the nation and the Democratic party. Just as the nation was divided over slavery and its expansion, so were the Democrats split when it came to land bills. Roland Jones of Louisiana perceived that no question divided the Democratic party as much as the public land question.[2] Grow had to agree. He watched how the homestead bill drew its divisive quality from the tempest over the Kansas-Nebraska bill, which had more than its share of divisive qualities. The two bills were inseparable; free soil and free land became interlocked.

Land to the Landless

The future of the homestead bill had never looked stronger than it did at the end of 1853. When Congress convened in December, representatives and senators from every part of the country were ready to introduce homestead legislation. In the House, Grow and fellow Pennsylvanian William L. Dawson jumped ahead of everyone with their bills; Bernhart Henn of Iowa and W.R.W. Cobb of Alabama followed. Meanwhile, Senators Chase of Ohio and William Gwin of California had similar intentions. Grow's and Dawson's bills were referred to the Committee on Agriculture, and since Dawson chaired that committee, he succeeded in getting first consideration for his measure. The next day he reported it back to the floor without amendment, but debate did not begin until the second week in February.

The moment for debate on the bill could not have been less opportune, for by now national attention was turned to the Kansas-Nebraska bill before the Senate. Harsh attitudes generated by the territorial bill affected the thinking in the lower house on the land measure. The ramifications of the Senate bill inescapably intruded upon the discussion of the House bill. Some representatives used the time they were allocated to address the homestead proposal as an occasion to vent their pent-up feelings on the territorial bill.

House opponents to the homestead bill raised old postulates, contrived fears, and concerns aired in the previous Congress. Was the bill constitutional? If enacted, would it not inevitably stimulate a westward flow of population? And could such a trend be controlled to avoid draining the industrial areas of skilled labor, thus increasing the cost of manufacturing? Finally, and probably the most poignant question asked: Would the free-land bill not encourage wholesale immigration? At a time when nativism, with its invectives against popery and the foreign-born, was at a peak of popularity, this question was not to be pondered lightly.

Despite such opposition, not one part of the country braced itself solidly against the bill. The idea of granting free land to actual settlers had not yet dug an unbridgeable abyss between any two sections. Germane to the southern position, however, was the irrepressible urge to renounce the homestead concept as inimical to the interests of slavery. Why should the South support a bill that attracted to the public lands settlers inclined to be hostile to slavery? This question became more widespread as the tension over the Kansas-Nebraska bill increased. When applied by hordes of northerners and immigrants, the doctrine of popular sovereignty that distinguished the territorial bill might destroy any hope of the South to perpetuate its peculiar institution. Southern radicals were not fooled. "Land to the landless," editorialized the *Richmond Enquirer* on March 15, 1854, "was the most unprincipled and pernicious measure yet bred in the prolific brain of demogoguism."

During the Thirty-third Congress, Grow strengthened his reputation as the most liberal crusader for homestead legislation, replacing Andrew Johnson, now governor of Tennessee, as the driving force behind the free-land movement. His hope to see his own measure taken up first by the House was overshadowed by a stronger desire to support any genuine homestead bill that stood a good chance of passage. The essential need was to legislate the homestead principle; amendments with liberal provisions were destined to follow.

On February 21, 1854, Grow delivered his second major address endorsing the homestead bill.[3] He repeated what he had voiced in the last session: that the true object of the government must not be the sale of public lands but their settlement and cultivation. He restated his conviction that through the homestead idea the government could eventually derive more gain from the lands than through their actual sale. The several hundred dollars a settler must pay to the government or, more likely, the speculator for the land could be better used to purchase imported goods for the comforts of life and the necessary stock and farm implements for cultivating his fields. His purchase of foreign goods would mean an increase in tariff revenues.

Grow envisaged an expansive federal program to encourage the mobility of people and institutions; immobility and stagnation were curses to progress. To avoid an overpopulated East with congested slums and many people out of work, the excess population must be permitted to move westward with the aid of a liberal land policy. He did not have to remind his colleagues that, as long as America remained the citadel of freedom, immigrants would continue to flock to its shores. Each year more arrived. "Is it not better to give them a home in your wilderness," Grow asked, "and thus fasten them to the country by a tie stronger than the oath of allegiance?" Why confine them to the eastern seaboard to become penniless wards of society? Give them land and they will produce. And those who remained in the cities would find it easier to obtain employment and a better quality of life. Free land could help build a society of good citizens and not one of drifters "to hang about the purlieus of your cities, a curse to themselves and to your own population."

Grow drew heavily from a repertoire of arguments validated by the land reformers. With an inducement of free land, the poor would alleviate a major labor problem in the industrial areas, he contended. Surplus workers contributed to a reduction in the cost of labor, thus creating hardships for themselves. With purchasing power of the masses at a minimum, manufacturers found it necessary to reduce prices or cut back production or both. Grow closed his remarks with a bit of agrarian wisdom: the wealth of any nation consists not in the sums of money paid into its treasury, but in "its herds, flocks, and cultivated fields."

Exactly one week after Grow's address, debate over Dawson's bill began in an atmosphere rendered glacial by hostility. Members harangued with such vituperative bias that it appeared the bill might be lost in a turbulent sea of words. Verbosity did not conceal conviction. Most lawmakers just found it impossible to keep their minds off the Kansas-Nebraska bill and kept alluding to it as they wrestled with the land bill. Some moderates began to share the suspicions of the radicals that the passage of the homestead bill would act to prevent slavery in the territories.[4]

The most provocative section of the bill, the qualification provision, flared emotions and sometimes tempers. Who was to benefit by this legislation? Only citizens? Was there to be a distinction between naturalized and native-born citizens? What about the immigrant? And what about women? Freedmen? How old must the settler be? Must he be single, married, or either? The question went on and on, often causing derision and despair.

To break a deadlock over the qualification provision, Cobb of Alabama offered his bill as a substitute amendment. He wanted to limit the benefits of the bill to single white men who were at least twenty-one years of age and who were citizens. The amendment required the settler to locate upon "agricultural" lands and not "unappropriated" tracts as designated in Dawson's bill. Since unappropriated lands included valuable mineral properties, it was unwise to give these away to common settlers, Cobb maintained. Dawson advised the friends of the homestead bill to adopt his bill in its original form. He charged that Cobb's amendment contained "so many propositions in a single sentence that its interpretation would be rendered very ambiguous." Other legislators agreed that Cobb's inability to show how mineral lands would be determined and set aside, and his insistence that only single men were eligible, made his amendment unacceptable. On March 2 it was rejected.

On the same day, Grow went after the southern opponents to the main bill.[5] More in this session than the previous one, his vitriolic tongue easily cast him as one of those free-swinging "freedom shriekers" whose flamboyancy was exceeded only by a passion to discredit, if not destroy, southern interests. He directed his venom at one of the leading apostles of southernism, J. S. Millson of Virginia, who did not like the homestead bill's potential for drawing population from the older states. Grow retaliated: "Why confine a man to misery and want beside your own doors and in your own State when he can find a happy home for himself and his children in a far distant land?" If a settler left his farm in one of the older states to take advantage of the bill, he would most likely sell his property to another farmer. Besides, Grow asked, what man who had a permanent home would leave it just to avail himself of new legislation? The bill was expected to assist mainly those laborers who owned no property and could not make a living in the older states, he argued.

Although Grow may have angered southerners with his rebuke of Millson, another Pennsylvanian probably amused them. Hendrick B. Wright, Democrat from Luzerne County, proposed to limit the land to "free white" settlers. Whatever his motives may have been, his amendment superimposed slavery upon the homestead bill and gave a new three-dimensional effect to sectionalism. Southerners and northerners alike reacted with astonishment. Many from the North embraced the amendment with mixed feelings, believing that concessions of some kind were necessary if the homestead bill were to receive southern support. A North-South coalition enabled the Wright amendment to pass, 101–78, and gave promise that a homestead bill in some form probably would pass the lower house. Some friends of the homestead idea, including Grow and Dawson, wanted no part of this ploy and voted against the amendment.[6]

The amendments of Grow, Cobb, and Henn were actual substitutes for Dawson's bill. The House never seriously considered the Henn proposal. In fact, the Iowan agreed to take his substitute off the floor and vote for the original bill. He suggested to Cobb and Grow that they do likewise, but both were still too critical of Dawson's measure to accept it without a struggle. His earlier attempt to amend the bill having failed, Cobb now offered another substitute that combined elements of graduation with those of the homestead bill and also extended the benefits to women. This new measure was also rejected.[7]

On the same day, Grow pressed for the adoption of his measure.[8] Even though be believed the bill of his fellow Pennsylvanian to be worthy of favorable action, he still did not like many of its provisions. He boasted that his substitute included all the amendments adopted by Dawson's committee and other provisions designed to guard the government against fraud and imposition while, at the same time, protecting the settler. He insisted on two points: that the settler pay the costs of survey and title transfer, and that no land hereafter surveyed by the government, except mineral lands and certain tracts the government might reserve for its own use, should be available at public sale. All should be open to entry by actual settlers only.

Grow's substitute differed from Dawson's bill in other ways. Whereas Dawson wanted to restrict the benefits to those who were citizens at the time the bill went into effect, Grow proposed that a settler merely declare his intention to become a citizen before he made an entry; once he completed naturalization he would receive his patent for the land. Opening the door to both present and future immigrants was the feature that made Grow's bill so objectionable. Second, he required the applicant to swear that the land was for his own use, another safeguard against the speculator. It also extended the privileges and rights provided for heads of families to any one of the settler's children who, upon the death of both father and mother, assumed the responsibility of caring for the rest of the family. Finally, the would-be settler had to agree not to bargain away any part of his land before he received his patent.

Because of his vital concern for the immigrant, Grow saw little hope for his bill. On March 6 the House rejected it. Moments later the lawmakers approved Dawson's bill, 107–72, after an attempt by William O. Goode of Virginia to table it. As he had promised, Grow voted in the affirmative.[9]

The voting did not reveal a truly intersectional character — North versus South or East versus West — but there were signs that such a pattern was in the making. Growing southern resistance was evident: among the fifty-one representatives from Virginia, the Carolinas, Georgia, Alabama, Mississippi, and Louisiana, only eight voted for the bill and thirty-six opposed it. A half dozen did not bother to vote. In the Northeast the results revealed mixed sentiments. Of the twenty-nine New Englanders, only seven voted for and nineteen voted against the measure. In the Middle Atlantic states, about a third of the representatives did not vote, and the vast majority of those who did vote did so in the affirmative. William H. Kurtz, York County Democrat, was the only Pennsylvanian to vote against the bill. A few northerners like free-soiler Gerrit Smith of New York may have voted in the negative because of the Wright amendment.[10] As expected, the best showing for the bill came from the West. Only a handful of negatives were recorded in all the states between the Ohio River and the Pacific.

The votes on the Wright amendment and homestead bill made

one thing obvious to the Democrats — sectional differences on key leg-islative issues must be cushioned if the party was to maintain its ma-jority. And if abolitionism and free-soilism were to be checked, then the South needed western support. But this posed a dilemma. In-creased southern prejudice against the homestead bill might jeopar-dize any chance for a permanent alliance with the West. On the other hand, southern endorsement of the homestead bill would open the door to immigration and more antislavery zealots. Homestead sup-porters waited to see how southern leadership planned to handle this "bases-loaded" situation. Yet a greater question, for the moment, faced the Democratic party: can a solidarity of Democrats everywhere re-sult from the Kansas-Nebraska bill? With that bill pending in the House, there was considerable doubt that unity could be achieved.

Touchstone of the Orthodox Democracy

Grow was looking ahead to his defense of the homestead bill when Stephen A. Douglas dropped his Nebraska bill on the floor of the Senate. At first, the territorial measure caused little stir. By the time everyone had a chance to examine each of its provisions, however, the stir had become a rumble of seismographic intensity that could be felt clear across Capitol Hill.

In its original form the bill simply organized the Nebraska terri-tory and designated slavery as a local option: "When admitted as a State or States, the said territory . . . shall be received into the Union, with or without slavery, as their constitution may prescribe at the time of their admission." This language was similar to that used in the Utah–New Mexico acts of 1850. Since Douglas's committee was not prepared to recommend either an affirmation or denial of the Mis-souri Compromise, the entire slavery matter remained up in the air.

Bewildered and unhappy, some southerners pressured Douglas to give a new form to his bill that would not only include the doctrine of popular sovereignty, but would also resolve the question of slavery restriction under the Missouri Compromise. Archibald Dixon of Ken-tucky, Henry Clay's Whig successor to the Senate, proposed a repeal of that part of the 1820 Compromise that prohibited slavery north of the 36° 30′ line. Like many others, Douglas was surprised by the amendment, which was definite and explosive. Perhaps it was a Whig maneuver to embarrass and split the Democrats, or maybe it was just a reaffirmation of the principles of the 1850 Compromise.[11] Either way, Douglas was worried. He had hoped his bill might remain vague and equivocal. He had assumed that the slavery restriction of the Missouri

Compromise would remain in force until it was invalidated by the courts, although it represented a potential contradiction of the popular sovereignty principle.

Grow claimed that Douglas had been caught off guard by Dixon's amendment and had tried to convince the Kentuckian to change his mind. This conclusion was based on a dinner conversation he had had with Douglas, Sen. John Slidell of Louisiana, and Postmaster-General James Campbell of Pennsylvania sometime between Douglas's reporting of the original bill and his later substitute, which made for two territories instead of one and which rendered the Missouri Compromise inoperative.[12] At this meeting, Slidell urged Douglas to move for the repeal of the 1820 Compromise. Later Grow told Benton that the Illinois senator seemed so unsure in his views on slavery and its expansion that he believed Douglas was leading the Democratic party from its moorings. The feisty Benton chuckled and replied that it was the other way: the party had been leading Douglas by the nose for years and that he would follow it to hell!

The Douglas bill went to the Senate in its final form on January 23, 1854. Backers and opponents in and out of Congress aired all the possible arguments, pro and con. Editorials reflected the division of opinion with glaring optimism or portentous misgivings. It was clear that responsibility for the measure rested with the Pierce administration and the Democratic party.[13] The bill was to become the symbol of party fidelity. Democratic mavericks were those who refused to honor the bill and the 1850 Compromise as a final settlement to the slavery question. These included the free-soilers, who had few remaining options. Either they endorsed the Kansas-Nebraska bill or they faced repudiation and exile. And what about the impact the bill might have on sectionalism? Right now, the optimists held the high ground. The *Baltimore Sun* assured its readers that the bill would not agitate the slavery controversy as long as the administration and the Democratic Congress remained resolute.[14]

Grow was disappointed with the bill and its author. For years he and Douglas had seemed to share a common, twofold goal for the West: developing that region with the aid of a homestead bill and minimizing the slavery issue in any territorial policy. As chairman of the Senate Committee on Territories, Douglas believed that he could achieve both objectives. But this was not to be. Grow watched political expediency again triumph, sure that the senator had allowed himself to be intimidated, cajoled, or duped by certain southerners who undertook to nationalize the slavery question. What future favors Douglas expected in return remained a mystery.

Douglas assured Grow that President Pierce considered the Missouri Compromise to be unconstitutional and ought to have been repealed in the 1850 settlement. Grow was dubious. It appeared certain that the senator from Illinois did not want his measure to shoulder this matter of repeal alone and blamed the president as a convenient expedient. On the Sunday before his final bill was introduced, Douglas, along with a bloc of southerners that included John Breckinridge, David Atchison, and Philip Phillips, met with Pierce. The president was not thrilled with the proposal to annul the Missouri Compromise, but the senators pressed him to go along. Reluctantly he obeyed. He realized that he needed these key men to support his domestic programs, foreign policy, and patronage. Party unity weighed heavily on his mind. Now, with the blessing of the president, Douglas was ready to ram his bill through Congress. If nothing else, he had to demonstrate his leadership before the party and nation.[15]

Whatever power game Douglas may have played, Senate discussion on his bill had an impact upon the homestead measure before the House. The two bills touched common ground at several points. In addition to dealing with western lands, each bill resurrected the old, knotty question concerning the extent to which the federal government could interfere with the internal affairs of the states. With its repeal of the Compromise of 1820, the Kansas-Nebraska bill underscored the principle of nonintervention, probably its most important feature. Southerners insisted that this principle had been recognized by both parties in the 1850 Compromise. At the same time, states'-rightists denied the right of Congress to use the homestead bill to squander the public domain at the expense of the individual states. They asked why the newer states should not have the power to deal with these lands as they saw fit.

Then there was the matter of immigration. Grow's attempt to extend the homestead bill's provisions to aliens and future immigrants paralleled the action waged in the upper house against the Clayton amendment to the Kansas-Nebraska bill. This proposal of John Clayton of Delaware, former secretary of state, restricted the franchise in the territories to citizens alone. Grow asked, since it had been the policy heretofore to permit all residents who had declared their intentions to become citizens to participate in the organization of the government, what reason was there now to exclude them? Disqualifying them was unjust. Being residents of the territory, he argued, was ample proof of their serious intention to become citizens.

Grow may have agreed with the *Baltimore Sun* that the Kansas-Nebraska and homestead bills were inconsistent, but for different reasons. The homestead idea sensitized southern apprehension that the public lands would be inundated with hordes of immigrants and the indigent unemployed from northern cities, most of them against slavery. Opening a new territory with the help of a liberal land policy meant defeat for the South in the numbers game. In no way could that section send enough of its sons and daughters to match the population flow from the North and from Europe. Southern support for the homestead bill therefore was suicidal, the *Sun* concluded.[16] Grow did not doubt that the bill would attract masses of potential settlers, but he was not so sure the majority of them would stand in the way of slavery. At first he believed that Kansas was destined to become a slave state. He cited the fact that there were 863,589 slaves already living north of the 36°30' parallel. The widespread claim that slavery could not spread into Kansas because of climate and soil was humbug. But the real inconsistency between the two bills, as he saw it, was that while one promised a boom to western development, the other represented a carefully designed political stratagem to extend slavery in the name of popular sovereignty.

In the first week of March, the Senate passed the Kansas-Nebraska bill 37–14. The closing debate, which continued through the night, pricked the nerve endings of most senators. Douglas, in a final burst of glory, harangued for three hours, massaging old arguments and throwing invectives at his critics. To some he was brilliant; to others his style was boorish, inappropriate, and ungentlemanlike. Knowing there were enough votes to pass the measure, the long night became a vigil for those who opposed it. Sam Houston was valiant in his last-minute effort to save the Missouri Compromise. Since he was willing to repudiate the Douglas bill for the sake of the Union, why were not others? But it was hopeless. The Douglas men greeted the new day with sighs of relief and contentment.

There was good reason to believe that the bill would not get through the House. Uncertainty started to appear as discussion on the homestead bill subsided and campaign time drew near. Opponents managed to relegate the measure to the bottom of the House calendar, with many bills ahead of it, though Douglas and the administration prepared themselves to use everything at their disposal to push the bill through in this session. Still, the bill did not come to a vote for several months. This delay afforded House members ample time to assess the opinions of their constituents, the actions of their legislatures, and the steady diet of verbiage coming from pompous editors and from the public forum. Washington's taverns, hotels, and rooming-houses buzzed with rumors and reports, as news from every part of the nation poured into the city. The word from the northern states was not good for the Democrats. Only one, Illinois, endorsed the Kansas-Nebraska bill. Some of the free-state legislatures repudiated it by huge majorities; a few, including Pennsylvania, New Jersey, and California, refused to take any action. For the first time in a long while the Whigs felt a dose of political adrenalin. Perhaps a comeback for the party was in the making. The fall elections in all the northern states would find the Democrats painfully divided. The bill was turning many of them to the free-soil doctrine. Weeks earlier, the *Baltimore Sun* direfully predicted that the bill would bring the Wilmot Proviso out of the woodwork.[17]

By the beginning of May 1854, the eyes of the nation viewed the House as the Armageddon of this territorial struggle. Foes of the bill had delayed action long enough. Now the Douglas and administration forces, led by William Richardson of Illinois, were ready for the final assault. But the person most responsible for driving the legislative chariot through the phalanx of opponents was Stephens of Georgia. A more conscientious spokesman for the South did not exist. He pontificated that the "principle of division" as regards slavery contained in the Missouri Compromise had been abandoned and repudiated by the North in the organization of all territories since 1848. The bill of 1854 was only carrying out, in good faith, the principle of nonintervention established in the 1850 Compromise.[18]

Week after week the oratory flowed back and forth across the lower chamber. Much of it was ornate, turgid, and often laced with emotion. But logic and smooth rhetoric soon gave way to serious plea bargaining, browbeating, and downright name calling. All discipline vanished as lawmakers exchanged threats and displayed their bowie knives and pistols. Suddenly a democratic forum became a menagerie of frightened, exhausted, and embittered souls. It was anyone's guess how the vote might go.

An inner group of rabid enthusiasts, which included Grow, Benton, and Lewis D. Campbell of Ohio, determined to bury the bill with words. They went straight to the southerners who charged that they had been cheated and cajoled by the North over and over again. Benton taunted them for keeping the slavery issue alive. Previous legislation, starting with the Northwest Ordinance, had put it to rest, he thought. Why drag it into Congress again? He believed the Kansas-Nebraska bill was a stupid piece of legislation, full of contradictions, that served no good purpose.[19]

On May 10 it was Grow's turn to speak. According to the *New York Herald*, his speech was recognized by friends of the bill as one of the "most effective and powerful blows that the bill has yet received from its enemies in the House."[20] Even the *Susquehanna Register,* the Whig paper that generally haunted Grow as a poltergeist, called the address a "powerful and eloquent effort, [which] does much credit to the manly independence as well as ability of its author."[21]

His appeal to good sense and his repeated references to precedents were intended to convince his colleagues that they should remember what Congress had done in the past regarding territories. He loved to hang his opponents on some forgotten fact or a quotation from a renowned figure of political yesteryear. If statistics were available to strengthen a hypothesis or conclusion, he used them. Few in the House analyzed a question as thoroughly as Grow. His preparation was always complete before he rose to address his audience from a position of documentary strength. What he lacked in diplomacy, tact, and finesse, he made up for in clarity, directness, and raw conviction. He was not without humor, but he could never match the wit of Giddings or Benton; few men could. Friends found something majestic in this rugged individualist with chiseled features, towering over his desk, straight and sturdy as a Pennsylvania pine sapling. He was as much the courageous, swashbuckling paladin of the antislavery North as Stephens was the level-headed, suave oracle of the orthodox South.

Grow scorned the idea of organizing two territories.[22] He believed one was adequate to protect the settlers and the contemplated railroad routes to California and Oregon. Unlike Kansas, Nebraska was one vast wilderness inhabited almost entirely by wild Indians who had little contact with whites. Why must the government hasten the development of this region, he asked, and assist in the extermination of the savage? If the humane factor is not strong enough, then the increased expenses of government should at least be considered.

But his greatest objection to the bill was its nullification of the Missouri Compromise. He sarcastically accused Douglas of just recently having discovered that a "great wrong and injustice" had been done to the South by the 1820 legislation, a wrong to which the South with "remarkable humility . . . has quietly submitted for more than a third of a century." Hogwash! "If the Missouri Compromise be an indignity and a wrong," Grow retaliated, "it was heaped upon the South by her own sons." A majority of southerners in both houses of Congress approved it, and a southern president signed it upon the advice of a cabinet, a majority of whom were from the slaveholding states. This great injustice, Grow continued, must have occurred after December 23, 1851, for on that day Douglas had told the Senate that the 1820 Compromise "had been acquiesced in cheerfully and cordially by the people for more than a quarter of a century." Apparently its success was applauded by the members of the last Congress from both North and South. In that Congress when Willard Hall of Missouri had introduced a bill to organize the Nebraska territory, the vast majority had supported it. Not a word had been voiced against the bill because it had not tried to repeal the Missouri Compromise. But what happened afterward? Why was the slavery controversy reintroduced? Who was to blame for the confusion and consternation that had descended upon Congress and the nation?

Grow attacked the southern view that since territories are common property among the states and since all citizens have common rights in them, slaveholders can enter the territories with their slaves. Historically the courts have ruled that there is no foundation for slavery in nature or reason, he argued. Slavery must rest for its support solely upon local law. Any citizen who takes his property into a territory subjects it to the law of the territory, which is dictated by Congress. Grow agreed with Henry Clay that no portion of the people of the United States can take slaves into the territories under the idea that these territories are held in common among the several states. In a derisive tone he added that no northerner who adheres to any opinion of the illustrious Kentuckian on slavery could be charged with fanaticism!

Grow repeated that he harbored no sentiments one way or another on slavery as it existed in the states under local laws. But being asked to take legislative action to open to slavery a vast empire from which it is excluded by federal law, he could only again invoke the wisdom of Clay: "I will never vote, and no human power will ever make me vote, to spread slavery over territory where it does not now exist."

Finally, he warned his Democratic colleagues that adoption of the bill would ensure an antiadministration majority in the next Congress. It would blot out the Democratic party as a national organization, "leaving but a wreck in every Northern State." He also urged southerners to stand against a bill that violated a "contract of freedom" entered into faithfully by their fathers in 1820. Should they vote for it, he warned, they will have destroyed the "last breakwater that stands between [their] rights and the surges of northern abolitionism." One sure way to end the intersectional rivalry over slavery, he concluded, was to observe in good faith all the compromises and reconciliations of its conflicts and henceforth banish it forever from the halls of Congress.

When Grow had finished, Benton, who sat nearby, got up quickly

to congratulate him,[23] as did some of his other friends. But his enemies saw a man who had damned the principle of finality in the last
Congress now declaring the 1820 Compromise a holy covenant! The
southerners were annoyed by his accusations as they recalled his chastisement of them over finality. In their eyes the Pennsylvanian was
casting himself in cement as one of those crazy malcontents bent on
destruction. In its editorial of June 1, 1852, the *Charleston Mercury* had
dubbed Grow as a Democrat who preferred a free-soil faith to party
fidelity, even if it proved ruinous to the party. The southerners saw
no reason to disagree with that opinion of the Pennsylvanian. His
consistent attack against southern leadership was to groom him as
a commander of the antislavery brigade in Congress. His wrath, arrogance, and wit, combined with genuine talents as a debater and
parliamentary tactician, made him more than a mere adversary to
southern interests. He became a dreaded scourge, a paragon of pa-
rochial northern bias.

Along with Campbell and the other obstructionists, Grow held
out to the end. And the end came on May 22 when Stephens, using
tactics that even flabbergasted some of the parliamentary experts,
rammed the bill through. The Georgian did not hesitate to take full
credit. The final vote was 113-100, close enough to raise expectations
that both sides would be forced to defend their positions before the
public. With elections near, it was conscience-clearing time, and for
the Democratic party the prospects of avoiding a cataclysm appeared
dim. For many it was a time of remorse; for many others it was a
moment to cherish. After the vote Grow recalled how the roar of cannon beyond the Capitol intensified the jubilation of the devotees of
slavery in what they regarded as a "final triumph" in a contest of more
than half a century.[24]

The Hunter Substitute

Just what effect the passage of the Kansas-Nebraska bill might have
on other legislation remained uncertain. A great deal depended upon
how soon and how well the Democrats could regroup. To many observers, including Grow, damage to the party was irreversible. Harsh
attitudes were bound to carry over into other legislative areas. For
the homestead bill the effect was immediate. Traditionally looked upon
as a Democratic measure, the bill faced a hostile Senate, where the
real power of slavocracy stood undisputed along with the lobbying
influence of speculators in land warrants and railroads. If there had

been any euphoria in the House following the passage of the homestead bill, it quickly melted in the heated atmosphere on Capitol Hill over Kansas-Nebraska. Senators carefully monitored the deliberations in the House on the territorial bill. Their delay in taking up the House-approved homestead measure, perhaps planned, may have been crucial. For by the time they were ready to debate the bill, the furor over Kansas-Nebraska had peaked in the lower house. The behavior of the obstructionists there undoubtedly reinforced the suspicions of the southern senators: free-soilers wanted free land to perpetuate the cause of abolitionism.[25]

On May 3 the land issue was reopened when President Pierce returned the indigent insane bill to the Senate with his veto message. With the West and a few southerners in opposition, this bill provided for the appropriation of large blocks of the public domain for the benefit of the indigent insane. Pierce vetoed it on the grounds that it was unconstitutional: if Congress can provide for the indigent insane, it can also care for the indigent who are not insane. Western senators naturally endorsed his action for the bill's enactment would have in effect withdrawn many acres from a prospective homestead act.

When Congress failed to pass over the veto, attention turned to the homestead bill. Some close observers intimated that it would slide through the Senate in some form.[26] There were just too many western Democrats whose support of the measure made it imperative that some favorable action be agreed upon by party leaders, North and South. Realizing that it was impolitic to shelve the bill, southern senators adopted a brilliant new stratagem of opposition. On July 10, 1854, Robert Hunter of Virginia introduced a substitute to "graduate the price of public lands, and for other purposes."[27] A distinguished disciplinarian who believed in a strict and rigid construction of federal powers, Hunter had won praise in the last session for his opposition to the homestead bill.

As amended, his substitute assured possession of portions of the public domain by heads of families and gave title after five years of occupancy and the payment of a sum graduated according to the time the lands had been on the market. The sum ranged from one dollar per acre of land that had been on sale for five years to twelve and one-half cents for that which had been on the market for thirty years. The second provision was for grants of alternate sections of land on the lines of railroads chartered by the states. Third, the states were allowed to take possession and acquire title to lands within their borders on the same terms as individual settlers. Although the prices for land were reasonably low, the essential homestead idea was abandoned.

Hunter's substitute accomplished what many had hoped for. It made the actual settler the prime beneficiary while it denied the speculator the unlimited opportunities he once possessed. Furthermore, it retained the practice of selling the land and weakened what many considered a socialistic scheme by homestead advocates to commit the central government to a dole system of giving away land instead of money or food.

Southern extremists were especially satisfied with the bill. It released the new states from the domination of the federal government by giving them supreme sway over their own lands without sacrificing the rights of the Atlantic states. The *Charleston Mercury* praised it as one of the "most important measures ever brought before Congress. It reaches and remedies nearly all the evils that have so long beset the question of the disposal of the public lands. The details of the bill may be criticized, but as a whole it is statesmanlike, comprehensive, and in its effects, promises to confer great benefits on the country."[28]

Those who wanted a free land bill were not fooled by this southern ploy to pass another graduation measure under the guise of a homestead bill. They objected to its introduction so late in the session and pleaded for a test vote on the House bill. This and all attempts to kill the bill through filibuster and motions to table failed. On July 21 the Hunter substitute passed the Senate, 36–11.[29] The lopsided vote resulted when some of the staunch defenders of homestead agreed that the substitute was the nearest thing to it that could get through this session. Chase of Ohio, whose amendment to allow future immigrants to become homesteaders had been defeated earlier, voted for the Hunter bill because he believed it secured benefits to the actual settler. Douglas likewise accepted the substitute as "satisfactory."[30]

Grow and homestead supporters in the lower house did not share the senator's view. They rejected the substitute, and stubbornly refused to consider the homestead bill any further during that session. A reporter for the *Daily Pittsburgh Gazette* summarized the general attitude of homestead backers in Congress after an interview with many of them: "There has been a most disgraceful trickery practiced to kill, reject, and cast out the real homestead feature and principle, and to foist upon the Senate and country the daring and insidious scheme of land speculation known as Hunter's substitute."[31]

Hunter took Pierce off the horns of an embarrassing dilemma. The president could neither approve nor veto Dawson's homestead measure without damaging further the fibers that held the Democratic party together. At best, the substitute was a disguised effort to quiet a popular issue at a time when other issues were clobbering the heads of party unionists. At its worst, Hunter's bill provided unequivocal proof that the South was moving toward an inflexible position on homestead. To land reformers like Grow, the future of the homestead bill dangled precariously at the end of a very thin thread.

But Grow was not moved to despair. Though the vagaries of legislative opinion on the territorial and land bills had defied the axioms of common sense, logic still had a place in politics. A philosophy based on the assumption that most men simply wanted a home of their own, without the pangs of slavery, was not bankrupt. Grow was not ready to abandon faith in political intelligence. It was characteristic of his political temper that he should, despite an occasional fling at emotionalism, appeal in the end to reason. Sound principles that mandated rational action had to spring from one's fidelity to convictions that separated right from wrong. Grow knew he was right, and he determined to pursue his concept of the truth—a quest that led to free soil, free land, and, unfortunately, secession and war.

6

Becoming a Black Republican

SITTING AT HIS Washington desk, Grow pondered the future of the Democratic party. He felt uncomfortable. The oppressive July heat, with its sultry days and nights and voracious mosquitoes from nearby polluted marshes, were enough to debilitate a herculean constitution, and Grow was no Hercules. He complained constantly of his health. But the young lawmaker did not need nature to make him feel miserable. The news from back home did this. Less than two months since the passage of the Kansas-Nebraska bill, signs already pointed to an election that presaged only terrible things for the northern Democratic party. Its total ruin was not beyond probability. Though he had forewarned that this might happen, Grow's prescience provided little solace. Everywhere strong political palpitations suggested a chronic illness of destructive power. Nowhere was this more evident than in the northern counties of Pennsylvania.

Grow was in a quandary. Everyone knew where he stood on the Kansas issue and how he felt toward the administration Democrats. He had made his position clear, yet he could not completely let go of the strings that tied him to his party. Grow promised to back William Bigler, the party's gubernatorial candidate for reelection, despite the fact that many "Nebraska" men were also supporting him.[1] Nothing in the North could be done "except negatively," Grow wrote to Bigler. The anti-Nebraska men appeared unapproachable on a suitable candidate. He disagreed with the governor, who believed that any attempt to repeal the part of the 1854 law that nullified the slavery restriction in the Missouri Compromise would be futile. "I think anything is possible in American legislation," Grow exclaimed.

The coalition of Nebraska men in Washington overshadowed anything that a state Democratic organization might do. Still, Grow and the party's free-soilers demanded that the Democrats of Pennsylvania be heard in the settlement of the great national issues. Reenactment of the Missouri Compromise was not out of order, in their opinion, and could be accomplished if all the anti-Nebraska forces were to combine in a countermovement. Free-soil Democrats and Whigs, abolitionists and Know-Nothings, all working together, raised an awesome and intriguing specter.

Among these groups the Know-Nothings seemed the most unpredictable. This nativist organization exhibited its political influence in Pennsylvania for the first time in the local elections of 1854. Its support of Robert T. Conrad, successful Whig candidate for mayor of Philadelphia, stunned the state Democrats. Now, with the demoralization of the Democratic party and the disintegration of the Whig party, the Know-Nothings had a golden opportunity to increase their numbers. But would they rally behind an antislavery countermovement when their primary fear and hatred were directed toward Catholics and foreigners?

With trepidation and cautious reserve, Grow looked to the campaign that lay ahead. Perhaps the free-soilers could take charge. By every standard the 1854 elections assumed greater portentousness as the months rolled by. Maybe a mandate was in the offing that would tell Congress and the Pierce administration that a correction in territorial policy was necessary. Whether or not Grow would be able to keep a foot in both the free-soil and Bigler camps remained to be seen. As he probed the ways to preserve the party, he determined to make principle the test, and the only test, of party fidelity. He grew weary of fellow Democrats who, he felt, cringed irresponsibly before southern expansionists. Should they continue to permit the extension of slavery to be riveted to the Democratic creed, then Grow's course was predictable.

A Storm Across the Northern Tier

The election of 1854 was a severe test for Pennsylvania Democrats. Success at the polls seemed as tenuous as gossamer. Only by denigrating the importance of the Kansas-Nebraska Act did party leaders see any chance of diverting voter attention from the controversial measure to local issues. Initially, therefore, the Democrats neither endorsed nor denounced the measure. Instead, at their state convention in March, they reiterated their stand behind the 1850 Compromise and the 1852 Baltimore platform. But this soft-shoe maneuver around an emotion-packed issue proved unsatisfactory.

The Whigs refused to allow their opponents to exit from the heat of the campaign without scars of humiliation, guilt, and defeat. Taking their cue from their national leaders, they chastised Douglas and his bill and declared that repeal of the 1820 restriction on slavery was the Democratic party's way of saying that it no longer felt obligated to defend old compromises on the wretched institution. The once-proud party of Jefferson and Jackson had finally capitulated to the sinister demands of slavocracy! One platform resolution of Pennsylvania Whigs scorned the 1854 act as a "high-handed attempt to force slavery into a vast new territory now free from it by law." This sentiment was echoed by the party's gubernatorial candidate, James Pollock of Northumberland.

Throughout Grow's congressional district the reaction to Douglas's bill was immediate and included mass rallies, torchlight parades, bombastic oratory, and fiery editorials. Here and there an effigy of the senator swung in the frosty air. The bill's catalytic powers influenced free-soilers of all parties. Politically conscious groups of traditionally opposed views suddenly found themselves welded together in a common cause. On February 14, a huge, angry crowd packed the courthouse in Towanda to protest the proposed legislation.[2] The winter chill failed to dull the enthusiasm of those assembled. David Wilmot harangued for nearly two hours in the opening volley of a speaking crusade that took him back and forth across the district and throughout the state. Forgotten by some, he was now back as the mischievous oracle of the northern counties. Probably no one in Pennsylvania stumped against the 1854 bill as much as did Grow's former law partner. In his July letter to Bigler, Grow intimated that the governor's success in the district would be no less than it had been in 1851 unless Wilmot campaigned actively against him. If this occurred, Grow prophesied, Bigler's vote would inevitably be diminished.

By the time Bigler received Grow's letter, Wilmot had already made his decision. Not only had he decided to work against Bigler, but he also planned to rally his free-soil troops behind Pollock. To old-line Democrats, Wilmot's defection was sacrilege, but his return was in response to public clamor. His zeal mirrored the sentiments of most district voters; according to the *Tioga Eagle*, "The Democrats have always stood up for preserving the Missouri line," an idea that enjoyed unanimity among district editors.[3] Both Democratic and Whig presses disapproved of the repeal. Anti-Nebraska demonstrations, similar to the Towanda meeting in February, took place in Wellsboro, Montrose, and scores of smaller communities. The entire district was afire. At these gatherings, Wilmot inspired his audiences to adopt resolutions instructing the state legislature to declare that the majority of Pennsylvanians opposed repeal. In the process he urged the defeat of those candidates who labored in behalf of Douglas's bill. After its passage in May, outrage in the district reached a new zenith. For Wilmot it was the turning point. He seemed to wash his hands of the Democrats and moved toward fusion of the anti-Nebraska forces.[4]

Just as Grow had predicted, Wilmot's assault against the governor and the Nebraska Democrats spelled disaster for them in the district. Bigler tried to keep the territorial question out of the campaign by insisting that it was a national issue and not related to his duties as governor. This was the party line, and through the summer old-line Democrats counseled Bigler to adhere to it. District opponents seized upon this politically untenable position.[5] Strictly speaking, the territorial question was in the national sphere, but it had pervaded state and local levels as well. For the governor's advisers to ignore this trend was an oversight, which gnawed away at his support base. Alarmists, worried that a landslide was imminent, urged Bigler to visit the northern counties to explain the troublesome 1854 act to the people.[6] E. B. Chase of Montrose, editor of the *Montrose Democrat* and former Speaker of the Pennsylvania House of Representatives, pleaded with him not to use his influence in favor of reopening of the slavery question.[7] He tried to tell the governor that the territorial issue, not Know-Nothingism, was the real problem in Susquehanna. Many in Bigler's camp believed the reverse, that nativism posed a greater threat to the party than reaction to the territorial bill.

Bigler accepted the invitation from Susquehanna Democrats and spoke at Montrose in late August. Weeks before his arrival, the *Montrose Democrat* had commented that, though the governor still had not taken a stand on the Kansas-Nebraska Act, it would continue to support him because it did not think he would ever endorse the measure.[8] Obviously the editor's intent had been to prevent further party erosion, but the governor's remarks only hastened the depletion of the party's ranks. He labeled the territorial question a work of Congress for which he would accept neither credit nor responsibility, and with which he had no official connection. When he declared that Congress had to assume the burden, he watched disappointment sweep across the many faces in the throng at the courthouse.[9] Personally believing the doctrine of nonintervention to be a good one, he professed more trust in the people of the territory to make decisions on matters that affected them directly than he had in Congress. Like many others, he did not think slavery would extend into the territories of Kansas and Nebraska. In a final effort to placate the free-soilers, he said that he would have organized the two territories in terms of the 1850 acts *without disturbing the 1820 line*. And he caused some cheering when he boasted that he was indeed opposed to the extension of slavery.

The majority in the audience, however, were not satisfied with the governor's assurances. Many were skeptical; some even demanded a rebuttal. Cries for Wilmot and Grow reverberated through the hall, but neither came forward. Only the previous day, the two had held captive a similar audience while hundreds were turned away. Unfortunately for the governor, some of the anti-Nebraska fervor manifested at this gathering carried over to the day of his speech. Chagrined, and obviously feeling helpless before a hostile crowd, Bigler felt compelled to ask the chairman to adjourn the meeting. In so doing, he reduced the Montrose trip to a recognized failure.

In contrast Grow stood on solid ground. When he returned from Washington, men of both parties had saluted him as a gallant legislative warrior. His able defense of the homestead bill, his celebrated repudiation of the territorial bill, and his chastisement of southerners had put him in the good graces of his constituents. During the campaign his congressional record was a shield against any criticism that resulted from his support of Bigler and the Democratic platform. His renomination and reelection was therefore assured from the beginning. As early as March he had received the approval of the Democrats of his county. Tioga and Bradford Democrats followed.[10] "His consistent and upright conduct," the *Tioga Eagle* commented, "has gained him the respect and confidence of his associates. . . . Grow's name has, in Congress, always been upon the side of Right."[11] The Whigs saw little need to put up a challenger. By the end of summer, the young lawmaker had received the endorsement of every convention in the district.[12]

Grow's position may have been solid, but his views were nonetheless controversial. A middle-of-the-road strategy was culpable and unpopular with his enemies and the extremists. Some early Republicans charged him with voting for nearly everything—Bigler, whiskey, Nebraska, slave pens—because of the pressure from the Democrats to crush the free-soil sentiment.[13] Undoubtedly Grow's support for Bigler was sincere, but the governor's endorsers considered it compromised by his other positions. Firmly convinced that such a relationship with Bigler was a sine qua non of the party's good fortune, he labored where other free-soilers feared to tread, and perhaps he overstated his case. Yet at the same time he did not want to see the northern Democratic party turned into a vassal of the South. To prevent this, he directed his campaign efforts to exposing all attempts to nationalize the slavery issue and then going after the perpetrators. He hoped his joint defense of the Democratic slate and the anti-Nebraska position would convince the Wilmot people that they had more to gain by staying with the party and working to free it of the slaveholders' deadly grasp. Besides, the memories of the failures of the free-soil bolts of 1848 and 1852 remained fresh in his mind.

By keeping a foot in both the regular and free-soil camps of the Democratic party, Grow helped resurrect the question asked in 1848: "Where does Grow stand?" Accusations that he was still a reluctant radical and an opportunist unwilling to burn bridges behind him do not tally with the evidence. His hostility to the Kansas-Nebraska bill and its sponsors was unequivocal and readily visible to most voters. Secondly, the Democratic state convention's decision to endorse the homestead bill and not the territorial bill met with his approval. Intraparty differences on great national issues were common. Grow agreed with Bigler that if Democratic members of Congress had voted unwisely, that was no reason why Democrats should strike down a Democratic governor if his administration had done well. And though the Harrisburg convention of Democrats had leaned toward acceptance of the territorial bill, majority sentiment was otherwise, which Bigler interpreted as a positive sign. Up to election day, Bigler and his close advisers continued to dodge charges that they were in any way responsible for the 1854 act. Most district voters anticipated that Bigler, tainted by hunkerism and the territorial bill, would lose to Pollock, especially since the Whig candidate had the legendary hero of free-soilism on his side. Not only did the governor face a redoubtable foe in Wilmot, but also he knew that a vote for him implied an endorsement of the territorial bill.

Actually, some critics saw no difference between Grow and the governor with regard to that bill. One voted against it; the other swore he would not have disturbed the Missouri line. The *Tioga Eagle* failed to see why anti-Nebraska men opposed Bigler while they enthusiastically supported the "orthodox" Grow.[14] Meanwhile, the Whigs called Bigler a doughface and saluted Grow for the great work he had done. Admittedly, the old-line Democrats of Bradford, including Col. D. M. Bull, E. W. Baird, William Elwell, and David Cash, did not help Bigler when they went beyond the party platform to endorse the bill and to congratulate those in Congress who had voted for it.[15]

The only challenge to Grow, and a slight one at that, came from some of the Tioga citizens who claimed that it was their county's turn, under the unwritten "doctrine of rotation" or "four years rule," to send the next representative to Washington. Bradford's Wilmot had enjoyed the honor for three terms, Susquehanna's Grow for two. But M. H. Cobb, editor of the Whig *Agitator,* a Grow supporter, and an anti-Nebraska man, did not believe it was time to make a change. Since the voters of the district wanted Grow reelected, the rule should be waived, Cobb wrote.[16]

Election returns in the district told the story. For the anti-Nebraska forces, it was a stunning victory but hardly a surprising one. Unopposed, Grow received more than 13,000 votes. His gubernatorial choice, however, did not fare as well. Bigler lost to Pollock by 4,000 — a dramatic turnabout from his 1851 showing, when he had carried the district over William Johnston by more than 1,500 votes. In that year all three counties had gone for Bigler; now they went for Pollock. The governor's best performance was in Susquehanna where Grow's stumping apparently helped and Pollock's plurality was only 693. Some Democrats complained to fellow Democrats that Grow was not supporting Bigler enough while, at the same time, they told the Whigs who were behind Grow that he was working hard for Bigler.[17] Most observers blamed the territorial bill for the district Democrats' drubbing at the polls, although there was strong agreement that Know-Nothingism had played a big part as it had elsewhere in the state. In Susquehanna, for example, anti-Nebraska candidates were defeated by Know-Nothings who had never identified with the bill.[18]

Statewide, the results sounded no clear signal. Alexander McClure noted, "The political contest of 1854 presented the most unique and conspicuous results to be found in the entire history of Pennsylvania politics."[19] Though Bigler lost by nearly 40,000, two other Democrats — Henry S. Mott, candidate for canal commissioner, and Jeremiah S. Black, candidate for the judge of the supreme court — were victorious. The Whigs did well on two other fronts. They easily outnumbered the Democrats elected to the national House of Representatives, and they took control of the legislature when it convened in January. Actually, since "quite two-thirds of the Whigs, and a very large proportion of the Democrats" had been absorbed by Know-Nothingism, nativism did seem to be in control.[20]

One thing was certain: the breach between the Nebraska and anti-Nebraska men forced a realignment of parties and factions. Roy Nichols referred to the period as one of "disintegration and reintegration."[21] Times were changing. Principles were casting long shadows over party dogma as traditional loyalties broke down. The parties themselves shattered and the debris gravitated toward nuclei of ideological attraction. What this reshuffling of political labels implied was a resharpening of attitudes toward slavery within the meaning of the Kansas-Nebraska Act, which, in turn, marked the beginning of a new phase of sectionalism. Some expected this phase to lead to an open break. Indeed no politician dared deny that the old national wound caused by the irritation over slavery had been lanced again.

Free Soil, Free Speech, and Free Men

Many anti-Nebraska men in Grow's district, flushed with enthusiasm and spite, moved quickly to translate their "victory" into a call for a new party. Soon after the 1854 elections, Charles F. Read and Homer H. Frazier of Susquehanna announced their plans to begin a paper, the *Independent Republican,* which was to serve as a medium for expressing Republican and free-soil sentiments in the county.[22] Published in Montrose, the first issue appeared on January 4, 1855, under the motto, "Freedom and Right against Slavery and Wrong." As one of the earliest Republican newspapers in Pennsylvania, it was a support organ for a political party still to be organized in the state as well as nationally. Watching the embryo of the new party develop, cynics doubted that a birth could ever occur; and, if it did, the life expectancy was presumed brief. Genetically the political fetus did not have a chance. There were just too many ideologically incongruent groups whose incompatibility was detrimental to parenthood. For this developing organization conceived and nourished by political man, the problems of birth and survival had to be explained and resolved logically.

What would it take to piece together these seemingly irreconcilable political elements into a meaningful and permanent relationship? A platform of makeshift compromises and arrangements? The total absolution of one's past political sins? A rejection of all spurious ideas? The acceptance of a simple thought, that slavery is evil in every respect and its defenders must no longer expect northern acquiescence and submission? Perhaps all of these. A fusion could occur only if old grievances were settled and achievable aims agreed upon. Whigs and Democrats were haunted by their associations with the Fugitive Slave Law or the territorial bill or both. At the same time, free-soilers, abolitionists, and Know-Nothings suffered from poor public profiles because of their professed radicalism. United by a common desire for power, these diverse elements were still torn by ancient feuds growing out of doctrines as numerous as the different tongues in the tower of Babel.

To find a politically suitable coagulant presented a major problem. Aside from their obvious quest for office, the first Republicans needed a more legitimate raison d'être upon which a lasting coalescence might be effected. The Wilmot Proviso, with its heralded principle of nonextension, seemed to be a natural choice. Accommodation to this familiar concept was intellectually easy, for it lacked both the rigors of abolitionism and the complacent tolerance of slavery. If anything, it gave a sense of continuity and thus of dependability; it reminded men they belonged in the stream of conscionable history and that their political lives had meaning only if they touched those moral laws that mandated that history. Besides, for the first Republicans in Grow's district, the proviso was still a homespun product.

But to blend free-soilism with Know-Nothingism and a host of other creeds was no easy task and, for this reason, some free-soilers across the state like Grow did not initially join the party.[23] The anti-Nebraska movement paradoxically had splintered the proviso advocates. One group, the followers of Wilmot, reflected philosophically the mood that followed the passage of the Kansas-Nebraska bill — doubt that the two major parties could ever be trusted to stop the encroachments of the slavery oligarchy. To them the national parties were defunct; a resurrection was out of the question. The second group, which included Grow, also mirrored the disillusionment that came after the territorial bill had become law, but they did not abandon the hope, faint as it was, that the integrity and ideals of the two parties might still be there. The first embraced separatism and the idea of a new party with all the anxiety and romance of a spurned lover on the threshold of both divorce and infidelity. The second considered the course of the first group rash and, at best, a calculated risk.

But once the movement for a new party in the district had begun, there was no way to slow its acceleration. Organizational meetings and gatherings were epidemic. By summer the formation of Republican groups became the most popular political game among both purists and hacks, with Bradford and Susquehanna leading the way. The Bradford Whigs were among the first to call for a "union of northern forces upon one common platform of Freedom."[24] Notwithstanding the diabolical reputation of some nativist Whigs, free-soil Democrats dared not reject the challenge. In their judgment the time had arrived to break away from the Democratic party, for it had ceased being a national party and had become instead a vehicle for the protection and aggrandizement of slavery. "We have acquiesced and compromised and succumbed so long," the editor of the *Bradford Reporter* commented, "that arrogance has taken the place of patriotism."[25] The remedy seemed to be in the new Republicanism, whose aim was to bring the government back to the designs of its founders. In late August free-soilers of all stripes met at Towanda, disavowed all connections with any of the old parties, and then invited men of those parties to unite with them behind a platform of "free soil, free speech, and free men."

At the same time, a similar action took place in Susquehanna. Meeting in Montrose, the first Republicans framed a number of proposals.[26] One resolution referred to President Pierce as a "corrupt tool of slavery," a tragic leader whose removal of Andrew Reeder as governor of the Kansas territory was an outrage and disgrace. Another labeled slavery a local, not national, issue and called upon the federal government to prevent its extension. To this end the delegates pledged never to consent to the addition of another slave state. Finally, the group appointed representatives to attend the Republican state powwow to be held on September 5 in Pittsburgh. Prominent among the delegates were the distinguished Judge William Jessup, who later became president of the Pittsburgh convention, and newspapermen Charles Read and Homer Frazier.

District Republicans returned home from the meeting to apply finishing touches to their organizations and platforms. For the most part they approved the work carried out in Pittsburgh, including the resolve to repeal the Fugitive Slave Law. They also endorsed the nomination of Passmore Williamson for canal commissioner. His draft had been the emotional high of the Pittsburgh conference, for he was then in prison for contempt of court. But second-guessers agreed that an emotional favorite is hardly guaranteed success and that Williamson was politically an unsound choice. On the eve of election, therefore, he was replaced by Thomas Nicholson of Beaver, a person more acceptable as a "union" candidate, though actually he was the choice of the Know-Nothings. He lost to the Democrat, William Plumer of Venango, in the opinion of McClure because he had entered the campaign much too late.[27]

But Nicholson did win in Grow's congressional district by more than 2,500 votes. The fact that he had carried all three counties shocked the Democratic organization. While the fusionists boasted of their victory, the old-line Democrats debased it as a Republican and Know-Nothing fraud.[28] Both Jessup and Wilmot came under heavy attack for responding to Know-Nothing demands. The former had helped stack the Republican central committee with Know-Nothing friends; he did not deny that he belonged to the American party. In the same vein, Wilmot, as chairman of the state executive committee, had worked for the nomination and election of Nicholson, another Know-

Nothing. The bitterness against Wilmot intensified along the broader lines of deserting his party, ignoring his bench duties, and stumping for everybody who claimed to be against the Democratic party. Chase of the *Montrose Democrat* went so far as to accuse him of drunkenness, debauchery, and blasphemy. When Wilmot sued, the editor gracefully retracted his statements.[29]

The fiery editor also had made some disparaging remarks against Grow, charging him with pursuing a "betwixt and between" policy for the past year.[30] A longtime friend, the editor had become increasingly impatient with Grow during the heated struggle for Speaker in the Thirty-fourth Congress, which convened in December 1855. When Grow finally decided to support Nathaniel Banks of Massachusetts, a Know-Nothing, it signaled to Chase that his friend's scruples had been lost and any remaining sentiments for the Democratic party had vanished. Recalling the hectic days of the 1854 campaign, the editor charged Grow with supporting the party and Bigler only enough to insure his own reelection and of a lack of resolve.

What really bothered the editor was Grow's promise that he would never vote for the nativist Banks. Chase believed Grow's principles had suddenly given way to opportunism. When asked why he had refused to participate in a Montrose meeting to discredit Know-Nothingism, Grow had simply remarked that he "didn't speak on that subject." Was his refusal to speak an indication that he did not wish to antagonize many of his friends, like Wilmot and Jessup, who were tripping over one another in their haste to enlist nativists for the Republican party? Grow's Democratic friends had hoped that his trip to Europe in mid-1855 might clear his boggled mind and refreshen his spirits to help him reaffirm his Democratic faith. Unfortunately, according to Chase, this did not happen.[31]

Besides making a trip to Europe after the adjournment of Congress in March 1855, Grow wanted to spend some time with his family. Chronically complaining of his health, he wanted rest and temporary relief from Washington's drudgery, its crowded hotels and restaurants, and the foul odors of its streets and sewers. He was tired and shaken by the political events of the past year. With the wreckage of the Democratic party all about him, it would have been easy for Grow to involve himself completely in the general pandemonium that characterized the realignment of political factions that summer. Although some of his free-soil friends urged him to join Wilmot and others to give direction to the budding Republicans, he chose instead to put his politics temporarily on hold, enjoy the comforts of the family farm and home cooking, and do some traveling.

After the madness of Washington and Congress, he welcomed the serenity and isolation of Glenwood. The rustic life was always refreshing to his body and spirit. What little time he had to spend with his family and friends before embarking for Europe, however, was partially taken up by business matters. With their increased property holdings, the Grows in 1855 controlled a good part of the economic life of the small village and community along the Tunkhannock. The brothers had organized a firm with Galusha handling all the legal problems. Edwin Grow managed the mercantile business in the village and Frederick operated a similar but larger store at Carbondale. The brothers still ran their profitable lumber business and recently had sold to A. F. Snover the hotel they had build a few years earlier. Most of the farming on the old homestead was entrusted to a brother-in-law, although Galusha enjoyed doing some of it himself. During the previous season he had personally worked a fallow of about 100 acres.

Before he departed for Europe, he decided to accompany his sister, Elizabeth, part way to her new home in Joliet, Illinois. She had recently been married to J. Everett Streeter, a former clerk in the Grow store and the son of Dr. J. B. Streeter and the brother of Farris B. Streeter, in whose office Grow had read law. The young groom brought Grow up to date on what was happening politically in the West. Everywhere the story was the same: the Democratic party was in deep trouble. Even in his own state of Illinois, Stephen Douglas was finding it difficult to face many Democrats. The anti-Nebraska men there, armed with judicious ardor, were anxious to erect a Republican temple upon the warm ashes of the old Democratic party. The formation of a new party against the South and slavery seemed the only issue of importance to the party ideologues and hacks. The homestead bill and the further development of the region momentarily mattered little to these westerners. To Grow's mind, this limited view was unfortunate.

On May 12 Grow departed for Europe. Traveling had always been one of his great desires, but his stated reason for going abroad was to study the political and economic systems of European countries. Once there, however, his letters to his family and friends suggest that he was primarily on a sightseeing tour.[32] Making the journey with him were Elihu Washburne of Illinois and two New Yorkers, Edwin B. Morgan and Benjamin Pringle, all members of Congress. The men may have been frustrated in being unable to follow the political events back home, or maybe they were relieved at not knowing what was occurring. Grow commented that only the letters he received kept him abreast of the more important developments. Occasionally the Americans were able to read New York newspapers.

Grow remained in Europe all summer, visiting England, France, Portugal, Spain, Switzerland, Italy, and Greece. His well-written and most descriptive letters portray the author as an astute observer who was quite sensitive to the lifestyles of the Europeans. For example, the lack of courtesy and respect extended to the average woman, especially in Italy, moved him deeply. Admittedly, he wrote, the woman in America had a long way to go to improve her general status, but she was still better off than her European counterpart. One woman who was indeed treated as a lady and who impressed him with her beauty, elegance, and charm, especially in conversation, was the Empress Eugénie, wife of Napoleon III. "I have fallen in love with French royalty," he wrote. Coming from a young man with a commoner's disposition, this confession may have been made in jest. Nevertheless, he bought a portrait of Eugénie and lamented the fact that he had no daguerreotype of her. As one of ten Americans invited to a royal ball in her honor, a high mark in his otherwise lackluster social life, he wore the most formal court attire—a military coat with gold lace, gilt buttons, white vest and cravat, sword, and chape. "I reckon if some of my bark peelers should see me with it on," he quipped, "they would wonder who it could be."

If fellow bark peelers would have been startled to see their friend in such ornate garb, the Know-Nothings who had voted for him in 1854 must have been simply livid to learn that he had attended mass at St. Peter's in Rome in the presence of the pope and a coterie of cardinals and bishops. What these nativists thought was of no concern to Grow; their anti-Catholic prejudice did not impress him. When it came to religious preferences, it is doubtful that he had anything but an open mind. He noted that the Sabbath was not celebrated in Europe as it was in America. Sunday was a day devoted to entertainment and amusement, with gambling and merrymaking commonplace. He remarked that religion was something that European men were content to leave to their women and children.

Grow arrived in New York on the *Pacific* in early October. After spending some time in Connecticut he prepared himself for the opening of the new Congress. Physically he felt fine. Politically, despite entreaties by the fusionists, he remained uncommitted to the new party. Although he still regarded himself as a free-soil Democrat, he began to sense that being a hyphenated Democrat of that stripe was no longer popular. Many years later he told his biographers that he had gone over to the Republican camp once Pierce had signed the Kansas-Nebraska bill.[33] But this profession of political faith has to be taken as a generalized statement to cover a larger time frame. Spiritually he may have crossed over, but present evidence does not indicate that he officially belonged to the new party before 1856. His name fails to appear in accounts of any of the district party's early organizational meetings.

Why did Grow not play an initial role in the formation of the Republican party in Pennsylvania? Too many things associated with the fusion movement still troubled him. Most striking was that the new party was founded strictly upon the evils of slavery, thus giving it immediately a sectional character that could only push the nation closer to the precipice of disunion. Because of this dangerous flaw, he had shunned the third-party movement in 1848 and 1852. In the second place, many of the Republican leaders were former Whigs whose policies and interests had been anathema to Grow. Was he to join forces with those who had been his political enemies? Moreover, the new party's Know-Nothing connection was easily too strong for a man who took pride in his humanitarian instincts and who welcomed the immigrant as a beneficiary of homestead legislation.

The assimilation of Whiggism and Know-Nothingism with ardent free-soilism, with all the implied contradictions and conflicts, called for special consideration by Grow. Were the new Republicans to be trusted? Were not some of their political philosophies mere mosaics of ancient prejudices, put together without regard for truth or consistency, to appeal not to common purposes and the good of the nation but to common fears and hates? This was especially true of the Know-Nothings, he believed, many of whom were jumping into the Republican ring only because there was no other place for them to go. When the opportunity arose on the House floor, Grow did not hesitate to clarify his association with the nativists. Samuel Smith of Tennessee had tried to link Grow to the Know-Nothings because so many of them had voted for him. The Pennsylvanian was promptly on his feet. He swore that he was not then and had never been a member of any secret political organization.[34] He admitted that many nativists had voted for him not because he was one of them but because there was no other candidate. Many Whigs also had voted for him because their party had not bothered to nominate a challenger. He had been the unanimous choice of voters of different political stripes who were opposed to the territorial bill, which Grow maintained was forced upon the North as a campaign issue. Chase of the *Montrose Democrat* agreed. He claimed that the Democrats had tried to keep the Nebraska issue and the fanaticism associated with it out of the local elections, but failed. The editor concluded that the repeal of the Missouri Compromise had been the "cause" of the defeat of local

Democrats, and Know-Nothingism the "agency" by which that defeat had been effected.[35]

Grow was not quick to join the new party for another reason. The Republican resolutions adopted in September in Pittsburgh fell short of his minimal expectations. They seemed to be the work of men afflicted by tunnel vision. The *Pittsburgh Gazette* was poignant in its observation that slavery dominated the platform.[36] No mention was made of immigration and naturalization, the tariff, or internal improvements. These omissions were deliberate in order to avoid clashes among the participating factions. But to Grow the absence of the homestead bill in the list of resolutions was unfortunate, especially since Pennsylvania's free-soilers had been consistently behind the measure and in November 1854 the Susquehanna Republicans had endorsed it. The issue that meant so much to him was being ignored by a state party that hoped to enlist his unequivocal support. At best, the Republicans impressed Grow with their manifesto of sorts against the Kansas-Nebraska Act, the Fugitive Slave Law, and everything and everybody identified with slavery aggression. Yet this was not enough. What was needed was a platform philosophy that transcended the parochialism of the North-South conflict over slavery and addressed itself to all the major issues of the day.

From 1854 to 1856 Pennsylvania Republicans faced an identity crisis not dissimilar to what other Republicans were experiencing. The Pittsburgh convention of 1855 was well attended, with sixty-four of sixty-five counties sending delegates, but it was an amorphous group. Many feared that once their masks were drawn aside, these Republicans would show their true colors as diehard Democrats and Whigs, Know-Nothings, abolitionists, and temperance enthusiasts. Because of the lack of a unifying national platform and the scarcity of finances, those in attendance agreed to campaign only on a local level; their sole nominee for a state office was Williamson of Philadelphia for canal commissioner. This strategy points to the local conditions under which the party assumed its earliest character.

The grass-roots development of the Republican party in Pennsylvania is of special interest to historians. Recent studies have examined local issues and stimuli during the party's formative years to determine whether any of them was more important than the antislavery impulse that was shaping a national party ideology.[37] It is evident that economic problems, xenophobia and anti-Catholicism, and temperance were very strong motivating factors in some communities. But were they therefore stronger than the nightmare of slavery's extension? One thing is certain: the old Jacksonian democracy that had prevailed for several decades in hundreds of townships throughout the state, including Grow's district, was breaking down after 1854. Within two years those townships became solidly Republican and would remain so for years to come. Was this turnabout the direct result of the repeal of the Missouri Compromise, or was it due more to the belief by thousands of former Democrats that the party had failed to improve their economic condition and quality of life? What were the true sources of the new radicalism that forced the realignment of political factions? Obviously, more local and regional studies are needed to provide a clearer picture of the formation of the Republican party in Pennsylvania.

Grow found himself in the unenviable position of an old-time radical trying to adjust to a changing radical situation. Uppermost in his mind, as always, was putting an end to the slavery agitation. But what he observed in the dialectics of the new radicalism and the revolutionary force and strategy of its promoters was something as potentially dangerous as the militancy of the southern expansionists. Lodged in the bosom of the early Republican creed was the insatiable desire to parade slavery before all other issues, and this disturbed him. Grow grasped the full implications of the party crisis, and by the summer of 1855 he suffered from a kind of schizophrenia. On the one hand, he was determined to keep his radicalism in stride by making additional claims for free-soilism and homestead against southern encroachments and obstinacy. This goal was in line with what his constituency demanded. On the other, he was forced to make personal peace with a district Democratic party that also opposed the extension of slavery, but not necessarily at the cost of party and union. Of course there was a third choice: he might join the Republicans, who were waiting in the wings for his services, and surrender his individuality to the dictates of the new party.

Grow pondered his future and that of the Thirty-fourth Congress. Unlike the existentialist Jean-Paul Sartre, who later wrote that "we should act without hope," Grow looked to the new Congress with confidence that the nation's lawmakers might continue to hope for the best and then adjust their deliberations and actions accordingly. Otherwise, it promised to be a bonanza for the radicals of both the North and the South and Armageddon for the unionists.

The Republicans Claim Victory

The Thirty-fourth Congress opened against a backdrop of political uncertainty in Kansas. Stories of violence, intimidation, and fraud became so commonplace that they stunned only the most naive. Politicians exchanged any shock symptoms they may have experienced for the scruples of charlatans. They saw the Kansas debacle as a political crucible that overflowed with golden opportunities. They realized that they could manipulate any body of facts from the situation to satisfy both their mania and the line of propaganda they wished to pursue. Many intentionally bifurcated the Kansas drama into simple black and white terms. Either they sympathized with the free-soilers there and blamed all irregularities on the proslavery settlers and their Missouri allies, or they supported the proslavery government in Kansas and repudiated the emigrant aid societies for importing crackpot abolitionists. There was no middle ground in this kind of disjunctive reasoning. It was an oversimplication of the realities, but politicians did not care. Slavery was the only problem that counted in Kansas and they planned to externalize it whether the settlers there approved or not.

As Washington began to fill with members of Congress, lobbyists, job seekers, and the press, observers correctly predicted that recent reports from Kansas would force new and strange alignments in the House.[38] The anti-Nebraska men, who represented a majority in that body as well as a kaleidoscope of political shades, met at the Willard and National hotels to map strategy. The prime target of the warring factions would be the speakership, which exerted influence second only to that of the presidency. They talked of organizing behind an antiadministration candidate, but nothing came of it. Too many believed themselves best capable either of filling the position of Speaker or naming someone who could. Again, the New York representatives preferred a free fight on the floor.

The anti-Nebraska men failed to reconcile their divergent views and agree upon a candidate for Speaker before the opening gavel in part because of their general inexperience. All were enthusiastic but most were novices in Capitol Hill politics. Only a handful of them had been with Grow in the Thirty-second Congress, including Israel Washburn of Maine, Lewis D. Campbell and Joshua Giddings of Ohio, and John Allison of Pennsylvania. The group was not impressive when compared with experienced lawmakers like Howell Cobb and Alexander Stephens of Georgia, John Phelps of Missouri, William Richardson of Illinois, Thomas Clingman of North Carolina, J. Glancy Jones of Pennsylvania, William Aiken and James Orr of South Carolina, and Fayette McMullen of Virginia — all strong defenders either of southern interests or the act of 1854. The group of free-soilers consisted of talented and promising men who soon would be heard from: Elihu Washburne of Illinois, Schuyler Colfax of Indiana, Nathaniel Banks of Massachusetts, John Sherman of Ohio, John Covode of Pennsylvania, and Justin S. Morrill of Vermont. Some of them were to become good friends of Grow and, along with him, to establish the nucleus of the first radical Republicans.

The House Democrats, a frustrated minority, seemed better organized than the opposition. They caucused on December 1 and decided to reaffirm their faith in the now infamous act of 1854. Second, they approved a resolution introduced by J. Glancy Jones that condemned Know-Nothingism as pernicious and antidemocratic. Finally, the Democrats agreed upon William Richardson as the logical choice for Speaker because he had played a pivotal role in uniting the party behind the 1854 act. He was able and well respected. Prior to the caucus, however, Howell Cobb had been recognized by some as the administration's steward on the floor and a likely candidate for another term as Speaker.

Grow did not attend the Democratic caucus, the first sign that he planned to join the opposition. The caucus's action with respect to the Kansas-Nebraska Act further insulated him against any lingering hope of ever working with the Democrats. Later, after the balloting for Speaker had begun, Jones of Pennsylvania informed the House that Grow had not been to any of the Democratic meetings and that he obviously was not voting for Richardson. He understood this to mean that his fellow Pennsylvanian no longer pretended to belong to the national Democratic party. He respected Grow for making his anti-Nebraska position honorably known. Beyond this, Jones did not wish to comment.[39]

Having made his break with the Democrats, Grow moved into the anti-Nebraska camp, bag and baggage. It was a camp with many tents, one for every political group that proclaimed an antislavery posture. Aside from this common trait, the camp managers remained confused in their collective aims and beliefs. At the time Grow was less moved by ideology-swapping than by a general floor plan to divest the Democrats of House control. The latter just seemed more important; perhaps his judgment was wrong. His attitude illustrates the saying of Bacon, "Truth emerges more easily from error than from confusion." Still, he looked forward to working with young leaders like Colfax, Covode, and the Washburn brothers who seemed so refreshing and visionary in contrast to the doughfaces and the irascible southerners who remained as unyielding as the gargoyles of a Gothic structure. The amorphism of his friends was giving way to collective action. They were burying their grievances and investing their emotions in a common cause. The contest for Speaker provided incentives to fuse their views on Kansas and to sandbag their ideological differences. And the longer it took to elect a Speaker, the closer the anti-Nebraska men moved toward the core of the new Republicanism. When asked to explain what this Republicanism was about, the elderly Giddings replied that he and his friends took the name "Republican" because they advocated the principles of Jefferson, Hancock, Adams, and Franklin.[40]

Several weeks passed before the group settled upon a candidate. The stormy drama was a prelude to the speakership contest in 1859. In the beginning the race was wide open. On the first ballot, no fewer than seventeen antislavery candidates received votes. The more popular contenders included Alexander Pennington of New Jersey, Lewis Campbell of Ohio, and Nathaniel Banks, a Know-Nothing from Massachusetts. At the end of the twenty-eighth ballot, Banks stormed ahead of the pack with eighty-six votes; Pennington had a mere eight. Campbell's supporters decided to back Banks. Never had the antislavery people seemed so hopeful and so united as after this ballot. "Republican" solidarity had been achieved.

At first Grow did not support any of the favorites. His choice on the initial ballot was instead an obscure, free-soil friend, Matthias Nichols of Ohio. He stayed with Nichols on the next five ballots; on the seventh, he switched to Banks. But on the fourteenth he returned to Nichols and remained with him until the twenty-eighth ballot, when he again turned to the candidate from Massachusetts, this time for good. Meanwhile, Grow received votes from Republicans Orsamus Matteson of New York and John Perry of Maine.[41]

The inconsistent pattern of Grow's voting illustrates the frustration of the anti-Nebraska men as well as his own. No one among them appeared in charge. The malaise deepened as lawmakers began to punctuate the tedious balloting with explanations of why the House could not organize. Easy-flowing oratory brought accusations to the foreground as old suspicions were rekindled. In this melee of words, the Democrats did their best to divide the opposition. They charged that free-soilism and Know-Nothingism were synonymous. The plan here was to raise doubt in a free-soiler like Grow to whom nativism was anathema. Attention focused upon Pennsylvania where the two isms in the recent elections had been equally strong. However, James H. Campbell of Pottsville insisted that the American party was not noted for free-soilism and chided the Democrats for harboring as much free-soilism as there was in the American party. A good case in point, he explained, was Grow, who had been elected as a free-soil Democrat. His remark prompted laughter, undoubtedly from those who hardly considered Grow a Democrat of any stripe.

Once Grow had decided upon Banks as his choice for Speaker,

he began to participate more in the floor debate with straightforward and cursory remarks. As expected, and much to the delight of his anti-Nebraska friends, he bullied and "bad-mouthed" the southerners. He went after those, like James Dowdell of Alabama, who threatened to break up the Union should the Missouri Compromise be restored. "Do you gentlemen of the South," Grow cried out, "stand here today to libel the memory of your fathers, by declaring that they put upon the statute book a law that it is dishonorable for you to submit to?" Should dissolution occur, he warned, those responsible would be proclaimed the "degenerate sons of noble sires."[42]

Grow did not stop. When McMullen of Virginia praised Richardson as the only Speaker nominee of a truly national party, Grow sneered and demanded to know how a total of seventeen northern votes for Richardson could qualify a party as being national. William Goode of Virginia angrily snapped, "I ask him [Grow] to name a single northern man belonging to his political organization who has voted for any southern man?" Admittedly Grow had no retort to that remark. Jones of Pennsylvania also jumped on Grow but with levity. He assured the House that seventeen was not a bad figure. "Paucity of our numbers," he contended, was no evidence to the want of nationality. After all, it required only ten men to save Sodom! He brought cheers and shouts of approval when he promised to help defend the rights of the South as any good Democrat should do.

Grow enjoyed his greatest verbal exchange with John Quitman of Mississippi, former governor of that state and hero of the Mexican War. The southerner became annoyed with Grow for his constant harangue over the repeal of the Missouri Compromise. At the same time, Grow chastised the Mississippian for making unfounded charges of northern aggressions against the South. "What are the northern aggressions that the gentleman speaks of?" asked Grow. Quitman interrupted to ask Grow whether he was not elected on the "principle of hostility to the institutions of the Southern States?" Angrily and with tongue in cheek, Grow responded that he harbored no hostility to southern institutions. He had been unanimously chosen by his constituents instead for his resistance to the repeal of the 1820 Compromise. Quitman continued, "You robbed us of California." Grow asked how this was possible when the people of California had exercised popular sovereignty because they had been neglected by the general government. They did what they had to do: they formed a government and excluded slavery. "And what did you do?" he asked Quitman. "The application of California for admission into the Union was resisted from the first . . . a protest of ten Southern Senators . . . because her constitution excluded slavery." Flush with resentment, Quitman denied the allegation and then dismissed Grow's basic assertion that the root of the difficulty to organize the House was the passage of the Kansas-Nebraska bill. "No sir!" he snarled. "The cause of the attitude in which the House now stands lies still further back . . . it lies still deeper." The one-on-one dialectic between the two men came to an end when Quitman was cut off by Colfax.

Grow saved some of his firepower for Alexander Marshall of Kentucky, who had alluded to an alleged collusion between Banks and members of the Pennsylvania delegation, making a testy situation testier. Misdirected statements and innuendoes like his served only to inflame further already outraged sentiments among wearied and frustrated lawmakers. Grow demanded to know who had started this story for he had heard nothing. The Kentuckian hesitated to mention names but he was upset enough to seek an adjournment until the matter was investigated. Marshall said that he had been led to understand that Banks had met with representatives from Pennsylvania and, for their support, he was now willing to waive his position on certain national issues. John Kunkel of Pennsylvania admitted that such a meeting had taken place; the tariff had been the principal topic of discussion and sixteen or seventeen men who were leaning toward Banks were affected. Although Banks was not noted as a tariff man, he apparently satisfied the protectionists for he not only secured Pennsylvania votes but the New England tariff states as well. Obviously a number of deals were struck.[43]

One of these deals had to involve Grow. For days he had wavered between Nichols and Banks before permanently committing himself to the latter. That he waited so long to make a firm commitment raises questions. To go from a position of no support to one of strong support implies something more than a sudden and casual change of heart.

Several explanations can be suggested. The first is that he had pledged not to vote for a Know-Nothing until it was plain that the candidacy of Banks had become a symbol of unity among the anti-Nebraska lawmakers. Second, Grow may have held back until a decent offer was made in return for his vote. The men for Banks, especially Anson Burlingame of Massachusetts, worked hard to corral free-soilers,[44] and it is reasonable to assume that the carrot was dangled. Once Banks had been elected, Grow received the chairmanship of the Committee on Territories. With Kansas, Oregon, and Minnesota waiting to enter the Union, this House appointment was recognized as one of the more important in this session. Was this the prize Grow demanded? Finally, there was the logistical argument.

The longer the antislavery forces diffused their loyalties and debated their candidates' strengths, the greater the likelihood the hard-line Democrats might succeed in organizing the House their way. To Grow this eventuality clearly meant southern hegemony, so little choice remained but to unite behind a suitable nominee. Once the decision had been made to support Banks, Grow ably defended him. In so doing, he solidified his position in the new antislavery party and quickly became a stalwart among the "Black Republicans."[45]

Writing to a friend shortly after the election of the Speaker, Colfax referred to Grow as a person who "possesses great influence" and who was the favorite among Republicans to chair the territorial committee.[46] The two congressmen became friends and close allies in their struggle for a free Kansas and a homestead bill. Colfax also wrote later that Grow had been one of a handful of men who met privately every other night to map strategy in behalf of Banks as Speaker. Others included Burlingame, Elihu Washburne of Illinois, Benjamin Stanton of Ohio, Israel Washburn of Maine, William Howard of Michigan, and E. B. Morgan of New York. Occasionally others would join them, but it was this inner group that, through their "incessant and persistent" efforts, prevented any breakup of the Banks coalition. Should any danger of a break in the coalition appear, Colfax commented, this self-appointed "committee" would act quickly. Encouraging constituents to telegraph their representatives to "Stick to Banks" was a favorite weapon. Waving a number of telegrams on the floor of the House seemed to have a sobering influence upon those who were considering a change in their vote. The committee applied this timely appeal not once, but scores of times.[47]

Symbolic of the earliest Republican organization in the House, this committee consisted of a free-soil Democrat, an American, several Whigs, and Republicans. Perhaps the intention was to make the group fully representative of the antislavery forces. Secondly, it was also multisectional: participants came from New England, the mid-Atlantic states, and the Northwest. In subsequent balloting on crucial legislation, the votes of the members of this group remained fairly consistent and basic to the Republican position.

Despite this phalanx of ardent supporters, Banks still did not have the necessary majority, but he was close. At Christmastime he had 101 votes; he needed 110. The nearest contenders were Richardson with 72 and Fuller, the American, with 31. The balance between victory and defeat was, therefore, controlled by the nativist Americans. Both northern and southern editors assailed them for their obstinacy. Southern Americans refused to support Richardson, while a dozen

northern Americans who had been elected on an anti-Nebraska platform remained opposed to Banks. "Why they're holding out is beyond
me," wrote a dejected Greeley, who printed their names widely in
the hope that some practical sense might be driven into warped minds
by their constituents.[48] "Half of these men could at any time elect
him [Banks]," editorialized the *Lewisburg Chronicle*, which feared that
such an adamant stance would pave the way for another triumph of
slavery by allowing the Democrats to organize the House.[49] On the
other hand, the Romney, Virginia, *Intelligencer* warned that should
Banks get elected, the South would hold the Americans responsible.[50]

The House tested the limits of absurdity when it passed a resolution, proposed by Felix Zollicoffer of Tennessee, requiring all the candidates for Speaker to state their positions on the great political issues
before the nation. The intent may have been noble, but the results
were ludicrous. Pennington said he had no idea that so unpromising
a candidate as himself would be asked to state his position on anything; after all, he was outside the popular triangle of Banks, Richardson, and Fuller. This brought a roar of laughter, as did Luther Ken-
nett's witty question whether each candidate believed in a future state
after death, and if so, did he see that state as free or "slave"! William
Barksdale of Mississippi, who had been badgering Banks with questions on slavery, took offense to this jocularity. He approached Ken-
nett angrily, but no blows were struck. Banks, with his friends seated
around him, did not feel obliged to answer the questions. Claiming
he had not solicited the support of anyone, he said of his friends, as
Othello said of Desdemona, "They had eyes and they chose me." More
laughter. But he did declare that he believed in the Wilmot Proviso
and that Congress had been wrong in repealing the Missouri Compromise. This brought applause from the Republicans and jeers from
the opposition. Finally, when Fuller was asked whether he wished
to promote equality of the races, he promptly replied to the amusement of many, "I do not sir — I acknowledge a decided preference for
white people!"[51]

Grow considered the inquisitorial examination inappropriate and
a waste of time. "Our business is to enact laws," he reminded his colleagues.[52] The House was not a political caucus, in his opinion, where
platforms and creeds were manufactured. It was not the place to probe
the hearts of men or to examine the doctrines of the Declaration of
Independence and the rights of man. "I have my own creed and political opinion," he added, "and do not recognize the right of any man
in this Hall to put any test of opinions upon me by any resolution
that he may offer." What was the object of Zollicoffer's resolution?

he asked. "It is to divert the plurality of this House from their purpose. Instead of going on to vote and elect a Speaker, the effect of the resolution will be to open a discussion between the candidates and different members of this House, that may last for weeks. It is to put the candidates upon the witness stand, to be cross-questioned by men who do not vote for the particular candidate, and never would." In Grow's judgment, this resolution was a ruse by the opposition.

At long last, at the beginning of February, the contest came to an end. A rule to elect the Speaker by plurality vote having been passed, the victory of Banks seemed assured.[53] After 133 ballots, Banks was declared the winner; William Aiken of South Carolina received 100 votes. On the eve of the final balloting, Aiken had replaced another Carolinian, James Orr, who had replaced Richardson as the Democratic candidate. As expected, the results met with mixed reactions. The *New York Daily Tribune* of February 9 called it the first great victory by freedom over slavery. Greeley hailed it as the victory he wanted, not a compromised victory of an anti-Nebraska candidate elected by deceived Nebraska men.[54] The *Augusta Constitutionalist* saw it as it was: an exclusively sectional triumph of the free states.[55] Its editor argued in vain that had the supporters of Fuller voted for Aiken, Banks would have lost.

Grow's own performance received mixed reviews. In his district the Republican press applauded him for his support of Banks but the hard-line Democrats disapproved.[56] When the Susquehanna Democrats met in convention on January 21, they chastised Grow and demanded that he switch from Banks to an anti-Know-Nothing Democrat. But their representative in Washington was not about to change colors. It had taken him a very long time to make up his mind — since the campaign of 1854 — and now he was sure his political sentiments were correct. His new party was to serve as a surrogate for unionism; the Democrats could no longer be trusted with the responsibility.

Grow's irreversible defection to the Republican movement came as no surprise to those who knew him. It had been only a matter of time. Like other free-soilers, he measured the movement in terms of the shifting attitudes of his constituents. The success of Wilmot's barnstorming for Pollock and his own unchallenged candidacy in 1854 had impressed him, for they had indicated the district's changing mood. He saw that the old bond between the rural electorate and Jeffersonian-Jacksonian democracy was losing its tensility or breaking down completely. The disenchantment of many Democrats with their party's inability to deal with the southerners and the slavery issue and to improve the quality of life for the toiling masses forced them to seek political refuge elsewhere. They did not wish to succumb to Whiggism nor to embrace the bigotry and proscriptive policies of Know-Nothingism. The Republican party promised hope and a new beginning. It was to be an open organization in favor of freedom and against the increase in slave power and the present national administration.

The speakership victory was therefore a glorious success for Republicans. More than ideology or dogma, the members' working together and staying together were responsible for that success. The victory was an antislavery mandate from within the House, a blush of resolve among the anti-Nebraskans. For Grow it was the beginning of a relentless struggle to block "southernism" everywhere. With many issues before the House, particularly those regarding the territories, the struggle promised to be everything that intimidation, vindictiveness, and name-calling could provide. Yet the dominant issue that faced the Thirty-fourth Congress was that of survival. With a presidential election at hand, a national sweep of Republicanism a possibility, and southern militants talking of disunion, the very foundation of the American political system seemed threatened.

No one sensed the seriousness of this crisis better than Grow. His career had reached a turning point. A new party, a leadership role in that party, and the chairmanship of a key committee suddenly advanced him to center stage in the House. Ambitious as he was, however, he was fully aware of the dangers that went with the opportunities. Was his belligerency toward the South to be tempered by dictates of statesmanship or would he succumb to a Jacobinism that many conservatives and moderates feared was to characterize the Republican control of the House? He realized that he was in the middle of a revolutionary situation that was about to explode over the Kansas issue. What his committee might do, therefore, was destined to go far in testing the integrity and durability of his party. That the Republicans intended to use slavery extension as a sectional issue in their efforts to strengthen their party, hardly anyone questioned. Some revisionists of the antebellum period contend that the partisan provocations of politicians created all the havoc that was necessary to keep sectional tension alive. Though slavery and cultural differences were important, these historians admit, it was the behavior and decision making of the politicians that created the most sectionalism.[57]

There is little doubt that Grow planned to exploit the Kansas problem. He resented the doughfaces and harbored a deeper resentment toward southerners who extolled the virtues of slavery. These biases exceeded any expectations he may have had regarding the successes of his adopted party. The men close to Grow — the cadre of dedicated visionaries and opportunists who had sustained the candidacy of Banks until he was elected — developed similar uncompromising attitudes. Their radicalism drew its nourishment from a stream of sectional consciousness that made partisan politics a trademark of the first Republicans. It is interesting to note that the three men who had accompanied Grow to Europe — Elihu Washburne, Pringle, and Morgan — received committee chairmanships. Was this part of the arrangement Grow had with Banks? Perhaps. At best, the appointments suggest a scheme to lay the foundation of a solid Republican edifice in the House. Voting patterns during the Thirty-fourth Congress reveal a high level of agreement among the fanatical supporters of Banks with respect to slavery, the territories, and the Democratic administration. The trend was to continue in succeeding congresses. Southerners were appalled by the appointment of these Black Republicans who lacked the experience to chair important committees. Even some northerners were annoyed with Banks for selecting relatively unknown men who represented essentially rural districts.[58] The makeup and character of the Republican leadership in the House was indeed odd. More important were questions involving the staying power and accomplishments of this leadership.

7

Leader of the Opposition

OBSERVING THE HOUSE debate over Kansas in the Thirty-fourth Congress, the sagacious Horace Greeley wrote that Speaker Banks and Grow were the "young chevaliers" of the new party. While one presided over the session, the other led the opposition.[1] Grow unquestionably accepted the newspaperman's comment as a compliment, but when Sherrard Clemons of Virginia later referred to him in the same manner, the Pennsylvanian angrily replied: "I am the leader of nobody but myself." His denial hardly reassured his opponents who equated him with the hard-nosed Republican position on Kansas.

Grow became a hell-bent spokesman and agent provocateur for the new party. As chairman of the Committee on Territories, he took charge of the Republican assault against President Pierce, his southern allies, and their bunglings in Kansas. News of his appointment rippled through the southern press. The *Charleston Mercury* declared that the new chairman was no friend to the South and that he greatly surpassed his predecessor Wilmot in "malignant antagonism" to the idea of state equality.[2] Another southern editor called Grow one of those socialists who, along with other Republican leaders, advocated programs that if carried out would inevitably destroy the Union.[3] Southern critics warned that all this irresponsible talk of things being *free*—free Negroes, free soil, free land, free labor, free thinking, free schools, and even free love—was enough to boggle the mind.

It was free Kansas that in 1856 caused the greatest uproar in Congress, and it was on this issue that Grow demonstrated his leadership qualities. No sooner had the contest for Speaker ended than Chairman Grow took the initiative. He stirred an inner group of ardent lawmakers for whom slavery seemed a far less important target than its protagonists. As suggested by Eric Foner, they were radical Republicans who consistently refused "to compromise with the South on any question involving slavery." To them southernism was the real enemy. The cotton-state militants interpreted Black Republicanism as the epitome of the North's calculated plan to destroy southern civilization. Each side saw the other as thoroughly insensitive, adamant, and evil. Argumentation stripped the issues of their national coatings and exposed acute sectional consciousness and frailties. Further negotiation and compromise became less real; political differences melted before endemically cultural values and traditions. As the *Richmond Enquirer* so aptly put it: two great systems, one free and one slave, were at war and only one could prevail.[4]

Kansas was the sword of this *Kulturkampf*. With every new horror story to come out of that territory, the Republicans honed the weapon's edge. Yet the party seemed caught in a crossfire of conflicting alternatives. If slavery remained integral to the territorial question, prospects for continued party growth looked encouraging. But some party men realized that the survival of the Union was at stake in this hypothetical proposition. If they were to swell their ranks, they could only do so through increased agitation and nourished sectionalism. And how much more division could the country take?

Will Kansas be Admitted?

Whether Congress would admit Kansas in this session and, if so, whether the new state would be free or slave was "the question of war or peace," wrote the *Tribune*, "and it lies with the House of Representatives to decide it."[5]

This was no easy assignment. When the year 1856 opened, Kansas had two rival governments, and it seemed doubtful that a peaceful settlement might be early and easily reached. In March 1855 several thousand armed intruders from Missouri had marched into the Kansas territory with boisterous pomp and threats of violence. With rifles on shoulders, pistols in belts, and bowie knives in boots, they had intimidated the antislavery settlers and taken control of the polls. They elected a proslavery legislature and chose one of their leaders, John Whitfield, as a delegate to Congress. This legislature then proceeded to adopt a drastic set of laws designed to protect slavery.

The wrath of northern settlers, many of whom were as heavily armed as the Missourians, was unbounded. They saw the takeover as a violation of the popular sovereignty pact. Repudiating the hated southern government, the free-state men held an extralegal constitutional convention in Topeka in October and with equal determination proclaimed their opposition to slavery. After their constitution was ratified by a small popular vote of their own people, they were ready to apply for immediate admission to the Union. But the Douglas people in Congress had no intention of admitting Kansas until its population reached 93,420, the apportionment number for a representative in Congress at that time. Meanwhile, violence continued to plague the territory.

At this tragic juncture in Kansas's brief history, President Pierce on January 24, 1856, sent a special message to both houses of Congress. Since everyone knew where Pierce stood on Kansas, there were no surprises in his remarks. First he explained that the organization of the territory had been delayed because of unjustifiable outside interference and the slowness of Gov. Andrew Reeder in reaching the territory and holding elections.[6] He attacked northern associations that had been formed to promote emigration to Kansas but whose designs and acts awakened "emotions of intense indignation in States near to the Territory of Kansas, and especially in the adjoining State of Missouri." Regardless of the wild cries that illegal votes had been polled, Pierce defended the territorial legislature on the basis that the election returns had been certified by the governor. He hardly believed it his duty to employ troops to preserve the fairness of balloting, but he promised to use force, if necessary, to uphold the acts of the legislature. "Whatever irregularities may have occurred in the elections," he argued, "it seems too late now to raise the question."

Grow disagreed that it was too late either to raise questions or to prevent a bad situation from becoming worse. Within a month of becoming chairman, he delivered a blistering attack against the president, the border ruffians, and their accomplices. This was the first of his two major addresses on Kansas in the first session of the Thirty-fourth Congress. Signaling the aggressive strategy of House Republicans to discredit the regular Kansas government and hold out for the adoption of the Topeka, or free-state, constitution, it was one of the most masterly speeches of his career. The address came on the heels of Grow's initial failure to block the seating of Whitfield, whom the Republicans wished to refute as much as the government he represented. Out of deference to his political allies, however, Grow had withdrawn his objection to Whitfield, but then added that the bizarre circumstances in this case were such that Congress should depart from its usual course of admitting delegates routinely on prima facie evidence.[7]

Grow methodically chipped away at some of the points made by

Pierce.[8] He assailed the president for trying to whitewash the matter of election irregularities by commenting at length instead on the delegate issue. How was it, Grow wanted to know, that six thousand men voted in March 1855 when the census showed only three thousand legal residents? He pointed out that it was commonly known that a large number of those eligible did not bother to vote because they were intimidated and threatened by men who had no lawful business in Kansas. "Is it to be supposed," Grow therefore charged, "that at a fair election in that Territory, but one free-state man would be elected to the Legislature out of thirty-nine members, and that he should be in the district furthest removed from Missouri?"

Grow's major thrust against the president's message came from his belief that what the free-state people had done was both fitting and legitimate. He rejected the president's claim that their actions were illegal and revolutionary. He proclaimed the "undoubted right of the people of a Territory to call a State convention, without any act of the Territorial Legislature or of Congress, for the purpose of transforming a Territory into a State." Simply, their actions were taken in response to the denial of their right to organize under the act of Congress because of intruders from Missouri.

Turning next to the usurping legislature, Grow scrutinized its official acts, "the first fruits of popular sovereignty as established by the repeal of the Missouri Compromise." Characteristically Grow's sarcasm, as shown in this remark, nearly matched his penchant for incriminating details. He illustrated how the bogus lawmakers had passed a bill that in essence disfranchised a large class of citizens and thereby deprived them of their right to hold office. This law required that before a citizen could vote he had to swear to sustain the fugitive slave act. Grow wanted to know, when had any government under the American flag demanded that its citizens support a particular law as a condition for exercising their freedom to vote? Under this undemocratic and un-American law, every person elected or appointed to office and every attorney who wished to practice in the territory had to take the same oath.

Grow further illustrated how these perniciously designed acts protected slavery far more than the rights of free men. For example, the penalty for advising or persuading a slave to rebel was death; for enticing or carrying away a slave, death or ten years' imprisonment; for aiding or assisting a slave to obtain his freedom, death. At the same time, to kidnap a white child was considered a crime of less severity. Where was the equity and fair-mindedness in such a system? Not content with enacting laws more efficient to safeguard slave property than those of any state in the Union, he continued, the legislature of Kansas reached the extreme by making it a felony just to *say* that a person did not have the right to keep slaves in the territory.

Grow was blunt: "Such are some of the laws of the Territory of Kansas which the President has announced must be enforced at the point of the bayonet, if necessary." In his judgment, these laws pointed to the consummation of one objective — the fulfillment of the prophecy by Senator David Atkinson of Missouri that should the Missouri Compromise be repealed, Kansas would become a slave state. Did anyone wonder, Grow asked finally, why Kansas was hemmed in by the state of Missouri? Why were the boundaries arranged in such manner that normal access to the territory would be through Missouri? What was Missouri's real interest in Kansas? To Grow the answers were obvious: "Slavery in Kansas secures slavery forever in Missouri. This is the motive which brings from Missouri men to preserve law and order in Kansas."

The upshot of Grow's remarks was that the free-state people of Kansas had the right to call for a constitutional convention to transform their territory into a state. Through their delegates the majority of voters had made it abundantly clear they were opposed to slavery. The sham legislature forfeited its right to represent them; under its workings squatter sovereignty was a "miserable delusion." The legislation adopted was sufficient justification for the free-state men to appeal to Congress to secure their rights and privileges.

To the critical onlooker Grow seemed a commanding orator, a stalwart parliamentary pugilist. Only thirty-two years old that spring, he had already reached a level of career promise normally not attained until a later age. Despite chronic health problems, he moved with vivacious quickness. He was sharp and clever and missed little that was said or done on the floor of the House. He followed debate with intensity, never hesitant to object to something that was out of order. Samuel Smith of Tennessee objected to his objecting so often. A blend of temperamental and intellectual qualities assured Grow continued success. His energy and his constant expenditure of nervous force were made particularly manifest by the viciousness with which he attacked his opponents. Whether an opponent was a barroom heckler or the president of the United States made little difference. He displayed evenly that sarcastic wit, that irritating method of insinuation, and that epigrammatic statement of a fact or figure that delighted his friends and infuriated his enemies. To succeed in the House at this time required style and alertness of intellect more than it did profundity. But it also required a mastery of the subtleties of parliamentary procedure. And this was not only Grow's shield, but also his weapon of attack.

His counterpart as chairman of the Senate Committee on Territories was Stephen A. Douglas, who needed no introduction. The Democrats looked to his oratorical and leadership abilities to uphold their party's position in Kansas. A week after Grow had addressed the House, the Illinois senator defended the Kansas-Nebraska Act without qualms, expressed scorn for the emigrant aid societies for pumping undesirables into the territory, and agreed with the president that the territorial legislature and its acts must be sustained with firmness and conviction.[9] To him the free-state movement was rebellious and treasonous, and those responsible for it were putting the settlers in Kansas on a collision course. The real issue, he said, was interference by outside groups, but to many colleagues his ideas were devoid of conviction and sincerity. Douglas struggled with his own credibility.

By the end of March a deadlock ensued between the Douglas and the free-soil plans for Kansas. There was little chance of the House consenting to the Senate bill (number 172) and less chance of the Senate accepting the Topeka constitution. This backdrop of sharply divided opinions depicted in a simple manner the initial lines of battle for the upcoming presidential election. For the Republican party it was not too early to plan campaign strategy. A national convention in late February in Pittsburgh had fired the first broadside when it adopted resolutions to resist the extension of slavery and to support the admission of Kansas as a free state. A month later in Washington, Republican and American members of Congress met to consider a possible union of all anti-Nebraska forces against the administration's Kansas policy. Many agreed with Greeley that regardless of what might happen to the issue of Kansas in Congress, the mandate from the people in the autumn elections was to be the decisive factor in determining the fate of the territory.[10]

Not immune to the need to seek additional support from his constituents, Grow returned home to defend his Congressional record and to answer charges made by his opponents. Democratic free-soilers wanted to know why he had to become a Republican in order to continue the struggle for free-soil principles. Grow always contended that the Democratic party had deserted him and Jeffersonian idealism. Chase of the *Montrose Democrat* had sensitized Grow's political ego with a constant barrage of complaints.[11] He had challenged Grow to face his constituents: "We're waiting for you to come, Grow . . . no more of those worn-out slavery speeches. . . . How do you stand?" The spiteful editor had scolded Grow for playing out a scenario written and orchestrated by old schemers like Giddings, Greeley, and Jessup. In his opinion, Grow's good judgment was being blinded by his antislavery fanaticism. Constituents in the district had more on their minds than slavery, Chase had written, and they demand that their representative in Congress "should at least . . . give his attention to something else besides niggers." Grow did not take kindly to criticism, especially when his principles were suspect or his motives maligned.

On Monday, April 7, more than five hundred men jammed the old courthouse in Montrose to see and hear Grow.[12] Many had come a great distance to the Republican rally. Some were free-soil Democrats who hoped to discover whether Grow's Republican arguments might be sufficient to release them from their traditionally Democratic moorings. Farmers and burghers huddled together in a stuffy hall and listened intently for nearly four hours to Grow express himself as a consistent believer in the free-soil doctrine. His tour de force was to convince his audience of his consistency, first as a Democrat, now as a Republican. To the charge that he had voted for William Cullom of Tennessee as clerk of the House, Grow responded that his support of Collum was consistent with his voting record. A number of Republicans had voted for the Tennessean. Although a Whig and a southerner, Cullom had been one of the biggest critics of the Kansas-Nebraska bill in the last Congress. Apparently Grow satisfied his listeners for they adopted him as Susquehanna's "favorite son" and recommended that he serve as delegate to the national Republican convention scheduled for June in Philadelphia.

Later that month, Grow returned to his duties in Congress and found a lackluster House disposing of lackluster legislative items. In contrast to the Senate, where Douglas's enabling bill was still twisting in a maelstrom of controversy, the lower house remained almost silent on Kansas. Its members instead discussed perfunctorily special claims, a deficiency bill, and the matter of the Washington aqueduct. On occasion, attendance was so poor that noses had to be counted to be sure a quorum was present. Much of Grow's attention was directed toward the work of his committee. It was only a matter of weeks before he would report its progress. Everyone anticipated a Kansas bill that would recognize its present free-state government and its admission into the Union with the constitution it had adopted.

What April lacked in excitement, the month of May compensated for in violent acts of criminality and insanity. Along with nearly everyone, Grow expressed horror when he learned of the brutal attack against Senator Sumner by Preston Brooks in the Senate chamber.

One Pennsylvania newspaper called the incident a good example of "Border-Ruffianism in Congress."[13] Northerners were enraged. Soon insolent approval of the assault on the part of southern congressmen and editors transformed that anger into deeper feelings of hatred, humiliation, and despair. Sumner had insulted South Carolina and the South, the *Charleston Mercury* charged, and Brooks and Keitt should not be chastised.[14] In the House, a committee of investigation heard witnesses and then submitted two reports. The Republican majority recommended that Brooks be expelled and Keitt censured; the Democratic minority declared that the members had no jurisdiction in the matter. Grow voted with other Republicans to expel Brooks and to censure Keitt for his supportive action. The House failed to expel "Bully Brooks" for want of a two-thirds vote, 121–95, but it did adopt a resolution "disapproving" of Keitt's action, 106–96. The southerners voted almost unanimously against expulsion and censure.[15]

News out of Kansas added another dimension to the already grim tragedy. The offices of Lawrence's newspapers, the *Herald of Freedom* and the *Free State Press,* had been ransacked and the presses thrown into the river by armed proslavery parties. One man had lost his life and property damage was extensive. Charles Robinson, Judge G. W. Smith, and George W. Brown were among the free-state people arrested and incarcerated at Lecompton for high treason. But the most scorching story to come out of the territory was of the retaliatory slaughter of five proslavery settlers on Pottawatomie Creek by John Brown and his sons. Until this abolitionist struck, the actions of the free-soil settlers had generally remained within the limits of endurance and the law, but now all the viciousness of men bent on freedom was turned loose. It was an eye for an eye. People saw what they wanted to see in these bizarre yet related incidents, but all had to admit to witnessing the collapse of the political processes in Kansas and the realities of a civil war there. No less ominous than the biblical Four Horsemen, the gathering evils of Kansas passed before the eyes of the nation. Writing to his daughter, Giddings warned against the terrible anger and hate that prepossessed some of his colleagues, so much that they were ready to fight and die for the cause of freedom.[16]

Against this awesome backdrop of calamities, Grow announced on May 29 that his committee was prepared to report. The committee had been ready for weeks, but with the national party conventions pending, he asked to be put on the calendar for June 23. By then the conventions would be over and Congress could get back to work. Meanwhile, he requested that all necessary reports and documents on Kansas and other territories be printed so they might be distributed prior to floor debate.

During June, the political world turned its attention to Cincinnati and Philadelphia where the Democrats and Republicans gathered to draft candidates and platforms. With regard to Kansas, there were no surprises: the Democrats pledged themselves to the Kansas-Nebraska Act, and the Republicans again went on record in favor of free territories. Both parties believed they had made good choices of presidential nominees. Buchanan, a household name among Democrats, was a conservative and relatively free of the Kansas debacle. The *Charleston Mercury* declared that he was entitled to the support of the South for he had never voted against its institutions.[17] At the same time, Republican John C. Fremont was "sound" on the territorial question and was not considered radical in his views on slavery. As leaders of both parties prepared for what was obviously to be the first real test of Republican strength, attention reverted to Congress, where another test — this one over the admission of Kansas — would shortly take place.

The Passion of Free Men

On June 23, 1856, Grow reported from the Committee on Territories. The combat readiness of the free-soilers and "Nebraskaites" was not at all abated by the pleasantries exchanged on that warm summer day. If anything, it was probably further sharpened by the tension from the populace of the city and by the annoying, rhythmic clink-clink-clink of the stonecutter's hammer as progress on the new Capitol wings continued. Washington had become a southern bastion. For the first time in years, strangers felt an uneasiness enhanced by a wanton display of weapons and bad manners. Three of the city's five newspapers defended Brooks. Since his attack on Sumner, a large portion of southern residents and transients had been in a state of frantic excitement, parading the streets and barrooms with indiscriminate threats and insults against northern men. The free-soilers reciprocated. In both houses of Congress, these rabble-rousers disturbed proceedings with tumultuous applause or disorderly shouts of displeasure. What may have been at best an unnerving situation at the beginning of the debate over Kansas soon became a war of incorrigible wills as neither side saw any reason to move toward compromise. And when this happened, alternatives were reduced to a paltry few.

Before he addressed the Kansas issue, Grow reported a bill "to enable the people of the Oregon Territory to form a constitution and State government and for the admission of such State into the Union."[18] Few opposed Oregon joining the community of states, but her admission immediately raised the knotty question of her population. According to the 1850 census, she had more than 13,000. Although no one was certain how many people resided in the territory, it did not have the minimum of 90,000 to permit its application to statehood. Despite this, Grow hoped that Congress would not use a population requirement against Oregon. He believed Oregon should be admitted if there was sufficient reason to believe that the residents could administer the state's law. After all, Grow advised his colleagues, other states, including Florida, Michigan, Iowa, and Wisconsin, had entered the Union without first having the necessary population as determined at the time of their application. Should Congress wait until Oregon's population approached the minimum, he warned, the number might double as the nation's population increased. So, unless the House membership were enlarged, Grow added, a figure of 200,000 might be necessary to send a representative to Congress. To him the delay meant keeping a territorial people in a state of vassalage. He argued that the power of Congress to organize territories was discretionary; the rule of establishing a population-representative ratio had no application to the constitutional power to admit new states. It is up to Congress to say when and how they shall come in, Grow concluded. "Congress may admit them with 500 or it may refuse them with 500,000 individuals."

This was a bold leap into the dark. For a man who had insisted upon the inviolability of the Missouri Compromise, Grow now opened the way for attacks against his plan of flexible options for Congress in admitting new states. Oregon was an acid test preparatory to the introduction of the Kansas bill. If Oregon were admitted without the required number of people, why not Kansas? Neither had populations anywhere near the number mandated, but the Republicans wanted both added to the Union as free states.

Southerners saw through Grow's plan. Percy Walker of Alabama accused him of deliberately wanting to destroy the traditional way of admitting new states. Zollicoffer of Tennessee agreed; Oregon must not be let in until it met the population requirement. And to make sure that everyone knew what that number was, he moved that the exact figure of 93,437 be included in the bill. George Jones, also of Tennessee, offered a similar amendment, but both amendments were defeated. John Millson of Virginia concurred with his fellow southerners that Oregon's admission must be delayed. The Virginian also ridiculed Grow's proposal. If the Pennsylvanian had his way, Millson cried out, Oregon and all the other territories would be carved up into smaller units for future states, with scarcely enough people to frighten a herd of buffalo. The horrible result might be a Senate with 200 members! Millson wanted no part of a "rotten borough" system that had plagued England. Finally, the southern Americans did not share Grow's curious psychological fixation of helping the immigrants: either he was giving them free land or, in this case, granting them a "natural right" to vote in the territory. Grow had opposed an amendment to the Oregon bill that restricted the suffrage to citizens.

Grow was glad to close debate on Oregon and move to the House bill (H.R. 411), to admit Kansas under the Topeka constitution. The debate had degenerated into a melee with wild accusations and a reopening of the slavery question. On June 25, Grow presented the Kansas bill as "the action of the people of Kansas Territory to throw off an odious and oppressive Territorial Legislature — one imposed upon them by usurpation and fraud." The southerners were led this time by Stephens of Georgia, the focus of the administration forces in the House. The Georgian remarked uncharitably that the Topeka constitution was not formed by any authority from either the territorial legislature or Congress.[19] It was formed, instead, "by men in open rebellion," some of whom at present were under arrest for treason. There was no evidence, he insisted, that a majority of the people in the territory were in favor of the free-state constitution. "It is an *ex parte* proceeding from the beginning to end — got up by a party — contrived by Governor Reeder." When he closed his remarks with a strong defense of slavery, the galleries echoed his sentiments.

Stephens submitted a substitute for the Kansas bill. Under the plan, similar to one offered in the Senate by fellow Georgian Robert Toombs, the president was to appoint a five-man team to go to Kansas, take a census of the eligible voters, and then make arrangements for an election of delegates to a constitutional convention. As expected, the plan met with the approval of other southerners.

Grow wasted no time in attacking the substitute. Like a courageous warrior, he prepared himself with renewed vigor to do battle with an old foe. Having been elected as a free-soil Democrat, he was on the administration side of the hall. His enemies sat within a rod's reach: Stephens, Millson, Marshall, Keitt, Smith, McMullen, and Quitman. To these southerners he symbolized the many evils of northernism. They suffered through the tirades of this fire-breathing radical who extolled the passions of freedom and placed the bloodshed in Kansas on the heads of the conspirators who repealed the Missouri Compromise. He was an Untouchable among Brahmins; he was the many-headed dragon of the Apocalypse. As Greeley observed, "Grow stands pouring the fundamental axioms of the Declaration of Independence into the amazed, reluctant ears of the platoons of slaveholders who immediately surround him."[20]

The Pennsylvanian came right to the point: "I have no faith in any measure of redress for the people of Kansas, which is to be placed in the hands of this Administration to execute."[21] He proceeded to explain how the president from the beginning had failed to protect the citizens of the territory under the Kansas-Nebraska Act. "When a public officer betrays his trust in one case, will you intrust the same charge to his keeping again? . . . I am opposed to any measure of relief the execution of which is to be intrusted to men who have trampled on every right most sacred to American freemen." Furthermore, Grow asked, how naive must a person be to believe that the president would appoint observers who were not wholly sympathetic to his views? Even a list of impartial appointees was no assurance that Judge Samuel Lecompte, chief justice in Kansas, would be impartial in his prosecution of illegal voters. This southerner, Grow remarked, was hardly a pillar of fair play. "A judge who orders the destruction of public buildings, printing presses, and private dwellings of respectable citizens, as nuisances, on the mere finding of a grand jury, is not to be trusted with the rights of American freemen."

With patented sarcasm, Grow hinted there was still a ray of hope for those who cherish freedom because Stephens and Toombs were now recommending that a team be sent to Kansas. Months ago southerners had resisted the appointment of any committee to investigate events in Kansas, alleging there were no frauds or violence against free-soilers in the territory, and even had there been the House had no power to redress them. Any violation of the law was a matter for the administration and the courts, not Congress. Now their legislative plan at least called for the appointment of a committee. Second, the previous demand that Kansas must have a minimal population of some 90,000 before it could form a state constitution had also been jettisoned in both houses. Still, Grow defied the opponents of the bill: "What objection can there [now] be save that her constitution prohibits slavery?"

He called for the immediate admission of Kansas; he saw no other way by which Congress could relieve the people of that territory and prevent constant harassment by nonresidents. Why delay its admission, he asked. Why bother to take a census as proposed by Stephens's substitute when it was conceded on all sides that it was now proper to let Kansas in without the necessary population? And to the opponents who wished more time to study the reports of the House investigating committee before reaching a decision, Grow sardonically quipped: "If there is a gentleman in this House who wants information with reference to the state of things in Kansas, before he casts his vote upon this bill, Barnum ought to have him as a specimen of a fossil, for he is the only man in the country that does not understand it. The whole country understands what wrongs have been committed in Kansas."

The Pennsylvanian rebuked two other contentions made by the Georgian. The first regarded Stephens's appeal to a higher law to sustain slavery. Without stopping to discuss scriptural authority, Grow maintained that if slavery rested on the Old Testament for its support, "then the same authority will support white slavery as well as black, and the amalgamation of master and slave." As a scholar quoting from text, he informed his colleagues that in biblical times there had been intermarriage between master and slave and that the slaves of the patriarchs had been white. If the Bible argument is acceptable, Grow concluded, whites can be seized and carried into bondage, and masters and slaves may amalgamate.

Second, Grow found no merit in Stephens's remark that Kansas could not be admitted until law and order were maintained there. "Sir," Grow countered, "law and order have not been violated in that Territory save by the officials of your Government." With the shout of law and order, he continued, printing presses had been destroyed and peaceable citizens had been arrested for treason and their homes battered down — all carried out with the blessings of the territorial government. "Law and order is the excuse of despotism," he exclaimed. It was to preserve law and order that freedom and patriotism were silenced in Poland and Hungary. After brutally suppressing the Warsaw uprising in 1831, for example, Field Marshal Paskevich sent to Czar Nicholas his memorable dispatch, "Order reigns in Warsaw." Grow drew a cynical parallel: "The satrap of this Administration in Kansas exhibits a like love of law and order with his prototype, whose example, with becoming propriety, he might well imitate if he succeeds in crushing out in Kansas the spirit of liberty, by sending a like dispatch to his superior, 'Order reigns in Kansas.'"

Besides discrediting the substitute offered by Stephens, Grow did what he could to keep his committee's bill from being driven to death by delays. He had already foiled one such move when at the onset of debate the bill's opponents threatened to send it to the Committee of the Whole. At this late point in the session, such action was tantamount to defeat. Grow and the Republicans did their best to ride the legislative rapids. Israel Washburn of Maine and Lewis Campbell of Ohio supported Grow by reminding the House that there were III calendar items for the Committee of the Whole; many of these were "special orders," which took precedence. Stephens assured his colleagues that sending a bill to the committee was not exactly condemning it to the "tombs of the Capulets" for the majority of the House could demand a vote on the bill at any time. Grow did not wish to take that chance. He stunned Stephens and other opponents by announcing his intention to call the question on the Kansas bill in a day or two.[22]

This did not prove to be easy. While Grow pressed hard for a vote, he also helped direct action against Stephens's substitute. In a last-minute flurry of amendments, stratagems, and parliamentary sand traps, both measures faced defeat. The scene on the floor must have appeared bizarre to those in the galleries. In the strongest gesture yet toward a repeal of the 1854 act, George Dunn of Indiana moved to amend the substitute with a provision to restore the status quo prior to the passage of the Kansas-Nebraska bill. It was an obvious ploy to kill the substitute and disconcert its author. Stephens naturally objected but the motion carried, 109–102. He then unsuccessfully tried to withdraw his measure. Thereupon, his substitute with Dunn's amendment — indeed, an unnatural graft — was defeated in a lopsided 2–210 vote. The Republicans naturally did not care for the substitute in its original state and the supporters did not want it with Dunn's amendment.

Motions to table or postpone the Kansas bill indefinitely failed, as did efforts to adjourn. The oppressive heat and humidity of early summer made the proceedings unbearable, but the majority determined to reach a decision. Houston of Alabama had left a sickbed to vote and he pleaded with his colleagues not to delay the balloting any longer. Floor consensus suggested that the vote would be very close, but both sides were confident of victory. When Grow called for the question, he may have acted in haste; several supporters, including his good friend Benjamin Pringle of New York, were absent. As it turned out, they would have made a difference. Then again, Grow's aggressive and brusque manner in debate may have alienated one or two others. In the general confusion, Grow and floor managers found it difficult to keep track of members who kept wandering in and out of the hall. The roll call seemed endless and tended to fray everyone's patience. By a single vote, 106–107, the Kansas bill was defeated. Immediately afterwards, and to the relief of most, the House adjourned for the day.

While the Republicans gritted their teeth, their opponents appeared jubilant. But their joy was short-lived. David Barclay, a Democrat from Pennsylvania serving his only term in Congress, asked the next day that the vote be reconsidered. He said that he had made a mistake in voting against the bill and feared that the House had committed a terrible error as well. The bill's defeat might imply that the House was approving all the criminal acts and indictments in Kansas, he said. He wanted now to vote for the bill. In response to a very angry Houston, who was grievously pained by people who can be "reached," Barclay assured his colleagues that his decision to switch was not the result of applied pressure. He had consulted no one.

Grow was quick to seize the advantage of Barclay's motion for reconsideration, which was passed by the slender margin of two votes. He pressed for an immediate adoption of the bill. He may also have been prompted by the absence of at least a dozen southern opponents. John McQueen of South Carolina moved to table the bill, but the motion failed. Both Stephens and Percy Walker of Alabama had asked McQueen to withdraw his motion. Walker commented that the Democratic side did not wish to prevent the bill from coming to a final vote. He said the only reason to delay the vote was to enable lawmakers who were on their way to the House to participate. On July 3 the question was taken and decided in the affirmative, 99–97.[23]

Of course, Grow and the Republicans knew that the bill had no chance in the Democratic Senate. But having it rejected by that body in a presidential election year was not all bad. Opponents insisted that the single aim of the free-soilers was to continue agitation over Kansas, and Senate rejection would help their cause.[24] When the bill reached the upper house it was sent to the Committee on Territories. On July 8 Douglas reported that his committee had agreed to a substitute. The Senate measure, introduced by Toombs and adopted on July 2, authorized the people of Kansas to form a constitution and state government. Despite a strong plea by Sen. Jacob Collamer of Vermont in defense of the House bill, the Senate approved its own version of the Kansas bill.[25] For the moment, at least, the plan to admit Kansas under the Topeka constitution was dead.

Still, the House was not through with the matter. Dunn of Indiana tried but failed to have the rules suspended to amend the Senate substitute. The House later adopted his amendment that repealed the Kansas-Nebraska act. Republicans displayed little enthusiasm for Dunn's measure. Several of its provisions were annoying to them, particularly those that sanctioned slavery in the territory until 1858 and recognized the fugitive slave law. Grow and others attempted to amend the proposed amendment, but Grow's main concern was not with the slavery provisions. Instead, he wanted an amendment that would release from prison those charged with treason and destroy the validity of the Kansas legislature. "If it does that," he commented, "it accomplishes all that is proposed by my amendment."[26] His enemies back home vilified him for supporting this "proslavery" proposal.

For the rest of the session, Grow continued to press on Kansas. During the third week of July he was ill, but he returned in time to take part in the heated debate over the army appropriations bill. He was one of the principal leaders in attaching to that bill a rider stipulating that the army should not be used by the president to enforce the laws of the Kansas legislature until Congress decided whether it was a valid assembly.

The rider's introduction by Sherman of Ohio set off a spirited exchange of charges and countercharges that involved Sherman, Grow, and Stephens. The three men argued over the many wrongs, real or imaginary, committed in Kansas. Whereas Grow reasoned that Congress had the responsibility to redress those wrongs, Stephens contended that the people of the territory had the same redress as the people of Pennsylvania — through the courts. "Congress has no right," the Georgian pontificated, "to inquire into, and pronounce judgment upon, the validity or legality of the organization of the Territorial Legislature."[27] He dared the free-soilers to produce evidence that any member of that legislature had been elected by force or violence. The whole outcry over Kansas was nothing but "clamor in the beginning, clamor throughout," and to simple clamor he would not yield.

The money bill with the Sherman proviso failed to make its way through the Senate, and Congress adjourned without making the appropriation. President Pierce immediately called an extra session to deal with the army bill crisis. The drama did not change: the House insisted upon the proviso and the Senate insisted upon its rejection. A conference committee stripped away some of the proviso's initial wording but retained the essential idea. The Senate still refused to accept the proviso and, in a close vote with a handful of members absent, the lower house went along with that decision.[28]

In a related matter, Grow moved to strike appropriations to sustain judges in Kansas who were, in his opinion, trampling down the liberty of the people. His amendment was adopted but it had no more chance in the Senate than did the Sherman proviso. Grow proposed that Congress use its power over the purse to end the injustices in the territory. Impeachment was hardly a workable option because the Senate, being the "guardian of slave power," was incapable of finding guilt in men who served the interests of slaveholders. Phelps of Missouri found it both untenable and amusing that Grow, who recently had voted for a Kansas bill that provided for judges, now wanted a bill that would not compensate them. Branch of North Carolina wondered if Grow's amendment violated the Constitution (Art. 3, Sec. 1) regarding judges and their compensation. Grow did not think the article applied to the situation in Kansas. Territorial judges were in office by the grace of the president, who could remove them at will. If he refused to remove them for just cause, however, Congress must then act in the best interests of the inhabitants.[29]

Grow was a thorn in the side of the administration forces. To the Democrats and perhaps to those in the galleries, he appeared to be an impetuous, unyielding, and obstructive youth who was blind to the inherent dangers of fanning the fires beneath the slavery controversy. Yet he influenced the legislative process. Not only did he occupy a most important committee chairmanship, but also he knew how to use that position to direct the designs of his party. As chairman he guided his faction on territorial questions, which had come to symbolize the increased sectional feelings within the House and nation. If having motions approved with consistency is a reliable index of legislative efficiency, as Bogue suggests, then Grow's power as a floor leader is easily substantiated.[30] With respect to the territories and related issues, Grow had a high percentage of his motions approved by the Republicans. Good or bad, they were accepted by men who had learned during the speakership contest that it is better to remain cohesive as a group on crucial questions than to fragment over individual preferences. The new party's presence in the Thirty-fourth Congress accentuated sectional loyalties reminiscent of party rivalries before the 1850 Compromise. The result was a standoff between opposing camps and a shift of attention from Congress to the forthcoming elections.

By the time Congress had adjourned in August, the presidential race was well under way. The public, wavering between fear and hope, held the power of mandate in its hand. But what did this really mean? Would a Republican sweep bring welcomed relief to the people of Kansas? Or would a Republican defeat at the polls assure the admission of a new slave state? Whatever the outcome, relatively few Americans wanted to concede that the territorial crisis would come to an end.

ℬ 8

Holding the Line on Kansas

H AD SOMEONE asked Grow in 1856 what he thought of the Democratic party, he probably would have answered like this:

Sir, the Democratic party, your party, is the greatest political survivor in our nation's history. It has outlasted tired old Federalists and Whigs, abolitionists, nullifiers, Free-Soilers, the crises of 1820, 1848, 1850, and 1954 — all because of slavery — and even southern secessionists. Above all, the Democratic party has been a political institution, an institution that has endured largely because of its rich Jeffersonian idealism and heritage. Recently, however, you have allowed your party to abandon this idealism, which makes as much sense as a Christian abandoning the Good Book. You have allowed one faction in your party — the South — to dictate not only the terms by which the party is to operate, but also the very conditions under which the Union is to persist. Sir! It is no longer the party I once believed in.

Grow shared with fellow Republicans the notion that in this election year the Democratic party was on an abortive mission. Unable to deliver to modern America a payload of genuinely acceptable pledges on slavery, the party, in their opinion, was pursuing a safe course by returning to the Baltimore platform of 1852 and the 1850 Compromise. It was telling Congress to leave the South and the subject of slavery alone.

This strategy of conservative Democrats logically would satisfy the vast majority of voters who stood between the radicals of North and South. At their Cincinnati convention the Democratic bosses dumped Pierce and sidestepped Douglas; each man, being too heavily blackened by his involvement in Kansas, had created a liability for the party. Instead, the leadership picked the urbane, irresolute, and conservative James Buchanan. He seemed the ideal choice to convey the

134

impression that while the Republicans were "subsisting exclusively on slavery agitation" and thereby feeding the fires of sectionalism and disunion, the Democrats were doing their best to keep the states together. For them the preservation of the Union was the "paramount issue" in this election. The preservative power of the platform's principle of noninterference in slavery by Congress and the candidacy of a political veteran whose reputation was as "wide as civilization itself" seemed an unbeatable combination.

Although Buchanan won the election, this campaign strategy was also hypocritical and defective. How strange it was for the Democrats to lambast those "sectional parties" for guiding the nation to civil war, but not to fault the bullies in the cotton states, who were not exactly immune to disunionist fever. Southern radicals did support Buchanan, and northern Democrats welcomed that support. But this clash of value judgments and the double-talk that accompanied it perplexed thousands of moderates and antislavery Democrats and strengthened the fibers of northern radicalism. To someone like Grow, the Democratic platform in 1856 simply reinforced the argument that the party had become totally submissive to slavocracy. Buchanan tried to bridge the obvious chasm within his party, but his oversights only deepened the rift. After his nomination, he was dismayed to discover that he had never written to Pierce or Douglas, enlisting their support.[1] Confusion and serious misgivings persisted. Hoping to create the illusion of being a united party, northern Democrats had no alternative but to bite the bullet, embrace their southern allies, play down the slavery issue, and reaffirm their trust in the holy bonds of the Kansas-Nebraska Act.

Mixed interpretations of the doctrine of popular sovereignty, which was fundamental to the act, added another embarrassment to the party. Most southern Democrats believed that a territorial legislature could not touch slavery, at least not until the residents adopted a constitution for statehood. Northwesterners and northeasterners agreed with Douglas and William English of Indiana that the settlers could have legislated against slavery much sooner. Such ambiguity fostered doubt and suspicion, despite assurances by English that differences between northerners and southerners were not material.[2] Southerners questioned the sincerity of northern Democrats who marched to the slogan, "Buchanan, Breckinridge, and Free Kansas." These same northerners placated their antislavery constituents with solemn pledges that the territories would be filled with multitudes of settlers from the free states, far in excess of those emigrating from slave states. The "will of the majority" was thus a built-in safeguard for popular sovereignty that assured freedom in the territories. Such irresponsible rhetoric infuriated the fireeaters, in particular, who were telling their constituents that "Kansas must come in as a slave state." The general voter found the issue of "union versus disunion" easier to grasp than a fistful of divergent opinions on popular sovereignty. The unequivocal concept of nonextension urged by the Republicans seemed perhaps a better choice for the antislavery voter.

Despite victory, the Democrats saw dangerous signs in the election results. Buchanan had failed to capture the majority of popular votes, and the Republicans had gained control in most of the free states. Everyone knew that the Democratic victory was lacking something that might contribute to the spirit of cooperation and mutual understanding so urgently needed in the management of national affairs. Maybe the wrong leaders had been chosen; perhaps there was an improper focus upon the issues. With the entire nation groping for the way to economic growth and stability, the Democrats may have expended too much energy in fighting their opponents over the Union and slavery. Expansion, railroad construction, disposition of the public domain, and the tariff were some of the economic stresses that demanded prompt action. Yet no sooner had the third session of the Thirty-fourth Congress convened than Democratic leaders resumed the battle over slavery.

If victory was a mirage, for the moment at least the picture looked bright. Buchanan's triumph, Democratic control of Congress, and even a favorable Dred Scott decision promised a reassuring grip on both the national government and Kansas. The Republicans faced extinction. Yet, in the final analysis, the Democratic party's real strength of stewardship lay in the resourcefulness and character of its leaders. The chances remained slim that they would or could overcome their party's weaknesses. Ideological and social pressures put before the lawmakers a strong temptation to play to the galleries. Campaigning never ceased; all issues were exploited politically. When this happened the cause for union became as elusive as a will-o'-the-wisp. The party approached bankruptcy, and the nation inched closer to civil war.

The radical Republicans contributed to this degenerative process. They rejoiced in the Democrats' disorder and feasted upon the party's carcass. Elated with their own showing in the elections, they seized advantage of Democratic weaknesses and determined more than ever to ride the momentum of the Kansas crisis to the eventual victory of the free-state forces. Struggling to make Kansas free was the single, symbolic objective upon which all Republicans agreed. Other issues such as the tariff and the homestead bill still divided them. But they must not yield on Kansas, or all would be lost. The attitude that, if the Union were to survive, it must do so on Republican terms, prevailed and simplified Grow's resumption of a leadership role in the House.

"First We Polked, Then We Pierced, Now We'll Buck Them"

Not overlooking their internal difficulties, the Democrats were as confident of victory in 1856 as they had been four years earlier. They appraised the opposition as a confederacy of disjointed elements that lacked spiritual integrity and unity. Fremont posed no threat. How did the Republicans, or fusionists, expect to win with a transparent romantic whose only credentials were swashbuckling and military exploits of questionable merit — a man whose own father-in-law, Thomas Hart Benton, did not plan to support him? Democratic leaders insisted that the nation was not ready for another Zach Taylor and a bunch of "freedom shriekers." With the Union so perilously close to disaster, the voter demanded a leader with balanced judgment and broad experience. Buchanan was that man, but his own state of Pennsylvania was very much in doubt. Republicanism was enjoying brushfire success throughout the commonwealth. The Democrats worried that if they lost Pennsylvania, their hopes of a national victory would appear dim.

Writing in 1928, George V. Larrabee, a friend of Grow's, recalled how as a youngster in 1856 he had listened to the young congressman: "It was in this campaign that Mr. Grow became famous all over the North as a great political campaigner and orator."[3] Actually Grow's reputation as a silver-tongued "stumpster" preceded his zealous crusade for Fremont and Republicanism. Larrabee probably meant that Grow had no difficulty in matching the fine oratorical skills of speakers like Horace Greeley, Hannibal Hamlin, and Henry Wilson — men with whom he shared a platform during this campaign. Even his staunchest critics had to agree with Larrabee that before a political crowd Grow had "few equals and no superiors."

Combining eloquence with showmanship, Grow performed with the zest of an actor and the gusto of a clown. In what was called by both Larrabee and the editor of the *Independent Republican* the greatest political rally ever held in Susquehanna County up to that time, Grow gave a good example of his craft. He delighted the huge throng, estimated at 10,000 with theatrics that revealed the lighter side of his demeanor, satisfying the audience completely. In those days political gatherings were entertainment as well as public forums. To be successful a politician had to move his listeners both spiritually and emotionally. He had to make those faces before him frown in anger, grimace with disgust, and light up with joy. The great speakers did it, and Grow was one of them.

On that beautiful but hot Saturday in September, thousands poured into Montrose to hear Grow and a panel of politicos. The boisterous, festive crowd looked forward to a weekend of politics and fun, highlighted by a torchlight parade on Saturday evening.[4] They came from all over the county — Jessup, Dimock, Auburn, Jackson, and Great Bend. One train, nearly two miles long, brought in delegations with brass bands, fife and drum corps, and soldiers in colorful array. They filled the streets and packed the taverns. Several thousand women joined the men who assembled before the speakers.

Grow, exuberant and flushed by the heat and excitement, proceeded to disrobe while William Jessup urged him on. The predominantly masculine crowd responded approvingly with every gesture Grow made. First he threw off his coat. Then he unbuttoned his vest. Next, he parted with his tie. The rules of propriety in the mid-nineteenth century apparently drew the line between decent and indecent dress for a gentleman with the dropping of the cravat, for when that item was discarded, a number of women, embarrassed, hurried away, but the men cheered. The editor of the paper that reported the event thought little of Grow's cheap burlesque, nor did he approve of his indictment of the Democratic party. Grow had said that while the Republicans intended to restrict slavery to its present confines, the Democrats planned to extend it over all the territories.[5] Larrabee remembered that it was at this Susquehanna meeting that Grow coined a saying he would often use with great effect: "The time will come in America when the sun will rise and set on no slave."

The 1856 campaign had begun early for Grow. While Republican and Democratic leaders attended their national conventions, Grow attended political rallies at home. He came fortified with stand-pat arguments against southern encroachments and the violation of liberties in Kansas. He clarified and justified his positions on the issues, and constantly urged a get-tough policy. In Carbondale, for example, he encouraged the adoption of resolutions condemning border ruffianism and the attack against Senator Sumner.[6] His stop at Montrose prompted a cryptic editorial comment that it would not be easy for him to solicit support from his old enemies, the Whigs and Know-Nothings.[7] At the same time, these groups wondered if his break with the Democrats was genuine or only cosmetic. On his last visit to the town in April, Grow had sensed their skepticism even though he had announced that he would have nothing to do with the Cincinnati Democratic convention. As late as August, some Whigs and Americans were saying he had not changed his true colors, that he was still a Democrat at heart. To a die-hard Democrat, however, the suggestion that Grow might still be part of the Democratic fold was utter nonsense. As chairman of the Committee on Territories, Grow had demonstrated his true grit.

Anyone who followed national politics knew Grow's thoughts on the issues. The old question, "Where does Grow stand?," which had been hauntingly used by his opponents since the 1850 campaign, no longer had to be asked. His record in Congress and on the stump was a testament to his political faith. He was the quintessential exponent of the radical Republican's conviction that the devotees of slavery had every intention of breaking up the Union should things not go their way. Just as his party declared it the duty of Congress to stamp out those twin relics of barbarism — slavery and polygamy — from the territories, Grow believed it incumbent upon all good Americans to expunge southern disunionists from the political system. His belief in the theory of a "plotted conspiracy" never waned; later in life he wrote, "This scheme for the dissolution of the Union would have developed in 1856 had Fremont been elected instead of developing in 1861 after Lincoln's election."[8]

Grow's hard-core repudiation of the so-called conspirators and the Democratic party that housed them gave instant definition to the antislavery movement in his district. He was lionized by enthusiastic crowds of his constituents. If knighthood were fashionable in America, Sir Galusha surely would have been one of the Republican party's first dubbings, along with Wilmot. He captured the rough-hewn spirit of pioneer radicalism that was so expansively invoked during his congressional tenure and transferred it to a new party. Sobriety, exuberance, vilification, and a sense of destiny marked his mission. In reality, however, most of his success came from whipping a prostrate horse, for the Democratic party in the northern tier counties was painfully close to death. While the desperate Democrats exploited the popular antipathy toward the amalgamation of the races, the free-soil Democrats, Republicans, Whigs, and Americans praised the virtues of an amalgamation of political causes against slavery expansionists and southern disunionists.

No one doubted that Grow would be renominated and reelected. As he carried his campaign from one end of the district to the other,

the question most asked was whether Grow would top his 1854 performance. Rallying support for the Republican cause and working to
consolidate the antislavery forces behind it best describe his 1856 efforts.
In vivid contrast to his indifference a year earlier, Grow now ener-
gized his role in structuring a permanently sound Republican organization. His old friend Wilmot was there, applying a steady influence; so were William Jessup and Ulysses Mercur. It was an all-out
effort to fuse Republicans, Americans, free-soil Democrats, and those
who still wished to be called Whigs. Writing to an apparent associate
in July, Wilmot was optimistic. If all opposition groups linked together against Buchanan, he predicted, Fremont would carry Bradford County alone by 3,000 to 4,000 votes.[9]

A number of district Democrats switched loyalties and became ardent Republicans, emulating Grow and Wilmot. One good example
was Simeon B. Chase, who, for four years, along with E. B. Chase,
had edited and published the *Montrose Democrat*. Throughout Pennsylvania such defections were common. Andrew Reeder of Easton,
former governor of Kansas, startled party leaders by announcing he
planned to support Fremont. John Read of Philadelphia and J. Ken-
nedy Moorhead of Allegheny did likewise. Despite these desertions,
John W. Forney, chairman of the Democratic State Committee, expressed guarded optimism over his party's chances in Pennsylvania.
But to be safe and also responsive to worried Democratic bosses, Forney recruited Howell Cobb and Herschel V. Johnson of Georgia and
John Floyd of Virginia to canvass the state, perhaps to convince
Pennsylvanians that southerners were not monsters ready to destroy
the Union.

Being a turncoat himself, Grow expected no mercy from his opponents. In a letter from Washington, dated August 11 and printed
in the *Independent Republican,* he complained that his signature was
being forged in some of the Buchanan literature.[10] The *Montrose Democrat* of October 9 accused him of quackery for being so vociferous over
slavery, yet supporting the Dunn bill, which established slavery in
the territories until 1858 and extended the Fugitive Slave Act.[11] He
was also charged with killing the Toombs bill, which, according to
administration forces, would have brought peace to Kansas. The meanest form of harrassment was the opposition's use of hecklers, drums,
and other musical instruments to annoy Grow when he spoke.

None of this flak interfered with his chances of victory. He did
not have to campaign so vigorously and he probably could have
been elected had he remained in Washington. But he stumped hard
through an ambitious and grueling itinerary covering each of Sus-

quehanna's twenty-seven townships. As a Republican of national acclaim who was running for reelection, he was in demand, and he loved it. He was never a front-porch campaigner. Meeting the people face to face was, he believed, a duty of everyone who held or sought public office. He valued his close relationship with his constituents. Early in his career he vowed he would never accept a political position unless it were elective. For this reason he refused a diplomatic assignment offered to him some years later by President Rutherford Hayes.

On the eve of the congressional election in October, the *Montrose Democrat* recapitulated Grow's campaign assertions: Congress had the constitutional right and duty to regulate affairs in a territory; the South had continually aggressed against the North, starting with the Pinckney resolutions or "gag rule" of 1836; the Topeka constitution had been a legitimate exercise of the sovereignty of a majority of bona fide settlers; the tragedy of the Sumner attack had been compounded by the Democratic party's refusal to expel Brooks; and he and Wilmot were acting with the interests of "pure" Democrats at heart. Viewing these declarations as pure rubbish, the newspaper summed up its attitude toward Grow: he was running on a Know-Nothing-Republican fusion ticket, supported by men who once had opposed him. The paper prayed that all good Democrats would vote against this charlatan and help elect Dan Sherwood.[12]

The abuse heaped upon Grow was neither uncommon nor equal to the severity with which Fremont was treated. All the candidates in 1856 were subjected to some degree of defamatory rhetoric and misrepresentation, but the hardest blows were aimed at the Republican nominee for president and his "nigger worshippers." Democrats reminded voters of his illegitimate birth and his pitiful record as a U.S. senator. They charged him with twice having voted against a proposition to abolish slavery in the District of Columbia and with opposing a proposal to extend benefits of the bounty land bill to widows and minor children of veterans. And was it not strange, they added, for the antisouthern Republicans to nominate a man who was a "southern man by birth, instincts, education and associations?" The falsehood that Fremont was a Catholic circulated faster than it could be denied. This damaging untruth was designed to dissipate the support of the Americans.[13]

Pernicious as it was, the propaganda paid off. Buchanan carried his own state by nearly 32,000 more votes than Pierce had four years earlier. His margin of victory over the Union slate, a fusion electoral ticket, was about 27,000. The state Democrats expressed relief. In Grow's district, however, the story was different. Here Fremont received 9,000 more votes than Buchanan, a not unexpected outcome. On November 18, at the courthouse in Montrose, the Susquehanna Republicans celebrated their fine showing. Despite the poor weather on this Tuesday evening, the turnout was good. The ladies of the town presented the prize banner to Lenox township, home of Grow, for the largest gain in the Republican vote between the October and November elections. The banner's inscription read: "The old Liberty Tree — let it *Grow*." The congressman accepted the award and quipped that the efforts of local Democrats like E. B. Chase undoubtedly helped the Republicans in Lenox.[14]

At this meeting, Grow gave one of his better speeches. He contrasted the growth and prosperity of free and slaveholding states and called for "Fremont and Dayton" in 1860. The audience approved. Wilmot also spoke, and seeing the two Republican warriors there reminded many of earlier elections when the two had campaigned together. Exuding abundant optimism, the two young men symbolized the irresistible appeal that marked early Republicanism. As Alexander McClure so aptly put it, the Democrats were confronted by a "tidal wave of impulsive politics" inspired by strong antislavery feeling.[15] Although they had "Bucked" their opponents into defeat nationally, the Democrats knew that a corner had been turned in the political history of the state and nation. Their victory might translate into a genuine concord of peace and union. What happened in the new Congress would suggest how successful they had been and how effectively the Republicans had been checked.

A Session of Watchful Waiting

But first the Democrats had to get through the third session of the Thirty-fourth Congress. If moderation were to be found somewhere after the elections, Capitol Hill was not the place. No sooner had the members returned from their homefront battles than the sectional bitterness reappeared in both houses. Much of the ill feeling was the direct result of the campaign, but a good deal of it was fallout from the previous session. Congress had adjourned on a sour note after an extra session in August to enact an army appropriation bill. The *Charleston Mercury* had called the efforts of House members to amend the bill Jacobinic in nature.[16]

Three months later, the Republicans were ready to resume their confrontational stance and bask in their moral triumph. Brooks, the southern militant from South Carolina, observed that the Republi-

cans had been beaten but remained unconquered: "Their organizations are undisturbed — the morale of their troops preserved — their
leaders confident, and still trusted."[17] The Republican Association
of Washington met on November 27 and expressed unbridled confidence.[18] The masses had supported them, the Republicans boasted,
and they would again support the party in 1860 for total victory. A
universal greeting among the Republicans went something like this:
"We have done nobly for a beginning — we can surely beat them next
time." They mocked the Democrats, who celebrated their Pyrrhic victory with a grand parade in the capital city, and took offense at one
of the more indiscreet banners borne aloft in the procession, which
read: "Sumner and Kansas — Let them Bleed."

Not unlike most short sessions, the third session of the Thirty-fourth
Congress was equally dedicated to politics and lawmaking. Controversy from the recent campaign marred the proceedings. Both sides
scrutinized the election returns, trying to find in the figures a mandate or sign to help them plot the future out of victory or defeat. The
lawmakers spent hours and hours before their colleagues and the nation, exhausting their political philosophies toward slavery and the
Union, and explaining what went right or wrong in the elections. It
was a steady barrage of warmed-over platitudes. Some of the legislators anxiously looked forward to the incoming administration and
the new Congress. Those who had failed at reelection planned to use
their time remaining in Washington to finish whatever they might
want done or to frustrate the legislative efforts of those whom they
disliked. In many ways this lame-duck session was to be a time of
waiting and a time of "calm reflection," as President Pierce suggested
in his parting message to Congress. For Grow it was a time of highs
and lows, of success and futility.

Grow did not delay putting the Republican prophesy of beating
the Democrats "next time" into action in the House. On the opening
day of the final session, December 1, he challenged those who wished
to seat the proslavery delegate from Kansas. John Whitfield had served
until August 1, 1856, when the House declared his seat vacant. He
then won an election in which, according to the Republicans, the free-
state settlers had refused to participate because to do so would have
implied recognition of the bogus legislature and its laws. Grow heat-
edly demanded to know why Whitfield should be seated since the legislature's laws and the elections held under them were still invalid.
Grow asked, What has changed? He took another snipe at the territorial legislature by referring to some of its acts as a "disgrace to the
age and the country!"[19]

Grow set off a sizzling discussion that lasted a week. Cobb, Stephens, and McMullen wanted a final vote on Whitfield delayed until a full House was present, but Grow gained a temporary victory on the first day by fighting off the southern filibusters and obtaining a vote against Whitfield, 97–104.[20] He even objected to the president's message being received until the delegate matter had been entirely resolved. Humphrey Marshall of Kentucky insisted that members had the right to hear the message. Samuel Smith of Tennessee, his pride somewhat scarred by Grow's earlier sarcasm, accused the Pennsylvanian of deliberately impeding the business of the House. Days later, not to Grow's surprise, the Democrats closed ranks and carried through a motion to reconsider the previous decision not to admit Whitfield. Grow then tried to have the entire delegate matter referred to the Committee on Elections, but this failed, 106–113.[21] Whitfield was given his seat and took the oath of office. When the House proceeded to draw names for floor seats before the delegate question had been settled, the first name drawn was that of Whitfield. A crescendo of laughter followed.

Levity may have eased the tension a bit but it did not exonerate Grow from helping to rekindle agitation over the Kansas issue. Everyone in the hall knew that he planned to steer the House into a collision over Kansas. The issue seemed to hang in the air like cannon smoke. Whereas the southerners tended to accuse Grow and his Republican cronies of starting a new wave of sectionalism, the latter pointed to the inflammatory passages in the president's message as responsible for reopening the questions of slavery and Kansas. Pierce's remarks were shocking, humiliating, and degrading to the office of the president, the opposition said.

In his December 4 message to Congress, Pierce devoted many words to condemning those "sectional organizations" that were pursuing a path leading nowhere "unless it be to civil war and disunion."[22] Their actions, he warned, were contemptible and revolutionary. With indiscriminate invective he lashed out against these northern interests for a history of aggressions against the constitutional rights of nearly one-half of the thirty-one states. These aggressions included the move for abolition, the refusal to enforce the Fugitive Slave Act, and the persistent violation of the 1820 Compromise. His clarion call for noninterference by Congress in the territories only reaffirmed his earlier statement that there was no constitutional way for the president to intervene in the election process in any territory. He trusted that the "peaceful condition" that now existed in Kansas might afford the opportunity for "calm reflection and wise legislation."

The president satisfied some but angered many. For the most part, southerners were pleased. Martin Crawford of Georgia and John Quitman of Mississippi agreed that the only Republican objective was to interfere with slavery in the states and territories. Sen. Albert Brown of Mississippi claimed he had already prepared his people for a great assault by the free-soil phalanx upon slavery in the states.[23] Robert Toombs of Georgia, however, still had his suspicions. Writing later to a friend, he admitted that he believed that for the past six months Pierce had been doing everything possible to make Kansas a free state.[24] On the Republican side, John Sherman of Ohio chastised the president for arraigning the Republican party upon accusations utterly unfounded. He understood the anger of a president who had been deserted by his party, his state, and maybe even his own town. But Pierce went too far in his rebuke of a growing party that the errors of his administration had called into being. In closing, Sherman advised his southern colleagues that Buchanan was elected only because the northern Democrats had campaigned for a free Kansas.[25]

Grow responded to the president's message by emphasizing the Kansas issue and applying it with steady pressure against the administration forces. For the Republicans the issue was crucial. Although calm may have returned to the territory, as Pierce had indicated, it was Grow's primary task to see that controversy remained alive. After his failure to prevent Whitfield from taking his seat, Grow scored in other ways. He succeeded in having a petition signed by 1,500 citizens of Kansas, remonstrating against Whitfield, sent to the Committee on Elections. He also helped Republicans adopt a House resolution that required the president to furnish statements showing how monies were used in Kansas to pay those in the service of the government and the expenses of all those involved in the arrest, detention, and trial of persons charged with treason.[26] This was a good example of legislative harassment.

From the Committee on Territories on January 31, 1857, Grow again reported in favor of the bill for the admission of Kansas as a state under the Topeka constitution in lieu of Senate bill 356, which authorized formation of a state government by the people of Kansas.[27] His committee was of the opinion that "there is little hope for the success of any measure of relief for the people of Kansas which is entrusted in its execution to an administration whose neglect duty, or complicity with the wrong doers, has brought upon them all their woes." The Senate bill, he explained, would relieve the people of none of their real grievances and would leave the usurping legislature and all its acts except test oaths in their original force. The only point of contest in the territory, his committee concluded, was simply whether slavery should be allowed or prohibited; one party advocated the Topeka constitution because it prohibited slavery, and for the same reason the other party opposed it. Grow and his committee had no intention of recommending any measure, in any degree, that had been sanctioned by a proslavery administration.

Grow's greatest success with Kansas in this abbreviated session probably came with the passage of House bill 799, which invalidated all the laws enacted by the sham legislature at Shawnee Mission and called for new elections, with stiff penalties for nonresidents who voted. Grow's committee had reported in the first session a bill to annul the laws of Kansas, but this proposal had been passed over and what is known as Dunn's bill was finally adopted as a substitute. His committee then prepared another similar bill, but House rules prevented it from getting to the floor. He did not wish to see his dedicated committee blamed for a delay caused by what he regarded as a "natural design" in the framing of the rules to give a minority control of the House. The bill he now presented was, in his opinion, the only sure way the people of Kansas might "render void and nugatory all the obnoxious laws of the Legislative Assembly of that Territory — to wipe away all evidence of its usurpation." Attempts to defeat Grow's bill by amendment and adjournment having failed, the House approved it 98–79.[28] Sixty-four of the negative votes came from the South. In the Senate, the bill was tabled after no agreement could be reached on whether it should go to the Judiciary Committee or the Committee on Territories. In either case, there was little hope of passage.

Kansas was not the only territorial matter to come before the House. Grow also managed to get approval for bills for the admission of Oregon and Minnesota. Neither bill faced any real opposition, for neither territory was entangled with the slavery issue. But the future of both bills in the Senate remained uncertain. It was hinted that Sen. James Green of Missouri might try to link Kansas with Oregon in order to bring Kansas under some sanction of Congress that would, indirectly at least, legitimatize the government there.[29] House members debated those provisions in the bills that dealt with voting privileges and boundaries. In the case of Oregon, there was general consensus that voting be restricted to citizens of the United States. John Letcher of Virginia succeeded in adding an amendment by which delegates to frame the constitution could be chosen only by citizens, but thereafter the matter rested with the state. Unlike his earlier position in support of immigrants voting in the territories, Grow did not oppose the amendment.

There was little difficulty with the Minnesota bill until Phelps of Missouri began to needle Grow on the boundary provisions. What followed was owing more to a personality clash between the two men than to any serious disagreement over the bill. Phelps may have been only evening the score for Grow's arrogance and obstreperousness over the seating of Whitfield. If nothing else, he intended to illuminate Grow's hypocrisy. Phelps informed his colleagues that Grow's Minnesota bill was about to violate the Northwest Ordinance of 1787, a pact that Grow held sacred, by taking a piece of the old territory and making it part of the proposed new state. How could the great defender of solemn compacts justify his stance? the Missourian wished to know. He had an answer: Grow planned to honor the sixth section of the 1787 ordinance outlawing slavery and ignore the fifth article describing the organization of future states. Almost in the same breath, Phelps added that he never believed the ordinance to have a binding influence either upon himself or the country. Besides, he hoped to vote for the Minnesota bill. He had only wished to make a point — at that, an embarrassing one for Grow.[30]

Angrily, the Pennsylvanian asked Phelps what he would do with a gore of land left outside of the five states organized from the Northwest Territory. Would he let it stand forever in an unorganized condition? Or would he organize it into a separate state and make six states out of the territory, which would be a more serious violation of the ordinance? Did it not make more sense simply to add that tract of land to an adjacent territory? Phelps responded by repeating that he did not take too seriously the 1787 law to which Grow had attributed so much sanctity. Grow snapped at the Missourian: "It comes with a bad grace from a member of this House for the State of Missouri to raise such a question here to-day, when the Platte country was taken from the Ordinance of 1820 and included within the limits of that State."

In the discussion that followed, an irate Grow was exceptionally abrasive and unyielding. He wished to bring the Minnesota bill to a speedy vote and the delays bothered him. The southerners were annoyed with Grow and accused him of cutting off debate deliberately. Speaker Banks and Washburn of Maine supported his efforts, causing Clingman of North Carolina to remark that until this Congress a member who had the floor would yield it for a question. But Grow refused to do so. Frustrated, the Carolinian stammered, "I have no interest in this debate."[31] His comments came after Smith of Tennessee had pleaded without success to obtain the floor. Banks ruled that Grow had the right to close debate. The following illustrates an interesting interplay of Republican leaders against southern filibuster:

Smith:	Will the gentleman from Pennsylvania (Grow) allow me to make an inquiry which will perhaps have some effect on the vote of the House on this bill? It is a question for information only.
Washburn:	I object to debate. The previous question has been called.
Speaker:	The previous question has been withdrawn.
Grow:	I renew it.
Smith:	Will not the gentleman allow me to ask a question for information? I am favorable to the bill.

Eventually Smith, who had threatened to vote against the bill, got the floor to ask his question. At Stephens's urging, Grow agreed to answer questions for information but refused to yield to anyone whose sole purpose was to make irrelevant remarks to keep discussion going. After some brief questions, the bill was put to the vote and passed, 97–75.[32] Smith did vote for the bill; Stephens and some forty southerners did not. Again, much of the negativism here was probably directed more toward Grow and the way the Speaker managed the debate than toward the bill itself.

Some of the emotionalism and personal test of wills displayed prior to the passage of the Minnesota bill carried over to other territorial business. A bill to authorize payment for property taken or destroyed in Kansas under the authority of law was struck down. It had called for the appointment of a commissioner, Abraham Lincoln of Illinois, to evaluate all claims against the government. Southerners were irked. William Boyce of South Carolina accused Grow of bringing the slavery controversy up again. With tongue in cheek, Grow tried to assure Boyce that this had not been his purpose.[33] He did manage to get funds appropriated for the completion of the capitol building in New Mexico and a "western district" of Kansas approved. But he watched another bill for the Utah capitol laid aside after Dunn of Indiana argued that nothing should be given to the people of Utah, who had no respect for the laws of the country. Many Republicans agreed; Grow did not press the matter.

If Grow revealed a streak of rascality in the debate over the Minnesota bill, he showed more of the same in a case that shocked Congress. On January 9, 1857, William Kelsey of New York read before the House an article from the *New York Times* stating that a "corrupt organization of members of Congress and certain lobby agents at Washington" existed in a land-stealing scheme involving the Minnesota

Territory. Some House members, including Grow, immediately questioned the accusation because of its source. Both Grow and Orr of South Carolina urged that an investigation be initiated to determine if the charges were valid. Kelsey succeeded in having a motion to investigate approved.[34] The Speaker then appointed a five-man committee to examine the evidence and report back the findings with recommended action, if any.

A month later, when the special committee prepared to present its findings, Grow asked that the report not be accepted. His objection hinted at a veiled cover-up. Some of the Democrats thought he might be attempting to protect some guilty party, since two names to emerge tainted from the investigation were William Gilbert and Orsamus Matteson, both Republicans from New York. The Republicans were helplessly pinned to their defenses. The *Tribune* warned that any scandal involving Republicans would be embarrassing and damaging to the party's image.[35] Even Greeley was suspected of being at least on the perimeter of the caper, but he emphatically denied it.

There is no evidence to suggest that Grow tried to whitewash anything. He made it clear he wished to screen no man from fair scrutiny but he objected to the mode of investigation. He charged the committee with exceeding its authority, violating the privileges of the House, and disregarding the constitutional rights of its members.[36] Citing previous litigation, he contended that the committee could not obtain testimony after a member of the House had been implicated without first securing authority from the House to do so. Apparently Gilbert had not been notified by the committee before witnesses gave incriminating evidence against him. Grow asserted that the evidence of one witness had been taken on January 16 and Gilbert was not notified until the 29th. He termed this irregular procedure contrary to parliamentary law. "A Star Chamber sits under your Capitol," he cautioned his colleagues, "with closed doors, and summons profligates from the streets to blacken the character of your members, trampling down the safeguards and protections that are given to the meanest criminal at the bar of a criminal court — the privilege of being confronted with the witnesses against him, and meeting his accusers face to face."

Grow was particularly annoyed with the committee for admitting evidence from two individuals, one of whom had been discharged by the doorkeeper of the House "for his profligacy" while the other had been fired from the pension office for malfeasance. Yet it was upon the testimony of these two witnesses, Grow cried out, that the committee had maligned the character of a House member. The whole

case was a farce and without precedent. Grow said he had voted for
an honest investigation, but had never dreamed the committee would
dare attempt to ferret out fraud and corruption by trampling on justice and the securities of personal liberty.

Grow spoke at length. His cutting remarks shattered any hope of
an early and amicable settlement of the problem. Charges and countercharges intensified the combativeness of members debating whether
to accept the committee's report. Grow still demanded to know exactly what kind of report was to be given. The chairman responded
that it could not determine this until the report was read and the report must be received to the extent that a member of the House has
been implicated. Grow insisted that the report could not be received
except by leave of the House. The chairman at least agreed that it
was for the House to determine whether or not the committee had
gone beyond its jurisdiction.

Great confusion followed. Two southern members of the committee, Orr of South Carolina and Henry Winter Davis of Maryland,
were discomposed by the rudeness of Grow's remarks. Orr defended
the actions of the committee and insisted that Gilbert had the opportunity to cross-examine the witnesses, but had refused to do so. Davis,
a member of the American party who later became a Republican,
was hard on Grow. With flowing oratory he rebuked the Pennsylvanian for demeaning the stature of the committee by calling it a Star
Chamber and a "packed jury" with "packed witnesses." He labeled
Grow's utterance as "contemptible." Letcher of Virginia also said he
had heard enough from Grow and wanted him to sit down. Keitt of
South Carolina sarcastically exclaimed that it was strange that Grow
and Gilbert, who were now clamoring that parliamentary privileges
were being abused, had earlier been in the forefront among those
demanding either the censure or expulsion of him and Edmundson
after the Sumner incident.[37]

Grow suffered a setback when the committee's report was finally
read and a motion to receive it was approved by an overwhelming
vote, 169-5.[38] Some of his friends supported it. Grow was one of many
members who did not vote on the report or on the action taken against
Matteson and Gilbert. Most likely, he was not even in Washington.
During the debate on the report, he had complained of being ill. Apparently he was a victim of the much publicized malady known as
the "National Hotel disease," which was blamed for the deaths of several Congressmen.[39]

In the closing moments of the session, when the tariff bill came
to a vote, Grow and many others were absent. With the object of re-

ducing an embarrassing surplus in the treasury, Letcher of Virginia appealed to everyone who wanted to save the country from commercial revolution to join him in a measure to decrease revenues.[40] There was no heated debate. In the recent elections, the tariff issue had received only casual attention. The Republicans had ignored it in their platform. Some of the Pennsylvania delegation raised questions, but Campbell of Ohio warned them that if they could not see beyond their iron and coal interests and prevent passage of the bill, then they must accept responsibility for whatever disaster might follow. On March 2, 1857, while most of Washington prepared for the presidential inauguration, the tariff bill reducing rates of the 1846 act passed the House, 123–72.[41] The law received considerable attention in the Buchanan administration. At the time the nation was prosperous, but the Panic of 1857 would change that and turn public concerns toward America's economic ills.

In his inaugural address the new president assured the American people that their country was indeed prosperous. "No nation has ever before been embarrassed from too large a surplus in its treasury," he boasted.[42] The nation's free-trade policy bound the sections together, but geographical hostilities and slavery agitation were threatening this unity and the steady progress of the American people. Buchanan hoped that the long sectional tumult was approaching an end and that "geographical parties" with their politics of intimidation would become extinct. He affirmed what the Kansas-Nebraska Act had ruled: that the people of a territory must be left free to form and regulate their own domestic institutions. The controversy over the application of popular sovereignty, which was gnawing at his party's sinews, was of "little practical importance." It was a judicial question and he promised that the Supreme Court would soon have something to say about it. This statement may have shocked some Republicans but, for the most part, they were not surprised by anything Buchanan had to say on the subject of territories.

The Thirty-fourth Congress ended as it had begun—divided on Kansas and undecided on slavery in the territories. With limited options available, the Democrats clung tenaciously to popular sovereignty while the Republicans reveled in their ability to hold the line on Kansas. It was a standoff; sooner or later a resolution had to come. Buchanan called time the great corrective, and the Republicans agreed; in the case of Kansas they believed that time was on their side.

Grow probably had mixed feelings toward the Thirty-fourth Congress. He was pleased that he had helped achieve Republican solidarity by using his committee to present a united front on Kansas.

The territorial question had broken down to one of slavery extension versus nonextension and the Republicans had aligned themselves accordingly. Whether they would be able to maintain voter interest in this question long enough to ensure their party's stability, however, worried him. Regional and local issues were starting to pressure Republicans to think beyond Lecompton and Topeka. At the national level, economic considerations also warned of possible cracks in the party's structure. Republican spokesmen feared that old differences between former Whigs and Democrats might surface as soon as the fervor over slavery in the territories died down. For example, holding out for the homestead bill, Grow had voted consistently against land-grant bills for railroads, a body of legislation that many Republicans favored. At the same time, some of Grow's party colleagues were either lukewarm in their endorsement of the homestead idea or opposed it entirely.

Another problem bothered Grow. Being identified with a free Kansas had made him a national figure. Winning accolades inflated his ego and expanded his ambitions. In the process of loyally serving his new party, however, he now faced a dilemma. If he continued to build a reputation upon Republican exploits in Kansas, he was doomed as a hypocrite for doing exactly what he had accused the Democrats of doing — nationalizing the slavery issue. On the other hand, were he to de-escalate the tension over Kansas, he ran the risk of weakening the base of Republican support that he needed for his homestead bill. Though not every Republican shared Grow's enthusiasm for homestead, theirs exceeded any that remained in the Democratic party. By the close of the Thirty-fourth Congress, Grow realized that all hope for the adoption of the free-land bill rested upon the success of the Republican party, which in turn drew its sustenance from the continued agitation over slavery. It was a situation that he had neither planned nor wanted, but he determined to make the most of it.

𝕮 9

"First Blow for Freedom"

AS A DYSPEPTIC whose health had been further frayed by the National Hotel sickness, Galusha Grow sought rest, relaxation, and plenty of fresh air after the adjournment of the Thirty-fourth Congress. By today's standards he was no athlete, but for the nineteenth century Grow was a fine sportsman. He prided himself in his ability to rough it in the rambling wilds near his home, to peel bark with fellow woodsmen, and to hunt game with his friends. His political enemies mockingly referred to him as the "Glenwood bark-peeler." Once he had confided to Charles Buckalew that spending time outdoors was good medicine for him.[1] So, while most of the political world turned its attention to news from Washington and Kansas, Grow enjoyed himself by shooting buffalo along the Big Sioux River in the Dakota Territory. He did take time from his macho pursuits to deliver an Independence Day address and to offer the usual toasts in "pure cold water."[2]

Yet he could not ignore political events back home, where his enemies were busy gnawing at his congressional record. Prior to his western departure, Grow had been maligned for his hostility toward the House committee investigating the Matteson-Gilbert incident; even some of his Republican colleagues had rebuked him for his quixotic stand. These attacks continued. In addition the *Montrose Democrat* had accused him of favoring the Collins steamship line in return for free passage to Europe.[3] His friends denied the charge and attempted to show that he had voted against any proposition that favored that line.[4] Grow needed no one to defend his actions. On Monday, April 6, 1857, at a fusion meeting in Montrose, he had attacked the *Democrat* for its statements and policies. At the same time, he had taken a swipe at the Supreme Court for its Dred Scott ruling; the gesture brought an immediate cry of "moral treason" from his enemies. "The mustachioed Glenwood shrieker," the *Democrat*'s angry and vitriolic editor charged, "vomited his venom and abuse by the hour."[5]

Grow followed the Pennsylvania gubernatorial race with dispassionate interest. In March, his friend Wilmot had been nominated by the Union State Convention as Republican candidate. His opponents were the Democratic nominee, William F. Packer, and the Native American, Isaac Hazelhurst of Philadelphia. At the time, Wilmot was the president judge of the Bradford and Susquehanna district and indeed recognized as the foremost Republican in the state. Most Republicans throughout the state and nation, however, greeted his candidacy with mixed feelings, knowing his chances of victory were slim. Still, he was willing to accept the position of standard-bearer to strengthen the cause he had so faithfully championed. The grand apostle of free-soilism seemed the right choice at a time when the Kansas issue stood at the apex of popularity. But his candidacy proved to be an anachronism. Wilmot's "abolitionism" and free-trade ideas were anathema to some issue-oriented Republican managers who were looking to conservative and business-interest groups to support their party. Thus his campaign faltered in Philadelphia, a center of proslavery Americans and old Whigs in favor of protectionism. Not only did Wilmot lose Philadelphia by an impressive margin, but also the state by more than 40,000 votes. As expected, he did much better in Grow's congressional district, receiving over 6,000 votes more than Packer.

If the Democrats seemed ecstatic about crushing Wilmot, they found additional joy in the election returns of other states. In New York, which the Republicans had swept in 1856, the Democrats captured the legislature and minor offices. They did the same in Ohio, another Republican stronghold, and nearly defeated Salmon Chase for reelection as governor. In other states, Republican majorities faded as Democrats benefited from the dissolution of the American party. Despite the financial panic, northern disgust with the Dred Scott ruling, and the prolonged agony in Kansas, the party of President Buchanan appeared intact and healthy. At worst, the congressional elections of 1858 promised to be what the Republicans had hoped for—a one-on-one confrontation. The outcome of those elections might very well determine which party would win in 1860.

Between the parties stood the many issues that beleaguered the nation in the autumn of 1857; the most intense was the Kansas problem. The territory remained afflicted by the presence of two intransigent governments, one at Lecompton and a free-state one at Topeka. Most northerners, regardless of party label, did not wish to see the Dred Scott decision used as license to spread slavery throughout the territories. The malignancy had to be removed before it stabilized in Kansas. Otherwise the Union risked a terminal metastasis.

Yet a northern president was not very accommodating. Buchanan's wish to assure his southern friends that he would be satisfied with any territorial settlement only helped widen party fissures. If patronizing the South, especially on slavery, was Buchanan's idea of party discipline, then his chances of keeping northerners in line seemed less probable. Party or no party, many northern Democrats were becoming increasingly vexed by slavocracy's demands. Was Kansas to be the test of party fidelity as the Kansas-Nebraska bill had been? A president who had not been involved in the bloody scuffle over the 1854 bill had to be downright presumptuous to believe that he could mandate a policy so unpopular to battle-scarred warriors like Douglas.

Republican leaders liked to see Democrats fighting with one another, and they planned to drive wedge after wedge into the Democratic organization until it crumbled. Their plans were encouraged by the anticipated resolve of the administration to admit Kansas under the recently drafted Lecompton Constitution. To defeat Lecompton, therefore, became the immediate and foremost objective of congressional Republicans as they gathered in Washington in late 1857. Since they constituted a minority in both houses, the Republicans realized that victory might be elusive. The new Congress promised to be a disarming ordeal for men caught between causes and the pressures of practical politics. The Republicans hoped to recruit and befriend, if necessary, frustrated Democrats and Native Americans in their drive to bring freedom to Kansas. Writing to Hannibal Hamlin, ex-Speaker Banks did not see how the Republicans could avoid a fight in the House over Kansas.[6] The villany of the whole scheme at Lecompton was "demonic." He was ready to do battle; so were Grow and the rest of the Republican leadership.

Constitution with Slavery or Constitution without Slavery

It is doubtful that the Republicans could have written a better scenario than the one being enacted at the start of the Thirty-fifth Congress. All the confusion and disorder they might have wished upon the Democrats lay before them. Both Douglas and Robert J. Walker, governor of Kansas, were ready to part company with Buchanan over the Lecompton constitution. This proslavery document, like the antislavery Topeka constitution, excluded all free Negroes from Kansas.

It denied the legislature the right to emancipate any slaves already there without the consent of owners, forbade amendment before 1864, and called for strict enforcement of the fugitive slave law. The convention responsible for the constitution also adopted a schedule that removed Walker and federal officers as of December 1, 1857, and established a provisional government to provide the machinery for new state elections. Most important, the convention called a referendum for December 21, at which time the people of Kansas were to vote either for the constitution with slavery or for the constitution without slavery. Thus, the vote was to be on the slavery clause and not on the entire constitution. Immediately the free-soilers called it a "heads I win, tails you lose" proposition. Even if the "without" vote carried, several hundred slaves would remain in the state with no possibility of emancipation until 1864.

Walker, who had labored hard to win the support of the free-state settlers, tried without success to convince the president that the convention had botched its job and that the referendum would be meaningless. Later he remarked that the administration was obligated under previous pledges to see that the entire constitution be submitted to the people, but the administration insisted there was no legal obligation, since the people of Kansas had not required their convention to submit the constitution to a popular vote. Douglas backed Walker and advised the president not to recommend approval of the Lecompton constitution. But the white-haired president, perhaps not understanding this new generation of ideological politicians, had made up his mind to support the document. The rest was left to Congress.

While not underestimating the serious breach within their ranks, the Democrats in Washington remained confident that their majorities in both houses would allow them flexibility. When Congress fully organized on December 7, the Democrats had an edge of seventeen over the Republicans in the Senate; in the House, an edge of thirty-six. There were five Americans in the upper chamber; fourteen in the lower. For the moment, Democratic solidarity seemed assured in the House, where James L. Orr of South Carolina was elected Speaker on the first ballot, receiving 128 votes. Nearly all Republicans supported Grow, who had been nominated by former Speaker Banks. The Pennsylvanian received 84 votes; he voted for Francis P. Blair of Missouri.[7]

The new Speaker seemed a strong person who inspired confidence. Although he came from the state that produced extremists like Lawrence Keitt and James Hammond, Orr managed to resist the options of the fireeaters. Perhaps he was not as skillful a parliamentarian as

Grow or Stephens, but his straightforward, common-sense logic won him respect from both sides of the aisle. He surprised no one when he asserted Democratic prowess by chairing the more important committees with members of his party. He named J. Glancy Jones of Pennsylvania to the powerful Ways and Means and Stephens of Georgia to Territories; these two men were to direct administration policy in the House. Grow was again appointed to the territorial committee, but serving with him this time were several of his southern antagonists, John Clark of Missouri, William Smith of Virginia, and Lawrence O'B. Branch of North Carolina.

In reality, the Democratic advantage in the House was tenuous. Agreeing on a Speaker was one thing; agreeing on the issues was something else. Behind the numerical superiority lingered bad signs. Southern Democrats remained dubious of any support they might receive from their northern colleagues. The Douglas people and the antislavery Democrats, on the other hand, prompted by an angry northern press, moved further away from the administration and the southern position on the Lecompton constitution.

In his first annual message to Congress on December 8, Buchanan insisted that the Lecompton convention was not bound by the terms of the Kansas-Nebraska Act to submit any portion of its constitution to an election except that which related to slavery.[8] The next day Douglas told the Senate that the president was absolutely wrong.[9] Furthermore, the convention had never been recognized by Congress. A week later, Walker, also bothered by the president's assertion, resigned as governor. He had accepted the office on the condition that the constitution would be subjected to a vote of the people of Kansas. He claimed that the president had agreed to this condition, but was no more optimistic than Douglas. Thus, in one stroke Buchanan had managed to alienate two men whose supporters soon warned that the survival of the Democratic party, and perhaps the Union, required the defeat of Lecompton.

The question of submission assumed a dynamic of its own and forced a coalition of anti-Lecompton, pro-Douglas Democrats and Republicans. This group faulted the president for defending the southern claim, made popular by Stephens, that the Kansas convention had the right to refuse to submit its constitution for ratification or rejection. "The propriety of submitting it or not is one for themselves to determine," the Georgian had written.[10] Southern ultras, furious with Douglas, stated their case unequivocally: anyone who touched the Kansas issue must automatically define his position as in favor of the South or against the South. The *Charleston Mercury* was also blunt: anyone who embraced Lecompton did so with a plea for slavery and the South.[11]

Republicans took these brazen remarks as further proof that the split within the Democratic party had broadened and soon would have to be measured geometrically. Their mission was clear: to remove any remaining fragments of Democratic unity by electrifying the Kansas issue. Buchanan was helping. Largely because of him, the Republicans strengthened their image by appearing as the defenders of democratic principles in Kansas against slavocracy's efforts to enslave the territory.[12] Everyone agreed that Kansas bonded the Republicans and divided the Democrats.

While the nation prepared for another holiday season, Douglas maneuvered openly with Republican leaders to effect an alliance that he hoped might lead to a union party to save the nation from southern secessionists. Douglas was a man with a problem. His popular sovereignty was in the balance; his reelection to the Senate was on the line. Among House leaders, Douglas met with Grow, Colfax, Banks, and Burlingame to map strategy on Kansas. He assured them of his determination to fight the Lecompton swindle even if it meant his defeat at the polls. His apparent break with the administration became as newsworthy as Kansas itself. Southerners were shocked. "The defection of Douglas has done more to shake the confidence of the South in Northern men than everything that has happened before," editorialized the *Charleston Mercury* on January 16, 1858. Republican glee was matched with suspicion. One Republican admitted being confounded by the senator's change of heart and wrote, "Personally I am inclined to give him the lash, but I want to do nothing that will damage our cause."[13] Other Republicans also expressed a willingness to accept Douglas's help even though it might be temporary. Colfax candidly observed that the Republicans knew the disgruntled senator was with them only on this one issue, but, with his aid, there might be at last a chance for justice in Kansas.[14]

Regardless of what Douglas did, Grow continued his politics of harassment. To southerners he remained the dreaded scourge, a paragon of northern bias. His abrasiveness clashed with Orr's civility. The two men bickered constantly over procedure; each had his cadre of parliamentary supporters. When he found himself being cut off from debate, Grow complained that the Speaker was "farming out the floor" to his friends on the Democratic side. His wit and sarcasm were as strong as ever. During the lengthy debate over the neutrality laws, Grow participated little, but he did punctuate the heated discussion with sardonic remarks directed toward the defenders of Lecompton.

Most of the heat came from southerners who were annoyed to learn of Commodore Hiram Paulding's seizure of William Walker and his associates in Nicaragua for violating American neutrality laws. Stephens criticized Paulding's misuse of military power there, calling it a "gross outrage of private rights." An opportunist who took advantage of the energy of events, Grow quickly paralleled the outrages against human rights abroad with those in Kansas. He was pleased to see the Democrats, especially Stephens, fault the government and the military for mishandling the situation.[15]

Though his primary attention in this session, as in the previous one, centered upon Kansas, Grow did address other issues — Minnesota, the public domain, military appropriations, the financial crisis, and the Matteson affair. There was a disinclination among congressmen, especially southerners, to proceed with legislation until the tangled Kansas question was settled. But beyond all the issues was the bedrock question as to whether members of Congress, as Americans, would meet those challenges as one people, resolute and self-disciplined, or as a truculent gang of bickering factions, out to get whatever they could for themselves. The fact that the Union was at stake did not bother many of them. None realized they were about to enter the most bizarre legislative stint of the antebellum period.

When Thomas Harris of Illinois proposed that Matteson be expelled from the House, his resolution was referred to a special committee consisting of Grow, James Seward of Georgia, and John Huyler of New Jersey. In its previous session, the House had passed a resolution expelling Matteson but tabled it since the representative from New York resigned his seat. Then Matteson was reelected and took his seat in the Thirty-fifth Congress. The proposition of Harris to expel, therefore, was based upon the proceedings of the previous Congress. But the committee asked, "What offence has Mr. Matteson committed against this House?" Seeing none, it recommended that the House take no action on Harris's resolution.[16]

Speaking in defense of the committee's report, Grow argued that the charges against Matteson were known by his constituents when he was elected. Grow then expanded his idea of personal rights, in this case, the rights of voters as well as those of elected officials. "It is not for this House," he remarked, "to erect itself into a judge of the personal merits of its members after they had been passed upon by their constituency — If so, then the theory of this Government is a fallacy."[17] To constitutionalists, this opinion was contrary to Article I, Section 5, of the Constitution which grants to each house the power to punish and expel its members.

To Grow, the time seemed appropriate to reintroduce the homestead bill, for the disposition of public lands was related to the Kansas problem. Enactment of the homestead bill might prevent the fraudulent distribution of land in Kansas. With Grow in the House and Andrew Johnson of Tennessee having been recently elected to the Senate, the prospects for the bill again appeared bright. As governor from 1853 to 1857, Johnson had urged his state's representatives to support the bill. He introduced a homestead bill on December 21; Grow's was presented on January 4, 1858.[18] Exactly two weeks later, Grow submitted another land measure, this one designed "to prevent the future sale of the public lands . . . until the same shall have been surveyed for at least fifteen years."[19] His intent was to give the actual settler a propitious start over the land grabbers and perhaps to accomplish by other means the good results contemplated in the homestead bill. The *Chicago Tribune* said that Grow deserved the thanks of every westerner for sponsoring a general plan to guard the public lands from the rapacity of speculators.[20]

The struggle over homestead in the first session took place in the Senate. After several months of postponement and delay, Johnson, with the help of William Seward, finally succeeded in having his bill considered. He defended it with a stirring address. In late May, however, the Senate voted to postpone further consideration, and Johnson's attempts to reconsider the vote for postponement failed. In the second session, most of the action on the homestead bill shifted to the lower house.

While Kansas and Lecompton engaged Grow's principal interest, another matter attracted his attention — a bill to authorize the issuance of treasury notes not to exceed $20 million. Grow moved to defeat the bill; in the heated discussion that followed, he revealed more of his economic philosophy. He also used the occasion to blast the administration for expanding its bureaucracy and having a "secret police force" of lackeys in local elections to influence the voters.[21] Increased patronage to implement the administration's whims and dictates, in his opinion, was the cause for enormous government expenditures. Congress was now being asked to pick up the bills. The immediate question was whether the government should go into the money market for loans to meet its debts or simply issue more "paper promises" to pay when there was nothing in its vaults to redeem those promises.

A hard-money advocate, Grow warned that putting additional treasury notes into circulation would make a bad situation worse. "Will not the paper currency which is proposed by this bill," he asked, "tend to keep from circulation the hoarded specie of the country?" He believed it would and contrasted the present crisis with that of two decades earlier. "In 1837 there was an expanded paper currency, with a very insufficient metallic basis." According to Grow's figures, the banks at that time had a circulation of $150 million, but there was only $80 million in specie throughout the nation. When the crash came, there was just not enough gold and silver to go around. Today, he continued, the situation had reversed itself; there was now $100 million more coin in circulation than paper. Yet the specie was being hoarded and the banks were suspending specie payments. The proper course of action, he urged, was for the government to authorize loans, which would draw forth specie from the vaults and closets.

Grow believed that many things were responsible for the emergency. The recent changes in the tariff added significantly to the foreign indebtedness and the economic mess. The injudicious tariff adjustments "forced upon the House of Representatives by the Senate," in his opinion, stimulated an overgrown and expanded credit system.

Smith of Virginia, an old adversary, expressed surprise to hear Grow recommend a hard-money policy, one traditionally held by Democrats. He congratulated the Pennsylvanian for still treasuring a relic of his past political creed.[22] Smith said that Grow illustrated the old adage that a renegade Christian is worse than ten Turks. "I suppose that no man in this House is so inveterate against Democratic principles and against the Democratic party, as is this gentleman, who was once a brother in full fellowship in the church." Smith might consider him a sound, reliable Democrat, except on the question of the territories, Grow responded. The Virginian angrily retorted: "I judge the gentleman by the company he keeps. . . . I judge him as hostile to Democracy when I see him doing the work of those who are esteemed as hostile to Democratic rule and Democratic ascendency. What is the object of the gentleman's labors? It is to break down the Democratic party and the principles they cherish."

Before he sat down, Smith had to rebuke Grow one more time. He was always struck by the Pennsylvanian's inability to deliver a single speech on the floor without alluding to the territorial question. "It is Kansas, Kansas, Kansas," raved the Virginian, "that fertile and exciting subject dances through all the mazes of metaphorical confusion in the imagination of the gentleman; and I suppose that when he sinks into the grave, and I trust he will be spared a thousand years, the cry will still be 'Kansas!'"

Indeed it was Kansas that continued to produce a potpourri of charges and countercharges from many members of the House. From their new quarters, they carefully monitored the mix of political statistics coming out of Kansas. The December 21 referendum on the Lecompton constitution showed more than 6,000 votes "with slavery," over 500 "without." On January 4, in another referendum, this one called by the free-state legislature, the constitution was voted down by more than 10,000 votes. Again, both sides cried "Fraud!" As expected, most southerners accepted the vote of December 21 and most northerners considered the January 4 vote as final. In light of the impressive January margin of victory, House Republicans were ready to seal the fate of Lecompton. The people of Kansas had made their decision, and a good one at that.

The next move belonged to Buchanan. Weary and confused, he solicited advice from both sides of the issue. His cabinet considered a compromise plan by which Congress would admit Kansas under Lecompton with the understanding that the first Kansas legislature would submit the constitution to a popular vote. Buchanan liked it, but dared not risk losing the support of southern members of the cabinet who objected to the plan. Despite the efforts of a delegation of House Democrats who urged him not to endorse Lecompton, Buchanan had made up his mind. He reasoned that since most Democratic senators and congressmen supported Lecompton, he could not reject it without rejecting his own party; the constitution was the legal will of the people of Kansas. On Tuesday, February 2, copies of Lecompton, with a message from the president recommending its endorsement, were sent to both houses of Congress. "It has been solemnly adjudged by the highest judicial tribunal," Buchanan wrote, "that slavery exists in Kansas by virtue of the Constitution of the United States. Kansas is therefore at this moment as much a slave state as Georgia or South Carolina."[23]

The administration hoped the constitution and the president's message would be referred to the "safe" House Committee on Territories, which was packed with Lecompton men. Stephens moved that this be done, thinking no one wished to discuss the matter. But the Republicans refused to adjourn. When Thomas Harris, an anti-Lecompton Democrat from Illinois, asked to introduce a resolution, James Hughes of Indiana refused to yield the floor unless Harris stated the purpose of his resolution. Harris refused. "That is my business," he exclaimed. The Buchanan people knew that Harris wanted the president's message referred to a special committee. Each side was testing the other's defenses.

When Grow obtained the floor he promptly yielded to Harris, as though on cue. Seward of Georgia protested, but then withdrew his objection in order that "we may see the intimacy existing between the gentleman from Illinois and gentlemen on the Republican side of the House."[24] The Lecomptonites knew what was coming. In a resolution worked out by Republican and Douglas strategists, Harris called for a special committee to investigate all the facts regarding the formation of the Lecompton constitution and the matter of fraudulent votes. Worried administration forces did not want such an investigation, for the delay would give the Republicans plenty of ammunition to use in the upcoming campaign. Here the matter rested for several days.

Late on Friday, February 5, Grow began debate on Kansas with scathing remarks on the president's message. He said it was "abounding in epithets and denunciations of the majority of the people of Kansas, without furnishing us with the facts that the official record ought to show."[25] After he had finished, Grow yielded the floor to Harris, who moved the question on his resolution for a special committee. Stephens hoped that Harris would not ask for a vote at this time, but Harris insisted. They counted noses and saw that they enjoyed a temporary majority. A number of the administration backers had departed early to prepare for dinner parties scheduled by the president and other officials. The Republicans pressed for a vote.

Stephens and his allies had little choice but to filibuster. They demanded roll call after roll call on motions to adjourn. The chairman ordered the doors closed and dispatched the sergeant-at-arms to find absentees. Both sides held firm as great confusion followed and the galleries buzzed with excitement. But enthusiasm abated as the spectacle dragged into the evening hours and the next morning. The voices of several clerks broke down while calling the yeas and nays. Members flopped down on sofas or fell asleep at their desks; spectators in the galleries stretched out on the floor. To a neutral observer, the scene would have evoked feelings of pity and shame. When one representative sarcastically asked the Speaker if it would be appropriate to call in a photographer to daguerreotype the scene, Orr responded sardonically, "Not yet."

But the most disgraceful behavior was still to come. While others slept, Grow assumed leadership of the anti-Lecompton forces, communicating between Democrats and Republicans and occasionally stopping to object to everything he believed to be out of order. About two o'clock in the morning, Grow crossed over to the Democratic side to confer with John Hickman, a Douglas supporter from Pennsylvania. Having finished his business, Grow was passing down the side aisle on his way back to his seat, when Quitman of Mississippi asked consent to submit a motion. Grow objected. Suddenly, fatigue exceeded patience, tempers shortened, and restraint gave way to testiness. After Keitt, half asleep and perhaps a little under the influence of beverage, as some members were, screamed at Grow to return to his side of the hall, all order broke down. Apparently the southerner had called Grow a "Black Republican puppy," and Grow responded defiantly that no slave driver was going to crack his whip over him. He would speak wherever he wished on the floor. Keitt put on his shoe, muttered something like, "We'll see about that," and went for Grow's jugular. They grappled. Keitt fell to the floor and a general free-for-all was under way. The two principal combatants soon learned who their friends were as lawmakers from every direction rushed to the battle center.

There was some agreement among participants and eyewitnesses as to what really happened in the melee. Someone, probably Grow, knocked Keitt to the floor; a half-dozen southerners surrounded Grow; the Pennsylvanian delivered a stunning blow to Reuben Davis of Mississippi; athletic John Potter of Wisconsin, swinging wildly but purposefully, rammed the middle of the group like a fullback; John Covode waved a spittoon high above his head, looking for a suitable target; the Speaker, who had a voice like a steam whistle, commanded the sergeant-at-arms with his mace to do something; and William Barksdale's wig was knocked to the floor. One of the warriors then ungraciously stepped on it. When Barksdale returned the hairpiece to his head, he put in on backwards. He looked ridiculous enough to convert nearly everyone's anger into laughter. In a few minutes the entire incident was over.[26]

Miraculously the fracas fell short of tragedy. Some hands were laid on knives and pistols, but none was used; a Republican reporter in the gallery was ready to lend his knife to a friend on the floor. After the fighting had stopped, a feeling that a great danger had been barely avoided injected a somber mood into the remainder of the session. The morning hours ticked on without further incident. At 6:25 A.M. an agreement was reached to adjourn until Monday when a vote was to be taken immediately on the motions of Stephens and Harris.

The press made the most of this contemptible exhibition. Republican newspapers for the most part exculpated Grow and praised him for standing up to the braggart who had been involved in the attack upon Sumner. Democratic editors were not sympathetic. The *Erie Weekly Observer* wrote that there is no connection between statesmanship and pugilism and that Grow had acted like a boor.[27] The *Lycoming* (Pennsylvania) *Gazette* called Grow a "red-hot abolitionist."[28]

Perhaps the most excoriating remarks came from a southern paper, which referred to Grow as a sneaking, rascally, abolitionary "Black Republican scoundrel who hails from some wretched locality" in Pennsylvania.[29]

Both Grow and Keitt apologized to the House, and the latter admitted he had started the brawl. Grow confessed that this physical encounter was his first but he prized self-defense as one of man's inalienable rights.[30] His constituency backed him. A group of assemblymen from his district left for Washington when they learned of the fight; if the district was to be involved in any knocking down of southerners, these men wanted a hand in it! The free-state people of Kansas hailed Grow as a true champion of free speech and presented him with a gold medal, upon which there was an arm and clenched fist with the inscription: "The first blow struck for freedom in Congress, February 5th, 1858." Critics cried that "muscle and pluck in Congress" should not be honored with public testimonials. Later in life, Grow wondered who had really floored the Carolinian.

Statesmanship and Compromise or More Muscle and Pluck?

Judging from the number of welts and bruises, the southerners may have lost the battle of fisticuffs, but they believed the war for Kansas was far from over. They licked their wounds and prepared for the next round. On Monday morning, without debate and parliamentary maneuvering, Stephens's motion to refer the president's message to the territorial committee was defeated, 114–113; twenty-two Douglas Democrats voted with the Republicans. Next, Harris's motion for a select committee of fifteen with investigative powers was carried, 114–111.[31] It was another administration defeat.

Still, there was cause for neither panic nor celebration. When he got around to it, Speaker Orr packed the special committee with a pro-Lecompton majority and punitively appointed Harris its chairman. The anti-Lecomptonites charged that they should have been given control of the committee since their position reflected the majority opinion of the House. Orr countercharged that the real issue was the president's message and, therefore, the administration forces were entitled to a majority of seats on the committee. Stephens was named to the committee; Grow was not. Had their margin of victory in rejecting Stephens's motion been greater, the anti-Lecomptonites might have pushed for another committee.

Meanwhile, could the administration "buy" two or three more

votes in the House? This would be the paramount question in the days ahead, editorialized the *Tribune*.[32] The harshness of the statement underscored what everyone knew—that the war over Kansas might be won or lost in the lower house. Increased administration pressure was expected; should it fail, painful concessions might be considered. Coercion seemed such a frail vehicle of rebuttal, but Buchanan allegedly had boasted that he would push Lecompton through Congress in thirty days. The Buchanan forces' arm twisting concerned the opposition. Charles Hoard, New York Republican, moved that a special committee be appointed to measure the extent of administration intrusion in the affairs of the House, but the motion failed.

It also appeared that the special committee might fail. Anti-Lecomptonites were convinced that Stephens had no intention of permitting a full investigation. The obvious plan of the administration Democrats was to hurry Lecompton through the Senate and then to ram it through the House without any reference to the committee of inquiry. In early March, therefore, Harris called for a question of privilege to bring attention to what he believed was the committee's refusal to execute the orders of the House. The Speaker ruled the matter was not a question of privilege; Orr maintained that Harris was entering an opinion or report of the minority of the committee, which was not allowed. Since the majority had not yet submitted its report, the House could not know whether its order had been obeyed. Harris appealed the decision; Stephens moved to table the appeal, but his motion was defeated, 97–112.[33] Again, both sides raised their colors.

Grow boldly led the anti-Lecomptonites. If a committee is not performing the job it was assigned to do, he argued, then it has violated the privileges of the House. Harris was therefore correct in raising a question of privilege. Grow then charged Speaker Orr with violating parliamentary law, in the first place, by appointing the special committee the way he did. "When a special committee is raised," Grow declared, "the friends of the subject on which it is raised are to compose the majority of the committee." Orr disagreed. In defense of his ruling, the Speaker claimed that the matter referred to the committee had been the president's message and not the Lecompton constitution. Grow came right back: "That is a difference of opinion between the Chair and myself."

Southerners rallied behind the Speaker, their ire automatically sensitized by anything Grow said. Stephens resented Grow's highhandedness. Warren Winslow of North Carolina, H. Winter Davis of Maryland, and Horace Maynard of Tennessee called the Pennsylvanian out of order. Maynard protested that Grow had no right to arraign the Speaker, but Grow persisted: "This committee, a majority of it, are opposed to making any investigation. A member [Harris] rises in his place and states that the committee have refused to make the investigation which the House has ordered, yet the gentleman from Georgia [Stephens] says we must wait until the majority of the committee have reported before we can raise the question."

The Grow-Stephens matchup was probably their finest. Whereas the Georgian tactfully and skillfully argued from a position of parliamentary correctness, the Pennsylvanian went beyond the usual subtleties of debate and probed deeper into the politics underlying particular actions and intentions. Both men were at their best. "I am in favor of investigating every material fact bearing upon the subject," Stephens responded to Grow's allegation. "I think the committee has done it, and at the proper time I shall be ready to show it." Grow reminded members that the committee had been instructed to investigate *all* the facts relating to the formation of the Lecompton constitution, not what were conceived to be only *material* ones. If it failed to do this, then it was wrong. Stephens rose to a point of order. When the Speaker agreed that Grow was going beyond the line of legitimate debate, the Pennsylvanian angrily snapped back that he did not intend to get out of line but he did not like being interrupted by the gentleman from Georgia, who had been allowed to proceed in his own way.[34]

Actually the House committee was waiting to see what the Senate might do. The president's message had been referred to Douglas's territorial committee, where the majority finally presented a measure admitting Kansas under Lecompton. This came as no surprise. Chairman Douglas, frustrated and wearied, managed to report the committee's minority position in opposition to the bill. Several weeks of debate followed. On March 22 crowds jammed the Senate chamber to hear the Little Giant assail the proposed measure as a detriment to popular sovereignty and states' rights. The next day, however, the bill admitting Kansas under Lecompton with guarantees of the right of amendment passed the Senate, 33–25.[35] The action now shifted to the House.

Astute observers surmised that a compromise formula of some kind had to be found. If the anti-Lecomptonites stayed together, there appeared little likelihood of the Senate bill getting through. Buchanan believed the bill would pass, but he was not that confident.[36] Several compromise plans had been already aired. One such plan in the Senate had called for uniting the admission of Kansas with Minnesota —

one free, the other slave — while John Crittenden of Kentucky proposed to resubmit Lecompton to the Kansas voters. Both plans had
failed. In the House, meanwhile, William Montgomery, an anti-
Lecomptonite from Pennsylvania, had introduced a bill that would
require the legislature of Kansas to apportion the territory into sixty
districts, from which delegates would be elected to review the constitution and to submit recommendations to a popular vote. Yet the
question remained whether any compromise proposal was capable
of softening the hard-liners on both sides of the issue.

Most analysts believed not. There was no way the Republicans
were going to admit Kansas as a slave state any more than the southern ultras were ready to see Kansas slip away from them. Neither
side wanted to be placated with crumbs. Meanwhile, the Republicans continued to agitate for "submission," a binding issue between
them and the Douglas Democrats. In his lengthy remarks of March 25,
Grow made a strong plea for resubmission. "The people of Kansas
had the right to expect that the constitution of the Lecompton convention would be submitted for approval or rejection," he asserted.
Further, the December 21 referendum had been a sham. "For if
everybody voted *against* what was called the 'slavery clause,' there still
remained the clause against which nobody was allowed to vote, viz:
'that the rights of property in slaves, now in the Territory, shall in
no manner be interfered with.'" This clause had not been submitted
to the people.[37]

Critics of resubmission viewed it as an obvious ruse, an afterthought
trumped up for political advantage by the opposition. Jabez Curry
of Alabama correctly speculated that if the Lecompton constitution
had been poorly drafted but had excluded slavery, it would have been
tolerated and defended by most of those who now denounced it. The
pressing issue was not one of submitting a constitution to satisfy the
conditions of popular sovereignty. Instead, the southerner explained,
the entire controversy on Kansas for the past four years had grown
out of slavery. It was that issue, and *only* that issue, that had pulled
the southern militants and Republicans miles apart and gave little
promise to compromise.

The ideological schism here paralleled the chronic division within
the Democratic ranks over Lecompton. On the evening of March 30,
a Democratic group from both houses met on Kansas; they failed to
approve a compromise plan and decided to stand by the Senate bill.
William English of Indiana, in behalf of the anti-Lecomptonites, had
resolved that Kansas be admitted upon the condition that its people
now and in the future may exercise their right of "altering, amending

or changing their constitution at pleasure." The administration Democrats opposed the idea and the conference broke up in a row.[38]

On April 1, before a packed chamber, Stephens rose and moved to take up the Senate bill. His manner was quiet and dignified, and his conduct fair and professional. The galleries buzzed with excitement, but on the floor better order and decorum had never been witnessed. With power, patronage, and money, the administration lobbyists were still trying to gather additional votes. But time was running out. Republicans moved about Grow for final instructions; Democrats looked to Stephens, Jones, and Montgomery. Veteran lawmakers wracked their memories to recall a more historic moment in congressional history. Stephens knew that the opposition had a substitute bill and made no move to block its introduction. It was Montgomery who offered an amendment to the Senate bill, which was similar to the one previously introduced in the Senate by Crittenden. In essence the Montgomery-Crittenden plan provided for the resubmission of the Lecompton constitution to the Kansas voters. The House approved Montgomery's amendment, 120–112. Ninety-two Republicans, twenty-two Douglas Democrats, and six Americans from the South had combined to defeat the administration. The amended bill then was carried by the same vote.[39]

When Speaker Orr announced the result of the vote on Montgomery's amendment, spontaneous applause and hissing echoed through the chamber. A frustrated Keitt demanded that the galleries be cleared. "There was no objection when the applause was on the other side," Grow rejoined. The irony of the outcome, observed the *Charleston Mercury*, was that all factions claimed a victory! The Lecomptonites boasted they had forced the Republicans to vote for the Lecompton constitution, simply by agreeing to submit the document to the people of Kansas. The Douglas men claimed they had defeated the administration and "honeyfoggled" the Black Republicans, who likewise bragged they had won another round from the South by defeating the administration in the battle over submission.[40]

Despite a strong plea by Douglas, the Senate, as expected, rejected the Montgomery-Crittenden proposal. The apparent plan of Stephens and the administration was to submit the bill with its House amendment to a conference committee that would rewrite it to their liking. Such a committee seemed the only way out of the dilemma, but this course offered no certainty. Though the Senate requested a conference committee, the House remained uncommitted. Whips of the administration labored hard to convert more Douglas Democrats to the idea. English had switched to a position of compromise. His conduct raised the suspicion he had never been sincere in his cooperation with the anti-Lecomptonites. He finally moved for a conference committee. Working with Stephens and the administration, English persuaded George Pendleton and Lawrence Hall of Ohio and Owen Jones of Pennsylvania, all Douglas Democrats, to support him. His motion squeaked by when Speaker Orr broke the 108–108 tie.[41] Four Lecompton Democrats and two Republicans comprised the two-house committee. On April 23, the so-called English bill emerged from the committee and was reported to the two houses.

Under the committee bill the people of Kansas were to have the opportunity to vote upon Lecompton in its entirety. But there was a hitch. If the Kansans accepted the constitution, they were entitled to land grants nearly equivalent to those given to most of the states recently admitted. If they rejected the document, however, they might not enter the Union until their territory possessed the minimum population required of a congressional district — about 93,000. William Howard of Michigan, the House Republican on the conference committee, pointed to the hypocrisy: if the population were sufficient to admit Kansas under Lecompton, why is it not sufficient under any other constitution? Obviously it was easier to enter the Union as a slave state than a free state, he concluded.

In the ensuing days, northerners and southerners tried to delay debate on the conference bill. Joshua Hill of Georgia, Quitman of Mississippi, and Howard were among those who requested a postponement. Some representatives just wanted to go home, while Howard argued that his Republican colleagues needed more time to study the new proposal. Stephens, who wanted no unnecessary delays, curtly informed Howard that the Montgomery-Crittenden amendment had been sprung upon the Democrats on April 1 and that they had not complained. Howard referred to the new bill as a "bribe," a charge easily taken up by Republican editors.[42]

The new Kansas bill seemed to mystify its enemies as well as its friends. Neither the southern ultras nor the Republicans wanted any part of it. On April 27, the correspondent to the *Charleston Mercury* called it another "one-sided" compromise that must prove disastrous to the South. Republicans charged the Democrats with dangling a carrot — in this case, land grants — and denying Kansans the right to proceed immediately to alter Lecompton outside of the provisions of the Constitution itself. Some supporters bemoaned their futility, for they anticipated the bill's rejection at the polls. Administration Democrats wondered why the opponents were denouncing the English bill since it allowed the people of Kansas to bury the Constitution through referendum and cancel the significantly reduced land grant.

Samuel Cox of Ohio admitted that he had supported the bill because Kansans could crush Lecompton at the polls.[43] His break with the anti-Lecomptonites signaled a favorable turn of events for administration forces. Another Douglas Democrat, John Haskin of New York, who had refused to abandon the cause vowed to expose Cox before his peers. Grow helped Haskin obtain the floor. The New Yorker accused Cox of having expressed in private strong feelings against both the conference bill and Representative English, which Cox denied. But his defection was only one of several desertions from the Douglas camp. Their votes helped the English bill pass the House, 112–103, on April 30. The same day the Senate approved the bill by a vote of 31–22, with the irreconcilable Democrats—Douglas, Charles Stuart of Michigan, and David Broderick of California—in the minority.[44]

Confident that the people of Kansas would reject Lecompton, Douglas supporters and Republicans waited for the election results. They wanted the rejection to be unequivocal. Writing to Gov. Charles Robinson of Kansas, Grow asked for a decisive referendum against the obnoxious bill.

Now we hope to see the Free State men make their assertions good against Lecompton by as large a majority as it is possible for them to give. . . . Let Lecompton be repudiated by an overwhelming majority at an election that the Administration fixes and the doughfaces will be exterminated next fall. We shall have the next Congress beyond a doubt and the Democrats even conceed [sic] it. Then Kansas will be admitted, if not before, for the condition in the English bill about population will not bind a future Congress in their action.[45]

Grow got his wish. When the vote was taken on August 2, 1858, the Kansans destroyed Lecompton by nearly a 10,000-vote majority. They were willing to wait for admission to the Union. Buchanan was happy that a bill of some kind had been passed before Congress had adjourned, although he had favored the Senate bill. But his party was in ruins. Southern ultras expressed bitterness over the loss of another possible slave state, while northern Democrats who had wavered between Douglas and the administration faced a credibility crisis with their constituents. Though the Buchanan forces insisted that the Kansas issue was now dead, Grow and the Republicans argued to the contrary. It will come back to haunt you "like the murderer in the play," Grow told the House Democrats. Certainly he and the Republicans had no intention of allowing the issue to slip away from them on the eve of the elections. They planned to maximize its potential in strengthening their cause before the voters and then resume the struggle once a Republican Congress had been elected.

The steadiness with which the Republicans in the Thirty-fifth Congress pursued the Kansas question was a natural follow-through from their position in the previous Congress. In his study of roll calls in the House during the first session of the Thirty-fifth Congress, Thomas B. Alexander describes the partisan and sectional patterns in the voting on various topics.[46] Republican consistency on slavery-related issues is obvious. And though there also seemed to be general party alignment on economic issues, as Alexander suggests, what is not so obvious is the range of opinions within the party regarding economic legislation. Sharp differences did exist. For example, public lands still remained as controversial as ever. While Grow continued to press for a homestead bill, many of his colleagues expressed more interest in other public-land proposals, including railroad and canal construction. When a hard core of Republicans voted for Morrill's agricultural college land-grant bill, Grow voted against it. A close examination of other issues, such as the tariff, may further illustrate what Grow and other party leaders had feared at the close of the previous Congress — the surfacing of conflicts among former Democrats and Whigs over what was best for the nation's economy. Worried Republicans warned that these differences had to be reconciled in the upcoming campaigns. They wanted to impress the voters with their unity of purpose and their single-mindedness on the issues, both political and economic. Otherwise, their hopes for significant victories in the elections would be considerably diminished.

❧ 10

"Free Homes for Free Men"

T HE REPUBLICANS pressed the Lecompton issue in the 1858
campaign, and they also broadened their base of voter appeal
by exposing the economic side of what they called Democratic incom-
petence. In their opinion the administration's wasteful and lavish ex-
penditures of public money, plus free-trade policies associated with
the 1857 tariff, were causes of the hard times. So, despite the new attention given to slavery in the territories by the Lincoln-Douglas
debates, not all Republicans cared to see the campaign contested on
the singular issue of Kansas. A more conscientious probe into the ingredients necessary to carry out the nation's expansion seemed more
logical. Railroad legislation, land policies, and tariff adjustments were
some of the crucial issues that demanded immediate resolution.

Just as the nonextension of slavery had been seminal in the formation of the Republican party, so a general agreement on economic
matters stabilized its structure in the next two years and assured its
success. Unfortunately for the Union, Republican successes of any
kind only fanned the fires of sectionalism. The alliance between the
Northwest and the East on the homestead bill, for example, weakened prospects for any continued cooperation between the Northwest
and the South since southerners were becoming united against the
land measure. While the Republicans capitalized upon this blow to
Democratic hopes of reunification, North and South tragically grew
more defiant toward each other.

The social philosophy of the radical Republicans was in essence
a program of legal, economic, and political reforms derived from the
principle of divide and conquer, which they held as the only practical
and rational guide to both platform strategy and public policy. Divi-
sions within the Democratic party had to be bared, pitted against each
other, and exploited. Toward this end anti-Lecomptonism among

Democrats helped, as did steady talk of disunion among southern extremists. However, probably none of the radical Republicans, including Grow, believed that strict adherence to this principle or to original Republican tenets was sufficient to defeat the Democrats. Militant oratory alone was not going to do the job. Victory seemed possible only if pledges were made to an assortment of groups, many of whom preferred sound economic proposals to hackneyed expressions against administration policy in Kansas and encroachments by the loyal sons of slavocracy.

If Republican radicalism persisted anywhere in 1858, it was in Grow's Fourteenth Congressional District. The *Tioga Agitator* charged that the resolutions adopted by the "People's Convention" in Harrisburg did not deal strongly enough with the real issues. The editor believed the platform to be "negatively Republican and positively mild — clever — harmless."[1] Certainly Grow saw little reason to ease up on the slavery question. As usual, he barnstormed the district with vigor and enmity, showing no moderation or retreat. He defended the Republican state ticket and echoed the local party's platform pledge to work against the "wickedness and imbecility" of the administration. Popular as ever, he experienced no difficulty in being nominated unanimously and elected comfortably for the fifth time.

The conferees who met at Towanda on September 7 to select Grow also advocated a revised tariff to increase revenues and provide maximum protection. The tariff, the party's strongest economic commitment, had to amuse the Democrats. Seemingly the free-trade views of former Democrats like Grow and Wilmot were being scrapped to accommodate former Whig protectionists now in the party. Maybe it was expediency, but it was also smart politics. The defeat of Wilmot for governor the previous year was a cold reminder that in Pennsylvania the protectionist argument was not to be taken lightly.

Much to Grow's disappointment, however, the homestead bill was not mentioned in the Harrisburg platform. Here again, the reason may have been to placate Know-Nothings who did not approve of Grow's plan to offer free land to future immigrants. Regardless, Grow had no intention of either abandoning the crusade for homestead legislation or modifying the liberal provisions of his bill. As with Kansas, he intended to be the driving force behind the land bill when the House convened again. The German philosopher Hegel once wrote that "political genius consists in identifying yourself with a principle." Grow's political wisdom was less a virtue of his own ability than his association with great principles and dynamic forces popular at the time. Free land to actual settlers was one of those great principles.

"Niggers to the Niggerless or Land to the Landless?"

During the second session of the Thirty-fifth Congress, which began on December 6, 1858, most of the homestead struggle took place in the lower house. It was one of several issues that aroused sectional tensions, but in reality much of the strain had been caused by the recent elections. For the Democrats the returns had been a total disaster; the political wreckage lay about them. Administration managers despaired of regrouping the party's factions. In his message to Congress, Buchanan tried to elicit a new enthusiasm for his program — a Pacific railroad, a national bankruptcy law, a revised tariff, and the acquisition of Cuba — but his credibility was gone, and in both houses Democratic leadership was so poor that no legislative program could be guaranteed.[2] Prospects for the next Congress appeared no brighter. Republicans were sure to control the House. The administration had suffered a serious blow when Alexander Stephens decided not to return to Washington for another term, and J. Glancy Jones, another floor leader, lost at the polls. What the Democrats did not need at this time was another embarrassing piece of legislation to test party strength. The homestead bill became exactly that when it became entangled with the Cuban issue.

Having introduced his homestead bill (H.R. 72), Grow spoke at length on January 26.[3] His arguments were familiar, his position steadfast. He deplored the diseased system of land monopoly: "It palsies the arm of industry and paralyzes the energies of a nation." Yet it would continue to agonize as long as Congress viewed the public domain as a mere source of revenue. He reminded his colleagues that President Jackson in 1832 had made the same observation. What the government must do, Grow continued, was to promote the welfare of the nation by giving the lands to actual settlers who would cultivate them. Under the present system, the settler obtained his land at government price only in comparatively few instances. In most cases the speculator benefited the most. The four or five dollars per acre that each settler put into the pocket of the speculator amounted to a great deal of money in every township, which could be put to better use in the building of schools, churches, roads and improving the general quality of life.

The doctrinaire part of Grow's thought was his faith in the philosophy of John Locke: each individual brings to society a right to property just as he brings the physical energy of his body. Hence society does not create the right, and it is wrong for government to deny man that which by nature was already his. Providing free homesteads

was only keeping in line with natural law, Grow believed. Give a settler a homestead and he would be able to surround it with improvements and institutions necessary for civilization. He will "convert the
haunts of savage life into a home for civilized men."

The enemies of Grow's bill prepared for battle. Immediately after
it was favorably reported out of the Committee on Agriculture, Millson of Virginia and Stephens of Georgia tried to table it, but the House
refused to do so by a 77–113 vote. This setback told the story: most
likely the bill would pass. In the discussion that followed, Grow led
the attack with characteristic decisiveness and wrath. He pounced upon
the southerners with the ferocity of Danton and the malignity of Marat.
When Millson complained that more deliberation on the bill was necessary, Grow was laconic: the bill had been debated in Congress for
eight years and no further debate was necessary. He repeatedly refused to allow Horace Maynard of Tennessee to offer an amendment.
Marshall of Kentucky, Smith of Virginia, and Jones of Tennessee
were likewise frustrated. John D. Atkins, a Buchanan Democrat from
Tennessee where nativism ran deep, objected to the measure because
it extended benefits to unnaturalized persons. The first section of
Grow's bill qualified anyone "who is the head of a family, or who has
arrived at the age of twenty-one years, and is a citizen of the United
States, or who shall have filed his intention to become such." The last
statement in this provision was the most controversial. Grow attempted
to make his position clearer. He pointed out that an alien could make
an *entry* under the bill, but he could not take *title* until he became a
citizen. Maynard had charged that Grow's bill would give possession
of land to foreigners at the expense of southern planters.

Despite frantic moves by the opposition, on February 1, 1859, Grow's
homestead bill passed the House by an impressive 120–76 decision.[4]
Southern strength was not sufficient to block passage. The voting
reflected sectional and party trends. Of the negative votes, sixty-eight
were from the South, including those of thirteen Americans, while
only eight were from the North. Only three southerners (Josh Jewett
of Kentucky, James Craig of Missouri, and George Jones of Tennessee) voted for the bill. Furthermore, for the Republican and American parties the bill became a party issue. Only one Republican, Matthias Nichols of Ohio, voted against it and no American voted for it.

The House action on the bill received praise throughout the free
states. The *New York Daily Tribune* of February 2 remarked: "Had this
bill become law fifteen years ago, it would have saved a vast deal of
public corruption." Grow was singled out and toasted by every friend
of homestead. As the *Daily Pittsburgh Dispatch* so aptly put it: "Mr.

Grow deserves honor from every poor man and every just man in the nation."[5] Yet this paper, along with others, did not think much of the bill's chances in the Senate.

The editorial pessimism was neither ill-conceived nor unjustified. Once the bill reached the upper house on February 2, it became entangled in a ruinous conflict with a bill to appropriate $30 million for Buchanan to negotiate the purchase of Cuba. Which bill was to receive precedence? As revealed by one Washington newspaper, the hot issue of the day was the Caribbean island.[6] While the Republicans viewed the Cuban bill as another proslavery measure, the Democrats saw it as a viable means to mend party fences. The administration wanted it, the southerners demanded it, and some of the anti-Lecomptonites, including Douglas, endorsed it. At the same time, Republicans and some of the Democrats favored homestead. Yet neither the forces interested in Cuba nor the proponents of homestead would find nirvana or the mythical pot of gold at the end of the rainbow in this session of Congress. Astute observers predicted that the Cuban bill could no more get through the House than the homestead bill could get through the Senate. Republican senators wanted some assurance of a decision on Grow's bill as a price for permitting a vote on the Cuban bill. Southern Democrats refused to go along with this scheme.

The argument over the preference between the two bills continued until February 17 when the homestead bill was again shelved through the undying efforts of the southerners. Mason of Virginia said of the bill, "I have not yet known in the Senate a bill so fraught with mischief, and mischief of the most demoralizing tendency."[7] With only two weeks remaining in the session, he urged that the homestead bill be laid aside and the more pressing appropriation bills be taken up. Seward reminded his colleagues that the homestead bill had been laid aside for ten years. Both Wade and Johnson of Tennessee tried hard, but failed to bring the bill to a vote. The latter, maintaining that his land measure and Grow's were essentially the same, agreed to support the House bill. This personal concession had no effect upon fellow southerners, who, by this time, reasoned that one homestead bill was as bad as another. Along with Mason, fellow Virginian Hunter, Clay of Alabama, and Slidell of Louisiana took charge in postponing the bill for the session. Clay did not want to waste precious time discussing a bill that tended "to reduce, at least, if it does not entirely destroy, the revenue derived from the sale of public lands." Vice President John Breckenridge cast the tie-breaking vote to table the bill.[8]

The Senate friends of homestead did not give up easily. Toward the end of the session, James Doolittle of Wisconsin and George Pugh of Ohio moved to take up the bill, but their efforts were frustrated.[9] Seward bemoaned the fact that a bill to give land to actual settlers and furnish homes to free laborers was being bypassed to consider another measure that would enlarge the domain of slave power. Angry with the opponents of the Cuban bill, Toombs of Georgia, a normally impassioned man, hurled invective after invective at Seward and his Republican allies. He accused them of cowardice, of "shivering in the wind," and "skulking" on Cuba. He despised their demagoguery in propagandizing the doctrine, "Land for the landless." If you really want to give land to the "landlackers," he told his listeners, consider the extension of the American empire through the Cuban bill.

Wade of Ohio was quick to his feet. "Are you going to buy Cuba for land for the landless?" he demanded to know. Bringing his fist down heavily upon his desk within an inch of Toombs's nose, he roared, "We are 'shivering in the wind,' are we, over your Cuban question?" The central question, as he saw it, was, "Shall we give niggers to the niggerless, or land to the landless?" Let us first vote on the land bill, he urged, then we can get to the "nigger bill" on Cuba. Laughter broke out when Wade charged the Democrats with scrounging the earth to find more Negroes. "They can no more run their party without niggers, than you could run a steam engine without fuel." Despite the vociferous rhetoric, both the homestead bill and the Cuban bill were dead for this session.

Oregon and Cheap Postage

A simple swap of legislative defeats was no consolation to Grow. The homestead bill must wait for a new Congress. For the young lawmaker, February 1859 was a month of highs and lows. Through it all, he carried on with usual skill as floor manager, sometimes with particular revenge but always with pointed clarity and sufficient balance of temperament to protect the forward position of his party. He and his fellow Republicans knew the tide was slowly but favorably moving in their direction. The Democrats remained as divided and confused as ever.

Grow's arguments against the Oregon bill were especially cogent, although he could not prevent its adoption on February 12. His position on Oregon had changed, but for good reasons. In the last Congress he had introduced an enabling act for Oregon, which passed the House but failed in the Senate. After that Congress adopted the so-called English bill, which denied the people of Kansas the right to enter the Union until they had at least twice the number of persons as Oregon then had. It was the population question all over again. Grow swore he would never sanction an unjust discrimination between territories. As long as the English bill remained, he demanded that the House Democrats be fair and consistent and not stretch the rules for Oregon. Clement Vallandigham of Ohio disagreed and refused to see any connection between Kansas and Oregon. Grow moved to amend the Oregon bill by a repeal of the English bill. "Either take off the restriction on Kansas," he exclaimed, "or apply it to all the Territories." Speaker Orr ruled the amendment out of order on grounds that it had nothing to do with Oregon. Grow appealed the decision but his appeal was laid on the table.[10]

In reality the population factor was of secondary importance to Grow. He demanded equality of treatment but he looked beyond mere numbers. Were the people of Oregon, or any territory, deprived of protection of their persons or property by executive interference or neglect of duty? Grow promised he would support their immediate admission regardless of population. Ironically, no one seemed to know what the population of Oregon was. Stephens estimated it to be well over 100,000, based on the assessor's list of taxable property. Using this bizarre mode of calculation, Grow jeered, the estimated population of a district in New York, where there is a concentration of wealth, might exceed the total population of the United States! Grow claimed that the largest number of voters ever polled in Oregon was only 10,121. Stephens smarted: "Probably they do not take the same interest in voting there that they do elsewhere."[11]

One feature of the Oregon bill that disturbed Grow was the exclusion of the Negro. When quizzed by Georgia American Josh Hill on the Negro question, Grow revealed more of his radical philosophy. Since he seemed so uncomfortable with the bill's racial restrictions, Hill asked, would Grow be agreeable to an increase of "colored" population in Pennsylvania?[12] Grow replied: "I would not exclude anybody that God Almighty creates on the face of the earth, from his birthplace. . . . I never would vote to exclude any human being from coming into the State of Pennsylvania, whatever his color, or wherever his birth." Hill then demanded to know whether Grow would put Negroes on an equality with whites. Grow's affirmative response: "In their personal rights, if they observe the laws."

If Republican solidarity appeared weakened by the Oregon bill, it again stiffened in the debate over appropriations as time ran short. House Republicans knew they could block these bills and thus embarrass the administration. A good example was the deadlock over the post office appropriations bill. In late February the House had sent H.R. 872 allocating support funds for the post office to the Senate. With only four days remaining, Sen. David Yulee of Florida grafted onto the House measure a provision abolishing franking and raising postage rates some 70 percent on letters and more on newspapers. His move proved to be a tactical error, although such a proviso was popular among many senators who hoped an increase in revenue might wipe out the postal deficit. They returned the amended bill to the House with an unexpressed dictum, "Raise the rates or we defeat the post office bill." Thus the pressure was placed upon House Republicans: either accept the increase or face the consequences for immobilizing the post office department.

A tacit ultimatum did not scare Grow, who branded the amended bill objectionable and unconstitutional. The Senate had exceeded its constitutional prerogatives by increasing the rates under the House bill. The Senate can no more raise postage rates, he asserted, than it can raise the tariff or originate a bill increasing the price of public lands. He therefore objected to removing the amended bill from the Speaker's table and promised to stand firm until a vote was taken on his resolution calling for the return of the bill to the Senate.

Grow thought he had reached an agreement to this effect with Chairman Phelps of the Ways and Means Committee. But Phelps claimed his understanding was that Grow would only make a statement on the bill as a point of order. Grow, furious, warned Phelps that, unless a vote were taken on his resolution, he would not consent to *any* money bill being taken from the table. This was indeed a bold threat for anyone to make unless he was fully confident of his influence on the floor. Grow was. On March 3 the House voted 117–76 in favor of Grow's resolution to return the post office bill.[13] No Republican voted against it.

The Senate made short order of the post office bill by returning it to the House, but the Republicans there refused to be intimidated. With only hours of the session remaining, the House passed a new bill without the Senate amendments. Again, the reaction in the upper house was generally negative: senators refused to consider the House bill. In desperation, however, they agreed to call for a conference committee. Grow did not object to the proposed committee, but he did object to taking up the amended bill again. He served on the conference committee, which recommended that the original House bill be accepted without Senate amendment, but with the conciliatory provision that neither house waive any of its constitutional rights. The

House approved the compromise measure but the Senate refused to follow. Toombs of Georgia, Mason of Virginia, and Bayard of Delaware, upset with the action of their conferees, ranted, raved, and objected until the bill died. Later, Buchanan commented that he believed this was the first time in the nation's history that any Congress had adjourned without passing legislation necessary to keep the government going until the new Congress convened.[14] This lack of action, he continued, "imposed on the Executive a grave responsibility."

Probably, few Democrats cared. Bloodied, bruised, and spiritually disarmed, they stared at their party in total disarray. Voting patterns on the money and homestead bills revealed a division too severe to be overcome by the healing powers of time. Secondly, the ruthless resolve of the Republicans in Congress proved to the Democrats what the 1858 elections had suggested: their opponents no longer had to hang their hopes upon the single star of slavery. At first this eternal issue had delineated the complexity of northern and southern cultures, but issues such as the homestead bill were to transform that sectional line of demarcation into an impenetrable barrier. Little wonder that in the next Congress, southerners denounced the homestead bill as a Black Republican "abolition" measure conceived and designed to destroy the South.

"We Shall Demand It — Until It Is Granted!"

Grow's good friend, Schulyer Colfax, said it. Every Republican entering the Thirty-sixth Congress agreed and dedicated himself to the task. The homestead bill had indeed become a party issue, and its future seemed brighter than ever. The evidence was obvious in the 1859 campaign. Everywhere he stumped, and he stumped nationally, Grow encountered a genuine craze for his bill, not only from Republicans but from many Democrats as well. After he spoke in Minnesota, both major parties there added homestead planks to their platforms.[15] Bipartisanship on this popular bill was not uncommon in the Northwest. After many years of toil, friends of homestead were ready to experience the climactic moment in the history of the bill.

When Congress convened in December 1859, the hope for the homestead bill hinged upon a probable alliance between Republicans and some Democrats. Neither party had a majority in the House. There were 109 Republicans, 10 short of organizing the House. The Democratic total was 101, but a dozen or so were anti-Lecomptonites. The balance of power rested with the Americans, who were not likely to support Grow's homestead bill. Assuming the Republicans would unite behind the bill, homestead enthusiasts expressed confidence that at least ten Democrats would cross over.

First, however, the House had to be organized. The election of a Speaker would have an important bearing on the Republican cause and particularly on the 1860 election.[16] But never had the atmosphere in the House been gloomier or the sectional tension greater. Against a backdrop of frenzy associated with the John Brown hanging and southern anxiety over Hinton Helper's antislavery book, *The Impending Crisis of the South,* lawmakers labored two months, stumbling through ballot after ballot, to find a presiding officer. One observer wrote: "Everything is at sea, and no person here knows the course, or can steer or is capable of taking command."[17] The melodrama was a repeat of the 1855 fiasco that finally ended when Banks was acclaimed Speaker. Members became demoralized, and some took heavily to the bottle. On one occasion, Josh Hill was so drunk that he nearly lost his balance while delivering a tirade.[18] Writing to Stephens, a Georgian lawmaker said it best for many of his colleagues: "I wish you were here instead of me."[19]

Grow and Sherman of Ohio were the two leading Republican contenders for Speaker. Speculation had given the edge to the latter. The Ohioan was popular among northwesterners who wanted to see their section of the country achieve recognition and power in the new Congress. Grow remained a favorite with old friends, like the Washburns, and Pennsylvania Republicans. Thaddeus Stevens of Pennsylvania, who believed the Speaker must be not only an expert on parliamentary procedure but also a person with nerve and fidelity to party principles, nominated Grow. But Grow's impetuous manner and bravado worried moderate Republicans who preferred a candidate more acceptable to Democrats. Some Republicans indicated they would not go into party caucus but were ready to support an acceptable candidate who was not an ultra on the issue of slavery.[20]

Grow had begun to campaign for the office long before the House convened. His critics probably believed that his campaign had started as early as the Thirty-fourth Congress. He allowed his name to be placed in nomination in the Thirty-fifth Congress when there was no chance of a Republican being elected Speaker. Having been the caucus nominee, however, Grow now enjoyed a slight advantage over other contestants. He had some support pledges from New Englanders and from Minnesota representatives who were annoyed with Sherman's opposition to the admission of their state. Yet in his own state Grow's support was not as strong as expected. The Pennsylvania delegation planned to present his name simply because he had been the caucus choice in 1857, but there were indications that the Pennsylvania members would not push his claims very hard. John Wien Forney predicted that Sherman, who was popular in the Keystone State, would become Speaker and that he would be elected clerk of the House. With the Forney, Cameron, and Grow forces battling each other, as well as the Buchanan administration, there was little likelihood of any support of a Pennsylvania candidate for Speaker.[21]

Grow, disappointed, realized that his strength lay scattered among the northern states. Despite his support of the homestead bill and a free Kansas, the West preferred one of its own sons. His campaign strategists approached Sherman's managers to convince them that their candidate could best serve the party as chairman of the Committee of Ways and Means, but they were not interested. At the same time, Marylanders speculated that the only way the Republicans would be able to organize the House was if all the antiadministration forces, including the southern Americans, united. Were this true, Grow was indeed not the candidate.[22]

Neither Grow nor Sherman was acceptable to Rep. J. B. Clark of Missouri, who introduced a resolution declaring that no man who had endorsed Helper's insurrectionary book was fit to be Speaker. Grow, and a number of Republican House members, had endorsed the book and recommended the raising of a fund to purchase copies for free distribution. Though his name appeared in the printed list of signers of the endorsement, Sherman claimed he had never seen or read the petition recommending the book. After the first ballot, Grow withdrew his name, desiring not to retard the organization of the House. He then joined other Republicans to support Sherman until the Ohioan withdrew to make room for William Pennington of New Jersey, who was finally elected.[23]

At a victory celebration following the elections of Pennington as Speaker and John Forney as clerk, Grow told a jubilant crowd that the eight-week contest was not a conflict between sections or among states. It was instead a "conflict on a principle of political economy" as to the "system of labor that can best develope [*sic*] the material interest of the country, and foster its giant industrial interests."[24] The center of this conflict was whether the territories would be filled with free homes and free men or with black slaves.

Now that the House was organized, Grow moved quickly with his homestead bill. He introduced it on February 15 and saw it referred to the Committee on Agriculture, of which he was a member. His defense of the measure was perhaps the most provocative to date.

Entitled "Free Homes for Free Men," the speech was later distributed by the Republicans in the 1860 campaign.[25] The arguments used represented old wine in new bottles. Then again, Grow and the bill's friends exclaimed, what might be said of the homestead bill that had not been uttered many times before?

What distinguished this address was the dynamic quality of its arguments and the near-frantic appeal for a liberal land policy. As before, Grow warned against land monopolies, explaining that under the current system any world millionaire could become the owner of untold acres of America's public domain. The unfortunate settler then paid an exorbitant price to some speculator for a small tract of land. Using statistics, Grow disclosed how pioneers had already filled the pockets of land grabbers with millions of dollars — hard-earned money that could have been put to better use by settlers, their families, and their communities. Reaffirming his contention that the government must not look narrowly upon the public lands as a source of revenue, Grow next lashed into the antiquated bounty system under which the government rewarded its veterans with land warrants. Grow said that bounties to soldiers should be made in money, not land warrants, which were generally sold to speculators. "If rewards or bounties are to be granted for true heroism in the progress of the race, none is more deserving than the pioneer who expels the savage and the wild beast and opens in the wilderness a home for science and a pathway for civilization," he said.

There was little discussion on Grow's bill. Its supporters realized their strength and avoided any prolonged debate, which would have aggravated the sectional bickering and delayed the forwarding of the bill to the Senate. A week after it had been favorably reported from committee, the homestead bill passed the House on March 12, 1860, by an overwhelming 115–66 vote.[26] It was a purely sectional decision. While the Republicans voted en masse for the bill, a single free-state representative, William Montgomery of Pennsylvania, voted against it. Among the southerners, only James Craig of Missouri supported it.

Seeing that he had more than enough votes, Grow had labored to prevent his bill from falling into the swill of militant oratory. Unbridled rage produced irrationality in both action and speech; threats and name-calling were commonplace. Weapons became commonplace for some, as the distance between North and South widened. And, if anyone believed in a policy of brinkmanship, it was Grow. If anyone stood on the precipice of personal disaster, it was Grow.

He was a targeted man. Armed himself, he walked the streets of Washington, from his residence on Seventh Street to Capitol Hill and Brown's Tavern, protected by his good friends Wade, Trumbull, Reuben Fenton of New York, and John Potter of Wisconsin. "Give me John Potter," he exclaimed. "He has killed his grizzly and is a battalion in himself."[27] Weeks earlier, Grow had been nearly drawn into a duel with his old adversary, Lawrence O'B. Branch of North Carolina. The ordinarily urbane and amiable southerner had accused Grow of defeating the post office bill with the intent of inducing the president to call an extra session, something that Buchanan did not want to do. In rebuttal, Grow had charged Branch with violating all parliamentary and gentlemanly courtesy because no member should impeach the motives of another. Branch was maligned and insulted and Grow remained defiant; he would make no retraction. Vallandigham of Ohio had also claimed Grow was to blame for the bill's defeat and had been rude and offensive. The Democrats were incensed by Grow's terse remark that the *New York Herald* did all the thinking for them.[28]

"Will you please name a time and place outside the District of Columbia," Branch had written to Grow on December 29, 1859, "at which time you will receive from me a communication in writing."[29] By noon the next day, Branch's letter had been delivered; by evening Grow replied, refusing the challenge on moral and legal grounds. Later he and Branch were arrested and placed under heavy bond to keep the peace.[30]

As usual, the litmus test for the homestead bill lay in the Senate. Southern opponents were ready with their favorite arguments. The southern press contributed its venom to the cause. The *Richmond Whig and Public Advertiser* of March 19 was particularly caustic: "The passage of the Homestead Bill . . . is an ominous event in the history of the country. That bill is based upon the unjust, loose, radical, revolutionary principle of Agrarianism, and is, therefore, at war with the political and social rights of the people, and absolutely infamous in its character. . . . Never was there a more odious and iniquitous bill passed by any deliberative body on earth."[31]

The Senate had a homestead bill of its own, introduced by Andrew Johnson early in the session. At least in two respects Grow's bill was more liberal than Johnson's. The former extended benefits to any person of twenty-one years or older, whereas the latter restricted benefits to heads of families. The Senate bill was also limited to persons who were inhabitants of the country, thus denying the future immigrant the opportunity to file under the act. In contrast the House bill offered its provisions to all foreigners, present and future, who declared their intention to become citizens and to complete their naturalization during the residence period under the act. This standing provision in Grow's bill made it most unpopular with nativists.

Which bill was the Senate to take up first? The Committee on Public Lands recommended that the Senate bill be substituted for Grow's. Johnson, who surmised that the liberal House bill stood little chance in the upper house, thought it neither "unparliamentary nor discourteous to the House of Representatives for the Senate to proceed regularly with the consideration of a bill that it had matured and made a special order." Wade wanted the House bill discussed first and persisted until he managed to convince his colleagues to put the preference question to a vote. By a margin of two votes, 26–24, the Senate bill was laid aside and the House bill taken up.[32]

As expected, the debate opened all the channels to old arguments and new anxieties. Southerners viewed the bill as an abolition scheme, a Black Republican ploy. Friends deplored the effort to graft the slavery issue onto the bill. In desperation, opponents attempted to prolong discussion by introducing amendments. Yet the Democrats, divided on the land measure, exhibited uneasiness over their position. With the national party conventions only weeks away, they realized that the great Northwest might be the key to victory in the coming election. No longer was there any doubt about the bill's popularity in that section, especially with the Germans and other immigrant groups. Western Democrats feared that the party's continued obstruction of a reasonable homestead bill would surely spell defeat of their state platforms and maybe the national one as well.

From this unenviable position, the Democrats adopted a course of action not unlike that of 1854 when the Senate approved the Hunter substitute in lieu of the House's homestead bill. On April 11, Johnson withdrew his original bill and introduced another as a substitute for Grow's bill.[33] Both the House bill and the new Senate substitute were then referred to the Committee on Public Lands, which was instructed to report a completely new measure. The Committee's chairman, Robert W. Johnson of Arkansas, called the new bill a compromise measure between the friends and opponents of homestead. The compromise conferred benefits only to heads of families and required a payment of twenty-five cents per acre at the end of a five-year "constant residence" period. The bill extended privileges to aliens, but it required them to complete their naturalization in less time than was allowed under the House bill. Finally, all lands that remained unsold at the end of thirty-five years were to be ceded to the states in which they were situated.

Even in modified form, the Senate bill aroused the fury of most southerners. They remained convinced that it would restrict slavery, encourage a flood of immigration to the northern and western states, and contribute to the preponderance of free states. James Green of Missouri, a leading opponent, called the proposed legislation unnecessary since, under graduation, public land was already selling for as little as twelve and a half cents per acre. The bill's enactment would reduce income from the sale of public lands, thus prompting a higher tariff for revenue. Not only would the homestead bill cripple further land grants to the railroads, Green argued, but it would also render worthless the bounty land warrants held by veterans. Finally, he predicted that only northerners would avail themselves of the bill's advantages. Along with many other southerners, he was willing to give the public lands to the states, which could then choose to enact homestead measures.

After much wrangling, both parties agreed to accept the committee bill. But the friends of homestead were not happy. Aware of their inability to carry Grow's liberal measure, the Republicans saw the Senate substitute as nothing more than a crafty production by southerners to mollify prohomestead Democrats. Wade attempted to substitute Grow's bill, but his efforts failed. The southerners knew they had sufficient strength to block legislation as liberal as Grow's, but in light of the coming election they felt somewhat compelled to pass some version of a homestead measure. On May 10 the bill passed the upper house by a lopsided vote, 44–8. Republican Hannibal Hamlin of Maine, the only northerner to vote in the negative, said the measure was simply "not a homestead bill."

Many southerners, realizing that the measure was devoid of the homestead principle, probably did not care what the House did. Homestead friends, on the other hand, hoped House members would insist upon their own bill. The *New York Daily Tribune* on May 11 predicted that the popular branch of Congress was not about to accept the "miserable make shift as a substitute for its vigorous and healthy measure." The newspaper had earlier rumored that the Senate would not completely kill the homestead bill because southerners had the president pledged to veto it.[34] Another paper had commented, "No man has talked more frequently, and more ably, and more generously, in favor of a liberal land policy than James Buchanan," yet there was little question that he had changed his views since becoming president.[35]

When the Senate bill reached the House, homestead supporters disposed of it quickly. Owen Lovejoy from the Committee on Public Lands asked that the Senate bill not be considered and the original

House bill substituted. The latter was adopted by a 102–63 vote and sent to the upper house. Again, every Republican voted in the affirmative. A week later, however, the Senate made short order of Grow's bill by rejecting it.

With each house insisting on its own bill and with the adjournment of Congress at hand, it appeared that the homestead bill again was to be shelved. Grow was quick to move that the Speaker appoint a conference committee to meet with a similar committee of the Senate to resolve differences and produce a measure satisfactory to both houses. A majority of the House agreed to Grow's motion. Barksdale of Mississippi tried to have the vote reconsidered, but he was thwarted by Grow. Southern opposition in the House was no longer a match for the Republicans.

The Senate agreed to conference and selected Andrew Johnson to head its committee; Grow chaired the House committee, but the two committees failed to reach an agreement when each insisted on its own measure. Both chairmen reported that they had done everything possible to produce a suitable compromise. Grow suggested new appointees for another conference committee. Colfax was selected to head this one while Johnson was retained as the Senate's chief representative.[36]

The second conference also failed. In his report Colfax carefully reviewed the principal differences between the two bills. Whereas Grow's extended the benefits to all persons at least twenty-one years of age, the Senate measure applied only to heads of families. Under the House bill, only ten dollars to cover the cost of survey and recording were required, while the Senate bill asked for twenty-five cents per acre. A third distinction focused on present preemptors. Under the terms of the House bill, they were immediately eligible to take up the land, but under the Senate bill they were excluded from the land unless, within two years after the enactment of the measure, they purchased their lands at the full government price of $1.25 per acre. If not paid for at the end of this period, the lands were subject to public sale. With this stipulation, Colfax cautioned, most preemptors would have to abandon their lands and all improvements.

On June 19, a third conference committee meeting brought success, to the surprise of both branches. Colfax was not thrilled with the product; neither was Grow. They informed the opposition that they would regard the thinly disguised "homestead" measure only as a step toward the advancement of a more comprehensive and liberal bill, which they intended to demand in the next session. "We shall demand it . . . until it is granted," Colfax reported to the House. "We have taken this bill," Grow echoed, "not because it is what we want, but on the principle that half a loaf is better than no bread."[37]

The House conferees had consented to a measure that resembled the Senate bill more than Grow's. They failed to impress the Senate conferees with the need to extend the bill to everyone over twenty-one years of age. By the compromise agreed upon, all the land subject to private entry was to be open for homesteads at twenty-five cents per acre, along with one half of the surveyed land that had not yet been offered at public sale (that is, the odd-numbered sections). The House bill had included all lands subject to preemption and virtually all government lands not set aside for special purposes. The House conferees did manage to save thousands of preemptors from losing their lands by lowering the $1.25 to 62½ cents per acre, payable within two years of the bill's enactment. The Senate also struck the section requiring the president to sell the public lands two years after their survey.

Both houses wasted little time in accepting the conference bill with overwhelming majorities. The vote in the Senate was 36–2, while in the House it was 115–51.[38] Along with most homestead supporters, Grow voted in the affirmative. If nothing else, the conference bill was the first piece of legislation resembling a homestead bill to get through both branches of Congress. The circumstances under which it passed, however, gave it a negative image in the West. The *Chicago Press and Tribune* did not soften its criticism of the bill, especially the provision that restricted benefits to heads of families.[39] Other limitations were similarly judged. Yet most westerners, for the present, were willing to accept whatever they could get. They did not abandon hope that homestead advocates would ultimately produce a land measure worthy of praise throughout the West.

With the adjournment of Congress near, all eyes turned to the White House. Buchanan did not keep the friends and enemies of the bill in suspense very long. On June 22 the president's veto message was received and read in the Senate. His action was not in line with his inaugural address, in which he had stated that his administration's cardinal policy was "to reserve these lands . . . for actual settlers, and this at moderate prices."[40]

Buchanan gave many reasons for his veto.[41] He contended that the small sum asked for the lands, twenty-five cents per acre, was tantamount to a donation. For this reason, he felt that the bill was unconstitutional: Congress has no power to give away the public lands either to settlers or to the states. He had expressed a similar view in his veto of the agricultural college bill. He further maintained that the homestead bill was unjust, both to veterans who held bounty lands because it reduced their value, and to the older states because it encouraged their citizens to go West, thereby reducing the price of property in those states. It was also considered discriminatory. Unmarried citizens were prohibited from availing themselves of the bill's benefits, while immigrants, without being the heads of families, were eligible. Buchanan thought that this inadvertent distinction between the two groups was bound to open new fields for speculation and secret agreements between the capitalist and the would-be settler. Most depressing, according to the president, was the fact that the bill tended to demoralize people and repress the noble spirit of independence. He declared that the honest poor man "desires no charity, either from the Government or from his neighbors."

The veto rekindled Senate debate. Andrew Johnson pulled no punches in his criticism of the veto message and cynically proclaimed that the president would veto any measure that looked like a homestead bill. Along with the Republicans, Johnson succeeded in preventing the southerners from postponing the bill until the next session. But the bill did not have a chance. When the question was put, the 27–18 vote fell short of the two-thirds needed to override a veto. All negative votes came from the South.[42] For the last time the South had stopped a measure that threatened to enhance the power of the free states.

Buchanan's action was condemned throughout the West and Northeast. "The veto of the half-and-half Homestead Bill, by Buchanan, is the crowning infamy of the Democratic administration," wrote the *St. Paul Daily Times*.[43] In Pennsylvania, many Democrats joined the Republicans in assailing the veto as further evidence of Buchanan's willingness to sacrifice the interests of his own state in order to maintain his friendship with the most reactionary group in the South. The *Daily Pittsburgh Gazette* felt "no act of the present weak, corrupt, and infamous National Administration has created more indignation throughout the community than the President's veto of the Homestead Bill."[44] In New York, the acrimonious Horace Greeley interpreted the veto as "one of the natural consequences of elevating to the Presidency a man who from past associations has no sympathy with the poor, and who regards only the interests of speculators. Does anyone suppose that Abraham Lincoln would ever veto such a bill?"[45]

In addition to the defeat of both the makeshift homestead bill and his proposed bill, Grow suffered another disappointment in this session of Congress. The Senate also killed his land bill, which had passed the House on May 22, 1860, by a heavy Republican majority.[46] This measure reserved the public lands for actual settlers for ten years after a government survey and availability for settlement. It had been before the House for two years, and in January 1859 had been adopted as an amendment to a preemption bill that was later rejected. Being popular in the West, the bill was intended to give the Republicans favor with westerners.

In spite of the defeat of the two land measures, the Republicans acquired a true advantage over their opponents as election time approached. The record spoke for itself: Buchanan and his Democratic allies were the real enemies of any liberal land program the West demanded. The president's veto message became a poignant Republican campaign document. In fairness to Buchanan, his reasons for vetoing the bill were well stated and traditional, but he deprived his party of the honor of passing a bill that meant so much to so many. His approval might have strengthened his party's chances in the West, particularly the Northwest, but that prospect must be weighed against the possibility that the southern senators who did not oppose the conference bill preferred to see the measure defeated by a lame-duck, northern president. Regardless, with Congress adjourned, national attention turned to the autumn elections. Though the slavery crisis attracted much of that attention, the homestead bill also would play a significant role in the campaign.

𝒮11

Triumph and Defeat

AMID THE TUMULT occasioned by Buchanan's veto of the homestead bill, the first session of the stormy Thirty-sixth Congress came to an end. It was time to elect a president. Party platforms and candidates in 1860 gave every promise of an extraordinary campaign. As it turned out, however, demagoguery overpowered statesmanship. Rancor and threats transformed the usually debatable issues into pretentious reasons for disunion and the presidential hopefuls into saviors and traitors.

Historians and most nineteenth-century contemporaries agree that the responsibility for the Civil War rested with a multitude of differences between the North and South. A growing literature supports this contention and describes those differences. Some causes were rooted in principles and ingrained in the spirits of men who scorned compromise and acted instead out of self-interest and fear. Northern radicals and southern ultras exhibited their bitterness on all fronts with arguments less ontological than emotional. Yet beyond the rhetoric of these ideologues there existed two seemingly incompatible social systems separated by the institution of slavery. Within this context, the homestead bill stood out as perhaps the most sectional issue in the 1860 campaign.

With typical zeal, Grow labored to see that the homestead bill was featured in both the Republican platform and the party's campaign strategy. Over the hills of Pennsylvania and across the prairies of the West, he stumped for its enactment. He was persuasive, bold, cunning, and predictable. Copies of his bill and supportive speeches were freely circulated and translated into the various languages of the immigrants. These efforts paid off. A rally for the bill meant voter strength for the party, and Republican victories implied ultimate success for the bill. Within two years of Buchanan's veto, Grow was able to bask in the long-awaited sunshine of that success as he watched a Republican-controlled Congress adopt, and a Republican president sign, the bill for which he had so valiantly struggled.

The time was May 1862, and Grow stood at the pinnacle of his legislative career. Having been elected Speaker of the Thirty-seventh Congress, the Pennsylvanian saw the homestead bill become law during the time he held that office. Despite what must have been his greatest thrill, it was also a time of despair for him. Amid the twin disasters, secession and war, the pendulum of fate marred the lives of many, including Grow. As Speaker and leading radical, he had to shoulder the responsibility of war legislation, much of which was unpopular with northern voters. A constituency wearied by the war's endlessness and brazenness demanded a change. Grow's defeat at the polls in 1862 seemed more a rejection of what he stood for than of himself. His health shaken, a tired, disillusioned Grow left office not knowing whether he would ever return. Twelve years of public service had come to an end with a suddenness that paralleled that of his nomination and election in 1850.

The State of the Union

The election of 1860 found Grow in his most characteristic role, that of a campaigner. In this capacity, he was one of the best. His brand of radical Republicanism was in strong demand as a counterbalance to the oratory of "patriotic" or "summer" Republicans — moderates and conservatives who wished to mollify the truculent southerners to save the Union. To him sound arguments on the issues delivered "with the fire of a thousand furnaces" seemed the right way to sustain his party's vilification of slavery, southern "traitors," and the Democratic party. But his wrath had to be expressed without alienating voters who were mainly interested in the economic issues prominent in the Chicago platform. Still, the hard line had to be consistently pursued; the "enemy" constantly watched. "The price of liberty is eternal vigilance," was Grow's motto. His popularity carried him into the West, where he ably promoted his homestead measure with the help of Carl Schurz, who appealed to German immigrants. As a result, many of them supported homestead and some sixty-nine of eighty-one German-language newspapers endorsed Lincoln.[1]

Grow's greatest efforts came in his own state, where he had to be careful not to let his exuberance with homestead overshadow other issues; to many Pennsylvanians the tariff was far more important than anything else, including slavery.[2] Delayed until late August because of ill health, he traversed the counties in crowded trains and coaches, hoping his voice and strength would not give out. He often appeared on the same platform as Andrew Curtin, the popular gubernatorial candidate, who spoke in nearly every county in the state. Candidates to Congress, including George Scranton, Edward McPherson, and James Campbell, were indebted to Grow for his efforts in their behalf. All three were elected. Undoubtedly his largest audience, estimated at 40,000, was at Lancaster, where he was accompanied by Curtin and Thad Stevens. Several days earlier he had been with Curtin in Pittsburgh. From that city, in a letter to Horace Greeley, Grow expressed confidence in Curtin's ability to carry the state by 20,000.[3] He also told the New York editor that the party's strategy in Pennsylvania was to canvass Republican and doubtful counties and to let the Democratic regions alone. The Democratic candidate for governor, Henry O. Foster, had impressive but scattered support throughout the commonwealth. Where he was strong, as in Berks and Montgomery Counties, he was very strong. Grow had asked Greeley to use the power of his *Tribune* to rally Lincoln backers behind Curtin. State Republicans sensed they were far less united with Curtin than with Lincoln.

As it turned out, Greeley's help was probably not needed. In October Curtin easily routed his able Democratic opponent by more than 30,000 votes. The jubilant Republicans knew, as did everybody who was anybody in politics, that the gubernatorial election had been a dress rehearsal for the presidential race, and Pennsylvania was presumed to be the pivotal state in the national contest. Therefore, the October election had practically settled the matter of who was going to win in November. All the Republicans had to do for the next several weeks was to keep their forces in line. What happened in November came as no surprise to leaders of both parties. With a 60,000 margin of victory, Lincoln's sweep was even more impressive than Curtin's. Grow had predicted that Lincoln would win by 40,000 to 50,000. In his district, Grow helped elect Curtin by more than 4,500 and Lincoln by more than 10,000. And there was never a doubt about Grow's reelection. He easily defeated his Democratic opponent, Henry Sherwood of Tioga, by nearly three to one.[4]

Despite this evident unanimity, Pennsylvania Republicans were still not united. "The election of Lincoln opened wide the door for factional conflict in Pennsylvania," Alexander McClure later wrote.[5] By the time the People's State Convention had finished its business in Harrisburg in February 1860, the forces loyal to Simon Cameron, contender for the presidential nomination, and those for Curtin were in open battle with each other. The two men were not friends; they were not even on speaking terms. Their estrangement polarized the conduct of their faithful followers. In crowded hotel rooms, wiser heads and the logic of practicality had momentarily prevailed. Curtin had come out of the convention with the nomination for governor, as expected, while Cameron knew that the delegation planned to support him for the presidency. But it had been a hard-fought compromise. When the Republicans gathered in Chicago, Cameron had no chance to receive the nomination; perhaps no one from outside Illinois really did. On the third ballot, with the Cameron people assured that their man would be given a cabinet position, Pennsylvania had swung to Lincoln. Cameron was less than fully satisfied, and bitterness between the two groups persisted.

The schism became more apparent with Cameron's appointment to Lincoln's cabinet. He was not the only Pennsylvanian mentioned as a possible member of the official family. David Wilmot, who had supported Lincoln before the Pennsylvania delegation decided to do so, was also rumored to be in line to become either secretary of treasury or secretary of war. He ended the rumor when he allegedly told Lincoln that he was more interested in going to the Senate.[6] Thad Stevens, who was emerging as the party's leader in the national House, was still a third possibility. Writing to the president-elect, Grow recommended that Stevens be given a cabinet post and indicated that this was the wish of many Republicans; but many Republicans were as negative toward Stevens as toward Cameron.[7] Grow must have realized that Lincoln would not appoint two Pennsylvanians to his cabinet.

McClure disapproved of Grow's suggestion and tried to convince Stevens that his role in the next Congress was far more important than that of a cabinet member.[8] When Lincoln finally decided upon Cameron as his war secretary, Stevens protested, as did McClure, Curtin, and Wilmot — a reaction the new secretary was not likely to forget quickly.

In all probability, Grow was also disappointed with Cameron's appointment. The evidence suggests that warm feelings never existed between the two men. Their differences went back to the early days of Grow's political apprenticeship when he had worked closely with Wilmot. Was Grow's backing of Stevens, therefore, an attempt to embarrass Cameron or simply a beau geste to help a friend? Probably the latter. It is doubtful that Grow's plan was devious — to see Stevens join the cabinet in order to remove him as a rival to his own leadership in the House. Grow may have just wanted a fellow radical in the new administration. Certainly the radicals were concerned lest the administration assume a moderate stance and frustrate their legislative designs. This preference for Stevens widened the gap between Grow and Cameron as the Republican split became more pronounced. On the eve of the "secession winter," one question haunted the party: was their in-house feuding destined to imperil their first national administration?

On December 3, 1860, the short session of the Thirty-sixth Congress convened in a city beseiged by talk of disunion. As deliberations wore on, the need for closer integration must have been all too apparent to the first tier of party leaders. With the first crack of the gavel, the Republican leadership in the House, steered principally by Grow, gave unmistakable signs that to the best of its ability it would drive the Chicago platform through the Democratic opposition.

Hardly had the chaplain's voice died away on opening day than Grow, as though on cue, began to press for an early adoption of the homestead bill.[9] With the tariff and free Kansas, it was one of the principal party issues that remained unresolved from the previous session. Its popularity in the recent election had impressed even the most skeptical observer. Grow acknowledged that the appeal of free land had not been confined to the newer states, but had proved important to the Republican cause in the Middle Atlantic states as well. In Pennsylvania, for example, free land had been popularized in the rural counties just as the protective tariff had been emphasized in the industrial areas. Owen Lovejoy did not believe he was exaggerating when he later remarked that the Republicans could not have elected Lincoln had they not been pledged to the free land bill.[10]

Yet the chances of the bill's being considered at this time appeared slim. The overpowering threats of secession held the nation hostage and forced Congress to examine ways to save the Union. Amid the confusion in and out of the House, nevertheless, Grow demanded a reopening of debate on the bill; on December 5 John Phelps of Missouri, accustomed to Grow's provocative and intimidating tactics, attempted to prevent debate but failed.

On the same day Grow assailed Buchanan for his homestead veto. Whereas the president had contended that Congress did not have the constitutional authority to give away the public lands, Grow argued that the bill's provisions in no way established a "grant," but required a payment of ten dollars for the 160-acre homestead. Admittedly the cost was nominal, but Grow calculated how the government had thus far "given away" more than 180,000,000 acres to states, companies, and individuals without receiving a cent. On this occasion Grow's commentary was brief. He did not wish to belabor the merits of the bill for they had been reviewed by Congress for more than ten years. The time had come for action and he urged immediate adoption. The House responded favorably, but the Senate refused to take action during the session.[11]

The bill had been overshadowed by the real crisis at hand — survival of the nation. Republican leaders faced the arduous task of asking for a firm posture against the South while at the same time leaving the door open for any reasonable compromise. Only the naive actually believed that survival was possible. Lincoln's obligation to enforce federal laws in all the states was on a collision course with the ordinances of secession.

If party images could be overlooked, there was precedent to halt the careening forces; both sections had repeatedly accepted the tradition of compromise rooted in the democratic process. It commanded the allegiance of those politicians who wanted no permanent association with either the radicals or the ultras. As disunion loomed bigger and bigger, Republicans knew the nation looked to them to resolve the problem. Could they? Would they honor the tradition of compromise? Was there to be a "compromise of 1860" comparable to those of 1820 and 1850?

Grow, like other northern radicals, supported a policy of boldness. In a party caucus he expressed himself against all southern efforts "to bully" the free states into concessions.[12] Conciliation must not be offered in response to disunionist alarms or threats. He asked, what better platform was there for the North and South to stand on than that of Union, the constitutions, and the laws? The Republican party and its president, in his opinion, were entitled to fair play. Grow's enemies considered him dangerous. As early as 1856 he reputedly had told the voters that they would be better off with the southerners out of the Union. Others shared this feeling. Shortly after Lincoln's election, the *New York Tribune* of November 9 proclaimed the right of secession: "If the Cotton States shall decide that they can do better out of the Union than in it, we insist on letting them go in peace." A number of other Republican journals, reconciled to disunion, embraced the proposal of peaceful dissolution. The gulf between radicals like Greeley, Grow, and Stevens, and moderates like Bates, Sherman, and Corwin, was to plague Lincoln in the days ahead.

Soon after the House had passed the homestead bill, Grow found himself engaged in the discussions over the state of the Union. Unlike his visibility in earlier debates over Kansas, he managed this time to keep a low profile. A conspicuously silent Grow eased his way around the House chamber, arranging deals and striking party policy. Long speeches and personal confrontations were no longer his style. Neither did he extensively participate in deliberations over the many conciliatory proposals that were presented almost daily. At times he punctuated floor debate with some point of order. Perhaps the moderates were pulling the reins on Grow to keep alive any last hope of revitalizing the Union. That hope, however, quickly faded as more and more southerners resigned their seats, folded their tents, and went home.

Grow's voting pattern illustrated the split between the moderate and radical wings of his party. He opposed the December 4 motion of Alexander Boteler of Virginia to create a special committee of one representative from each state to study the serious political condition of the nation and to submit recommendations. When resolutions from this Committee of Thirty-three came to the floor, Grow was one of fourteen who voted to table them; the effort failed. He also voted against joint resolutions that proposed certain amendments to the Constitution. Perhaps the most controversial of these, a proposed amendment that would have been the Thirteenth, would safeguard slavery in the states where it existed. On February 28, 1861, Grow joined sixty-four other Republicans to oppose this constitutional guarantee to the South, but a number of Republicans, including Sherman, Corwin, Morrill, Colfax, and Grow's fellow Pennsylvanians, Scranton, McPherson, and Moorhead, supported it. The proposed amendment was passed by a 133–65 vote and then passed the Senate, 24–12.[13] Though the two-thirds vote was attained, the amendment was never ratified by the states.

Grow was negative toward both the work of the Committee of Thirty-three and the compromise proposals of Sen. John Crittenden of Kentucky, but he joined most other Republicans to adopt a resolution repealing the personal liberty laws. While it is true that Lincoln favored enforcement of the fugitive slave law, there is no evidence to suggest that his willingness to accept a constitutional amendment protecting slavery in the states was openly opposed by Grow. In the weeks following the presidential election, both men were consistent in their opposition to compromise. It was owing to the president's influence, perhaps, that the Crittenden proposals never had a chance. Many Republicans were disappointed, but not Grow. To the Democrats it appeared obvious that the Republicans were divided on the eve of their first administration. While the party's rank and file were having second thoughts regarding their choice of Lincoln, the *New York Herald* commented that their leaders, "blinded by partisan feeling or corrupted by a thirst for spoils and power," were leading the nation to ruin.[14]

Grow was undoubtedly one of the leaders this Democratic newspaper had in mind. He remained the prototype of radical intransigence that had been described a year earlier by a *Chicago Journal* correspondent:

I regard Galusha A. Grow of Penn. as one of the strongest, if not the ablest man on the Republican side. He is a tall man, of about 35 years of age. But a few grey hairs have crept in among his glossy black hair, while his whiskers and well-formed moustache are as black as the raven's wing. He is about 5 ft. 11 inches high, rather slim, but straight as an arrow. His expressive face indicates culture and thought, and his sharp black eyes, denote spirit and intellect, and though he has not yet addressed the House at length, yet what he has said evidences a strong mind, a fearless heart, and a deep devotion to principle, while his clear tones, easy and distinct enunciation, and unequivocal language, command the attention and carry conviction to his auditors. He is a skillful tactician, thoroughly acquainted with Parliamentary law and the rules of the House, and his points of order are always well taken and sustained by the best authorities. He is gentlemanly in his intercourse with members of the House, and is much feared by the Democracy, as he never speaks at random, but always hits the mark with vigor and force which are irresistable [*sic*]. But for the belief that his elevation to the Speaker's chair would militate against the chances of Mr. Forney, from the same State, for the Clerkship, Mr. Grow would have been the Republican candidate for Speaker. Still, I am glad that this line of policy retains so able and fearless a leader and so eloquent and powerful a debater on the floor, a position he is so preeminently qualified to grace.[15]

As chairman of the territorial committee, Grow faced the legislative problem of organizing the territories of Dakota, Colorado, and Nevada. He shocked many by urging the adoption of territorial bills that contained no prohibition of slavery. After seven years of almost exclusive agitation on the question of slavery in the territories, the Republicans suddenly decided to abandon the cardinal principle of their political creed. The radicals in both houses, James Blaine commented, offered neither explanation nor apology for their "extraordinary change of position."[16] Grow admitted that he agreed with James Green of Missouri, chairman of the Senate Committee on Territories, that there should be no reference to slavery in any of the bills. Ironically, Republicans and Democrats in both houses agreed not to delay the organization of the territories by rekindling old embers around the slavery issue. Grow was asked repeatedly by William Simms of

Kentucky whether the bills included the Wilmot Proviso. Apparently the Kentuckian could not believe what he was witnessing. Grow politely assured him there was no reference to slavery prohibition in any of the bills. Thus, without controversy, the territorial bills for Dakota, Colorado, and Nevada were passed easily.

Why the unexpected switch in Republican positions after the radicals and Lincoln had been inflexible on the territorial question? Slavery exclusion clauses in territorial bills had been a trademark of Republican consistency. Douglas did not hesitate to remark that the organization bills left slavery in the three territories precisely where his 1854 law had left it in Kansas.[17] Greeley explained the bills as an attempt "to soothe the prevalent madness" in Congress and to strengthen the southern unionists, but the legislation did not stop the secessionists from taking a walk. With a Republican administration only days away, the radicals knew there was no chance of slavery being planted in these territories. The Republican anomaly, though treated by some as a strong indictment of the party that had been forged in the fires of the territorial issue, became a mere academic question. The Republicans viewed the territories as basically free. Since no southerner was likely to take his slaves there, any effort at this time to renew the ruckus over whether slavery should be excluded seemed purposeless. Besides, with the admission of Kansas as a free state in 1861, the territorial question was no longer important.

Lincoln's inauguration found Washington hoping for the best but fearing the worst. War seemed imminent; seven states of the lower South had already seceded. Apparently Grow was involved in preparations by the incoming administration to meet the crisis. In an interview with Ida Tarbell years later, Grow described a plan that leading Republican figures had made weeks prior to the start of the war. According to Grow, he had met in March with Wilmot, Fenton, Postmaster General Montgomery Blair, and other cabinet members at Blair's residence in Silver Spring, Maryland. At this meeting, Grow claimed, he and Blair had presented a plan to offer Gov. Sam Houston of Texas a commission as a major general in the Union army if he could assume full command in Texas and bring that state back to the Union side. Grow further claimed that Lincoln had accepted the plan and commissioned G. H. Giddings, who once lived not far from Grow in Susquehanna County, to deliver the secret plan to Houston. Grow was sure his friend Giddings had accepted the mission, had journeyed to Texas, and had seen Houston, but it was already too late. Texas had seceded and the secessionists were in control. The obstinate governor refused to take an oath to the Confederacy and was subsequently removed.[18]

Grow went home, but his stay was cut short by the attack upon Fort Sumter. On April 15 Lincoln issued his proclamation convening Congress in special session on July 4 and calling for 75,000 volunteers. Three days later, Grow met up with some of these men at Harrisburg while on his way to Washington. They attracted attention, for they were in their blackened dress of the mines and factories. This small band of heroic workers from Pennsylvania arrived with Grow in Washington and were quartered in the committee rooms surrounding the hall of the House of Representatives. Here they remained until they received their weapons and equipment for combat.

Until the arrival of the Seventh New York and the Sixth Massachusetts Regiments, the nation's capital was cut off from railroad and telegraph service to the free states. Washington had the appearance of a deserted city, Grow wrote.[19] Few people wandered in the streets; soldiers stood as sentinels at approaches to the city. Residents feared local secessionists or mobs from Baltimore or Alexandria might trigger an uprising at any time. They organized themselves into two military companies called the Kansas and Clay Brigades. James H. Lane of Kansas was in charge of the first and Cassius M. Clay of Kentucky headed the other. Grow joined Clay's, which was housed at the dance hall adjacent to the Willard Hotel. The War Department furnished these undisciplined "minute men" with guns and ammunition, which fortunately did not have to be used. The civilian army continued in service until the two military units arrived from Annapolis. From that time, Washington became a gigantic armed camp.

The Speakership

"We are making history and not reading it," editorialized John Forney on the eve of the special session of Congress.[20] "We have too much at stake in the present, too much to contend for in the future, to pause and glorify the past." He asked those who wished to commemorate the Fourth of July simply to renew their allegiance to the principles of the past. It was a time of rededication of one's faith in the American dream.

To those who walked the streets of Washington that summer day, that faith, that rededication, seemed to hinge upon the military cordon that separated them from the rebel forces nearby. Looking through his windows, Vice-President Hamlin watched some 20,000 New York soldiers march by, their uniforms and bayonets glistening in the sun.[21] Long trains of government wagons with canvas tops, drawn by horses and mules and heavy with every kind of army supply, moved slowly along Pennsylvania Avenue. Now and then a battery of artillery or a squadron of cavalry swept over the same swampy thoroughfare. This awesome display of firepower was indeed impressive.

But Washingtonians were oblivious to another kind of firepower that was being demonstrated inside the House of Representatives. The newly elected Speaker of the Thirty-seventh Congress, showing the wrath of an angry god, highlighted his opening address with these words: "No flag alien to the sources of the Mississippi river will ever float permanently over its mouths till its waters are crimsoned in human gore; and not one foot of American soil can ever be wrenched from the jurisdiction of the Constitution of the United States until it is baptized in fire and blood."[22]

For several minutes, the packed galleries and the floor maintained a crescendo of thunderous applause and shouts. Thaddeus Stevens, who had nominated the Speaker, smiled sardonically as only he could do, while C. L. Vallandigham of Ohio shrugged his shoulders in total disbelief. The noise and confusion in the hall matched that which gripped the city outside — a city torn between the joy of celebrating the nation's eighty-fifth birthday and the horror of seeing it prepare for a holocaust.

The Speaker was Galusha Grow. At thirty-seven, he was rapidly approaching the zenith of his brilliant career. His scorn for the Confederacy and the fiery patriotism that laced his inaugural remarks surprised no one who knew him. His friends supported him for his strong antislavery convictions, his leadership on the floor, and the recognized skills demanded by the office he now held. His opponents, however, interpreted his attitude of righteous indignation toward the South as a battle cry. Some of them had favored more moderate contenders for the position of Speaker, such as Colfax of Indiana or Frank Blair of Missouri. The three Republican choices represented different rays of the party, with Grow farthest to the left. The *New York Times* of July 2 had given the edge to Blair, who seemed most popular among the younger members of the party and most able to strike a deal with the backers of Forney, a candidate for the clerkship. Another paper praised Blair as the best qualified because of his "national" attitudes, which were needed to unite the various factions.[23] Colfax apparently had decided as early as July 3 to withdraw from the race, announcing that his candidacy had been declared contrary to his wishes. His biographer suggests that he withdrew because he was afraid of losing.[24] One thing was certain: the Republicans had agreed not to tolerate any protracted conflict over the speakership. There was too much to be done.

On opening day of the session, Grow was easily elected. After the first ballot he had seventy-one votes, nine short of victory. Blair, in second place with forty, withdrew and urged his supporters to switch their votes; twenty-eight did. Stevens broke up the House when he begged his lone supporter to switch his vote. Grow won with ninety-nine votes. He had voted for Blair, who, along with W. A. Richardson of Illinois, escorted the Pennsylvanian to the Speaker's chair where Elihu Washburne administered the oath of office. Grow then thanked his supporters and attacked the malcontents who, in his opinion, were conspiring to destroy the U.S. Constitution.

Any hope of sectional reconciliation died with the election of Grow. The organization of the House with Blair as Speaker and Forney as Clerk might have slowed the progress of the radicals. But it is doubtful that the moderates could have succeeded very long in the Thirty-seventh Congress. The attack against Sumter gave the radicals all the leverage they needed to impress the whole world that they had been right all along in their assessment of the "traitors." Now it was the responsibility of those in office to protect the Union and the Constitution. Southern militancy had to be first matched and then checkmated by northern radicalism. With Grow in the chair and Stevens directing strategy on the floor, the radicals could not miss.

When it came time to make committee assignments, Grow did what was expected of him — he appointed radicals and friends. A few of the latter had leaned toward compromise. In a true Jacksonian manner, Grow believed in using patronage and spoils to the fullest advantage. Although he was serving his third term, Vallandigham of Ohio received only a minor committee assignment, perhaps because he had been a gadfly to the Republicans or simply a member of the minority party.[25] Stevens chaired the powerful Ways and Means, which assumed the function of the later Committee on Appropriations. The appointment had to amuse McClure, who earlier had said that Stevens was "utterly unfitted" to administer the nation's finances.[26] Other chairmen included Elihu Washburne, Fenton, Potter, Lovejoy, Colfax, Covode, Blair, and John Ashley of Ohio.

There was little doubt what direction the new House would pursue. Grow's enemies called his appointees abolitionists and disunionists. Even members of the cabinet raised questions about Grow's appointive powers. Secretary of the Navy Giddeon Welles was annoyed with Grow for not consulting with him on appointments that affected his department.[27] Secretary of the Treasury Chase was similarly concerned.[28] Regardless, the radicals worked together with moderates and Democrats to support the emergency war measures, including

Lincoln's call for troops, a law that recognized the "insurrection," and the "Crittenden resolution," which declared that the war was being waged to defend the supremacy of the Constitution and to preserve the Union.

It was Grow's fortune to be Speaker during one of the nation's critical moments. The Thirty-seventh Congress faced an awesome task. It had to raise, organize, and equip military forces, and to find the means to support them and the government as well. Yet its performance record was impressive. Before it adjourned in early August, the special session had passed more than sixty bills, and productivity was to continue into the second and third sessions. Fortunately the Republicans enjoyed a comfortable majority and were able when necessary to ride roughshod over the Democratic opposition. A call for the question often ended the Democrats' efforts at prolonged debate.

Though they protested and harangued, the Democrats helped establish a bipartisan war policy. They refused to take responsibility for starting the war, but now that it had begun, they were willing to support measures to fight it. Only Vallandigham spoke out against coercion and argued in favor of compromise and northern concessions to the South. And though the Democrats may not have made many positive contributions to the acts of this Congress, some of them supported legislation providing for the railroads, the Department of Agriculture, and free land to settlers. In general, they united as a party on issues relating to war priorities, blacks, and constitutional rights, and were divided on economic issues.[29]

Speaker Grow was firm, calm, and precise in construing the rules. Even the Democrats came to respect him as a presiding officer. He may have been the first to descend from the rostrum and take part in debate as he did in the fight for the homestead bill in 1862. Rep. William Holman of Indiana said of Grow: "No man who was ever Speaker more largely or more beneficially influenced the general course of our legislation."[30] In his *Speakers of the House,* Hubert Fuller suggests that Thad Stevens dominated both Grow and his successor, Colfax. There is no question that Stevens was the domineering personality on the floor. For that matter, he became the driving force behind Republican strategy off the floor as well. In party caucus, where his word was law, he "brooked no insubordination." In debate, his views usually spirited the extraordinarily unnatural proposals of his party — namely, emancipation, confiscation of rebel property, and reconstruction. His line became the party line. His obtrusive and arrogant behavior reminded Republicans and Democrats of Grow's manner as floor leader. Now, as Speaker, and showing a great respect for the rules of order, Grow did not hesitate to reject his friend Stevens, but it was more with regard to procedure than thought that Grow made his challenge.

One good example occurred on July 18, 1861, when Henry May of Maryland asked for the floor to defend himself against charges that he had had "criminal intercourse" with the rebels in Richmond. John Hutchins of Ohio objected to the way in which May attacked the military authorities in Baltimore. Stevens said May was out of order, but Grow ruled that May was entitled to the floor. Stevens put his protest into the form of a motion, which the chair refused to entertain. When Stevens appealed the decision, Grow insisted he had no control over the train of remarks May might pursue and, therefore, could not rule him out of order. The chair was overruled, but May was permitted to continue.[31]

Though the relationship between Grow and Stevens was noncompetitive, that between the Speaker and Lincoln is more difficult to ascertain. The difficulty arises when the radicals' growing antipathy toward the president is assumed. Grow's radicalism might therefore be suspect as preventing any genuine harmony between the two men. But the evidence does not support that suspicion. To the contrary, the men seemed to get along admirably, at least during Grow's speakership. If Grow harbored any bad feelings toward the president, he forgot them later in life. He then spoke warmly of Lincoln and considered him the nation's greatest president. "Every time I met him (and for two years I was with him several times each week) I was deeply impressed by the grandeur of his character, brought into strong relief by the lights and shadows of the war." As a judge of men and public opinion, Grow believed Lincoln to be almost infallible, a leader who never rubbed Congress the wrong way and who handled men masterfully. In contrast, Grow doubted seriously whether Seward, had he been president, would have been able to keep Lincoln's cabinet together for two weeks. To Grow the chief executive remained always fearless and patient. The slaughter of soldiers agonized him, but he never relinquished hope. In one of the darkest moments of the war following the humiliation of Bull Run, Lincoln told Grow one evening: "My boys are green at the fighting business, but wait till they get licked enough to raise their dander! Then the cry will be, 'On to Richmond,' and no 'Stonewall' will stop them!"[32]

Lincoln was influential in seeing that Grow did not enter the army. Aside from his brief stint in Clay's Brigade, which his enemies derisively referred to as a "knife-and-fork brigade," Grow saw no military service. After the adjournment of the special session, he did write to

Ben Butler and asked to be appointed to Butler's staff so that he might acquire field experience before the regular session. Butler welcomed Grow to join his staff at the rank of major.[33] Lincoln and some of Grow's friends advised against the idea, and Grow heeded their advice.

As Speaker, Grow had to change his life style. Among his expected duties was the entertainment of diplomats and other dignitaries. For a bachelor who liked his privacy, this seemed a strange and onerous responsibility. He asked his brother, Frederick, and his sister-in-law to come and live with him in Washington. As it turned out, Helen Grow became a wonderful hostess. She was the former Helen Fuller of Voluntown, Connecticut, who had married Frederick more than a decade earlier. Also assisting Grow on special occasions with honored guests was Lincoln's secretary, John Hay, who acted as liaison between the White House and the Speaker. Hay and Grow became good friends.

Grow liked to be in the company of soldiers. He welcomed them to the nation's capital, entertained them at his home, and introduced a number from his home district to the president. With Helen Grow he spent a great deal of his free time visiting them in the camps and hospitals. The Grows took gifts and flowers and tried to comfort the men who were homesick or in pain. Often they joined the cavalcade of civilian carriages that crossed into northern Virginia, where the persistent smell of death prepared them for the horrors of war. Hour after hour they searched for familiar names and faces among the trains and wagons carrying the broken bodies of the wounded and dying. Some of the casualties were from home units, like the Susquehanna Volunteers—Company K of the Thirty-fifth Pennsylvania Regiment, which had taken a good beating at Fredericksburg. Much of Grow's geniality and concern was sincere; some of it was simply political showmanship. The fighting men saw him both as a politician determined to crush the rebels in a noble cause and as a plain Tunkhannock bark peeler who still yearned for the friendly forests and streams back home. The war years in Washington were hard on Grow. Later he would not miss them half as much as the earlier years.

When he returned to the House to begin the regular session, Grow braced himself for what proved to be a critical time for the Union and the Republican party. The stupendous problems of the war and the limited accomplishments of the Union armies worried him. Pressures on party leadership increased as voters demanded to know why it was taking so long to defeat the rebels. Blair of Missouri had criticized General Fremont, a hero to many radicals, and also Congress for refusing to vote for more troops. When Lincoln removed Fremont from command in October, the anger of the radicals was intense. Democratic officers were moving into key military posts. One of them, Gen. George B. McClellan, came under fire from the radicals, who complained to Lincoln of the general's inability to push back the enemy. Finally, both houses of Congress called for a joint committee "to inquire into the conduct of the present war." To this committee, Grow appointed D. W. Gooch of Massachusetts, G. W. Julian of Indiana, John Covode of Pennsylvania, and Moses Odell of New York. The members went after officers not sympathetic to the radical program, as the Inquisition had gone after heretics.

By this time Grow was convinced that Congress would have to come to some understanding over slavery as a war issue. Some members contended against emancipation and the confiscation of rebel property; the unity that had been manifest in the special session no longer existed. There was an obvious breach between the Republicans and representatives from the border states as well as skirmishes among the Republicans themselves. Some Democratic editors plainly assessed the political situation as a simple tug of war between abolitionists and conservatives, with the president in the middle. They predicted that the abolitionists would triumph and pull Lincoln to their side.

Anyone who believed that Grow, as Speaker, might be impartial in this power struggle had to be ignorant of the fanaticism that guided House extremists. No sooner had Congress convened than Grow and a dozen other radicals, including Stevens, Bingham, and Morrill, caucused to determine what strategies were to be pursued with respect to antislavery and emancipation bills.[34] It was a brain trust similar to that which had directed anti-Nebraskans to the election of Banks in the Thirty-fourth Congress. Fearing that the sharp differences over slavery between them and the more conservative wing might widen, this inner group did not bother to invite all members of the party. But they soon learned they could not have everything they wanted. Eventually the caucus agreed on a middle course of freeing the slaves of rebels as a war measure. Lincoln's plan providing for gradual emancipation by voluntary action by slave states, with federal support for colonization and compensation, did not sit well with the House radicals. Yet they supported a joint resolution requested by Lincoln that called for federal assistance to any state that adopted a plan of gradual emancipation. A month later the radicals were jubilant when both houses passed an emancipation bill for the District of Columbia. In the lower house amendment was not allowed and debate was limite

It seemed that the radicals were saying with Jesuitical adroitness that they wanted no interference with their plan to free the slaves. On April 16 the president signed the bill.

Like so many Republicans, Grow had moved quickly from a position of noninterference with slavery to one favoring emancipation. He knew that his support of abolition was not going to bring smiles to the faces of many of his constituents. Negative reaction to emancipation in his district was probably more than the Republicans had anticipated, yet he was also committed to a total-war concept that identified the slavocrats as the treasonous perpetrators of the rebellion. Whatever his party could do to destroy their world, including the freeing of every black, had to be done. With characteristic candor he instinctively followed what were to him the moral laws of history; he probably believed his selection as Speaker to be less political than providential. His missionary zeal surprised no one, especially those who knew him well. They did not have to ask where he stood on the issues.

Deliberate in his workings with party members, Grow still was not always sure how things might turn out. Though he was generally careful to have radical representation on special committees, the results were often less than he desired. Final reports led to intraparty squabbling, with Thad Stevens usually in the center of these conflicts. Arrogant, dictatorial, and sarcastic, he antagonized Republicans as easily as Democrats. Grow was often unable to avoid clashes among his friends. He admitted that he could correct the errors he made in the chair, but he could not correct those made by colleagues on the floor. When the committee investigating government contracts released its findings, a fiery discussion led to charges and countercharges and opened the way to sharp rebuke of the War and Treasury Departments.

Critics' scrutiny of government dealings with war contractors put Cameron on the spot. Sloppy practices by his department were embarrassing to the administration. The committee's report of December 1861 indicated that Cameron was guilty of mismanagement. Furthermore, he had hired an intimate friend, newspaperman Alexander Cummings, to purchase army supplies, to charter vessels, and so forth. The committee felt that Cummings was totally unfit for the job and that his appointment was "unjustifiable and injurious" to the public interest.

The problem was too big for Lincoln to ignore. For some time he had contemplated the removal of this secretary of war who had become such a liability. Cameron not only brought trouble by the actions of his office, but also by favoring a plan to arm the slaves against the rebels, which became part of a report Cameron attempted to circulate without Lincoln's knowledge. The President managed to have the report recalled. Cameron then consented to omit the controversial suggestions. Democrats made the most of the faux pas. They speculated that the wily Pennsylvanian wanted to put slaves into the front lines and reward them with 160 acres each for the scalps of their masters! Lincoln had little choice but to accept Cameron's resignation. The coup de grace came later when the House adopted a resolution of censure against Cameron. His biographer writes: "Following Lincoln's call for troops, Cameron's performance was that of a nervous, confused, embarrassed executive who had completely lost control of the situation."[35] Grow said of the Secretary: "No one who knew Simon Cameron well could doubt his patriotism and loyalty to the Administration, but it was evident from the first that he was not the right man for the great task of carrying on the fiercest civil conflict of all time. No one knew this better than he."[36]

Grow was one of the first Republicans to raise the ire of the secretary of war. After Lincoln had issued a call for troops, Cameron refused to accept those beyond quotas assigned to the states. His action annoyed governors who were caught in the frenzy of war fever and asked that they be allowed to send more men. Writing to Cameron on May 5, 1861, Grow expressed his own frustration:

You have no conception of feeling, universal in the Northern mind, for the prosecution of war. . . . If the Administration fails to prosecute the war . . . it will sink to the popular heart below that of the Buchanan Administration.[37]

Grow advised the secretary to receive all the men who offered their services but to detain them in the states until they were called for. In his judgment the enthusiasm of the hour ought not to be repressed by flat refusals on the part of the government. Spurred by ardent patriotism, Grow's frankness was more than Cameron wished to honor. He undoubtedly included Grow among those Republican leaders who had plotted against him. If he had tried to win their favor by advocating the use of ex-slaves in the army, then he failed.

Of no small importance in this session was nonmilitary legislation, especially that dealing with the public domain. The Thirty-seventh Congress was noted for its eagerness to dispose of the public lands. It established policies that were to continue long after the war, perhaps with as much impact upon the nation's economy as the war itself. One such policy was the college land grant, which provided a generous chunk of public land to the states for the support of education. Justin Morrill dedicated himself to this measure with as much enthusiasm as Grow generated for the homestead bill, but their legislative plans became antagonistic. In the Thirty-fifth Congress, Grow had voted against the agricultural college land-grant bill, which was passed and then vetoed by Buchanan, as he had voted consistently against grants to railroads. Anything that rivaled his homestead bill invoked his immediate displeasure. Yet, as Speaker, he did not try to block its adoption, even though it was destined to remove large areas from entry under homestead. Both the Grow and Morrill measures had beome strong features of the Republican program. With the party in full command, it was a foregone conclusion that each would be adopted in some form.

Despite Lovejoy's candid remark that the Republican party stood pledged to the enactment of the homestead bill, it encountered many objections. Some of these came from representatives of the border states who aired traditionally southern arguments. But Republicans asked whether this was the best time to give away land when federal finances were under serious strain. And were those men who did not enter military service to enjoy an advantage under the bill over those who did? Some easterners who preferred the college land-grant bill saw no harm in postponing action on homestead and delayed the bill in December.

Grow was concerned. On February 21 he broke with tradition and left the rostrum to deliver his final plea for the enactment of the bill. His remarks were brief.[38] The bill had been discussed for so long, he said, that it should be "matured enough for the immediate action of the Representatives." It had been passed by the House five times in the last ten years. He repeated many of his old arguments and then challenged those eastern Republicans who wanted the public lands reserved as a basis of credit: "The retention of the lands by the Government will in no way enhance its credit. The standard of credit with a nation is not the amount of unproductive property that it may possess, but the ability of its people to pay taxes."

Grow was willing to give soldiers every possible opportunity to benefit under the bill without discriminating against others. He opposed his good friend Potter of Wisconsin who wanted to combine a bounty of cash and land for soldiers with the homestead idea. Under a July 1861 law, soldiers were already receiving money bounties. Grow admonished his colleagues that, while they were providing with an open hand for the soldier on the tented field, they ought not forget the heroes of the wilderness who were paving the way for a new civilization.

Exactly one week after Grow's comments, the bill was overwhelmingly passed in the House, 107-16.[39] Apparently the Speaker's midnight plea worked. Whatever opposition to the bill remained simply melted away. Most of the negative votes came from the border states; the remainder were largely cast by those who either wanted land bounties or desired to reserve the public lands as a source of proceeds. The Senate did not begin debate on the House bill until early May. Little opposition was anticipated. Probably the biggest concern among the senators was making sure that homesteads would not be available to the rebels. So, in the first section of the bill they inserted a qualifier stating that the bill's benefits would go to those who had "never borne arms against the United States Government, or given aid to its enemies." They also struck out the money bounties to soldiers and forbade one person to enter more than 160 acres. The House bill had carried a bounty of thirty dollars cash for each three-months' soldier, one hundred dollars for those enlisted for the whole war, and awarded each soldier a quarter-section in addition. It was this provision that Grow had been reluctant to see included. Most likely, he urged his friend Wade to use his influence against the provision in the Senate. On May 6 the upper house passed the amended bill by a 33-7 vote.[40] Grow was eternally grateful to Wade for helping to eliminate the bounty clause.

The House refused to accept the Senate amendments and asked for a conference. Potter was upset with the action taken against the military bounty. Grow continued to press for a quick settlement; the chances of the bill being talked to death were nil. Neither was there to be a veto. A month before his inauguration, Lincoln had declared: "In regard to the homestead bill, I am in favor of settling the wild lands into small parcels so that every poor man may have a home."[41] After a short parley that satisfied everyone's dignity, the conferees reached an agreement. In a letter to the *Bradford Reporter,* Grow wrote that he had just signed the final bill and, thus, the "long struggle for the land for the landless [was] at last consummated."[42] On May 20, 1862, Lincoln applied his signature.

In its final form the Homestead Act was in essence an embodiment of the provisions characteristic of Grow's standing bill. Title to the homestead was acquired by continuous residence, improvements over a five-year period, and the payment of a nominal fee. The applicant had to swear he or she was the head of a family or twenty-one years of age, had not borne arms against the United States or given aid to its enemies, and that the application was for "his or her exclusive use and benefit." The applicant also had to be a citizen or had to have filed a declaration of intention of becoming one. He was not to enter more than 160 acres. At the end of the five-year residence he received a patent for the land, provided he had not abandoned his claim for more than six months at any time.[43]

For Grow the homestead drama ended happily. Signing the bill for which he had so consistently labored for ten years had to be most rewarding. Through this measure, he hoped, the public domain would go to the toiling millions where it belonged. Despite its many limitations and shortcomings, the act did make a significant contribution. It transformed potential economic independence into reality; many persons with little capital but with abundant enthusiasm and a thirst for adventure acquired land. In his careful analysis of the Thirty-seventh Congress, Leonard P. Curry suggests that the Homestead Act fostered the illusion that the United States was a nation of sturdy, independent yeoman farmers, when in reality it was rapidly becoming an urbanized, industrial society; the era of the yeoman farmer had passed.[44] Certainly Grow harbored no unrealistic impressions of those poorer classes who would avail themselves of the act's benefits. To him the nation's development was the history of the common man. Granting a parcel of the public domain to the actual settler did more than pay homage to a contrived image of a rural America. It was a direct response to a growing desire to develop the West with federal policies that recognized man's right to the soil, and it continued to strengthen an agricultural economy that would be needed to feed an industrial society. Grow never abandoned the idea that free government and the pillars of state must ever rest upon the hearthstone. He was sure the Homestead Act promoted that idea.

The difficulty with the homestead bill was mild compared with the storm that developed over the ship canal bill. This legislation was written to provide easy passage for armed and naval vessels between the Mississippi River and Lake Michigan, and for the enlargement of locks on the Erie and Oswego Canals in New York State. The Republicans were sharply divided on the issue of federal funding for canals. Pennsylvanians, including Grow, opposed the measure. Why should their citizens be taxed, they asked, to underwrite canal projects in other states when Pennsylvania had always financed its own lines of communication? Abram Olin of New York and Washburne of Illinois, Republican supporters of the bill, were annoyed with the Pennsylvanians. Olin charged the railroads in Pennsylvania and New York of milking western farmers by levying exorbitant fees. In the past year, he estimated, rail rates had increased between 30 and 40 percent. He was particularly upset with Stevens and accused him of trying to "joke" the measure off the floor. Not wishing to appropriate the money, the Pennsylvanian had introduced an amendment that would have given his state $100 million to "slackwater" the Susquehanna. At least that river had water, he quipped, whereas the poor Illinois River, not known for its abundant flow, would have to draw water from Lake Michigan until the lake became bone dry!

Washburne took his frustration out on his good friend Grow. The Speaker had been charged with stacking several committees with opponents of the ship canal bill. As a measure designed to strengthen the defenses of the lakes, the bill had been sent to the Committee on Military Affairs. Grow had replaced two of the committee's members, Francis Blair and James Jackson — both of whom had departed for military service, with men who opposed the bill — namely, Edward McPherson and George Yeaman. He also replaced John Clernand of Ways and Means with Horace Maynard, another opponent who would vote against appropriations. Washburne went further and accused Grow of ignoring the Northwest and its eight million people when he appointed his standing committees. The Speaker was absent the day his friend vented his anger, but upon returning he refuted Washburne's allegations. Almost every state of the Northwest had been given a chairmanship of an important committee; he did not feel he had slighted that section. Fenton and Cox came to Grow's defense. Cox added that not everyone in the Northwest was in favor of the ship canal bill. Dejected, Washburne watched as a number of Republicans helped defeat the bill.[45]

Controversy also characterized the debates over conscription and the legal tender act. Again, the Republicans were divided. Those in favor of the money bill said that it was a necessary war measure. For a hard-money enthusiast like Grow, the authorization of non-interest bearing greenbacks was a difficult pill to swallow, yet he apparently did nothing to prevent its adoption. He did not leave the chair, as he had in the case of the homestead bill, to join the opposition. Still, its immediate impact upon the nation lacked the sting of the military bill. Demostrations and protests spread through the North as the enforcement of the conscription law produced difficulties and anxieties. Despite these exhibitions, the Republican leadership was again sure it had done the right thing to bring the rebellion to a speedy end. Unfortunately, at the close of the Thirty-seventh Congress in March 1863, the Union was not near to victory, and some Republicans, including Grow, had already paid dearly for the fact at the polls.

Aside from contributing to the success of the radical Republicans, Grow's speakership also signified the beginning of a new legislative era. Before secession, government policy had catered to rural interests, hard money, and low tariffs; states' rights and laissez-faire had been watchwords. It was a time when many former Democrats from small towns and farm communities who were now Republicans — like Grow — had served their political apprenticeships. In 1856 Speaker Banks had been criticized for appointing these relatively unknown rural representatives to key committee positions. Their provincialism paralleled their free-soilism; their unity revolved about Kansas.

Soon they had to tailor their views to meet the demands of a generation that refused to see the future simply in terms of slavery and an agrarian economy. Recognizing this, the Republicans, without fettering their antislavery bias, structured their platform philosophy to accommodate more of the electorate on economic issues. After secession the party was able to give the North the programs it had long desired. The result was something that looked like Clay's American system — high tariffs, internal improvements (a railroad to the Pacific), and a national banking system. Though these programs were designed to appeal to business and manufacturing interests, Republicans argued that all Americans benefited from them. The Homestead Act and the Morrill Land-Grant Act emphasized the party's commitment to labor by providing free farms and educational opportunity.

For Grow it was not difficult to make the philosophical transition from being a rural Democrat to Republican Speaker of a wartime Congress. His liberalism for years had called for greater involvement by the central government. To effect federal legislation by nationalizing the issues was his way of promoting the common good, as in the national homestead policy. Still, there were hard decisions for him. Supporting greenbacks was one thing, but defending vindictive measures against the South seemed so much out of character for someone who had always crusaded for the rights of man. Even within the context of waging a war effort, Grow realized that, by negating some of the views he once held, he was only helping his political enemies back home.

Fall of a Gallant Champion

While the month of May 1862 may have been the high-water mark of Grow's legislative career, it was also a time when political fortunes turned against him. The winds of war swept out of Virginia and into the northern tier counties of Pennsylvania, where they agitated a disturbance in the political climate. In early 1862, a Republican-controlled legislature in Harrisburg had passed an apportionment bill that was a revision of the Apportionment Act of 1861.[46] Under the new law, Susquehanna County with its population of 36,000 was joined to Luzerne and its 90,000 to make up the new Twelfth Congressional District. Luzerne Democrats cried foul and charged Republicans with gerrymandering to consolidate their power and to "abolitionize" Luzerne.[47] Determined to fight back, they aimed their guns at Grow, who was looking forward to his seventh consecutive term. For the first time he was without a constituency that was amenable to his radicalism. The old "Wilmot-Grow district" was gone.

As the election of 1862 neared, Grow found himself under increasing attack by Democrats and moderate Republicans. In a real sense, it was guilt by association. Confiscation acts, emancipation, and violations of civil liberties were becoming increasingly unpopular with the majority of Pennsylvanians, who believed that congressional radicals had gone too far. Grow had to share part of the directed criticism. His enemies recalled how, in a meeting in Montrose, Grow had refused to speak unless a black stood beside him. Demonstrations and incidents involving Susquehanna blacks who exhibited a fresh attitude of freedom and importance worried many whites, irrespective of their party affiliations. Republican leadership also expressed concern as a serious backlash to radical exuberance endangered the party's future. Alexander McClure opposed the Emancipation Proclamation and felt that conservative Republicans of the middle states would not sustain it.[48] Along with Curtin and some of the moderates, McClure renewed efforts to explore forming a coalition party with Forney and the Union Democrats to support the administration and the vigorous prosecution of the war. In 1861 a number of prominent prowar Democrats had been placed on the Republican ticket in the state elections. The combination had worked then. Now, a year later, many believed the same kind of magic should be tried again.

But Grow was too set in his radical ways to move toward any political center. A. J. Gerritson of the *Montrose Democrat* accused Grow of using threats and patronage, especially among post office appointees, to spurn the union movement. Republicans like Grow, Wilmot, and Stevens suffered from tunnel vision. Gerritson suggested that these radical hard-liners, branded by the "nigger question" and infatuated with their own bigotry, self-righteousness, and invincibility, had rejected union sentiment and now faced defeat. And defeat was sure to come, the editor prophesied.[49]

No doubt Grow's unyielding position on the South and his accommodating attitude toward emancipation helped upend him with moderate and conservative voters. The *Luzerne Union* labeled him an abolitionist demagogue who had poisoned the northern mind against fellow Americans in the South. It made reference to an address in Scranton in which Grow had allegedly said that he hoped to see the South made a desert waste, burned to such a crisp that a carrion crow could not fly over without starving. Stevens had made a similar comment in Congress. The paper instructed its readers not to vote for this dangerous man, Grow, the "prince of fanatics," unless they cared to watch their tax dollars used to compensate slaveholders so that four million blacks might be turned loose to feed upon Union armies and northern industries. The *Union* dared Grow to go to the mines and factories in the district and explain to the Irish and German workers how he planned to permit blacks to compete with them for their jobs. The Democratic message in Luzerne was clear: "We are not opposed to blacks being set free, but we don't want them here!"[50]

Susquehanna Democrats were no kinder. On the eve of the congressional election, Gerritson of the *Democrat* summarized all that was wrong with candidate Grow.[51] Not only did he, as Speaker, feast the abolitionist Wendell Phillips but also, as a member of the Thirty-sixth Congress, he had called John Brown an "avenging angel" and had endorsed Helper's book. He was reported to have said, "Not to be an abolitionist is to be a wicked and diabolical instrument of the devil." Even his raving over the Homestead Act came under fire. The timing was poor, the editor contended, for the legislation gave an undue advantage to the "lazy stay-at-homes" over the brave men who went to war. Furthermore — and this was not to be overlooked by any proud Pennsylvanian — one of the first acts taken by Speaker Grow was to remove Buchanan's portrait from the Capitol rotunda!

What may have been the strongest indictment against Grow in the campaign involved a military bounty. Gerritson made the most of the incident. He accused the Grow brothers, who had prospered somewhat by Galusha's living off the public trough, of promising to subscribe $1,000 toward payment of a county bounty to military volunteers but then backing down to $100. The story went something like this: Galusha apparently had subscribed the $1,000 in the name of the Grow brothers, a pledge that ingratiated him with many voters. This gesture had been made, Gerritson insisted, to win back support of those who opposed his renomination because of his public insult of a prominent Montrose Republican, B. S. Bentley. This gentleman and many of his friends turned against Grow after his remarks at a town meeting. The editor claimed Grow's electioneering had worked, but no sooner had he recaptured the confidence and commitment of local Republicans than he insisted he had only meant to pledge $100. "Grow cheated his party into nominating him," Gerritson concluded. The story received a good amount of play.

As an opposition candidate, the Democrats named Charles Denison, a popular young attorney from Luzerne, who had neither a public record to defend nor a personal program to espouse. They also pledged to waive all mere party questions in favor of the Union cause. So deeply ran their convictions that being called "traitors" by Grow and Company did not hold up with the voters. Denison kept a low profile, obviously expecting the gathering momentum against Grow's radicalism to assure his victory. He was right. Grow's catastrophic defeat was symbolic of the retreat some Pennsylvania radicals suffered in 1862. Grow carried Susquehanna by 1,117 votes, but lost to Denison in Luzerne, as expected, by 2,884.[52] The Luzerne Democrats were ecstatic. The majority for the Republican candidate for Congress in 1860 had been 1,347. Thus, a county gain of 4,231 votes in just two years was nothing short of spectacular. Lincoln also carried Luzerne, but Foster defeated Curtin.

Election losses are generally not explained by any single cause. Reapportionment, the slowness of the war, and the uncertainty of emancipation contributed to Grow's defeat in 1862. Grow, an experienced politician, indeed understood election upsets as part of the game. Some of his friends tried to show that his defeat had resulted from causes other than his personal unpopularity and the "fanatical abolition ideas" he advocated. Much was made of the allegation that most of the soldiers, had they been home to vote, would have supported Grow. Democrats countered by suggesting instead that Republican pressures actually had kept some of the men at home or had furloughed them so they would vote for their party's candidate.

Other Grow supporters charged Cameron with having caused their hero's political demise. Friend and editor Ernest Hempstead later wrote: "Deliberately and undoubtedly with the intent to destroy him politically, Mr. Cameron had Mr. Grow's home county of Susquehanna torn from its fellows for many years, Bradford and Tioga, and placed with Luzerne County."[53] Fact or not, Hempstead's explanation is not so far-fetched. Cameron had to sense a serious threat to his suzerainty in Pennsylvania from Grow's meteoric success in Congress. Changing the Speaker's congressional district months prior to election time might temporarily slow that success. No one denied that Cameron had a controlling hand in the state legislature and that bad blood between the two men had been aggravated by Cameron's bid for a cabinet position and his dubious efforts as war secretary. If the two agreed on anything in 1862, it was their hope for a successful war against the South and the adoption of a homestead bill.

Gerritson of the *Democrat,* however, gave most credit to the Democratic organization of Susquehanna for the "squelching" of Grow. The party had cut its losses by holding firm. The Democratic vote for Denison in the county, he pointed out, had been greater than the combined Democratic votes of Tioga and Bradford in their congressional races. "Had the Democracy in this county become reduced as it is in those counties, Grow, and not Denison, would have been our member elect from the new district."[54] A corollary to this observation was that had the old Susquehanna–Tioga–Bradford district not been broken up, Grow would have won by another landslide.

Later, in his farewell message to his constituents, Grow admitted he welcomed a rest from public office.[55] Physically, the last twelve years had been an ordeal. His health was so impaired that one newspaper predicted he might not return to the rigors of politics.[56] But his parting words were not those of a man who was ready to quit a life that he loved so much. Certainly his defeat by Denison did not shake his self-confidence. He was too much a man of action to accept his first setback at the polls as a deathblow to his promising career. He liked the limelight and the attention too much; the cheers from a responsive crowd sustained his spirit as milk nourishes a child. He looked forward to new battles and challenges. He had acquired a national reputation that might someday propel him to high office. He would be back.

Presiding over the third session of the Thirty-seventh Congress, which convened on December 1, 1862, Grow found Republican radicalism as postulated and determined as ever, despite recent Democratic gains. It remained the heart of party ideology, the kinetic force directing public policy. War measures continued, including the controversial conscription bill. Even Lincoln seemed to be coming around as he refused in his message to Congress to retract his emancipation proclamation.

The Democrats had little hope of accomplishing anything in this session. With people like Vallandigham seen as bêtes noires for their condemnation of war programs, the radicals felt comfortably secure. But the Democrats believed that the conservative majority of Americans would turn against the war policies of the Republican party once its destructive and partisan aims were unveiled.[57] The recent election results seemed to support that belief, and Grow's defeat was a good example. Yet it is questionable that he saw his loss to Denison as reflective of a national mood shift against the leadership of his party. And though a sudden change might be in the making, his own posture as a radical was not likely to change. Grow was not to share in the glory of his congressional friends as they reaped the harvests of military victory. When he completed his duties as Speaker in March 1863, the best he hoped was that another elective office awaited him. But the wait was to be a long one.

After Congress adjourned, Grow returned to Glenwood exhausted and in poor health. The evidence of war was everywhere. Many of his friends and neighbors were serving in the military. It is not known how serious he may have been about joining them. He admitted that he had sent a substitute until he could pass a medical examination. Apparently that time never came, for he never was in uniform.

When he arrived home he found his mother seriously ill. Elizabeth Grow, now in her seventies, was a courageous woman who raised a large family and, at the same time, operated several businesses. But the rigors of widowhood and frontier life had taken their toll. Aware of her failing health, she asked Galusha to arrange her affairs and make provision for the division of properties among her children. Samuel Grow, who was several years older than Galusha, presented a temporary problem. He had been unsuccessful in the cotton milling business in Connecticut before settling upon the Grow homestead near Glenwood with his wife, the former Helen Lindley. Elizabeth Grow was glad to have the couple stay with her and planned to give them a share of the estate, but Frederick argued that, since his brother had already enjoyed and lost a fair share, he was not entitled to another share. If their mother wanted to give him additional money, Frederick urged that the money be protected by being put in trust or carefully invested. Samuel and his wife insisted that the money be given to them without conditions. Galusha believed that the decision rested entirely with his mother, who finally consented to Samuel's wish. Thereupon, Frederick angrily departed for a few days, only to return to reconcile with his mother. Galusha was glad the family quarrel had come to an end while his mother was alive. She had always been proud that she had been able to keep her family together.[58]

Shortly after the incident involving the estate, Elizabeth Grow died. Her death grieved Galusha considerably; he had been close to her. With her burial his depression deepened. The endless war, the uncertainties of the family businesses and his political career, and nagging health problems produced a painful period in Grow's life. He tried surveying again but found that he lacked the old stamina. Practicing law was out of the question, and as for a return to politics—well, he was not sure he was quite ready. Being appointed delegate to the Republican National Convention in Baltimore in 1864 was the closest he had come to anything politically exciting since he left Congress. Many of his old friends were there, and so was Simon Cameron, whose increased prestige nationally and in Pennsylvania was a bad omen to Grow. Should this wily manipulator of machiavellian statecraft emerge as the undisputed ruler of Republican politics in the state, Grow's political future was in serious doubt. Up to this time most of his career had been successful and independent of machine politics. But that trend was about to change. His defeat in 1862 was the first indication of that change.

ℬ 12

The Search for a Constituency

GALUSHA GROW, a prominent politician who so often had deplored the sins of capitalism, nevertheless found it worthwhile to turn entrepreneur in an expanding, industrial America. His family business had prepared him to seek bigger stakes and his successful friends encouraged him. In the years following his defeat for reelection in 1862, he ventured into several areas of economic activity. He engaged in the lumbering trade in Luzerne and oil properties in Venango, and, after his return from Texas, he became a producer of coal at Brady's Bend in Clarion County.[1] Still, politics remained his first love. He was always ready to return to the role he wanted most: to serve a constituency.

Yet for three decades the door to elective office remained closed to Grow. Without success he tried several times for the U.S. Senate, the governorship, and even the vice-presidency. His failure was due not to any lack of popular appeal; on the contrary, Grow enjoyed a steady following throughout the commonwealth. Although Andrew Curtin and Thad Stevens were the most charismatic Pennsylvania Republicans with the masses during and immediately after the Civil War, for the balance of the nineteenth century no state Republican exuded as much universal magnetism with the rank and file as did Grow. He sensitized their political palate with emotion-packed speeches that always seemed to end with some scathing remark against those Democratic "traitors" who had left the party's traditional moorings to accommodate the slavocrats. Whenever it came to "waving the bloody shirt," no one did a consistently better job than Grow; he was the living ghost of the hellish days of sectionalism. And he gloried in the support given him by the working classes in his unforgettable struggle for free homesteads.

Grow's inability to win his party's blessings for the offices he sought

221

resulted instead from the longstanding, intense rivalry between the Curtin and Cameron forces for control of Pennsylvania's Union-Republican organization. The two men were mutual irritants in a party that boasted of its diverse personalities and incongruent philosophies. If Grow leaned in any direction, it was toward the Curtin wing. In 1866–1867 the three men became competitors in the race for the U.S. Senate. Cameron walked away with the caucus nomination and emerged as the czar of Republican politics in the state, as Grow and Curtin smarted from defeat.

Cameron's victory made the former Speaker's future in the party at best tenuous. Cameronism and the dynasty it built proved too much for a man who loved his independent roles and who cared little for the craft and machinations of modern politics. Subsequent defeats for the vice-presidency and, again, for the Senate added to his despair. A sought-after sabbatical in Texas as president of a railroad temporarily removed him from the center of contention; his political role became innocuous. Similarly, Curtin's "Siberian exile" as minister to Russia removed Cameron's other old nemesis. For the moment, both Grow and Curtin were gone, but in 1872 they were to haunt Grantism and the Cameron machine.[2]

Three Strikes and You're Out!

In 1866 Grow was busily engaged in watching over his business interests in western Pennsylvania. He had become a victim of the oil fever. A wild, unprecedented era of speculation in the state's oil lands and stocks had begun in 1864 and continued well into the next year. Increased confidence in the petroleum industry prompted many to seek instant fortunes. Not only were ordinary citizens and men occupying high positions in the financial world affected, but leading political figures as well. Grow was so excited that he took up residence at Reno, Venango County.

In December 1865 he had helped organize in New York City the Reno Oil and Land Company, a joint-stock company with a capitalization of $10 million. This company purchased 1,200 acres on the Allegheny River four miles from Oil City and proceeded to drill wells and lay out the town of Reno. The property was the largest body of oil land held by one company in the entire oil region. Grow became its first president and one of its thirteen stockholding directors. He knew little of the oil industry and was probably made president to add prestige to the company. Joining Grow on the board of directors were two old Republican friends from Congress, Sidney Dean of Rhode Island and Augustus Frank of New York. Most of the directors were bankers.

Grow's vice-president was Charles Vernon Culver, a resident of Franklin, Venango County, and a current member of Congress. He had selected the Reno property, being convinced of its oil potential and suitability as the site for a model oil town. Culver was a free-swinging operator whose banking firm of Culver, Penn, and Company owned an interest in a string of banks in the oil region. He was criticized for spending more time with his banks than on the business of legislating. When his firm failed in March 1866, panic seized the region; five banks closed and depositors suffered heavy losses. Grow and his associates were embarrassed by the failure, which was due in part to the strong investment in building Reno, plus a federal tax of one dollar on each barrel of crude. It was more than the industry could withstand in a depression year for the oil fields. Despite these setbacks, the Reno Company continued to work its wells.

Grow's entrepreneurial adventures cast him in the unlikely role of land speculator. It must have been strange for the masses to see their hero associate with money men. His political adversaries were amused to watch the former Speaker strutting the dusty streets of Reno in his silk hat and keeping an eye on oil prices. But Grow wanted a piece of America's economic dream; if necessary, he was willing to forget all the bad things he had said about speculators and moneyed interests. As a result, his capitalistic proclivities may have tarnished his image somewhat with the working class, but they stood him in good stead with the business community that was destined to play a major role in the future of the Republican party. His prospects of gaining an elective office brightened considerably in the oil region. Within the year he was mentioned by oil men as a promising candidate both for the U.S. Senate and the vice-presidency.

Yet hardly anyone in 1866 expected Grow to become the next senator from Pennsylvania. October election returns strongly indicated that the majority in the legislature were either instructed or pledged to support Curtin. Democratic chances of electing a senator were slim without a coalition with one of the Republican contenders. Most observers predicted a contest between Curtin and Cameron and their respective organizations. Between the two men, the wartime governor bore the heavier task of convincing the radicals that he was in tune with their programs and that the charge that he harbored Democratic proclivities was unfounded. Radicalism in this election year was synonymous with true Republicanism and therefore a prerequisite for victory. Among all the major aspirants for the Senate seat, Curtin seemed the most vulnerable. He had to outradicalize the radical contenders.

Curtin's rivals included Grow, Cameron, Stevens, Forney, and James K. Moorhead of Pittsburgh. These men realized that a coalition of some kind was necessary to stop the former governor. The field narrowed when Forney withdrew before the end of the year and urged his supporters to back Stevens. But few people took the candidacy of Stevens seriously, including Stevens himself. Most likely his availability was a result of nothing more than his sardonic wit. Among the serious contenders, only Cameron possessed an organization comparable to that of the Curtin-Quay forces. With the holiday season coming to an end and a new legislature about to convene, it appeared that the contest would be another Cameron-Curtin shootout.

Before the ratification of the Seventeenth Amendment, the selection of U.S. senators was anything but a genuine expression of the popular will. The procedure was exciting and intriguing, but not very democratic. Senatorial hopefuls canvassed candidates for the state's General Assembly. Flagrant promises, intimidations, and downright bribes were part of a vicious game played by unscrupulous men who adjusted the rules to serve their selfish purposes. Often the legislative candidates bound themselves to specific senatorial hopefuls and sometimes they were instructed by local conventions to do so, but once the victorious candidates arrived in Harrisburg, it was not uncommon for many to experience a change of heart in the party caucus. Here the party strategists played out their final, masterful roles in determining their party's choice for the Senate. The more successful ones had completed the groundwork for eventual triumph long before the caucus met.

A favorite story told in Crawford County about Simon Cameron illustrates how the old Winnebago chief was turning a new leaf in his how-to book on party discipline.[3] Indeed, he was the apostle of modernity in politics. While Grow and Curtin were perambulating the state in the senatorial race of 1866–1867, outdoing one another with radical platitudes and eliciting the huzzahs of frenzied crowds, Cameron was on their track, quietly manipulating the local politicos. He was selecting his friends as legislative candidates in counties where nominations had not yet been made, and where they had been, he was "bringing a material influence to bear upon them." So, as Grow and Curtin pontificated, the wily old Cameron worked among the shadows. He selected the candidates, and the Grow-Curtin supporters helped elect them. In this way Cameron packed the legislature.

How amused he must have been to see his opponents coming to Harrisburg at the opening of the General Assembly to fight out in caucus a nomination that had been virtually decided months earlier. How frustrating it must have been for Grow and Curtin to watch their "instructed" candidates suddenly switch loyalties.

Though he was the favorite in a number of counties and had worked diligently to get a number of his friends into the legislature, Grow operated at a serious disadvantage. What organization he had was amorphous. It had neither the means nor the network structure to match the businesslike character of the Cameron and Curtin operations. It lacked managerial leadership. There was no McClure, Quay, or a young Don Cameron to guide campaign strategy and to garner votes. Many of Grow's backers were newspaper editors and small officeholders whose influence waned before legislatures and conventions and whose fidelity often succumbed to political pressure. It was not uncommon to find him defeated before the party caucus convened. In the opinion of the *Tioga County Agitator,* Grow had been out of the picture for months before the Senate candidate was nominated in 1867.[4]

The only chance Grow had, and a slight one at that, was for a prolonged battle between Curtin and Cameron that would demand a compromise candidate. As Curtin's hopes dwindled, such an occurrence seemed a remote possibility. Several days prior to the meeting of the Union-Republican caucus in January, Cameron expressed confidence he would win; any last-minute combination against him appeared hopeless. A conference that included Grow, Curtin, Stevens, and Forney reviewed the possibilities of such a combination and even entertained the thought of bolting the caucus and, with the help of Democrats, uniting behind their own candidate.[5] But nothing came of this. While the malcontent conferees assessed their chances, Cameron, with the support of governor-elect John Geary and the skillful maneuvering of Quay and the younger Cameron, moved closer to nomination. In caucus he won easily and then went on to defeat Democrat Edgar Cowan by a straight party vote, 81–47. "His victory was a superlative example of the triumph of a hierarchical political organization over mass popularity," Cameron's biographer has written.[6] By this strong party endorsement, he emerged from his victory as the grand master of Republican politics in the state.

After he had licked the wounds from his first major defeat on his way back to elective office, Grow looked ahead to new opportunities. He determined to make a conscientious bid for the second spot on the 1868 Republican national ticket. Writing to his good friend John

Covode, he was characteristically blunt: "After looking the field all over, I have decided to be a candidate for Vice-President."[7] Perhaps it was another case of egomania — Grow was often impressed with the exuberance of his self-importance. He did not specify whether he was referring to the national or the state field of potential contenders. Regardless, his candidacy was conditional upon affirmative answers to two basic questions. Could he win the support of both the Cameron and Curtin factions? And did he have sufficient radical following outside Pennsylvania? His enemies and even some of his friends did not think so.

Nonetheless, Grow received plenty of encouragement. In June 1867 the *Titusville Morning Herald* urged a "Grant-Grow" ticket and ran a banner in subsequent issues.[8] The *Herald* was one of the first newspapers in the state to endorse the former Speaker. His plan was first to have all the "northern" papers of the state come out for him as soon as possible. It was in the northern counties where his base of support had been consistent. He then hoped to enlist the aid of papers in the eastern regions, particularly the *Philadelphia Inquirer*. He outlined this strategy to Covode. Meanwhile, he wanted the Westmoreland congressman to persuade editors in Indiana and Westmoreland counties to support his candidacy. Grow's technical game plan had not changed. With the aid of the majority of Republican editors, he hoped that public opinion would be sufficiently aroused to prompt county conventions and delegates to the state convention to support him. By the end of the year many Republican papers had come out for Grow. In the northern tier counties three-quarters of them were for him and for Grant. The *Harrisburg Patriot and Union* reported that Grow had as many as forty newspapers behind him.[9]

As 1868 neared, Republican leaders, despite serious reservations of many radicals, intensified their efforts to commit their party to the hero of Appomattox. The general's open break with President Johnson made their task easier. With the tide running so heavily in favor of Grant, much attention was directed toward the second place on the ticket, but there was no strong movement among state organizations for any one candidate. With the Republican national convention in Chicago close at hand, a number of states put favorite sons in the field. The list included several of Grow's closest friends: Colfax of Indiana, Wade of Ohio, and Fenton of New York.[10] Other possible choices were Hamlin of Maine, Henry Wilson of Massachusetts, and James Speed of Kentucky. Since Grant was from Illinois, it was reasonable to assume that second place would be given to one of the eastern candidates. Regardless, many of these men were notorious radicals. If the radicals were to control the convention and if they wanted a fellow radical as vice-president, then Grow would have to be seriously considered. Who better represented the radical animus of the party with greater consistency?

But Grow first had to win the endorsement of this party in Pennsylvania, which would not be easy, especially should Curtin decide to run. The "alliance" of Cameron and Curtin forces for the senatorial election implied that Curtin would receive the approval of the Cameron organization. In reality, there was no certainty of this happening; old wounds never totally heal.

The Curtin people felt considerable disappointment over the way their man had been denied the Senate seat. Grieved and frustrated, the former governor had retreated to his home at Bellefonte to rest, spend time with friends, and attend to business interests. Like many Republicans, he feared the worst in the upcoming presidential contest. Pennsylvania had been lost to the party by the election of the Democratic state ticket in 1867, and, with Democratic successes in several other "Republican" states, an ominous trend appeared. Republican leaders believed Grant could stop this trend and restore Republican power in the country. The Curtin people, who were sure that Republican losses in 1867 were the direct result of Cameron's dictatorial management of the party, also believed that a strong vice-presidential candidate like Curtin would assure Republican victory in Pennsylvania. If nothing else, his nomination would be vindication and partial compensation for the damages suffered in Harrisburg a year before.

On the eve of the Republican state convention in Philadelphia, Curtin's friends decided to bring out the former governor as the party's choice for the vice-presidency. The announcement of his candidacy reinspired many Republicans with renewed enthusiasm. The news was good for them but bad for Grow. Had Curtin's candidacy been born many months earlier, it might have discouraged Grow from proceeding with his own. Since both men opposed Cameronism, it was realistic to presume that a Curtin vote was a Grow vote and vice versa. Again, at best Grow loomed as an alternative choice should Cameron decide to block Curtin. As he bit the bullet, Grow prepared for another strain in the cold war between the party's two strongest factions. The detente reached in Harrisburg was about to meet its first real test in Philadelphia.

Grow's friends remained hopeful and continued to portray him as the best of all candidates, a national figure, a hero among the radicals. A favorable press described him as the one contender who was not obnoxious to any party faction. His record of true dedication to Republican principles spoke for itself. The editor of the *Tioga County Agitator,* a leading advocate of Grow's cause, stated with optimism that Grow would walk into the convention with more committed delegates than anyone.[11] From that standpoint, he was the people's choice.

Whatever strength Grow may have had, however, vanished before the orchestrated pro-Curtin tidal wave that swept through the Academy of Music, where the politicians gathered in early March. Both Curtin and Grow addressed the assemblage. The latter spoke at length, attacking the Democratic party with the usual viciousness.[12] But words were not going to gain him the candidacy. While the delegates cheered Grow, the managers for Curtin busied themselves in harvesting last-minute votes. Grow never had a chance. The Curtin men demonstrated a unity of purpose and resolve that made Grow and the Cameron people flinch. Taking a page from Cameron's own textbook, they steamrolled Curtin's nomination through the convention with dispatch. Furthermore, they reversed the usual practice of allowing congressional districts to elect delegates to the national convention by forcing through a resolution that instructed the Pennsylvania delegates to Chicago to vote for Grant and Curtin. To chair that delegation they chose Alexander McClure, not Cameron.[13] In a final gesture of magnanimity, they offered Grow the chairmanship of the Republican state committee.

By these decisive steps, the Curtin organization may have regained some of its lost posture in state politics, but these actions raised the ire of many Republicans.[14] Some delegates swore they would not vote for Curtin. According to McClure, one of the field commanders behind the Curtin blitz, the vindictive Cameron did everything he could to discourage other state delegations from supporting Curtin. The *Philadelphia Post* also expressed dismay with Curtin's nomination by the "Black Crook" convention. It editorialized that the former governor was no radical and, therefore, he should not expect radicals in the state or at Chicago to endorse him.[15] What really galled the *Post* was the manipulative way in which the Curtin gang compelled the entire state organization to adopt their candidate. Their action meant that those delegates not committed to Curtin would be dropped. About one-third of the convention delegates had voted against this unorthodox and tyrannical resolution (85–47).[16] Finally, the *Post* exclaimed, had the party known weeks earlier that Grow's name would have to be withdrawn, Benjamin Wade's strength in the convention would have tripled when Russell Errett of Pittsburgh, a Cameron supporter, attempted to substitute Wade for Curtin. With the impeachment trial of Johnson at hand, many believed that the president would be convicted and removed from office and that Wade, president pro tem of the Senate, would serve as interim president. This move was sure to elevate his candidacy as vice-president. When Johnson was acquitted, however, Wade's chances diminished.

If being selected state party chairman was supposed to have been some kind of compensatory victory for Grow, he surely must have viewed it as a bittersweet one. And, if he believed he could have won at a game in which the rules were mandated by managerial expediency, then his naivete exceeded the dictates of good reason. Grow was a vain person. To suffer such a crushing defeat, especially after months of campaigning had indicated he was the popular choice, had to be humiliating. It was his second defeat in less than two years and it worried him.

Though he was courageous in conviction, Grow was also a politician of a generation that was slowly and grudgingly dying. Nearly a quarter century had passed since he first stumped with Wilmot along the Tunkhannock, lambasting opponents wherever a crowd gathered to listen — under torchlight, in smoke-filled taverns, or in the shade of a quiet glen. Then there were his famous appearances before county conventions, debating the issues with rivals and seeking delegate support. Was there still a place in modern America for a campaign format of this kind? Certainly Grow believed there was.

He was and always would remain an integral part of the Civil War drama. He never allowed himself or his followers to forget that holocaust. Using as his constant backdrop a panorama depicting the whole history of the North-South conflict, he persisted in doing battle with the enemies of the old order — Democrats who had betrayed their Jeffersonian and Jacksonian heritage. His audiences loved it; they demanded more. His enemies called it repetition ad nauseam and wondered if Grow suffered from early senility. He continued to rest his case with "red-neck" Republicans, poor rural northerners who, like himself, had switched from the Democratic to Republican party in the mid-1850s. He prided himself in having strong bonds with the working classes, the immigrant, the freedman. Grass-roots politics meant everything to him. Through masterful oratory and party rags, he believed in bringing the issues to the masses and the downtrodden in a language they understood. To Grow this was the only approach a responsible politician should take. But politics in an industrial America were changing. Either he had to adjust his values and adapt to this change, or honor the charge that he was nothing more than what Sen. Boies Penrose once called him — "an old fogy."

Grow dutifully applied himself to the task of organizing the 1868 Republican campaign in Pennsylvania. Staying on the good side of Curtin and Company was probably his one chance to remain in the higher echelon of the party. Operating from his headquarters in the old Continental Hotel in Philadelphia, Grow conducted himself as everyone knew he would—tough, brassy, and merciless with Democrats.[17] There was nothing sophisticated about the Republican campaign—no serious probe of issues, only a frontal assault against all who opposed the radicals. Ornate phrases and hackneyed slogans, some of them from earlier addresses, distinguished Grow's chairmanship rhetoric. In his message to the voters, dated May 27, 1868, and published in the Republican press, Grow called the opposition party "an organization that was unfaithful to the country in the hour of its direct peril and false to liberty and the rights of man. . . . Had the policy of the Democratic party been successful, the genius of impartial history would have written on the tombstone of the present generation an epitaph of indelible, unfading and endless disgrace . . . that it preferred the Republic should die rather than endure the sacrifice necessary for it to live."[18]

Judging by the election results in Pennsylvania, Grow must have been satisfied with the performance of the state organization. Grant and Colfax carried the state by nearly 30,000 votes. Curtin had never placed higher than fifth place in the balloting for vice-president in Chicago and had withdrawn after the third ballot. But he went on to stump for the ticket in his state and other states. The Republicans were also pleased to have Gen. John Hartranft, a Cameron man, re-elected as the state's auditor general. Finally, the party carried both branches of the legislature. All in all, it was a banner year at the polls for state Republicans.

No sooner had the Republican victory celebrations ended than Grow again became a candidate, this time for the U.S. Senate. With the term of Democrat Charles R. Buckalew about to end and the Republicans in control of the legislature, the man they nominated was sure to go to Washington. For a fleeting moment it appeared that Grow might be that man. Well-known Republicans in the state were scarce. Thad Stevens and David Wilmot had died during the year, Curtin was being groomed for minister to Russia, and J. Donald Cameron was being prepared (at least by his father) for a position in Grant's cabinet. No one else of Grow's political stature was left in the field and, therefore, many Republicans believed the former Speaker deserved a shot at the Senate vacancy. His national reputation built upon radicalism and true Republicanism remained as impeccable as ever.

But these assets were not good enough. When the legislature convened in January 1869, the choice of the next senator seemed to depend upon factors other than good qualities and past performance. Ability, integrity, and experience of the candidates mattered little. Instead, expedience, personal favor and geographical considerations prevailed among the party managers. With respect to Grow, one thing was certain: the Camerons did not want him. The consolidation of party power by father and son precluded anyone who had opposed them from attaining high office. Grow was cast as a true troublemaker. In addition, the older Cameron was reluctant to have a colleague join him in the Senate who might challenge him for the patronage of the state, and Grow was ornery enough to do this.

Letters to Simon Cameron suggest that a few of his lieutenants were interested in Grow's candidacy. Confirming that Grow's real strength was in the northern counties, E. O. Goodrich of Towanda hoped that Cameron might favor Grow's election. He believed the former Speaker could be trusted and that his endorsement would fortify Cameron's position in the north. Goodrich assured Cameron that there would be no problem with the patronage: "Grow has no claims upon your support." H. Cobb of Wellsboro seemed confused over Grow's actions. He bluntly asked Cameron: what is Grow's status? what is he doing? whom is he allied with? Cobb knew that Cameron could name the next senator from Pennsylvania. Whoever he might be, Cobb preferred that he be as "radical, true and able" as Grow. Still, Cobb was annoyed with Grow for failing to trust his friends more and for operating in a mysterious fashion. G. C. Harbison of New Castle, also admitting that Cameron was the master of the senatorial situation, had no preference in the contest but confided that Grow could receive the endorsement of Cameron people in Lawrence County. One Republican who did not like Grow was Henry Johnson of Meadville. He was sure the candidate had been conversing "with the enemy" in neighboring Mercer County where the anti-Cameron movement was as rampant as in his own Crawford County.[19]

Another individual who opposed Grow's candidacy was Col. Thomas A. Scott of the Pennsylvania Railroad. In the Civil War decade he was proving himself as effective in Pennsylvania politics as he was in the state's transportation system. His railroad, one of the more powerful monopolies in the state, was capable of exerting tremendous political pressure. Scott was not to be ignored. His choice for the Senate happened to be John Scott of Huntingdon. Not related to the colonel, this prominent attorney had been a war Democrat and had voted for Lincoln in 1864. In the colonel's judgment, this young man showed every potential for best serving the business community of the commonwealth.

The Camerons decided to ally themselves with the colonel and throw their support to his candidate. Seeing this alliance develop, Grow did not waste time pulling out of the campaign. According to McClure, Scott had the nomination wrapped up before the legislature convened.[20] Grow compared his political record to that of Scott's and must have wondered what he had to do to win his party's approval. Admittedly he did not labor as assiduously to gain the Senate seat as he had the vice-presidency. But it did not matter. There was no way he could have grabbed the nomination away from the Scotts and the Camerons.

In a span of two years, Grow had been denied a chance for elective office three times. Whatever his qualifications for these offices, his failure each time resulted from his rejection by either the Curtin or the Cameron organization. Political mavericks and independents are anathema to structural politics. Politicians who are popular with the voters are snubbed if they do not conform to the rigid dictates of party policy or refuse to serve the interests of bosses and managers. Riding high on public approval was the only way Grow knew how to play the game. He was often accused of overplaying the circuit game by appearing before too many local conventions to plead his case. His strategy was always simple: Why have a party superstructure when you can communicate directly with the voters? The direct approach was commendable, but too limited in a process that was becoming more complex. Organization was vital, and Grow lacked a viable one. What he had was second-rate and ineffective and suffered from a leadership paralysis. As chairman of the state committee in 1868, he had relied on the mechanics of existing organizations and played the role of coordinator rather than originator of party policy. His defeats in 1867, 1868, and 1869 were as much an education in the art of contemporary politics as they were milestones in a rapidly fading political career.

"Bridge over the Bloody Chasm"

Grow had every reason to show bitterness toward Cameron for turning a deaf ear to his senatorial supplications in 1867 and 1869. The man who controlled the Republican party in Pennsylvania was irrevocably against the man who thirsted for office. Out of frustration perhaps, Grow may have even blamed Cameron for some of his health problems, although there is no evidence that he did. In 1871 he went west, traveling through California, Washington, and Victoria, British Columbia, in hopes of allaying some of his chronic maladies. By the end of the year he was in Houston, Texas, where he assumed the duties of the presidency of the Houston and Great Northern Railway Company, a position he held for several years.

Grow's sojourn in Texas was only a sabbatical from the heated politics of Pennsylvania. He was a carpetbagger who had no intention of spending the rest of his life in the South. He knew he would return to resume his political career someday when the situation back home was different and his chances of holding elective office vastly improved. Simon Cameron was already in his seventies. How much longer must he remain Grow's antagonist? The opportunity arose sooner than Grow had expected. The older Cameron was not dead, but his empire was in trouble. For an instant it appeared that this great party organization and everything it symbolized was about to collapse from an internal explosion. When the Liberal Republicans surfaced in 1872, Grow joined them.

The Liberal Republican movement had its origins in Missouri where the party divided over the political disabilities of those who had sympathized with the South during the war. According to Carl Schurz, one of its prime originators, the movement had two main groups: revenue reformers and Germans en masse.[21] In a broader sense, it was a general revolt against political privilege and corruption embodied in the Grant administration. As the movement spread to other states, it attracted reformers who wished to end the disgraceful misrule of the South, strengthen the civil service, and purge all levels of government of corruptionists.

In Pennsylvania the struggle within the Republican party assumed a familiar form—a war between the Cameron and Curtin forces. The central figure in this new round of party fisticuffs was Alexander McClure.[22] Although both an editor and an attorney, McClure was more at home playing a freelance wheeler-dealer in political circles. Active in state politics since the 1840s, he had been one of the Republican party architects. Now he seemed willing to ruin that party in an election year to destroy Cameronism and its corrupt defense of Grant. For this revolutionary action, McClure and those who backed him, lost grace with many party stalwarts. It was a gamble that, if lost, could drive the dissidents into oblivion. Purgative action was sure to follow. The Honorable Jeremiah S. Black of Pennsylvania, while regarding the movement as having little significance, exclaimed never-theless that those Republicans who planned to attend the national Liberal Republican convention in Cincinnati would have to "burn their bridges behind them and sink their ships."[23]

In 1871, McClure announced his opposition to Grant and declared his candidacy for the Pennsylvania Senate. Cameron interpreted Mc-Clure's actions as directed against him and sensed that a split in the party might seriously impair Republican chances in 1872 in both na-tional and state elections. When Curtin gave unmistakable signs that he might resign as minister to Russia, party leaders and editors hy-pothesized that the former governor planned to join the revolt against the Cameron-Grant forces in the state. The president did not help matters. He attempted to keep Curtin in the diplomatic service by offering him another mission and then tried to placate McClure with a position as U.S. district attorney. To his opponents, Grant's mo-tives were obvious. By April 1872 the party rebels in Pennsylvania were ready to organize a Liberal Republican movement and send a delegation to the national convention.

McClure arrived in Cincinnati to find great confusion. The gather-ing consisted of politicians, editors, and reformers who had little in common except their dislike for Grant. Many of the leaders—Samuel Bowles, Murat Halstead, Horace White—were amateurs in practi-cal politics. McClure remarked to Henry Watterson that he wanted nothing to do "with those cranks."[24] In contrast, George W. Julian, seeing many of his free-soil friends present, observed that he had never seen a "finer looking body assembled."[25]

After caucusing, the Pennsylvanians prepared to support a ticket of David Davis of Illinois and Horace Greeley after casting a cour-tesy vote for Curtin on the first ballot. The former governor was still in Europe and apparently unaware of what McClure was up to. But a Greeley-Gratz Brown movement drew away many Davis supporters. McClure did not have much confidence in Greeley as a presidential choice and held back his delegation's endorsement until the New York editor had received a majority of votes.[26]

In his recollections, McClure maintained he had received "hun-dreds and hundreds" of letters from state Republicans who sympa-thized with the movement and who promised "to fall in with the pro-cession as the campaign progressed."[27] He also admitted that at the close of the campaign he had destroyed those letters, including ones from J. K. Moorhead, William Stewart, Morrow B. Lowry, and Ga-lusha Grow. The wily McClure, who chaired the Liberal Republican state committee, boasted of the widespread support among rank-and-file Republicans. Much of that support was generated after the Cincinnati convention, for the *Pittsburgh Daily Gazette* of April 25, 1872, claimed that not one prominent Republican of Allegheny County had identified with the movement. Moorhead and J. W. Riddle, Republican candidate for mayor of Pittsburgh, ultimately did declare for Greeley.

Grow's participation in the Liberal Republican movement was at best peripheral. Some of the letters destroyed by McClure might have given us a better indication of Grow's involvement. He did declare in favor of the Greeley-Brown ticket and in a letter from Texas predicted that Pennsylvania would give the ticket a majority of 30,000.[28] This obviously impromptu remark reveals Grow's initial enthusiasm for the planned coup against Cameron. It also suggests a naivete regarding the actual state of political affairs back home.

Grow planned to stump for Greeley in the northern counties, but there is little evidence that he did. In a letter to McClure, he expressed disappointment at being unable to fulfill a speaking engagement because of a throat ailment.[29] Maybe the problem was acute enough to keep him on the sidelines for most of the campaign. At least one newspaper in the oil region claimed Grow had barnstormed in behalf of the Liberal Republicans. While he was in the western counties looking for support in his bid for the U.S. Senate years later (in 1880), he was charged by the *Venango Spectator* for trying to unsay all he had said in 1872 when he had accused the Cameron dynasty of "innate rascality and hypocrisy."[30] If Grow did any stumping in 1872, it was limited, for he is not mentioned in the leading newspapers as being on the campaign circuit.

In its issue of August 15, 1872, a leading journal commented that Grow joined the movement because of his warm friendship for Greeley and his desire to "bridge over the bloody chasm."[31] The first part of the statement may have been true, but the second part is questionable. After he had been nominated by the Democrats at their Baltimore convention, Greeley came to be associated with the campaign cry, "bloody chasm." A caricature in the *Harper's Weekly* shows him reaching across the corpse of a Union soldier to clasp the hand of an apparent southerner holding a gun.[32] It was a symbolic gesture of the psychology of forgiveness that had taken root in this presidential election year. Bonds of friendship between former enemies were to assure victory against Grant. Cynics pointed to the irony of ex-Confederates willing to do battle for a man who once had maligned them with his vicious pen. Perhaps it was this strange honeymoon between Liberal Republicans and southern Democrats that discouraged Grow from rolling up his sleeves and giving a 100 percent effort in the campaign. If he showed consistency in anything it was in his scorn for the secessionists.

As pointed out by the *Pittsburgh Daily Gazette,* the real contest in Pennsylvania was not between Grant and Greeley, but between the Democratic choice for governor, Charles R. Buckalew, and the regular Republican nominee, John F. Hartranft.[33] Beneath this, as McClure later wrote, the real issue was Cameronism "from the beginning to the close of the campaign."[34] The gubernatorial election preceded the presidential one by a month. All knew that a regular Republican victory would assure Grant's reelection as well. Hartranft's defeat, on the other hand, might have meant that Cameron would decide not to run for reelection to the Senate. It was a bitterly contested campaign in which charges of fraud and corruption were hurled back and forth between the candidates and their supporters. When it was over, Hartranft had swept the state by more than 35,000 votes. Several days later, McClure admitted the game was up. If any doubt remained, Grant's plurality of 130,000 ended it. The Cameron organization had survived, radical Republicanism had been sanctified by the rank and file, and the Liberal Republicans had been trounced. Grant and Hartranft were in and Cameron eased his way to another term in the Senate.

Like other radical Republicans, Grow had mixed emotions about the 1872 elections. The Liberal Republican movement had failed in Pennsylvania because Republican voters were less interested in reform and political housecleaning than in maintaining the status quo and keeping the "bloody flag" hoisted. Grow had no reservations about the successes of radicalism at the polls, but he lamented the fact that its stewardship would remain under the Camerons. The men who had associated themselves with the 1872 revolt did so for different reasons: revenge against Cameron, hatred for Grant, a genuine desire for reform. In Grow's case it had to be a matter of revenge. Yet he must have suspected that a displacement of the Cameron-Quay ring by a Curtin-McClure junta would not automatically return him to a favored status within the party. After all, it was the latter combination that had pulled the rug out from under him in the 1868 race for the vice-presidency. There were no assurances the two men could grant Grow what he wanted the most — a constituency. Meanwhile, he decided to remain in Texas. What irreversible damage he had suffered politically for his scant affiliation with the Liberal Republican movement remained to be seen after his return home.

❦13

The Warrior Returns

O FTEN IN DEFEAT there is salvation. In the spirit of *nil desperandum,* Grow looked to the day when he might return to the political battlefields of Pennsylvania. Had some Republicans had their way, Grow and others like him who had supported Greeley in 1872 would have been booted out of the party. Unlike Curtin and McClure, Republicans who continued to blacken their careers by flirting with Democratic candidates and policies, however, Grow was one former Liberal Republican who penitently returned to the party fold.

What he wanted was to see his integrity as a Republican leader restored and to gain elective office. He succeeded in one goal and failed in the other. A constituency continued to elude him, but he stepped forward as a party Brahmin, an oracle whose opinions were regarded with authority and respect, at least by the Republicans. Grow brought the party gospel to the people. He was often asked to address the issues, particularly the money question. He granted interviews to reporters and wrote position papers for leading newspapers. His recognized talents as a disputant and his genial qualities commanded voter attention. If nothing else, his writing and public speaking strengthened his visibility and made him a ready candidate at all times. In a real sense, Grow personified the very essence of true Republicanism. Because he was not shackled by the onus of organizational ties, he remained the unsung hero to many Republicans, a symbol of what their party really stood for.

A Carpetbag for a Constituency

When Grow returned from Texas in 1875 he found the political situation as topsy-turvy as ever. The Cameron machine still functioned in its accustomed manner, but the Republican party in Pennsylvania had its back against the wall. The reelection of Grant and the defeat of the Liberal Republicans in 1872 had not ended the party's internal strife. Dissensions continued. Scandals associated with the Grant administration further worsened the party's standing in the state. Sweeping Democratic victories in 1874 told the story of voter dissatisfaction.

One thing that frustrated Pennsylvania Republicans and helped weaken party unity was the manner in which the president managed or "mishandled" the patronage. Grant seemingly ignored Pennsylvania's share of the political pie, which annoyed the Camerons. For instance, when Wayne MacVeagh, son-in-law of Simon Cameron and a favorite choice for postmaster general, was snubbed in favor of Marshall Jewell of Connecticut, state Republican leaders cried foul. At their state convention in May 1875, they vented their grievances with Grant and declared they were "unalterably opposed" to a third term for any president.[1] Party leaders instead leaned toward Gov. "Black Jack" Hartranft for president in 1876. Though popular, he was far from being the favorite among the rank and file. By the spring of 1876, the most popular presidential candidate of Pennsylvania Republicans was probably James G. Blaine. His candidacy presented a dual threat. Not only did it challenge the machine's choice but also it appealed to many state Republicans who had bolted in 1872. Was there to be another revolt?

Disruption within the party was nothing new. What was significantly different in 1875 was that socioeconomic forces changed the party's platform strategy. The "bloody shirt" and the tariff were no longer sufficient to attract the loyalties of voters. Economic concerns, especially among labor and farm groups, demanded that the major parties redirect their attention to the problems of industrial America. The Grange movement, labor violence in the coal fields of Luzerne and Schuylkill Counties, and the ruthlessness of the Molly Maguires generated a blunt awareness of these problems. The paralyzing national panic that broke in 1873 set off a chain reaction of money houses collapsing and thousands of businesses going bankrupt. Hundreds of thousands of workers suddenly found themselves out on the streets. Speaking to Democrats of Berks County, Henrick B. Wright, chairman of the Pennsylvania Democratic state committee, wanted to know how long this deplorable state of affairs was to continue: "Our furnaces have gone out of blast, the wheels of our manufactories are not in motion, the wages of labor . . . reduced, and the products of the farm are at a discouraging price."[2]

Whereas Wright advocated the use of greenbacks to fight the slump, Grow called for the return of the currency to a specie basis. He believed resumption would save the public credit from dishonor, lighten the burden of taxation, and place the nation's industries on a solid and sure foundation thus helping the workingman. He viewed irredeemable paper as a terrible detriment to the productive energies of the nation. Republican state committee chairman Henry Hoyt asked Grow to take the hard-money message to those who cared to listen. Not all state Republicans agreed with Grow on the money issue. In the lame-duck session of the Forty-third Congress, Republican leaders had succeeded in passing a hotly debated Specie Resumption Act, effective in 1879. But the Pennsylvania Republicans had refused to endorse the legislation at their Lancaster meeting. So, disunited in other ways, the state Republicans now found themselves further divided on the most critical issue of the day — money.

They closed ranks in the 1875 gubernatorial race. There was no real opposition to the renomination of Governor Hartranft. At the state convention in Lancaster in May, he received the unanimous endorsement of the delegates. Though the Republicans hailed him as one of the state's greatest governors, the Democrats charged his administration with faulty management of the state's finances. They accused Robert W. Mackey, state treasurer, of permitting funds to be used by his Republican friends (the "Treasury Ring") for private speculations. Hartranft did not escape the wrath of his opponents, but his close supporters circled the wagons in his defense. He received outside help from the newly elected governor of Ohio, Rutherford B. Hayes, a hard-money advocate who accompanied him on a whirlwind tour of the state. Hartranft won by a plurality of 12,000. The lack of enthusiasm for his opponent, Cyrus Pershing, may have even exceeded the shortness of funds that plagued the losing candidate's campaign.

Since Grow hoped to ease his way back into the confidence of party leaders, his timing could not have been better than the 1875 campaign. The apparent unanimity surrounding the nomination of Hartranft left the door ajar for former deserters and prodigals who wished to seek forgiveness and expiation. Grow's quest was not that of an office-seeker. Had it been, his chances would have been nil. His absence of four years destroyed any presumptive claim to public office he may have entertained. Being asked to come out of retirement to help the party was a penance he did not mind making. His addresses on sound money cast him in the role of a teacher, a bearer of truth, and he liked it. He had studied carefully the money issue only to confirm what he really believed — that inflated currency was ruinous to government, industry, workers, and farmers. With sudden brazenness and skill, Grow cut his way back to the hearts of hundreds of voters as he lectured them on the merits of hard money. Despite success, he still longed for a constituency.

Sometime after the election of Hartranft, Grow decided to run again for Congress. As early as February 1876, the old warrior was known to be anxious to take another shot at an elective office. One Democratic paper commented that Grow seemed humble in his aspirations, but very thirsty for office.[3] Its editor, Eugene Hawley, warned that should Galusha fasten himself upon a "Court House Ring" ticket, the people of Susquehanna would see that his carpetbag was again packed and his one-way fare paid for a quick exit out of town. The "ring" referred to the Republican organization of present and former officeholders, especially those from Philadelphia, who controlled the party machine.

Grow's credibility as a candidate was a bit shaky. "Where does he stand with the party?" was the question commonly asked. Both the party Stalwarts and Half-Breeds might claim him, for he had worked diligently for the party in 1875 but had always enjoyed the reputation of being a freelance Republican who was never enamored with machine politics and politicians. The state organization seemed to have no apparent opposition to his candidacy, perhaps because this election was for only a seat in the national House. Many of his old friends, remembering his radicalism and zest, welcomed him back as someone they could trust.

By early summer, however, Grow realized he was in a dogfight. The automatic sweep of county and district delegates that he was so used to receiving in the years from 1852 to 1860 was not about to happen in 1876. The Democrats were sharpening their cleats; many Republicans opposed him. Yet he remained ebullient and confident. He wondered how he could lose in a still Republican district to the incumbent, Democrat Joseph Powell, who was hardly known. After his victory, Grow hoped to become Speaker again. He believed the nation and his party needed a man of his experience to serve in Congress. This was his way of saying that statesmanship was essential at a time when the party seemed more interested in building its organization and programming its politicians.

In reality this attitude reflected Grow's idealistic reaction to pressures of economic change, which he and other politicians scarcely understood. He realized that industrialization demanded the development of American qualities of initiative, responsibility, and self-sacrifice on the part of political spokesmen. But he did not apparently perceive these qualities as related to a partnership between industry and party, involving reciprocal rights and obligations, because that would subvert the traditionally democratic system he wished to preserve. Where he saw hope and challenge, others saw political gain. The *Wyoming Democrat* prompted speculation that Grow was brought back from Texas at the insistence of Tom Scott, who wanted dutiful Republicans in Congress to appropriate more land to his Texas and Pacific Railroad.[4] True or not, the suggestion implied that statesmanship of any kind was less important than deals between business leaders and officeholders.

If the Democrats were looking for a chink in Grow's usually impenetrable armor, they found it in the *Democrat*'s charge that he held investments in Texas. Grow denied he had any such holdings, but a campaign issue was born. Writing to H. G. Seaman on August 31, Grow tried to set the record straight: "I own no land in Texas and have no interest in any railroad in that state or anywhere else. I have no interest of any kind whatever that would be affected in any way by the passage of what is known as the Texas and Pacific Bill."[5]

Editor Hawley kept the matter alive. He responded to the letter by indicating that Grow had not paid any property tax in Susquehanna since 1872.[6] Does this mean he has no property? asked Hawley. Of course not. Galusha simply had a convenient arrangement whereby his property investments were held by the Grow brothers. Hawley strongly hinted that perhaps the Texas Ranger, as he liked to call Grow, enjoyed a similar arrangement with friends in Texas for his land holdings and stock in the Texas and Pacific.

Grow's letter, which was published upon his request, was viewed by his enemies as a defensive maneuver to save face. But there was nothing defensive in the way he lashed out against Hawley. The continuing feud between the two had been going on for some time. In a public meeting in Montrose, Hawley claimed that Grow had called him a "common, malicious and willful liar," for stating in his paper that Grow was an officer or stockholder in the Texas and Pacific. The angry editor reciprocated by referring to his antagonist as a "cowardly pettifogger." He challenged Grow and anyone else to produce the newspaper in which the so-called lie was made. None was produced. Hawley denied that Grow had ever asked him to correct the statement ("it would be impossible for me to correct a thing I never had stated"). The fiery newspaperman, who was a leader in the county Democratic party, called Grow a Greeley follower and reminded his readers that in 1862 and before a public audience Grow had insulted B. S. Bentley, a Montrose Republican who had criticized him.

Grow's sharp tongue might have cost him votes as it had in 1862, if he had gained the nomination. He received a majority of delegates at the Republican county convention, defeating James E. Carmelt, but he lost his bid at the district level. Bradford Republicans were not that impressed with the former Speaker. No longer was Wilmot available to help deliver the county to his friend and former law partner. In the district's congressional conference, Bradford had the most votes, six, with the remaining ten votes scattered among the remaining three counties—Susquehanna, Wyoming, and Wayne. Unless two or three of those counties united, Bradford's conferees had things pretty much their way. Their choice for Congress was attorney Edward Overton, Jr., of Towanda. Perhaps the key figure in Grow's defeat was George G. Waller of Wayne, who was determined to prevent Grow's nomination. Wayne's conferees did not intend to go with Bradford, but at the third conference held at Montrose, three of Wayne's delegates were induced to back Bradford and Overton. Afterward, the *Democrat* declared that there was not one Republican paper, either in the district or out of it, that did not lament the selection of Overton over Grow.[7] As it turned out, Overton went on to win in 1876 and again in 1878.

With the election of Rutherford B. Hayes, the first phase (1861–1877) of Republican rule came to an end. The president's epochal removal of the last federal troops supporting carpetbag governments officially closed the period of Civil War and Reconstruction. During that time entrenched Republicanism had built its case upon such issues as the preservation of the Union, Democratic treason, the tariff, and the Homestead Act. The consolidation of the party had assured initial success, but after the war the party suffered from ailments that threatened its hegemony over state and national governments. In Pennsylvania, the party endured election defeats and meager majorities. This state of affairs demanded tighter party organization, discipline and aggressive leadership.

Yet, the tendency toward the centralization of party power only perpetuated divisiveness. A tighter organization generally means less freedom, and less freedom spawns dissent. Party leaders had hoped that better organization would offer voters an open give-and-take of power opinion without endangering the organization. In other words, a free exchange of ideas must not interfere with the smooth running of the party. But conflicting views continued to cause dissension. Machine politicians scorned and chastised reformers who were determined to curb the spoils system. To a large extent the political left and right in the Republican party of Pennsylvania were measured in terms of how one stood in relation to the state organization, and not to the socioeconomic issues.

At a time when industrial tycoons became instant legends and creative capitalism a social virtue, it was not easy for idealists to discredit the spoils mongers who used public office as their private preserves. Making money from politics seemed a natural adjunct to the freedom of enterprise. After all, an alliance between businessmen and officeholders, though it might be corrupt, was still a small price to pay for the advances industrial America was making. Rationalization of this kind destroyed any respect for ideological values. Principles remained a part of the Republican portfolio, but they were dusted off and invoked only when absolutely necessary. Within a pragmatism of flowering materialism and hero worship, who cared about lofty principles? Who wanted to or could understand them? Grow was cryptic and not altogether cynical when he remarked on the eve of the 1878 gubernatorial campaign that "men will follow personal candidates when they can't track the logic of ideas."[8]

A Personal Campaign

Sitting in the office of the U.S. marshal in Pittsburgh, Grow talked about the upcoming gubernatorial race with the federal officer and a reporter from the *Pittsburgh Telegraph*. He seemed rested, even pensive. "What is needed is a personal campaign," he observed as he toyed with his silk hat.[9] In his opinion, the party needed a candidate for governor who could best combine the "three important elements" of the electorate — 40,000 to 50,000 frustrated voters, 15,000 blacks, and many greenback-labor men. Without them, "we will meet defeat." The party had not polled its full vote since 1872, Grow went on. A personal campaign was the best way to start the cheering for victory. The party had to select the right candidate. "It wouldn't be the proper thing in me, understand gentlemen, to say I am that man, but if any other man is suggested who can better draw those elements than myself, let him be nominated, and I will assist him." When asked about the attitude of the Philadelphia Republican ring toward a personal candidacy, Grow cheerily responded, "Philadelphians, as a rule, run things by the machine. 'My man or a Democrat' is the motto of too many of them . . . the Republican candidates are too often machine men."

Grow wanted the nomination. As early as January 1878 he was

in Washington, sounding out Pennsylvania Republicans on the gubernatorial contest and his chances in it. The same month, in a letter to the *New York Tribune* that was the opening salvo of his campaign, he gave his reasons why an "army of tramps" existed.[10] Thousands of unemployed and destitute men were begging instead of working because after 1873 their ability to consume had fallen behind the nation's capacity to produce. The stoppage in railroad building and the general stagnation in business caused an honest and willing labor force to beg for its bread. Discontent among the unemployed and workers in general was demonstrated by violence that spread across the state in 1877. This discontent, plus a growing sentiment in favor of the remonetization of silver and the agitation of temperance leaders, were principal signs of a promising election. These were the hard issues, which Grow believed a viable candidate dared not sandbag. A party hack handpicked by the bosses and a platform of rebuilt cliches were not going to do the job. The voters were going to show greater interest in the candidates and how they presented the issues than in the platform itself. Grow's association with the Homestead Act had endeared him to the laboring class, which his stand on temperance had strengthened. Above all else, he considered the fact that he had never held either an executive or a legislative office in the state to be the best feather in his war bonnet. If the Democrats charged corruption in state government, then Grow was free of any blame.

By February, Grow's candidacy gained momentum. In typical fashion he stormed the state with impunity, like a Christian warrior armed with rapier and the gospel of truth. As usual, he made a deep impression. His strength lay in his popularity with the rank and file, his abilities and personal integrity, and his freedom from all entangling alliances. His friend Ernie Hempstead of the *Crawford Journal* was one of the first to endorse him. The editor referred to Grow as being both "original and modern" in his Republicanism — a man who helped make the party when half of those now running it were still in their nurses' arms.[11]

On the other side, Grow's opponents saw him as an ass, running about and doing his own electioneering. There is nothing more distasteful to the voters, the *Scranton Republican* observed, than a candidate who tries too hard.[12] But his opponents also expressed concern that he was picking up delegates; his personal campaign was indeed working. At one point Grow boasted of having sixty delegates committed to him. In fact, a good number of counties had instructed delegates to vote for him. Those in the northern tier and the northwest, with the exception of Erie, seemed solidly behind him. Still, the machine's choice for the job, Col. Henry Hoyt of Luzerne appeared to have the inside track. Democratic cynics noted that the Camerons never cared for instructions from constituents and looked instead to influence the delegates to the state convention. Once secured or "bought," the delegates voted as instructed by the Camerons. Thus, what did Grow really have going for him?

In May the Republican state convention assembled at the new opera house in Harrisburg. Visiting delegations marched through the streets, many with their own bands. Curious onlookers stared vacuously at the spectacle so commonplace in their city. Grow and Hoyt stayed at the Lochiel Hotel, where they received friends and heard the latest political gossip. What Grow soon heard stunned him: there was absolutely no way he could receive the nomination. Hoyt was to be the party's choice for governor. Rumors had circulated earlier that Cameron and Mackey were scheming to back Democrat Andrew H. Dill for governor, while the forces friendly to Sen. William Wallace, who favored Dill, were willing in exchange to see that Don Cameron went back to the Senate. Grow had been dubious; he claimed he had been told by Hartranft and Mackey that Cameron planned to take little interest in the nomination.[13]

As it turned out, not only did Cameron take a special interest in the campaign, but, along with Mackey and Hoyt, he also took charge of the convention. Prior to the assembling of the delegates, these men met with Matt Quay to dismantle all barriers to party harmony. In addition to Grow and Hoyt, other candidates included James Beaver and James P. Wickersham. One of the decisions reached at this meeting was that Grow could have the office of lieutenant governor if he wanted it. Grow's bugleman at the convention, ex-Speaker James H. Webb of Bradford, liked the idea, but Grow rejected it. This tribalistic maneuvering remained as distasteful as ever. The nod then went to Charles W. Stone. The scenario was near completion; Grow's personal campaign was on its final cycle. William H. Koontz of Somerset nominated Grow for governor with a fine address, but it was no use. Hoyt received the nomination on the first ballot by a vote of 161 to 47 for Grow, 29 for Wickersham, 12 for Beaver, and one for Morrell. The nomination was then made unanimous, amid cheers, the waving of hats, and the playing of bands. The machine had triumphed again.

For Grow, it was a familiar story: first in the trenches, last in the victory parade. His friends were disappointed. "Proceedings yesterday," the *Pittsburgh Telegraph* reported after the nomination of Hoyt, "will disgust rather than interest the honest masses of the Republican party in Pennsylvania."[14] But Grow did not allow this latest setback to deter him from assisting in the campaign. As before, he was anxious to take the circuit in defense of the ticket and resumption. "The Republican party is well organized in Pennsylvania," he commented, "forgetting all personal issues and moving forward as a solid body to win the fight." His rah-rah attitude after he had been once again pummelled into the campaign dust suggests either that Grow was a masochist or did not know when to stay down. Another explanation is that he was determined to stay true-blue to the party and suffer abuse if necessary, but never abandon hope that someday the organization would recognize his worth and allow him a high elective office. His tragedy was martyrdom. He was the conscience of the party, a diehard who seemed willing to sacrifice himself for the sins of his party. In early August he proudly announced that he would open the Republican campaign in Oil City.

It was one of his ablest addresses.[15] Enthusiastic crowds poured in from nearby Franklin, Meadville, and Titusville. This area was the heart of the oil industry in northwest Pennsylvania, where Grow was popular, where some of his money had been invested, and where the money question was as serious as any place in the state. And it was the money question that Grow principally addressed.

What he gave the Oil City crowd was a very basic lesson in money and its relationship to the nation's economy. His language was simple, so that the average worker in the audience could understand. Many of the ideas expressed were repetitious of earlier statements. Some were cliches: irredeemable paper money had been a bad national experience; only coinage had real value because of its intrinsic worth throughout the world. Producing a paper bill from his pocket, Grow told his audience that without law the piece of paper he held had no real value. A twenty-dollar gold piece, on the other hand, spoke for itself everywhere. The coin represented actual labor necessary and indispensable for its production, and the world knew what that was worth. Hard money was the creation of trade and commerce, not of governments.

Grow contended that the panic of 1873 could not have been caused by the fixing of a definite time for resumption of specie payments; this did not occur until 1875. Nor could its real cause have been a lack of sufficient circulating medium, because the volume in 1873–1874 was greater than at any previous period. Instead, the panic occurred when industrial production exceeded the consumptive power of the masses. In Grow's opinion, an expanded currency of irredeemable paper, made necessary by the exigencies of war, stimulated a "spirit of wild living" because a nation's markets can absorb only so much. When the masses stopped buying, production dropped off and men were thrown out of work. To meet the current emergency, Grow urged government outlays for public works and a decrease in foreign imports. The period 1871–1873 witnessed a great influx of foreign goods and the export of much specie. Republican victories were necessary to protect both American industry and labor against the free-trade tendencies of the Democrats. Grow's opponents scoffed at this rhetoric, countercharging that his own record on the tariff was pitiful. If the economy were as bad as Grow contended, the Republicans had only themselves to blame since they had been in control of the federal government since 1861.

In 1878, despite his failure to capture the gubernatorial nomination, Grow played the role of a loyal party servant. He supported Hoyt and a strong money plank, and continued to wave the bloody shirt. There was a good chance he could have had a congressional seat, but he declined the nomination in a short address before the Republican county convention.[16] Overton was then renominated and later reelected in one of many Republican victories in the state. The party retained its control of the legislature, and Hoyt's majority was more than 22,000.

At the beginning of the new year, Grow assessed his political future. Now that he had proven his fealty to the party's leadership, he might be more persistent in his desire for a top elective office. His popularity had soared because of his campaign efforts. President Hayes offered him the ambassadorship to Russia, but he declined.[17] He remained loyal to his vow that he would never occupy an office unless it were elective. His friends, who understood him not as a party martinet but as a devotee of higher principles, were glad he turned the appointment down. They wanted him to stay active in state politics as a counterforce or watchdog to any possible encroachments by the party's leaders. To his friends Grow was the avatar of party righteousness.

Throughout most of 1879 Republican solidarity in Pennsylvania appeared healthy. At the state convention in July at Harrisburg, Grow was selected president of the assemblage. In a stirring address, he praised the economic progress and industrial employment that resumption had revived.[18] But he cautioned his fellow Republicans against a new political crisis — the return of Democrats to power in the Congress. By their recent refusal to appropriate tax dollars for the support of the army, the Democrats were again showing their treasonous colors and taking up where they left off in 1861. Realistically, Grow warned, they might move toward the repeal of laws that Republicans had dutifully enacted to protect the civil rights of the people. This repeal process would be "revolutionary and destructive." Trying to lift their conscience, Grow probably surmised, was like trying to lift the *Merrimack*. The delegates translated Grow's concerns into strongly worded anti-Democratic planks in their platform, which also favored payment of the national debt in coin and paper currency redeemable in coin.

If the state Republicans seemed united in the summer of 1879, they appeared less so six months later. When Don Cameron and the Stalwarts decided to support Grant for a third term, the breach with the Half-Breeds was suddenly reopened. In late December the state committee called for the party convention in early February. The Stalwarts hoped to stack the convention with Grant delegates before the Half-Breeds had the opportunity to build a strong case for their man, Blaine. The plan worked. Grant came away with almost unanimous backing by the Pennsylvania delegation to the national convention in Chicago. Yet Cameron, Quay, and the determined Stalwarts failed to win the nomination for Grant. After thirty-four ballots, they watched their efforts go for naught as the delegates began to drift toward James Garfield, who eventually became the nominee. After the smoke had cleared, all Pennsylvania Republicans at least accepted Garfield outwardly, but the Half-Breeds did not forget the sneaky maneuver of the party leaders. The ill feeling carried beyond a victorious election and into the new year. When the Republican-controlled legislature addressed the first order of business, the election of a U.S. senator, the ramifications of the 1880 duplicity became clear.

Taking on King Caucus

Grow was the first prominent Republican to enter the senatorial race of 1881. His momentum and popularity increased as he campaigned for Garfield and Chester Arthur. While he praised the party's ticket, he also canvassed the state to gain instructions to county conventions for himself. At the end of the 1880 elections, by his own count, Grow had nearly a majority in the next legislature instructed for him.[19] Because of this obvious support, the press favorable to him insisted that this time he had every right to be nominated. Skeptics believed that Cameron and Quay would eventually put someone, or several candidates, in the field to oppose Grow. The *Venango Spectator* editorialized that the Republican bosses would lay Grow out "as cold as a wedge" and immolate him upon the "shrine of Cameronism."[20]

But Grow was not intimidated. He had worked hard for the nomination and the number of instructions he claimed to have proved the success of his barnstorming. To cheering audiences, he had given the Democrats a good cleaning and rinsing and had hung them out to dry. If accusing them of tying their destiny to the exploits of the Greenback party did not arouse the crowds, Grow always had the bloody shirt available. He presented his claims with a logic and format peculiarly his own in every public place — schoolhouses, churches, theaters. His hair and whiskers were frosted with time, but he had lost none of his firepower from the rostrum.

In December 1880 rumors were rampant on the senate question. There was no shortage of possible candidates. Governor Hoyt, Lieutenant Governor Stone, Matt Quay, and John Cessna, former chairman of the state central committee, to mention a few. Hoyt was as popular in the eastern half of the state as Stone was in the northwestern region.[21] Perhaps the wildest rumor was the one that had Cameron dragging out Grant, if necessary, to stop Grow. The former president, still quite popular, had a home in Philadelphia. He had been the choice of the Cameron-Quay organization at the bloody Republican convention in Chicago but had been denied a third-term bid. Grow considered the president ineligible although the state constitution was not specific on the residency requirement.

Grow's ego-inspired confidence assured him that he would be the next U.S. senator from Pennsylvania, replacing Democrat William A. Wallace. Interviewed by a reporter from the *Philadelphia Press,* Grow admitted that Quay and Hoyt were trying to field a candidate against him. "They just think they can sit in their offices and decide who is to become Senator," he remarked.[22] Grow added that the two men had promised, apparently in good faith, a year ago, that they would not oppose him. But he was not looking to their support as much as he was relying upon every member of the legislature to obey the instructions of his constituents. He rested his case with the election process — as long as it was not interfered with. His principal lieutenants, among whom were Charles S. Wolfe of Union and E. Reed Meyer of Bradford, hoped to control the party caucus; they believed they would come within five votes of nomination on the first ballot.

Several days before Christmas, however, a caucus of the Republican legislators from Allegheny County met at the Monongahela House in Pittsburgh and decided to present for senator the name of Henry W. Oliver, a respected businessman and a friend of Cameron's with similar interests and views on protectionism. Though his candidacy had not been active and he was generally unknown among Republicans outside of Allegheny County, Oliver had played a role in drafting the tariff planks in the 1876 and 1880 party platforms.[23]

It surprised no political observer when Oliver's last-minute entrance into the race aroused the ire of Half-Breeds and issue-oriented independents, thus forcing them into either supporting Grow or coming up with a candidate of their own. They were still furious with Cameron and Quay for calling the state convention so early in 1880 to endorse Grant. Now this. Certainly they planned to block Oliver and back Grow, if necessary, but it was no secret that Wolfe wanted the Senate seat for himself. Would he double-cross Grow?

Meanwhile, Grow's credibility among the party's dissidents had been weakened by his Texas retreat during the Liberal Republican rebellion and his support of Hoyt in 1878. In western Pennsylvania, where he had always enjoyed a dedicated following, his name had lost some of its magic in anti-Cameron circles. To some Republicans, "Old Galush" had returned from the South only to join the party ring that had spat upon him in 1869 and that he himself had rejected three years later. The *Venango Spectator* curiously asked what the party had done recently to regain the confidence of a man who had been bold enough in 1872 to support the Democratic presidential nominee, Greeley.[24] "I don't care anything about Grow," remarked newly elected Pennsylvania Sen. Lewis Emery of McKean County.[25] The feisty lawmaker admitted that he was on Grow's bandwagon simply because he was against Cameron's machine. Soon he was to jump off that wagon and rally behind Stone. It remained problematical to both Republicans and Democrats whether Grow would stay on his independent course or compromise his position by supporting the organization's candidate as he had in 1878. One thing was certain: since 1872 Grow had been tiptoeing through his own mine field. Rather than destroying any of his enemies, he had stood constantly on the brink of destroying himself.

With the start of the new year, Grow's political fortunes appeared far less encouraging than they had a month earlier. Instead of picking up additional legislators, he risked losing some pledged to him. His enemies, saying that he was already beaten, ridiculed him for mismanaging his lieutenants, who were conducting Chinese warfare by simply beating gongs instead of working on uninstructed lawmakers. When a delegation of Grow's friends indiscreetly asked Sen. Don Cameron to persuade Oliver to withdraw, Cameron replied: "Gentlemen, I am in favor of Mr. Oliver and Mr. Grow won't be Senator!"[26] The Stalwarts' position was plumbed. Perhaps some of them had rationalized when they questioned the soundness of rewarding unfaithful members of the party with high office. Whether he like it or not, Grow found himself straddling a fissure. On the one side he faced the party's old guard, who believed he had erred in 1872 by deserting them when good Republicans were needed; on the other, he found many independents who viewed his timorous role in the Liberal Republican revolt and his labors for Hoyt in 1878 as indication of his good intentions not to antagonize the Cameron gang too much.[27] As a result many Republicans who had initially backed Grow now became extremely cautious.

On January 3, 1881, a test vote was taken for chairman of the House Republican caucus. The Oliver faction selected John M. Pomeroy of Franklin County; Grow's supporters endorsed I. D. McKee of Philadelphia. Pomeroy received sixty-nine votes to McKee's fifty-one. Though not a decisive prediction of the vote on the next senator, the election did suggest Grow's deteriorating candidacy. His vulnerability was perhaps greatest among the representatives from the Philadelphia area, where the machine was not particularly friendly to him. Some lawmakers from the western counties felt increased pressure from party leaders and constituents to drop Grow for someone else, preferably a westerner. Three men who had instructions for Grow — W. R. Montgomery of Mercer, Ellis Morrison of Lawrence, and S. B. Meyers of Venango — decided to back Pomeroy after they had "listened" to machine managers.[28] But most of Grow's supporters remained faithful and confident. They regarded the late date fixed for the party caucus, January 13, as to their advantage; they needed time to recruit lawmakers who still wanted to be "convinced." Actually, time worked against Grow.

Both sides were assured of victory. Grow and Oliver had rooms at the Lochiel Hotel, where the heaviest caucusing took place. In Grow's headquarters in Parlor A, a placard read: "For United States Senator, Honorable G. A. Grow, Father of the Homestead Bill, Advocate and Defender of American Industry, Champion of Free Soil, Free Speech, Free Men." Surely, these superlatives covered all the bases. While the former Speaker entertained his friends in a parlor, Oliver welcomed his in the hotel's bridal chamber.

The vicious politicking and the balloting that followed made this intraparty struggle as tense as any in recent years. Politicians are generally subjected to unremitting scrutiny; thus, they are forced to polish their images until the shine often blinds anyone who wishes to probe beneath the surface for a glimpse of more substantial qualities. But appearances do not always matter. In the 1881 senatorial race, images, the abilities of the candidates, and their understanding of issues were once again relegated to a subordinate status. The real story was that of rival organizations. The election resembled a Shakespearean tragedy, and not just because more pathetic characters crowded the stage than the audience wanted to sort out. The election also contained the old anti-Democratic theme, sustained by deception, fraud, chicanery, and a political witchcraft that horrified voters into believing that what they were seeing could not really be happening.

On the eve of the legislature's convening, the candidate situation had become murkier. Either to scare the Oliver people into making some sort of deal or to reduce Grow's strength, the Philadelphia representatives proposed another candidate, A. L. Snowden of their city. Grow's managers did not look upon this move with disfavor, for their man was not counting on more than three votes from Philadelphia. At the same time, the scare tactic, if this is what it was, did not ruffle Oliver's backers; the Philadelphia gesture was doomed to failure. Meanwhile, two of Grow's supporters from Allegheny County, William Flynn and John Knowland, under constant pressure, switched to Oliver.

When the lawmakers assembled on January 12, it was obvious that no candidate of either faction controlled a majority. A Republican meeting that evening at Senator Cameron's proved encouraging to Oliver but disappointing to Grow. The Cameron-Quay forces made it clear that they had enough votes to block Grow, which they intended to do, and to frustrate the chances of any other candidate the independents might advance. Grow claimed he had sixty-one votes, seventeen short of election. In addition, he learned that he was no longer the overwhelming choice among Republican editors. Finally, Snowden's decision to drop out and the determination of the Philadelphia delegation to support Oliver utterly demolished Grow's frontal assault. All he could do was to spike his guns and retreat to higher ground.

Realizing their hopeless predicament, the Grow faction decided to bolt the party caucus scheduled for the next day. By this means they hoped to prevent the presence of a majority necessary to form a caucus and so arrest any possible action. The *Pittsburgh Evening Telegraph* commented that Grow and his friends never questioned the caucus as long as they believed they had a chance to control it.[29] They posted a notice calling for a Republican meeting at Grow's headquarters. Forty-five attended and adopted a resolution that it was not in the best interests of the party to go into a caucus for the election of a senatorial candidate. Instead, they intended to give their individual preferences in the Senate, the House, or in joint assembly.[30]

When the caucus met the next day, forty-seven Republican members of the legislature had endorsed the resolution. Though the party strength in that body was 154, fewer than 100 senators and representatives attended the caucus. General uneasiness prevailed. Those in attendance adopted a motion to prevent any candidate from receiving the nomination unless he polled a majority of all Republicans in the legislature. The first ballot gave Oliver fifty-one votes, Snowden twelve, and Grow ten; twenty-two votes were scattered among eight other contenders. On the second ballot, Oliver received sixty-three; on the third, seventy-nine. Since he now had a majority, he was declared the party's nominee.

Republican reaction to the bolt was divided between joy and censure. James Freeman Clarke was reported to have said, "If anything in American politics is Heaven born, it is a bolt." Those who praised the Harrisburg bolt hoped the bolters would hold out to defeat every lackey the machine put forth. To the critics, the uprising was "an inexcusable revolt within the party and that those engaged in it must retrace their steps or take their place outside of the organization."[31] Their party was one of law, and neither compromise nor concession attained through threats and bolting was forgivable. They saw Grow becoming the bête noire of the party. His lance level, he was ready to slay the dragon of Cameronism and with it the Republican party. Don Cameron did not like what he saw. It was Chicago in 1880 all over again, but more serious. The defeat of Oliver might mean the end of the Cameron dynasty.

The longer the bolters held out, the more desperate became the efforts of the Stalwarts. Compromise seemed out of the question. Quay appealed to President-elect Garfield to intervene by offering the veteran argonaut, Grow, a cabinet position, but Garfield showed little interest.[32] Blandishments of promised patronage from the incoming administration to the bolters were hoped for, but would they be forthcoming? Pennsylvania businessmen were becoming fidgety. Writing to the older Cameron, a manufacturer from York warned against Grow and pleaded with the aging oligarch to insist upon Oliver.[33] But insistence was no assurance of victory. Actually, Oliver's boom developed faster than many Republicans had anticipated. Though rumor had it that Don Cameron was not that enraptured with the Pittsburgh industrialist, the party boss had little choice but to stick with him. Oliver may have been made a candidate just to block Grow, and once this had been accomplished the Stalwarts were in a position to urge a more preferable choice, perhaps Quay. But now it seemed too late.

At the same time, many of Grow's friends believed their man had played his cards poorly. By bolting the caucus, he had abandoned any chance to become senator. Had he gone into the caucus, they argued, he probably would have exceeded Oliver's vote on the first ballot. The ten votes he received in the caucus, combined with the block he already had with the bolters, easily surpassed the fifty-one given to Oliver. In the opinion of the *Titusville Weekly Herald,* Grow's courage gave out when he needed it most.[34] He walked out when he saw he could not control the caucus and subsequently he failed to be nominated. In contrast, Oliver accepted the challenge and eventually emerged the caucus winner. Because of his courage and determination, some Republican editors were satisfied to declare Oliver the choice of the party.

Grow remained serenely hopeful. Neither he nor Oliver expected or desired aid from the Democrats, who enjoyed the Republican debacle and resolved to stand as a phalanx behind Wallace. On January 17 Grow's friends prepared a statement giving the reasons for the bolt. They demanded higher qualifications for such a distinguished position than business experience and financial success. In their view the caucus had tried to force the selection of a man who was inexperienced in public life and was previously unknown outside his county. The bolters insisted they were Republicans in support of a man of unquestioned fidelity to the party. They were merely transferring the contest from the caucus to the joint convention of the two legislative houses in order to determine if the will of the people would be respected.[35]

On January 18 the question of who was to become the next senator from Pennsylvania went before the legislature. The vote for the three major contenders was inconclusive:

	Senate	House	Total
Oliver (R)	20	75	95
Grow (R)	12	44	56
Wallace (D)	16	77	93

Since no candidate had a majority, the Senate and House went into joint assembly. Under both federal and state law the joint assembly was to meet every legislative day and vote for a senator until one was chosen. On January 19 two ballots were taken and the totals matched the earlier ones.[36] No one was about to give in. The Democrats had it in their power to break the deadlock, but their policy seemed to be "look wise and say nothing." A strong rumor circulated that an alliance might be made between the regular Republicans and Democrats, with a fair apportionment being traded for a U.S. senator. But many Democrats expressed a repugnance at aiding any arrangement that would promote success of the Republican machine. From January 19 to February 9 the legislators dutifully met, cast their ballots, and reaffirmed the deadlock. More anger resulted. With each ballot costing the taxpayer about $2,500, responsible lawmakers argued that the tomfoolery had gone far enough. It was time to call a halt.

Everyone agreed, but no one would make the first gesture. With an inner resolve, Grow quipped that his troops had enlisted for the war and would stay all winter if necessary. His grit matched Cameron's obstinacy. But some of Grow's warriors were exhibiting signs of battle fatigue; the struggle had become one of endurance. Unswerving principles pulling at both ends of the Republican line continued to test its strength. Pressure from constituents, however, prompted the bolters on January 24 to submit a list of seven names, any one of whom they pledged to support if mutually acceptable to Oliver's managers. These were Thomas Bayne and George Shiras, Jr., both of Allegheny; C. S. Wolfe of Union; Wayne MacVeagh and Joseph Wharton of Philadelphia; Sen. John Stewart of Franklin, and Grow.[37] The regulars were not impressed; all seven were objectionable. Oliver and his backers viewed this peace offering as proof that Grow was finally weakening and that his cronies were ready to hang the white flag.

Meanwhile, rumors continued. One had Wolfe scheming to combine Democratic and Republican votes for himself, with little success. Another was that Garfield wanted to appoint Sen. Don Cameron his secretary of war, so Pennsylvania Republicans could elect both Grow and Oliver. A third rumor was of a movement to adjourn the legislature so that the governor might appoint someone for the interim.

The break came on February 9. On that day, the twenty-first ballot produced little change in the voting pattern but, more important, Oliver broke the Gordian knot by withdrawing from the race. He informed the Republican members that he was no longer a candidate and that his supporters were free to choose their next senator from among worthy Republicans. He had sent a note to Grow conveying his decision to withdraw, thus hoping that the ex-Speaker would pull out as well. Grow officially withdrew his name and thanked those who had supported him.[38]

Cameron apparently had met with both combatants and advised them to sheath their swords. Neither had a chance of victory. The party czar then submitted his own list of suitable candidates, including Quay and Gen. James Beaver of Bellefonte. It was said that Grow had walked away from that meeting indicating he had no objection to Beaver. Some of Grow's friends, upon learning of his talks with Cameron, feared that some political plum had been offered to Grow. Their fears were inflated by a story that Grow had agreed to Beaver after Cameron's promise of the gubernatorial nomination the next year, a slot for which Beaver had already been booked.[39]

Inoculated with Cameron phobia and upset with Grow's personal maneuver, the bolters held a caucus to map their next move. It was a stormy three-hour session. In the words of a reporter for the *Harrisburg Patriot,* the swearing of an army on the march was piety compared with the quality and quantity of expletives hurled about by Grow's former allies.[40] The bolters dropped Grow, rejected Beaver and Wolfe, and decided upon Bayne of Allegheny. They agreed to stick with him until at least two-thirds of them wanted someone else.

Meanwhile, about fifty regular Republicans met at Cameron's and unanimously endorsed Beaver. A pair of new faces had been introduced to the voting, but the old animosities remained. On the first ballot in joint assembly, Beaver and Bayne polled almost identical votes. There were also about a dozen other candidates in the field. Despite Beaver's fine qualities, the fact that he had been picked by Cameron killed whatever chance he might have had. The Republican party was back to square one.

The horrible thought of another hopeless impasse produced serious consideration of compromise. A proposal for a conference committee between the warring groups was agreed upon after acrimonious debate, but at least it was a step in the proper direction. As it turned out, each faction appointed a representative group to meet daily in joint session and ballot for the party's nominee. As many as twenty candidates received votes. The conference committee had its problems, especially since the bolters wanted to abide by the two-thirds rule. It appeared that the deadlock would go on forever. Finally, on February 22, both sides agreed to nominate John Mitchell of Tioga County, who on the same day defeated Wallace in joint convention. The long ordeal had ended.

Mitchell was a congressman and Half-Breed from the anti-Cameron belt of the state who had managed to avoid many of the party's quarrels. The bolters claimed him, therefore, as one of their own and believed they had defeated Cameron and the machine. Regular Republicans insisted that Mitchell had been satisfactory to Cameron, who never relinquished his right to reject anyone who was personally obnoxious to him. And that is where the matter rested; both sides claimed victory. According to McClure, it was Col. Samuel Dick of Meadville who served as Cameron's close adviser and arranged the compromise that led to the selection of Mitchell.[41]

Time was needed to survey the party wreckage and determine the severest casualties. Certainly machine rule had suffered. The Cameron-Quay organization had experienced unprecedented indignities, which were bound to affect relations with the party's reformers. King Caucus was again on the line; a better, more democratic way of selecting senators had to be found. Those who had hoped the nomination of Mitchell might restore party unity soon discovered that Republican togetherness rested upon the conviction that no one during the seven-week struggle had sacrificed a single principle. Group conscience was no deeper than the shallow opportunities of individual leaders.

Tired, chagrined, and beaten, Grow lay on a couch, his palms under his head, talking sotto voce to a reporter for the *New York Tribune.* His words took on a dreamy, almost elegiac, tone. The reporter stared at a man in his late fifties, hair and beard of a grayish-white, tall, thin, rather loosely jointed, and with a goatlike look, and listened to a sad story of how ninety committed representatives showed up in Harrisburg only to be devoured by machine managers.[42] It was a tale of woe Grow had told before. Again, he had been a front-runner who lost in the home stretch. His candidacy had been the crossroads of two intersecting lines of thought. While he had believed himself to be the candidate whose knowledge, independent views, and deep roots in the political loam of Pennsylvania and Washington would strengthen the party's position in the Senate, many independents had viewed him simply as the most available person with credentials who could be used as a symbol against Cameronism.

There was little question that, prior to the opening day of the legislature, Grow had been the party's only legitimate candidate, and a popular one at that. And it was quite possible that the Cameron ring was sorry afterward that it had blocked him. Quay allegedly believed Grow had more strength among voters than anyone in the state; an alliance between him and Cameron would be invincible.[43] But Grow had not gone to the organization for the senatorship; instead, he had appealed directly to the people, as was his custom. He had to be stopped, therefore, to preserve the integrity of the machine.

Watching the final balloting from the rear of the hall, Grow had to wonder what was next in store for him. How many more political Everests must he climb to prove his worth to his own party? In the months following this last humiliation, he turned his attention to his coal interests in western Pennsylvania. He refused interviews and seemed content with what he was doing. Friends wondered what it would take to return the gracious veteran to political life. Some believed the Independent Republican movement of 1882 might spur him into action. After all, it was another revolt against Cameronism and its gubernatorial candidate was John Stewart, one of the 1881 bolters. Though many had hoped Grow would actively campaign in Stewart's behalf, there is little evidence he did. It seemed he had taken another political sabbatical.

ℬ 14

Congressman-at-Large: The Last Hurrah

G ROW'S ENEMIES ridiculed the way he had quietly removed himself from the political scene, and frequently asked "Where is Grow?" Some observers believed in 1882 that he would make his presence felt in the Independent Republican movement, which was offbeat enough to appeal to his rebellious instincts. Others figured he had been so badly stunned in the senatorial race that an unpretentious retirement was the only dignified way out of an embarrassing situation. But his friends expressed confidence he would be back. They contended that, together with his allies, Grow had dragged the Republican party from the sands of uncertainty to its current solid position. He had given too much of himself to the party to leave it with a brush of finality; he was not about to run away from it as he had in 1872.

His friends were right. Grow did return to participate in the 1884 presidential campaign. Hope of redemption, revenge, service, vanity — not necessarily in that order — all prompted the old warrior back into action. Visions of elective office continued to blind him; he had been mentioned in 1882 as a possible gubernatorial candidate. His name was as commonplace as the Republican party itself; anybody who knew anything about Pennsylvania politics knew of Grow. His reputation remained anchored to his successes as a champion of homestead legislation, a maverick of the first order, and a staunch radical in Congress who figuratively had stood indignant southerners upon their heads or literally had knocked them to the floor.

At a time when more and more loyalty was being exacted to ensure party regularity, Grow had found it easier than most politicians to defy the dictates of party machinery. He had earned the right to be either accommodating or obnoxious, or both. Among leading state Republicans, no one boasted more scars from running the gauntlet of elective office than Grow, and none had enjoyed such consistent fortune in being able to touch the political conscience of the electorate. If anyone represented what might be called the self-righteousness of Republican behavior, it had to be Grow. He made Republicans feel glad they were Republicans. His candidacies had excited those voters who expected to see a silver lining in every political cloud.

Yet time had taken its toll. Tethered to a traditional radicalism and battered by repeated onslaughts of party bosses, Grow found himself becoming an irrelevant anachronism to many voters. He was nostalgia; his political world rested more in the past than in the future. As the twentieth century neared, the country needed new ideas and new leadership. Its institutions had to adopt manageable systems that were developed upon quantified knowledge drawn from many fields of learning. Social Darwinism had penetrated the very marrow of intellectual America; it pointed to continued progress in a complex society. To snub these precepts was to reject science and modernity.

A generation that had not experienced abolitionism, or the massacre at Pottawatomie, or the attack on Sumter looked askance at older politicians who scoffed at the logic of party order and relied instead upon elegant oratory and personal pizazz as springboards to immortality. The days of Webster, Clay, and Douglas—the great debaters and guardians of Union—were gone. There was still room for individuality, but not at the cost of group success. More than ever, political organization was necessary as a vehicle to give fresh ideas their marketability. Independent action by party members was taboo. Those first Republicans, like Grow, who had envisaged their new party as a pacesetter in the van of progress, now had the opportunity to use that party to advance the great ideas of the day. Either they marched forward, arm in arm, as progressives engaging the future or they had to leave the trail to those who would. Reveling in yesterday's memories and refighting former enemies would not open new vistas.

Tribute, Triumph . . .

In 1884 Pennsylvania Republicans were fragmented over the choice for president. Some spoilsmen favored the incumbent, Chester Arthur, while the majority leaned toward the ever popular "Plumed Knight," James G. Blaine. Reformers and other opponents raised questions about Blaine's reputed dishonesty. Whether these disparate elements were obstinate enough to frustrate efforts at party harmony remained to be seen.

As expected, Grow came out early for his friend Blaine. Of all the presidential candidates, he called Arthur the weakest, an opinion shared by many fellow Republicans. Along with F. F. Lyon, Grow was chosen as a Blaine delegate from the Fifteenth Congressional District. Talk that he might run as congressman-at-large died once he had been selected delegate. Prior to the Republican state convention in April, he was also considered the delegate most likely to become its chairman.[1] If nothing else, this consensus in favor of Grow suggested that cooperation, not discord, would prevail in Harrisburg. The Blaine people would dominate the convention, and it was reassuring to them that the party bosses were not scheming to block Blaine's candidacy. Quay did not plan to interfere with the people's choice for president, while Cameron was persuaded to take himself to Europe. Neither man attended the national convention in Chicago. Thus, tension between the Stalwarts and Half-Breeds in Pennsylvania had been momentarily reduced.

Grow became the unanimous choice for permanent chairman at the Harrisburg meeting; apparently the regulars believed that he was a good enough Stalwart to preside. Upon taking the chair he gave a characteristically spirited address in which he asked for a protective tariff that would secure for the worker a comfortable living and warned against Democrats who based their convictions and theories of free trade on "imaginary" facts. Cheapness of commodities, he said, was not to be sought at the expense of the wages of the American worker. With normal convention hullabaloo, the delegates cheered Grow as he reviewed the achievements of the party and urged harmony among its members. The delegates were off to a good start. They declared in favor of Blaine, six to one, and adopted a platform that called for the continuation of the present tariff, the suspension of coinage of the standard silver dollar, and the promotion of civil service.

In his acceptance address, Grow had used the coal industry to illustrate how protectionism worked to the benefit of labor. His critics found this dictum both amusing and at variance with his recent behavior. According to a Harrisburg newspaper, Grow had been in Washington nearly all winter lobbying for a free-trade reciprocal treaty with Canada on coal.[2] How hypocritical it was of Grow, as president of the Coal and Iron Ore Reciprocity Association, the paper went on, to endorse a protective tariff plank while at the same time hoping that coal might be placed upon the free list. His action obviously indicated a desire for the best of two worlds. The same paper also found it ironic that Grow, pontificating on the benefits of protectionism to labor, should now find the workers at his own mine in East Brady out on strike because of the poor wages he paid them.[3]

With fifty-nine other Pennsylvania delegates, nearly all of whom were solidly behind Blaine, Grow journeyed to the national party powwow in Chicago, where he hoped he would be elected president of the convention. His state delegation was for him; so was Quay back home. In a letter to his old friend, Elihu Washburne, Grow promised that, if elected, he would do what he could for a business item of importance to Washburne.[4] But he failed to gain the chair. The best he did was to serve on the rules committee, from which he made a recommendation that delegates to the next national convention be elected in the same manner as members of Congress. Grow was named as the Pennsylvania representative to the committee to notify Blaine and his running mate, Black Jack Logan, of their nomination. The *Philadelphia Evening Telegraph* commented that Grow "always gets to the front just in time to get left."[5] He was pitied as much as he was admired.

His disappointment did not keep him from laboring hard for Blaine and the platform. He barnstormed the commonwealth as though he were a candidate. Everywhere he went his message was clear: America can only prosper under Republican leadership, which will see that both industry and labor benefit under any plan of protection. He explained how a tariff for revenue only opens the country to foreign manufacturers. The highest wisdom of statesmanship was the enactment of laws that permit American workers to produce the commodities consumed by the American people. Next to human bondage, the greatest crime of nations was a policy that degraded or impoverished labor. Just as government has the responsibility to enact land legislation to enable actual settlers to benefit from their cultivation of the land, so government must adopt protective measures to allow the workingman to attain the maximum from his labors.

Grow had to be pleased with the response of Pennsylvania voters; Blaine carried the state by a plurality of more than 80,000. But the Democratic "reform governor" of New York, Grover Cleveland, won the general election in a close contest. It had been a campaign marked from the beginning by one of the worst displays of mudslinging in American political history. Cleveland was accused of being a drunkard and the father of an illegitimate child, while Blaine was caricatured as the "tattooed man," blighted by innumerable acts of dishonesty. Personalities and not issues had dominated the campaign. Blaine probably lost the general election in New York, a pivotal state with thirty-six electoral votes, where a Republican clergyman foolishly proclaimed in Blaine's presence that the Democrats were a party of "rum, Romanism, and rebellion" — an accusation that obviously offended the Irish Catholic voter. Blaine did not repudiate this slur. New York went Democrat in the election.

In a way, Blaine's defeat was Grow's defeat. For the first time since Buchanan, a Democrat sat in the White House, while former Confederates from a regenerated South occupied key positions at all levels of government. Republicans suspected that the Democrats might repeal the war-born amendments to the Constitution and turn the clock back to 1860. Grow expressed this fear in some of his speeches. From his standpoint, the old enemy had attained through the ballot box what it had failed to attain on the battlefield — political power. But his fear proved unrealistic because the bloody shirt had lost some of its former magic.

Secondly, in spite of Blaine's victory in the commonwealth, the Republican party in Pennsylvania had to be rebuilt. This meant a return to a tighter organization by managers loyal to Quay and Cameron. So much had rested upon the success of Blaine's candidacy. His sweeping victory in the state occurred because the will of the people had been exercised without the usual interference by bossism. Blaine's supporters had been optimistic as the campaign camaraderie briefly sparked a unanimity, which they hoped would glow in the aftermath of victory. But after Blaine lost, many Republicans speculated that his defeat would prompt Stalwarts to cry "I told you so!" before proceeding to recapture their total command of the party. The long ensuing struggle was bound to tear the party apart along the old seams. Skeptics correctly ruled out peaceful coexistence among the rival factions. Subsequently, the jockeying among managers for position and the lingering stench of Cameronism dispelled all rumors that the party was approaching nirvana. Quay had his back to the wall, but he emerged from the intraparty struggle much stronger than most of his antagonists. But the party was badly shaken.

Grow's political career was one of the coffins buried in this time of trouble. Though he still longed for elective office, his enthusiasm began to wither. No matter how hard he twisted and turned, he remained stuck in the turnstile of political fate. Though he was casually mentioned several times as a possible candidate for the U.S. Senate, party bosses showed little interest. In a sentimental, almost romantic, way Grow appealed to Republicans as an institution might; he was respected, admired, but taken for granted. To his critics he was still the same old Grow — a braggart intoxicated with the flare

and monotony of his own demagoguery. In his speeches they saw
hackneyed phrases whose freshness could not be revived by the ideas
they contained. To his friends, in contrast, he remained the crusty
old knight who symbolized the spirit of the Union and the glory of
the party. Grow always appreciated the moral support of his friends,
but after the defeat of Blaine he was out of spirits.

Contributing to Grow's depression at this time was the death of
another crusty old knight, Reuben E. Fenton. In August 1885, several days before his sixty-second birthday, Grow journeyed to James-
town, New York, to pay his last respects to a dear friend whose early
political career closely paralleled his. Both men entered Congress as
enthusiastic Democrats and left it as uncompromising Republicans.
Their similar philosophies drew them together. Each supported homestead legislation, a cheap postal system, and the repeal of the fugitive
slave law. And they were among the first in the House of Representatives to speak out against the Kansas-Nebraska bill. Their youthful
exuberance, patriotism, and abhorrence of slavocracy were sufficiently
unrestrained to drive them into the streets of Washington, if necessary,
to do battle with their opponents. Fenton went on in 1864 to become
governor of New York and U.S. senator from 1869 to 1875. No doubt
Grow envied his friend's political successes, but he never let this mar
a warm and lasting bond between them. Grow spent a great deal of
time in New York and was often seen in the company of Fenton.

Grow's opportunity came in 1893 with the death of Congressman
William Lilly of Mauch Chunk. For nearly a decade Grow had been
something of a political recluse, but he was still able and willing to
run. After canvassing other possible candidates to replace Lilly and
observing that the Republican press was endorsing Grow, party leaders agreed not to interfere with his nomination. There were definite
advantages to having his name on the ticket. A popular candidate
like Grow was apt to call out the old Republican guard, and his presence in the House was sure to strengthen the Republican position
at a time when the party needed all the help it could get. McClure
thought Grow's candidacy was merely a sop to the antimachine elements.[6] And it is reasonable to presume that Quay went along just
to avoid another intraparty quarrel.

By the time the Republican state convention assembled in Harrisburg in early January 1894, Grow was the only viable candidate
for congressman-at-large. Delegates wasted no time in nominating
him by acclamation. One lone challenger humbly withdrew his name.
The applause began and then swelled as Grow walked from the back
of the hall down the center aisle with the suppleness of a young man.

Before he reached the speaker's platform, the applause had become an ovation as men rose in their seats and waved their hats. It was a tumultuous tribute to a courageous man. After thirty years of humiliating setbacks and defeats, Grow stood on the brink of elective office with the full blessing of his party.

With tears in his eyes, he graciously thanked the cheering delegates and then electrified them with one of his patented addresses. He arraigned President Cleveland and Secretary of State Walter Gresham for their un-American and unconstitutional "policy of infamy" in trying to return Queen Lilioukalani to the throne in Hawaii. He blamed the Democrats for the nation's economic plight and called their programs a handicap to America's industries. He referred to their party's Wilson bill as a tariff hybrid—not sufficient to raise revenue, not protective enough for manufacturers and their workers. Unwilling to miss the opportunity to single out the southern Democrats, he charged them for historically embracing a political philosophy based upon the principles of slavery, secession, and free trade.[7]

Had the script been written by Grow himself, it could not have been better. The whole party seemed to close ranks behind his candidacy. His selection, in the opinion of many, reflected far more credit upon the party and commonwealth than upon Grow. The action taken was not only proper but long overdue as well. Wesley R. Andrews, editor of the *Meadville Daily Republican* and an ally of Quay's referred to the nomination as a "master stroke of both good policy and good sense."[8] He viewed it as symbolic of a new liberal spirit in party management that pointed to the day when "clans" within the party would be abolished.

Grow's candidacy was more than a beau geste or belated honor to the "grand old man" of the Republican party. Republicans hailed it as a conscious effort to focus state and national attention upon their battle over the tariff. Grow was supposed to buoy up the spirits of the Republican minority in the House and to reinforce arguments against the Wilson bill. Who was better able to represent the concerns of Pennsylvania's industrial community than Grow, the elder statesman who years earlier had performed so well in the crusade for hard money?

With the election scheduled for February 20, campaign time was limited. Nearly seventy years of age, Grow canvassed the state as best he could. Crowded coaches and uncomfortable hotels were beginning to take their toll. Ex-Congressman Samuel Miller of Mercer County promised he would never again go campaigning with Grow, for the former Speaker had insisted that Miller give him a total rubdown after they appeared together in Greenville.[9] Yet Grow had lost little as an orator. His wit and sarcasm had not been blunted by time. Hundreds of listeners had heard him many times before. Others for the first time watched a sprightly veteran of the game — his face of fixed determination, his silver hair and whiskers transfigured by the glow of gaslight — dissect the issues with the cutting skill of a surgeon. Republicans everywhere greeted him warmly. After an address in Pittsburgh, where he had appeared at the old city hall with William McKinley, the high priest of protectionism, Grow was casually mentioned as a possible vice-presidential candidate. "McKinley and Grow in '96" seemed a reasonable combination if the tariff was to be the key issue in that election year. Even the Democrats of Susquehanna believed that Grow was the best Republican choice, but the *Montrose Democrat* quickly added that good Democrats should vote for their party's nominee, James B. Hancock of Venango.[10]

Grow won in a landslide — 485,804 votes to Hancock's 297,966.[11] Republicans boasted that Grow's plurality was the greatest achieved by any Republican candidate in any previous state election and dusted off his pre–Civil War title of "Great Majority Grow." The Republican press interpreted this overwhelming victory as a protest against the Wilson bill and free trade.

On March 2, 1894, Congressman Grow was sworn in as a member of the Fifty-third Congress. When William Holman of Indiana, the "Father of the House" until Grow arrived, moved that the oath of office be administered even though the credentials had not yet been sent by Harrisburg, no one objected. Holman was the only one present who had been a member of the House when Grow was the Speaker. Also on the floor was Daniel Sickles of New York, who had served with Grow in the Thirty-fifth and Thirty-sixth Congresses. On January 21, 1892, Holman had been one of several representatives to pay tribute to Grow and Samuel J. Randall at a ceremony in which portraits of the two former Speakers from Pennsylvania were presented to the House. The legislature of Pennsylvania had commissioned artist W. A. Greaves of Warren to do the portraits. Others who honored Grow on this occasion included David Henderson of Iowa and fellow Pennsylvanians Charles W. Stone and Myron B. Wright. Grow was present at this memorable event; Randall had died two years earlier. Regarding Grow, Henderson perhaps summed it best: "As Speaker of the House he was fair, firm, and fearless, showing a keen regard for the laws of the country, the laws of this body, and the higher law which touches every heart from the divine source of all law."[12]

Grow reentered Congress at a time when the nation's economy was on the downside. Times were painfully bad. Cleveland had hardly made himself comfortable in the White House for his second term when the panic of 1893 destroyed any hope of recovery. Thousands of business houses had suddenly collapsed. The market bust seemed a natural climax to everything that was falling apart. The agricultural depression deepened as farm prices continued to fall. Populists demanded a new deal and looked among America's industrial masses for allies. Acute labor distress and strikes plagued basic industries, bringing gloom and misery to many communities. Violence became a logical aftermath. In Ohio, "General" Coxey prepared his ragged army of the unemployed for its heroic march on Washington "to right the nation's wrong." On top of all this, the president faced new deficits. Under the Sherman Silver Purchase Act, the treasury issued legal tender notes for the silver bullion it bought — notes that were redeemable in gold. The repeal of this act in 1893 satisfied Wall Street, but it did not stop the run on gold. At the time of Grow's election in February, the draining of gold had dropped the reserve to an alarming $41,000,000. Fear paralyzed money groups as rumors circulated that the nation might have to go off the gold standard.

In due time Grow addressed many aspects of the ailing economy, but his first remarks were in defense of his own amendment fixing the lowest rates in a pension appropriation bill for disabled veterans. The lawmakers applauded when he concluded, "There is no reason why the animosities engendered in the conflict [Civil War] should not be buried with the honored dead, remembering only their heroic deeds."[13] Was Grow finally putting the bloody shirt to rest? Many hoped he was. His statement was in sharp contrast to his Harrisburg acceptance in January when he scourged the southern Democrats. Economic exigencies seemed far too important to give the replay of the war equal time. Grow was smart enough not to become mired in old political mud. A new generation of political leaders, inspired or intimidated by such works as Henry George's *Progress and Poverty* (1879) and Edward Bellamy's socialistic novel *Looking Backward* (1888), confronted the nation's ills with remedies that indicated that American politics was clearly becoming more ideological. The socioeconomic imbalances in society forged both a new conservatism and a new liberalism that attended to the poor, the unemployed, and the disenfranchised. The preponderance of social problems made the exact relationship between government and capitalism the crucial debate question of the day. The old issues of sectionalism and Union were no longer relevant.

Grow had to make strategic and tactical adjustments. The greater picture behind every issue was not an illustration of northern and southern interests in conflict. No longer was he able to talk about the tariff, for example, as a sectional problem. Such a simplistic explanation was not going to wash with fellow representatives, many of whom were toddlers at the time of the war. They wanted to treat the great problems as products of contemporary society and not as relics of a bygone age. "Let's forget the war," they might say, "and get on with the business at hand." If he wished to politicize the tariff, Grow now had to stress party differences. He had to convince his listeners that a Republican tariff was better than the Democratic proposal, not because free industry and free labor preferred it over a plan sponsored by southern extremists, but because it was good for the country.

The tariff had been a major issue in the two previous presidential elections. High-protection Republicans, through their McKinley tariff of 1890, had succeeded in raising rates to their highest peacetime level — an average of 48.4 percent on dutiable goods. Although it was designed to provide greater protection, its prohibitory rates lowered total customs receipts and caused mounting discontent. Combined with the gold drain, the sharp decline in revenues increased deficits and wiped out the surplus of 1890. Democratic victories in 1892 had forecast a move to frame a new tariff that would provide sufficient revenue and moderate protection. To appease the Populists and the poverty-conscious Democrats who scorned a developing plutocracy, the proposed Wilson bill also included a 2 percent tax on incomes over $4,000. The bill managed to get through the House without difficulty while Grow was campaigning. Though he had taken his seat too late to try to prevent its passage, he hoped to influence Senate opinion on it.

His extended remarks on the tariff began on June 7 in an address characterized by impressive statistics and heavy charges against the Democrats. He spelled out what he believed to be the doctrinal differences between the two parties on this crucial issue. Whereas the Democrats viewed the tariff primarily as a means to raise revenue, even at the cost of flooding American markets with cheaply produced foreign articles, the Republicans saw the tariff as a way to protect home production by encouraging domestic markets to absorb products of domestic labor. Imports, he continued, must not be used to reduce wages of American workers who produce the same goods; articles not produced in this country should be admitted free unless there was a good reason to impose duties. In later commentary he attacked the income-tax provision in the Wilson bill by insisting that there was no reason for such a tax in times of peace. Throughout our entire history government had been satisfied in peacetime to collect revenues from duties on imports "without resorting to an income tax or any of the other taxes known and recognized as war taxes."[14]

Grow's poignant rebuke of the Wilson bill failed to match, in quantity at least, the everlasting speech that Quay delivered by installments in the Senate. The senator's filibuster was purposeful as well as boring. The result was what counted, however. The Senate amended the bill more than 600 times before adopting it in July. The next month the House approved the bill and then passed special bills placing sugar, coal, barbed wire, and iron ore on the free list as a protest against the Senate rates on these articles.[15] Outraged by what he regarded as a betrayal of Democratic pledges to the voters, Cleveland permitted the bill to become law without his signature. After all, a poor Democratic measure was better than keeping the McKinley tariff. The new act did reduce the rates on dutiable goods to 41.3 percent.

The amended bill, christened the Wilson-Gorman bill, was no more an answer to the nation's hard times than the McKinley tariff had been. Farm prices continued in a downward spiral while labor unrest intensified. The Republicans took the 1894 tariff to the voters, referring to it as a sham, a fraud, a piece of legislation that benefited no industry but injured many, and an instant step to disaster. The Republicans cleverly pointed to the new law's reduced duties on Havana cigars, liquors, silk dress goods, carpets, cut glass, jewelry, and pearl buttons—all to the benefit of the more affluent classes. In the next session of Congress Grow asked that duties on these luxury items be restored to fend off increased losses in revenue. The deficit was rising at the average rate of about $4 million per month. "So it would seem," declared Grow cynically, "that this new system of finance is not a great success." He alluded to the lack of protection under the new law. With the reduction in the glass schedule, for example, labor in this country's glass industry had been reduced 22½ percent.[16]

Whether it was the new tariff or continued hard times, the Democrats paid dearly for being in office. In the 1894 elections they suffered severe losses. In Pennsylvania the election was called a popular revolution against Democratic leadership, free trade, and the alliance between a corrupt Tammany Hall and a solid South. The revitalized Republicans, now enjoying a more than two-to-one edge in the national House, looked forward to the next presidential race with renewed hope. Grow had coasted to another easy victory, receiving 571,085 votes and surpassing Benjamin Harrison's 1888 Pennsylvania total by nearly 45,000.[17] He was reelected in 1896, 1898, and 1900 by impressive majorities; in 1902 he refused to run for another term. Grow's landslide victories were simply consistent with general Republican successes in Pennsylvania. (See Appendix Table D)

During the remainder of Cleveland's administration, Grow redoubled his attacks against the Democrats for decreasing revenues and increasing deficits. Soon after McKinley's victory in 1896, Grow took one last shot at the outgoing administration.[18] The prostration of business after Cleveland's election, he argued, had caused too great a reduction in revenues, with the 1894 tariff being the real culprit. Grow showed how exports for 1895–1896 were nearly $200 million less than they had been in 1892–1893, the last years of the McKinley tariff. Had the Republicans continued in office, he contended, their tariff would have raised sufficient income to meet the expenses of the government and reduce the national debt. With alacrity he called the Democrats "Bourbons" who had learned nothing. He compared the Buchanan and Cleveland administrations by indicating how each had consistently produced deficits.

Grow's well-known position on the tariff and hard money was in general accord with that of most Republicans. On most issues he aligned himself with the mainstream of modern Republicanism. He voted for the building of a canal across the Isthmus of Panama, restrictive immigration, reciprocity with Cuba, and the creation of a Department of Commerce and Labor. In an age of American expansionism, ardent nationalism, and labor militancy, it was difficult for lawmakers to maintain a steady course without occasionally veering toward extremism, either of the right or left. Grow was no exception. Unlike his earlier days in Congress, when he hardly ever trampled the ideological middle road, he now tried to cultivate a more balanced statesmanship. His views were popular among Republicans and probably among most Americans as well. Perhaps he had mellowed. Sometimes he appeared as a flag-waving imperialist, an antiunion capitalist, even a reactionary. Then again, he was merciful, a champion of freedom, a true progressive who favored the direct election of senators, aid to the special education of deaf children, and rejection of the literacy test for immigrants.

His successes as a businessman and an investor obviously had an impact upon his thinking toward labor. No one prided himself more on respecting the rights and welfare of the workingman than Grow. His support of a protective tariff, hard money, and homestead legislation had always rested upon their benefits to the masses who worked hard for a living. Yet he harbored reservations about workers organizing themselves against management and about the government interfering in collective bargaining. For him the freedom of contract was a sacred bond in the normal relationship between employer and employee. "Compulsory arbitration between employer and employee would be a usurpation of the inherent rights of both by the law," he said in the Fifty-seventh Congress.[19] In anticipation of the opposition to the prolabor laws of the 1930s, Grow insisted that government had no more right to compel capital to pay labor a certain wage than it could compel labor to work at a fixed rate of wage.

Grow did not oppose the right of workers or their employers to organize. But no group had any powers or rights greater than those of the individuals comprising it. He opposed the principle of closed shops advocated by Samuel Gompers and the American Federation of Labor and was against boycotts and violence of any sort. Nor did he consider a workers' strike anything but a total waste. He estimated losses in the 154-day anthracite coal walkout in 1902 to be over $200 million. Grow hoped that, by some method of profit sharing between labor and management, harmonious cooperation between the two would be secured, strikes prevented, and the condition of the workingman greatly improved.

In foreign affairs, Grow became an outspoken defender of American interests. When the Venezuela–British Guiana boundary dispute of 1895–1896 created in America a strong anti-British animus, he sided with the jingoists. Meeting with a delegation of Quakers who feared the prospect of war between the United States and Great Britain, Grow assured them there was no such immediate danger. But if London insisted upon claiming more territory on the American continent than Britain was entitled to by purchase, his country should do as she did when a burdensome tea tax was placed upon its citizens by Great Britain—resort to the arbitrament of cannon![20]

With respect to Cuba, Grow joined a frenzied public, prodded by a yellow press, that demanded freedom for the oppressed islanders. On March 31, 1898, a little more than a week before President McKinley sent his war message to Congress, Grow expressed the belligerent mood of the lawmakers: "The time is near at hand when the government should recognize the independence of this people as a sister republic struggling as did our fathers for the great principles of our own Declaration of Independence. When that is done, this government must be ready to see to it that recognition secures the independence of the people."[21]

Anticipating armed conflict, Grow had some advice for his government: Do not begin the war in Cuba during the rainy season or the climate might become the major killer of American soldiers. He was of the opinion that nature had been responsible for more deaths of Spanish troops than the rebels. Once American troops had been sent into combat, Grow urged Congress not to meddle with the management of the war. As far as he was concerned, the military was doing a fine job.[22]

Through the years Grow had enjoyed a rather good reputation with soldiers and veterans. He had supported increased payments in a military pension plan. During the discussion on the war in the Philippines, Grow rushed to the defense of the army, which had been accused of committing atrocities against the civilian population. The controversy arose after unarmed American soldiers in 1901 had been massacred on Samar Island, southeast of Luzon, by the natives. John Williams of Mississippi wanted to know if an army order had been issued in retaliation against the Filipino population. Were women and children being deliberately victimized by the barbarities of war? Grow denied that any such order had been issued and added that, if "children" have weapons in their hands and are acting as soldiers, what did it matter if they were only ten years old? Would you pat them on the head and play pussycat with these potential murderers? Grow warned his colleagues that atrocities were a natural adjunct to war and that the duty of every commander in the field was to protect the lives of his soldiers, even if this meant resorting to brutalities in answer to those administered by the enemy. Pointedly, he asked: "How are you to deal with barbarians when they are prosecuting a warfare upon our soldiers, unless you adopt what will prevent their barbarities?"[23]

With no hesitation he accepted the challenges and responsibilities of America'a expanding empire. He criticized the anti-imperialist claim that the extension of American sovereignty and the establishment of colonial governments were not in the best interests of the country. On December 10, 1901, in a lengthy address before the House, Grow outlined his version of the new manifest destiny. The nation's mission was to promote the peace of the world, he said, and, so far as possible by precept and example, to aid in securing civil and religious liberty for all mankind. Delivered with regard to the Philippines, the speech may have been the strongest he ever gave on foreign affairs.[24]

He underscored the nation's responsibility to occupy the position vacated by Spain and to establish for the Filipinos a free government that would secure their personal and civil rights. This responsibility was not to be shirked. Grow reviewed the constitutional powers of Congress to acquire territories and to provide governments for them. Congress was obliged to give the Philippines a government that would best suit its people. All colonial governments were not the same; what might work for the Filipinos might not work for the Cubans. Though he doubted that the American people would ever consent to the admission of the Philippines to the Union because of cultural differences, the islanders should enjoy the same freedoms and rights granted to the inhabitants of any other American territory. He embraced the view that the Constitution did not follow the flag but that the powers of Congress did. Under the general power to acquire territories and the specific power to make all necessary rules and regulations regarding these possessions, Congress had the duty to establish a political system consistent with the spirit of the constitution. Grow drew a loud applause when he concluded: "Today the American Republic holds the torch of the world's advancing civilization, having carried it westward across the Pacific Ocean and planted it on the eastern confines of Asia. . . . the American people, true to their manifest destiny, marked out by the mighty events of four hundred years, shall faithfully discharge their responsibilities to liberty and the right of a common humanity in the onward progress of the race to a higher and better civilization."

. . . *and Tragedy*

Grow left Congress as gracefully as he had entered it and continued to receive honors. Pennsylvania delegates to the Fifty-seventh Congress framed and presented to him a preamble and resolution, which was unanimously adopted, engrossed in parchment with signatures of senators and representatives. "We witness his departure from these halls with regret," the resolution read, "and declare that his great public services entitle him to the honor and esteem of his countrymen."[25] Personal testimonials were numerous. "He is our oracle and we go to him freely for advice," commented Robert Hitt of Illinois. "There is more horse sense in him than in any man I ever knew."[26] In June 1903 a parade and celebration in Montrose were held in his honor. One of the attending dignitaries was Daniel Freeman, reputedly the first homesteader under the 1862 act.

After a political career that had spanned more than a half century, the "Sage of Susquehanna" finally retired to his home at Glenwood. He derived much pleasure in visiting with friends, granting interviews to journalists, and composing his memoirs. But misfortune struck at what he probably cherished the most — his reputation. A bizarre and sordid series of events that included mystery, blackmail, and scandal disrupted his tranquility and remained newsworthy years after his death. During his life Grow had retained an unsullied name. What happened in the two years before his death was a tragic postscript to an illustrious career.

The story, bearing all the qualities of a contrived soap opera, involved three beautiful women and politicians who had attained national fame.[27] Some time in the 1880s, through Reuben Fenton, his good friend and ex-governor of New York, Grow met Mrs. Augusta Cloney, a veteran's widow of considerable charm. Grow took a liking to the widow and began to shower her with gifts. She and her daughter Katherine DeFossez, an opera singer, moved into a brownstone house on Twenty-sixth Street in downtown New York City that was purchased for them by Grow. The well-furnished salon, as Mrs. Cloney called it, became a popular meeting place for artists, musicians, writers, and politicians. Grow spent many pleasant hours there.

Mrs. Cloney adopted a young girl named Kate, who referred to Grow as "uncle." For years Grow lavishly gave Kate money and jewelry and provided for some of her education. He also purchased a summer home in the Catskills for the women; there Kate met her future husband, George Williams. On May 20, 1903, the couple were married.

Never having known who her father was, Kate was led to believe that Grow was her parent. By 1905 events had become entangled. Grow — distraught, ill, and confused — confided in his close friend James T. DuBois of the State Department, that in the company of two attorneys, Kate and Mrs. Cloney's daughter had accused him of being the girl's father, and had demanded payment. Otherwise, they threatened to file charges against him. Shocked and terrified, Grow withdrew bonds valued at $61,000 and began paying off the extortionists.[28] According to DuBois, Grow did not want to press charges because of the potentially damaging publicity to himself and the girl; he did not wish to see Kate hurt, and he was physically unable to go through a trial.

This strange story did not become public until after Grow's death on Easter Sunday, March 31, 1907. As executor of Grow's estate, DuBois explained why Grow's reputedly sizable estate was smaller than expected.[29] In the last two years of Grow's life, in fact, DuBois had appealed to the Pittsburgh industrialist Andrew Carnegie to place the financially pressed Grow on his pension list. Carnegie donated $2,000 to Grow's welfare. Meanwhile, after researching the evidence, DuBois and Grow's attorney concluded that Grow was not the father of Kate Williams.[30] Apparently, his generosity had led to the swindle when he was too feeble to fight back.

Grow was buried next to his mother at the family plot in Harford Cemetery. Members of the family and a few friends attended. The flag was half-mast in Montrose and Washington. An impressive monument of Vermont granite, designed and erected years earlier by Grow, bears an inscription of words taken from Thomas Gray's "Elegy":

> The paths of glory lead but to the grave.

In Retrospect

Galusha Grow's political career was indeed remarkable; certainly few have been longer than his. He campaigned for James K. Polk in 1844 and left Congress the year the Wright brothers made history at Kitty Hawk. But a reputation in politics must not be measured in time alone. While endurance and tenure deserve recognition, achievement is more memorable. Grow's major contributions to the political history of the nation and Pennsylvania characterized him as a fighter. He fought for free homesteads and a free Kansas, and against Democratic and Republican leaders who, in his opinion, subverted the integrity of their parties and betrayed the trust of their constituents. During his initial terms in Congress (1851–1863), he enjoyed being called a radical. His political faith was conceived in a womb of Jeffersonian-Jacksonian egalitarianism, nourished by free-soilism, emancipated and born in time to help lay the ideological foundations of a progressive Republicanism. Noted for his patriotism, devotion to duty, and a propensity to wage war against party bosses and machine politics, he became one of the most popular politicians of nineteenth-century Pennsylvania.

If anything, Grow will always be remembered as the prime champion of the homestead bill. His devotion to this single issue superseded everything else he did during his first twelve years in Congress. He insisted that the key to the economic development of the nation was the proper disposition of the public lands. The cornerstone of his program was the opening of the West with a liberal land program and filling it with actual settlers. Being praised as the "Father of the Homestead Act" was what Grow cherished most. To nineteenth-century America the 1862 act was an integral part of the story of winning the West. For millions it symbolized a dream, a chance at a new life, and the opportunity to become independent and productive.

Grow's plan was simple enough; its principal premise was nothing new. By emphasizing the government's obligation to give legal effect to what is naturally and morally right, Grow proved himself a staunch defender of the natural-rights doctrine. Repudiating all ideas of state paternalism, he assumed that man has the fundamental right to that in which he has "mixed" the labor of his body, as by enclosing and tilling the land. Settlers who worked the common lands had an inborn right to own them. Certainly this argument was consistent with the liberal charge that heretofore governments had often been guilty of parceling out land to individuals who were not primarily interested in working it. Now it was time to change the policy. Plowing more fields implied greater production, which in turn meant a higher standard of living for most Americans. Free homesteads, Grow maintained, would drive capital away from land investments and into industrial undertakings. Rapid settlement of the West was sure to create new markets for manufacturers. Thus all facets of the nation's economy — farming, manufacturing, and transportation — would benefit under the homestead idea.

Regrettably for Grow, the slavery question stood in the way of homestead legislation. The two issues became hopelessly entangled in a quagmire of sectionalism. Southern interests in the territories clashed with the measure that would have opened the western lands to settlers who were likely to be antislavery. Furthermore, many southerners believed that the abolitionists were behind the homestead bill, for it would dispose of the public domain in small units and thus block the extension of the plantation system. Free soil and free land to the South therefore became a two-headed monster, the Siamese twins of northern aggression.

Grow feared from the start of the territorial debate that agitation over slavery would reduce the likelihood of a homestead bill being adopted. For this misfortune he faulted the Democratic party, which, now under the sway of southernism, could no longer be a spokesman for free homesteads. Once he was sure the Democracy had capitulated to the slavery expansionists, he became a free-soiler and finally a Republican. He valued the new Republican party as an outgrowth of Jeffersonian democracy. And, since land reform for the benefit of the actual settler had been part of the democratic creed, common sense demanded that the homestead bill be made a goal of the new party. Its ultimate success depended upon party success. As a plank in the Republican platform, its adoption was assured by the election of Lincoln and the secession of southern states.

Next to the homestead bill, Grow has to be remembered as a free-soiler who helped organize the Republican opposition in the U.S. House and became one of its radical spokesmen. The year 1856 was a turning point in his career. For his support of Banks for the speakership, he received the coveted chairmanship of the Committee on Territories. Before this time he had figured more as an orator advocating certain issues than as a molder of parties. But the quick turn of events that followed the Kansas-Nebraska bill and the elections of 1854 significantly altered the course of his political future. Suddenly he was a member of an inner group of anti-Nebraskans in the House who welded an opposition party that pledged itself to the election of Banks and a free Kansas. Though he had not been associated with the party's beginnings in Pennsylvania, Grow now moved forward as one of its prominent strategists in Congress. He was recognized by some as its principal mouthpiece on Kansas and slavery-related issues. Indefatigable and combative, he loved the rough and tumble of debate with short-tempered southerners. This reputation, in addition to his talent for the pointed phrase and his consistency on the slavery-extension issue, fashioned him into a powerful foe of southern interests.

As chairman of the territorial committee, Grow directed the assault against the Democratic administration's policies in Kansas. He personified the glibness of northern radicals who saw no reason why slavery should be accommodated in that territory or, for that matter, anywhere else. Their militancy matched that of southern fire-eaters who also failed to honor any compromise. The extremism of these two groups intensified as talk of disunion increased. Grow must be remembered as one of the Republican irreconcilables whose egocentric aggressiveness savoring of contempt for the slavocrats forced upon the nation war as a viable option. Their leadership seemed assured with Republican victories in 1860, and more so with Grow's election as Speaker. He was among the first of the party's radicals and, had he remained in Congress after 1863, his leadership role undoubtedly would have expanded.

During his term as Speaker, his defiant attitude toward southern belligerency did not mellow. In his valedictory of March 1863, he urged that the war be fought until the last rebel surrendered. The loss of life to save the Union, in his opinion, was better than continued sectional strife. The southern conspiracy against the Constitution had to be totally destroyed. For many years afterwards, Grow clung to the conspiracy theory. He was one of the last Republicans to abandon the "bloody shirt," and then did so reluctantly. His unyielding position easily enabled him to orchestrate programs of the radical Republicans by appointing many of them to key committees and several chairmanships. While he recognized the managerial dominance of

Thad Stevens on the floor, he continued through caucus and private meetings to exert a strong influence on party strategy. Yet he was reasonably successful in working toward bipartisanship in policies regarding the conduct of the war. His contemporaries judged him a good and fair Speaker who performed well in a crisis situation that was unparalleled in the nation's short history.

In Pennsylvania politics, Grow will always be remembered as a nonconformist who, for most of his career, battled bossism and the dictates of machine politics with a vengeance that bordered upon paranoia. He shunned the thought of becoming a simple party man. His conception of a party was that of a group of dedicated men bound by certain principles upon which all decisions were to be made. He linked great principles with great men. The crude idea of doing something for the "good of the party" was anathema to this Jeffersonian idealist and purist who believed that no politician whose convictions were those of his constituents ever had to worry about what might happen to him at the polls. Any time he saw party leaders sacrificing democratic and party principles, he did not hesitate to pursue an independent course. He sympathized with the Liberal Republican bolt in 1872 and created his own in 1881. By challenging party machinery with the deadliest weapon, indifference, Grow was a persistent problem for the bosses, who accused him of everything from senile devilment to dishonor. But this independent spirit consistently made him popular with the mass of voters. They found in him what they believed every politician should have—honesty of conviction, courage, and a strong sense of public service. He seemed always ready as a candidate, an alternative to those candidates groomed by party managers. If the Republican party needed a conscience, Grow was willing to provide it. In the opinion of his colleague in Congress, Samuel Cox of Ohio, Grow rose to prominence by energizing the "pietistic humanitarianism" of his party.

As admirable as Grow's pluck may have been, it was a poor means for reconciling his idealism and unassailable convictions with political realities. Unable to work out his differences with the Camerons and Quay, he forfeited the fruits of his ambitions. The result was a series of defeats that denied him the opportunity of attaining high office. By the time he returned to the good graces of the Republican bosses, he was no longer a threat to any of them. As congressman-at-large he became the party's grand old sage, a mentor who inspired younger men and faithfully followed the party line on most issues. The unprecedented number of votes he received affirmed his continued popularity with the general voter.

Grow retired from his respected career with all the laurels of the traditional hero. The party that he had served so well for a half century stood at the zenith of its power and prestige. Grow was satisfied that, despite the bosses who still guided its workings, the party was not without conscience — one that seemed to reflect many of the tenets he held dear.

Appendixes

PENNSYLVANIA ELECTIONS FOR U.S. HOUSE OF REPRESENTATIVES,
1852–1862[a]

Congressional District	1852	1854	1856	1858	1860	1862
1	D	D	D	D	R	D
2	W	W	UN	UN	R	UN
3	D	W	D	UN	R	UN
4	D	NAM	D	UN	R	UN
5	D	D	D	UN	R	UN
6	W	D	D	A-LEC D	R	D
7	D	D	D	UN	D	UN
8	D	D	D	UN	D	D
9	W	W	UN	U	R	UN
10	W	W	UN	UN	R	D
11	D	W	D	UN	R	D
12	D	W	D	UN	R	D[b]
13	D	D	D	D	D	UN
14	D[b]	F SOIL D[b]	R[b]	UN[b]	R[b]	D
15	D	W	D	UN	R	UN
16	D	W	D	UN	D	D
17	W	W	D	UN	R	D
18	W	W	UN	UN	R	D
19	D	W	UN	UN	R	UN
20	D	W	D	D	D	UN
21	W	W	R	UN	R	D
22	W	W	R	UN	R	UN
23	D	W	UN	UN	R	UN
24	D	D	D	UN	R	D
25	W	W	R	UN	R	—
Totals	D 16	D 7	D 15	D 3	D 5	D 12
	W 9	W 16	UN 6	UN 20	R 20	UN 12
		F SOIL D 1	R 4	A-LEC D 1		
		NAM 1		U 1		

SOURCE: *Congressional Quarterly's Guide to U.S. Elections*, 1985.

　　a. Party Symbols: D = Democrat; W = Whig; R = Republican; U = United; UN = Union; NAM = Native American; F SOIL D = Free Soil Democrat; A-LEC D = Anti-Lecompton Democrat.

　　b. Grow's district.

APPENDIX TABLE B

VOTE FOR PRESIDENTIAL ELECTORS AND GOVERNOR IN GROW'S CONGRESSIONAL DISTRICT,
1840–1860

| | | Presidential Electors | | | | |
	1840	*1844*	*1848*	*1852*	*1856*	*1860*
Bradford	Dem.	Dem.	Whig[a]	Dem.	Union	Union
Susquehanna	Dem.	Dem.	Dem.	Dem.	Union	Union
Tioga	Dem.	Dem.	Dem.	Dem.	Union	Union

| | | | | Governor | | | | |
	1841	*1844*	*1847*	*1848*[b]	*1851*	*1854*	*1857*	*1860*
Bradford	Dem.	Dem.	Dem.	Dem.	Dem.	Whig	Union	Union
Susquehanna	Dem.	Dem.	Dem.	Dem.	Dem.	Whig	Union	Union
Tioga	Dem.	Dem.	Dem.	Dem.	Dem.	Whig	Union	Union

SOURCES: *Crawford Democrat* and *Crawford Journal*.

a. Free-soil bolt.

b. Francis Shunk, the Democratic governor elected in 1847, resigned in July 1848. Another election was held.

APPENDIX TABLE C

CONGRESSIONAL ELECTION RETURNS, 1850–1862

	Congress	*Candidates*	*% of Votes Cast*
1850	32nd	Grow	54.6
		Adams	45.4
1852	33rd	Grow	94.2
		Horton	5.8
1854	34th	Grow (unopposed)	100.0
1856	35th	Grow	71.3
		Sherwood	28.7
1858	36th	Grow	76.9
		Parkhurst	23.1
1860	37th	Grow	71.4
		Sherwood	28.6
1862	38th	Denison	54.2
		Grow	45.8

SOURCE: *Congressional Quarterly's Guide to U.S. Elections,* 1985.

APPENDIX TABLE D

1. Pennsylvania Election Returns, 1894–1900
(Percent of Votes Cast)

	Feb. 1894[a]	Nov. 1894	Nov. 1896	Nov. 1898	Nov. 1900
Grow, congressman-at-large	60.0	60.0	61.0	56.0	61.0
Republican gubernatorial candidate		60.0		49.0	
Republican presidential candidate			61.0		61.0

2. Victorious Republican Candidates for U.S. House of Representatives
(Percent of Votes Cast)

Congressional District	1894	1896	1898	1900
1	70	70	72	71
2	75	78	84	80
3	65	D[b]	70	53
4	71	78	73	75
5	74	76	80	76
6	65	39	54	70
7	55	61	53	57
8	D	50	D	D
9	D	D	D	D
10	71	75	68	72
11	51	62	46	50
12	56	52	D	54
13	54	53	D	52
14	64	88	61	89
15	64	62	55	57
16	54	56	49	53
17	49	50	D	D
18	62	61	58	59
19	52	D	D	50
20	63	44	49	62
21	57	60	56	62
22	77	69	67	70
23	78	77	68	75
24	57	57	55	59
25	62	59	51	55
26	53	50	D	54
27	61	59	D	51
28	51	50	D	D
Average	62	61	61	62

Source: Smull's *Legislative Handbook*.

a. Special election.

b. Indicates Democratic victory.

1. The First Hurrah

1. *The Liberator,* Aug. 23, 1844.

2. Article written by "H.K.E." for the *Hampshire Gazette,* quoted in the *Montrose Democrat,* Jan. 8, 1852. Most likely the author was Henry Kingman Edson.

3. There are a few items on Grow in the Amherst College Archives, Amherst, Massachusetts.

4. Ibid.

5. The best available source on Grow's early life is James T. DuBois and Gertrude S. Mathews, *Galusha A. Grow, Father of the Homestead Act* (New York, 1917), a study based on Grow's reminiscences and autobiographical notes; additional autobiographical information is also included in two articles by Rufus R. Wilson, entitled "Personal Recollections of Hon. Galusha A. Grow," *Saturday Evening Post,* Jan. 19, Mar. 2, 1901.

6. See Calhoun's famous letter to the British foreign minister, Richard Pakenham, written on April 18, 1844, in *The Works of John C. Calhoun,* ed. Richard K. Cralle (New York, 1854), 5:333–39.

7. For discussion, see Lee Crippen, *Simon Cameron, Ante-Bellum Years* (Oxford, Ohio, 1942), pp. 46–49.

8. Malcolm R. Eiselen, *The Rise of Pennsylvania Protectionism* (Philadelphia, 1932), p. 159.

9. Whereas Grow was more than six feet tall, slender but muscular, with angular features, Wilmot was of shorter stature, on the heavy side, with a full red face, which was fair and very smooth.

10. Alexander K. McClure, *Old Time Notes of Pennsylvania* (Philadelphia, 1905), 2:588.

11. *Niles National Register,* June 28, 1845; James Buchanan to Mr. Herr et al., Mar. 31, 1845, in *The Works of James Buchanan,* ed. John B. Moore (New York, 1960), 6:136–38.

12. Milo M. Quaife, ed., *The Diary of James K. Polk* (Chicago, 1910), 1:184.

13. For discussion of the Kane letter and its impact, see Charles Sellers, *James K.*

Polk, Continentalist, 1843–1846 (Princeton, N.J.: 1966), 119–21; Eiselen, *Pennsylvania Protectionism*, pp. 160–63.

14. James D. Richardson, comp., *A Compilation of the Messages and Papers of the Presidents, 1789–1897* (Washington, 1896–99), 4:373–82.

15. Polk, *Diary*, 1:110.

16. Francis P. Blair and John Rives, eds., *Congressional Globe*, 29th Cong., 1st sess., Appendix, pp. 767–71.

17. *Pittsburgh Daily Gazette and Advertiser*, Aug. 14, 1846.

18. Quoted in *Niles National Register*, Aug. 1, 1846.

19. Quoted in DuBois and Mathews, *Grow*, p. 35.

20. *Montrose Northern Democrat*, May 27, 1847.

21. Ibid., Apr. 22, May 6, Aug. 26, 1847.

22. Unpublished essay on Grow, Ernest Hempstead Papers, Crawford County Historical Society, Meadville, Pennsylvania.

23. *Bradford Reporter*, Dec. 20, 1843.

24. Wilmot was well aware of the rumor that Buchanan may have been in sympathy with Colonel Bull and the anti-Wilmot forces (Charles Buxton Going, *David Wilmot, Free-Soiler* [Gloucester, Mass., 1966]), p. 153; Cameron also may have been hoping for Wilmot's defeat (Crippen, *Cameron*, p. 94).

25. *Montrose Northern Democrat*, Aug. 27, 1846.

26. *Cong. Globe*, 32nd Cong., 2nd sess., p. 115.

27. *Bradford Reporter*, Sept. 23, 1846.

28. Ibid., Oct. 21, 1846. His margin of victory in Susquehanna was slightly more than that in Bradford, suggesting the fine work of Grow and others in a county where the anti-Wilmot forces were strong.

2. *A Compromise Candidate Goes to Washington*

1. Buchanan to Foster, Nov. 19, 1846, in *Works*, ed. Moore, 7:117–18.

2. John S. Jenkins, *The Life of Silas Wright* (Auburn, N.Y., 1847), pp. 223–26.

3. Buchanan to Charles Kessler et al., Aug. 25, 1847, in *Works*, ed. Moore, 7:385–87.

4. *Cong. Globe*, 29th Cong., 2nd sess., p. 550.

5. Bernard De Voto, *The Year of Decision 1846* (Boston, 1942), p. 299.

6. Quoted in DuBois and Mathews, *Grow*, p. 46.

7. Letter to his constituents, Sept. 27, 1850, in Going, *David Wilmot*, pp. 431–33. The bibliography on the Proviso is extensive. For a summary, see Eric Foner, "The Wilmot Proviso Revisited," *Journal of American History* 56 (1969): 262–79.

8. Calhoun to Mrs. T. G. Clemson, Dec. 27, 1846, in *Works*, ed. Cralle, 4:328.

9. For a good analysis of the free-soil movement of 1848, see Joseph G. Rayback, *Free Soil, the Election of 1848* (Lexington, Ky., 1970).

10. *Montrose Independent Republican*, Feb. 8, 1855.

11. A critical summary of the senator's record on the proviso can be found in the free-soil newspaper, *The Champion of Freedom* (New York), Oct. 7, 1848.

12. Joshua Giddings to his son, Apr. 15, 1848, in the Joshua R. Giddings Pa-

pers, Ohio Historical Society, Columbus. Hereafter cited as Giddings Papers, OHS; Charles F. Adams to Giddings, Feb. 8, 1848, in ibid.

13. *Bradford Reporter,* Feb. 16, 1848.

14. *Montrose Northern Democrat,* Jan. 20, 1848.

15. *Democratic Union* (Harrisburg), Mar. 11, 1848.

16. Crippen, *Simon Cameron,* p. 101; Jon L. Wakelyn, "Party Issues and Political Strategy of the Charleston Taylor Democrats of 1848," *South Carolina Historical Magazine* 73 (1972): 72–86.

17. Horace Greeley to Giddings, Feb. 29, 1848, in Giddings Papers, OHS. Greeley's position opposed that of most Whig leaders. See James G. Blaine, *Twenty Years of Congress* (Norwich, 1848–86), 1:73.

18. Salmon Chase to Giddings, Feb. 29, 1848, in Giddings Papers, OHS.

19. Entry of June 9, 1848, in unpublished diary of Charles F. Adams, microfilm, Massachusetts Historical Society, Boston. Referring to the Whig Convention, Adams wrote, "a more high-handed piece of abominable villainy never was attempted in this Union."

20. Going, *David Wilmot,* p. 303.

21. *Cong. Globe,* 32nd Cong., 1st sess., Appendix, pp. 627–29.

22. *Northern Democrat,* June 29, 1848.

23. Wilson, "Recollections of Grow," *Saturday Evening Post,* Jan. 19, 1901. In later life, Grow summarized his early health: "Speaking in the open air a great deal superinduced a pestiferous bronchial affection which finally clasped hands with an old-fashioned dyspepsia, and the two together, in spite of my six-foot-two and strong wiry frame, forced me to live like a monk" (in DuBois and Mathews, *Grow,* pp. 96–97).

24. John F. Coleman, *The Disruption of the Pennsylvania Democracy, 1848–1860* (Harrisburg, 1975), pp. 36–37.

25. David Wilmot to Horace Willey, Aug. 19, 1850, in David Wilmot Papers, Bradford Country Historical Society, Towanda, Pa.

26. *Susquehanna Register* (Montrose), Sept. 19, 1850; *Bradford Reporter,* Sept. 21, 1850.

27. Her memoir is in the Galusha Grow Papers, Susquehanna County Historical Society, Montrose, Pa.

28. Wilson, "Recollections of Grow," *Saturday Evening Post,* Jan. 19, 1901.

29. *Tioga Eagle* (Wellsboro), Sept. 25, 1850.

30. *Susquehanna Register,* Sept. 26, 1850.

31. Ibid., Sept. 26, 1850, Apr. 21, 1851. In September 1851, Wilmot was unanimously nominated president judge of the Thirteenth District, comprising Bradford, Susquehanna, and Sullivan counties. He won the election by more than 2,000 votes.

32. Ibid., Oct. 3, 1850.

33. Ibid.

3. The Youngest Radical on the Floor

1. "Reminiscences of Washington," *Atlantic Monthly* 47 (1881): 544.

2. Quoted in DuBois and Mathews, *Grow,* p. 91.

3. *Bradford Reporter,* Apr. 23, 1853.

4. *Susquehanna Register,* Jan. 15, Apr. 19, 1852.

5. Wilson, "Recollections of Grow," *Saturday Evening Post,* Jan. 19, 1901.

6. Ibid.

7. For a recent and fairly comprehensive account of Kossuth's tour, see Donald Spencer, *Louis Kossuth and Young America: A Study of Sectionalism and Foreign Policy, 1848–1852* (Columbia, Mo., 1977).

8. Richardson, ed., *Messages and Papers,* 6:2650.

9. *Cong. Globe,* 32nd Cong., 1st sess., p. 22. Giddings predicted that the free-soilers would capitalize upon the Kossuth affair (Giddings to his son, Dec. 29, 1851, in Giddings-Julian Papers, Library of Congress).

10. *The Liberator,* Jan. 9, 1852. A week later this paper wondered what Kossuth thought of the hypocrisy of Webster, Foote, Clay, and Cass, the architects of the fugitive slave law, as they honored him as a great freedom fighter.

11. Jan. 4, 1852, in Giddings-Julian Papers.

12. Wilson, "Recollections of Grow," *Saturday Evening Post,* Jan. 19, 1901.

13. *Cong. Globe,* 32nd Cong., 1st sess., p. 180.

14. *Tioga Eagle,* Feb. 12, 1852.

15. Roy F. Nichols, *The Democratic Machine, 1850–1854* (New York, 1923), pp. 26–29; diary of Charles F. Adams, entry of Dec. 6, 1851.

16. A good treatment of the southern position is found in Howard C. Perkins, "A Neglected Phase of the Movement for Southern Unity, 1847–1852," *Journal of Southern History* 12 (1946): 153–203.

17. *Cong. Globe,* 32nd Cong., 1st sess., Appendix, p. 421.

18. Ibid., 32nd Cong., 1st sess., p. 5.

19. Ibid., 32nd Cong., 1st sess., pp. 5–12.

20. Ibid., 32nd Cong., 1st sess., pp. 381–83.

21. *Keystone,* Apr. 17, 1852. Twelve of the twenty-four-man delegation from Pennsylvania did not vote: seven Democrats and five Whigs.

22. *Cong. Globe,* 32nd Cong., 1st sess., Appendix, pp. 627–29.

23. Ibid., 32nd Cong., 1st sess., Appendix, pp. 663–71.

24. *Crawford Democrat* (Meadville), Mar. 16, 1852.

25. Allan Nevins, *Ordeal of the Union* (New York, 1947), 2:27.

26. Roy F. Nichols, *Franklin Pierce, Young Hickory of the Granite Hills* (Philadelphia, 1931), p. 203.

27. *Crawford Democrat,* Sept. 28, 1852.

28. Blaine, *Twenty Years,* 1:99.

29. Buchanan to Gen. Porter, June 4, 1852, in *Works,* ed. Moore, 8:451–52.

30. Buchanan to Theodore Leonard, Isaac Cooley, Elam Bennett et al., June 14, 1852, in *Crawford Democrat,* June 29, 1852.

31. Buchanan to Franklin Pierce, June 21, 1852, in *Works,* ed. Moore, 8:453.

32. *Bradford Reporter,* Sept. 11, 1852.

33. *Susquehanna Register,* Sept. 16, 1852.

34. *Bradford Reporter,* Oct. 23, 1852; *Montrose Democrat,* Oct. 21, 1852. The poor showing of the Free Democrats in the district was typical of the setbacks suffered by the third party throughout Pennsylvania and the rest of the Northeast. The re-

turn of many free-soilers like Wilmot and the New York Barnburners to the Democratic party was a reason for the decline in the vote for the Free Democrats. Frederick J. Blue, *The Free Soilers: Third Party Politics* (Urbana, Ill., 1973), pp. 264–68.

35. Blaine, *Twenty Years*, 1:105. Perhaps *The Liberator* said it best: "They sacrificed their principles, their constituency, their honor, for the sake of slave-driving votes, and defeat, disgrace, and political ruin have been their reward" (Nov. 5, 1852).

4. Man's Right to the Soil

1. For discussion, see Schuyler Marshall, "The Free Democratic Convention of 1852," *Pennsylvania History* 22 (1955): 146–67.

2. Salmon P. Chase to E. S. Hamlin, Aug. 13, 1852, in *Diary and Correspondence of Salmon P. Chase,* in *Annual Report of the American Historical Association* (Washington, D.C., 1902), 2:244–45; Richard H. Sewell, *John P. Hale and the Politics of Abolition* (Cambridge, Mass., 1965), pp. 147–48.

3. *Bradford Reporter,* Mar. 18, 1858.

4. *Daily Pittsburgh Gazette,* June 16, 1852.

5. Frank More, ed., *Speeches of Andrew Johnson* (Boston, 1866), pp. 12–77.

6. Adequate histories of early land policies include Benjamin H. Hibbard, *A History of the Public Land Policies* (New York, 1924); Frederic L. Paxson, *History of the American Frontier, 1763–1893* (New York, 1924); Roy M. Robbins, *Our Landed Heritage* (Princeton, N.J.: 1942); George M. Stephenson, *The Political History of the Public Lands from 1840–1862* (Boston, 1917).

7. Joseph Gales and W. W. Seaton, comps., *Annals of the Congress of the United States, 1789–1824,* 18th Cong., 1st sess., p. 583.

8. Thomas Hart Benton, *Thirty Years View* (New York, 1854), 1:103–04.

9. Greeley's agitation for land reform is reviewed by Jeter A. Isely, *Horace Greeley and the Republican Party, 1853–1861* (Princeton, N.J.: 1947), pp. 27–30.

10. Clay's report from the Committee on Manufactures recommending distribution is in Joseph Gales and W. W. Seaton, comps., *American State Papers; Public Lands,* 6:441–47.

11. *Cong. Globe,* 28th Cong., 2nd sess., p. 69.

12. Ibid., 28th Cong., 2nd sess., p. 241.

13. Grow's claim was that in its final form the Homestead Act of 1862 was essentially an embodiment of the provisions characteristic of his bill, which he consistently kept before the House since he first introduced it in the Thirty-third Congress.

14. *Cong. Globe,* 29th Cong., 1st sess., pp. 473, 492, 1077.

15. Frederick J. Turner, "Social Forces in American History," *American Historical Review* 16 (1911): 229; Joel H. Silbey, *The Shrine of Party; Congressional Voting Behavior, 1841–1852* (Pittsburgh, Pa., 1967), pp. 118–19.

16. *Cong. Globe,* 31st Cong., 2nd sess., p. 743.

17. Andrew Johnson to J. Patterson, Apr. 4, 1852, Andrew Johnson Papers, Library of Congress.

18. *Cong. Globe,* 31st Cong., 2nd sess., pp. 312–13.

19. Ibid., 32nd Cong., 1st sess., p. 58.

20. Ibid., 31st Cong., 2nd sess., Appendix, pp. 106–107; 32nd Cong., 1st sess., Appendix, pp. 686–89.

21. *Charleston Mercury,* Mar. 17, 1860.

22. George Fitzhugh, *Sociology for the South* (Richmond, 1854), p. 86.

23. *Cong. Globe,* 32nd Cong., 1st sess., p. 530.

24. Ibid., 32nd Cong., 1st sess., pp. 386–90, 1298.

25. Grow's address is printed in full in *Cong. Globe,* 32nd Cong., 1st sess., Appendix, pp. 424–26.

26. Remarks made by Grow before the Susquehanna County Legal Association, Apr. 11, 1892, in Grow Papers.

27. Michael F. Holt, "The Politics of Impatience: The Origins of Know Nothingism," *Journal of American History* 60 (1973): 309–31.

28. *Mississippi Palladium,* Jan. 22, 1852.

29. *Daily Pittsburgh Gazette,* May 17, 1852.

30. *Cong. Globe,* 32nd Cong., 1st sess., p. 1319.

31. Ibid., 32nd Cong., 1st sess., Appendix, p. 519.

32. Ibid., 32nd Cong., 1st sess., p. 1351. For an analysis of the vote, see Fred A. Shannon, "The Homestead Act and the Labor Surplus," *American Historical Review* 41 (1936): 637–51.

33. *Cong. Globe,* 32nd Cong., 1st sess., p. 1681. Westerners friendly to the bill continued to apply pressure upon the Senate. Schuyler Colfax to William Seward, Aug. 7, 1852, in Schuyler Colfax Papers, Library of Congress.

34. DuBois and Mathews, *Grow,* pp. 95–96.

35. Wilson, "Recollections of Grow," *Saturday Evening Post,* Mar. 2, 1901.

36. Ibid.

37. DuBois and Mathews, *Grow,* p. 97.

38. *Cong. Globe,* 32nd Cong., 2nd sess., p. 115.

39. Ibid., 32nd Cong., 2nd sess., Appendix, p. 205.

40. Thomas B. Alexander, *Sectional Stress and Party Strength: A Study of Roll-Call Voting Patterns in the United States House of Representatives, 1836–1860* (Nashville, 1967), p. 82.

5. Free Soil and Free Land

1. Richardson, ed., *Messages and Papers,* 6:2730–36.

2. *Cong. Globe,* 33rd Cong., 1st sess., p. 913.

3. Grow's address is printed in full in ibid., 33rd Cong., 1st sess., Appendix, pp. 241–43.

4. *Public Ledger* (Philadelphia), Mar. 2, 1854.

5. For debate on the bill, see *Cong. Globe,* 33rd Cong., 1st sess., pp. 500–501, 523, 525–26, 533–36.

6. *House Journal,* 33rd Cong., 1st sess., pp. 456–57. Only eight of the twenty-five Pennsylvanians voted for the Wright amendment. Eventually, fifteen of the delegation voted for Dawson's bill.

7. *Cong. Globe,* 33rd Cong., 1st sess., pp. 546–47.

8. Grow's complete bill is printed in ibid., 33rd Cong., 1st sess., p. 547.

9. Ibid., 33rd Cong., 1st sess., pp. 547–49.

10. Frederick Douglass to Gerrit Smith, Mar. 13, 1854, in *The Life and Writings of Frederick Douglass,* ed. Philip S. Foner (New York, 1950), 2:281–82.

11. *Baltimore Sun,* Jan. 21, 1854; *Washington Union,* Jan. 22, 1854; *Richmond Enquirer,* Jan. 24, 1854.

12. DuBois and Mathews, *Grow,* pp. 137–39.

13. Joshua R. Giddings, *History of the Rebellion: Its Authors and Causes* (New York, 1864), p. 372.

14. Jan. 24, 1854. Writing to Howell Cobb on Apr. 2, 1854, Douglas predicted that the fury over his bill would soon subside. Meanwhile, he asked his southern allies to stand firm and leave the Democrats of the North to fight the great battle. *The Letters of Stephen A. Douglas,* ed. Robert W. Johannsen (Urbana, Ill., 1961), p. 300.

15. DuBois and Mathews, *Grow,* p. 139.

16. *Baltimore Sun,* Mar. 7–8, 1854.

17. Ibid., Jan. 30, 1854.

18. Apparently Stephens never abandoned this view. Alexander Stephens, *A Constitutional View of the Late War Between the States* (Philadelphia, 1870), 2:172–75.

19. *Cong. Globe,* 33rd Cong., 1st sess., Appendix, p. 557.

20. Quoted in the *Montrose Democrat,* May 18, 1854.

21. *Susquehanna Register,* June 1, 1854.

22. Grow's remarks are in the *Cong. Globe,* 33rd Cong., 1st sess., Appendix, p. 972.

23. Grow recalled the address when interviewed many years later by Ida Tarbell. Ida Tarbell Papers, Allegheny College, Meadville, Pa.

24. Remarks before the Susquehanna County Legal Association, Apr. 11, 1892, in Grow Papers.

25. *Daily Journal* (Wilmington, N.C.), May 1, 1854.

26. *Baltimore Sun,* June 19, 1854. This paper predicted that the anti-Nebraska senators would support the bill as an antidote to the slavery provision in the Kansas–Nebraska bill.

27. *Cong. Globe,* 33rd Cong., 1st sess., p. 1658.

28. *Charleston Mercury,* July 25, 1854.

29. *Cong. Globe,* 33rd Cong., 1st sess., pp. 1819, 1832–33, 1844.

30. Ibid., 33rd Cong., 1st sess., pp. 1740, 1843.

31. *Daily Pittsburgh Gazette,* July 27, 1854.

6. *Becoming a Black Republican*

1. Galusha Grow to William Bigler, July 19, 1854, in William Bigler Papers, Historical Society of Pennsylvania. The "Nebraska" men were those who supported the Kansas-Nebraska Act.

2. *Bradford Reporter,* Feb. 18, 1854.

3. June 22, 1854. At its Harrisburg convention, the free-soil Democrats, many of whom had endorsed Wilmot for governor, rejected the Pennsylvania Democracy and its candidates and formally accepted the Whig slate.

4. Going, *David Wilmot,* p. 454.

5. John Negley to William Bigler, July 13, 1854, in Bigler Papers.

6. George Sanders to William Bigler, July 1854, in Bigler Papers.

7. E. B. Chase to William Bigler, July 20, 1854, in Bigler Papers.

8. *Montrose Democrat,* Aug. 3, 1854.

9. *Susquehanna Register,* Aug. 31, 1854.

10. *Bradford Reporter,* June 10, July 22, 1854; "To run a candidate against him [Grow] would be futile as it is for Whiggery to be honest," *Tioga Eagle,* July 27, 1854.

11. *Tioga Eagle,* June 22, 1854.

12. *Bradford Reporter,* Sept. 16, 1854. The editor saw this as ample evidence of the "direct repudiation" of Douglas's scheme.

13. *Independent Republican* (Montrose), Feb. 8, 1855.

14. *Tioga Eagle,* Oct. 5, 1854.

15. *Bradford Reporter,* June 10, 1854.

16. Quoted in ibid., July 29, 1854.

17. Ibid., Sept. 30, 1854.

18. Ibid., Oct. 14, 21, 1854; *Montrose Democrat,* Oct. 12, 1854. For the next two years nativism continued to play a major role in state elections. Thaddeus Stevens to Edward McPherson, Aug. 24, 1856, in Edward McPherson Papers, Library of Congress.

19. McClure, *Old Time Notes,* 2:212.

20. Ibid.

21. Roy F. Nichols, "The Kansas-Nebraska Act: A Century of Historiography," *Mississippi Valley Historical Review* 43 (1956): 187–212.

22. *Bradford Reporter,* Dec. 23, 1854.

23. A. J. Mason, editor of the *Conneautville Courier,* refused to support the first Republican ticket in Crawford County because it was under the control of Know-Nothings who had denounced free-soilism several years earlier. *Conneautville Courier,* Sept. 19, 26, 1855.

24. *Bradford Reporter,* Aug. 23, 1855. One of the earliest "Republican" organizations occurred in Susquehanna County in November 1854, when a number of free-soilers considered proposals adapted by Republicans in other states (*Susquehanna Register,* Nov. 30, 1854).

25. *Bradford Reporter,* Aug. 23, 1855.

26. Ibid., Sept. 1, 1855.

27. McClure, *Old Time Notes,* 2:240.

28. *Montrose Democrat,* Oct. 25, 1855.

29. Ibid., Mar. 8, June 21, Oct. 25, 1855, Apr. 17, 1856.

30. Ibid., Feb. 21, 1856.

31. In a letter of Feb. 26, 1856, Grow denied he had abandoned any of his principles and accused Chase of perverting the facts. Published in ibid., Mar. 6, 1856.

32. DuBois and Mathews, *Grow,* pp. 151–52. The letters are printed in the *Montrose Democrat,* Sept. 13, 27, Oct. 11, 1855.

33. DuBois and Mathews, *Grow,* p. 148.

34. *Cong. Globe,* 34th Cong., 1st sess., p. 1161.

35. *Montrose Democrat,* Oct. 19, 1854.

36. *Pittsburgh Gazette,* Sept. 6, 1855.

37. See Michael F. Holt, *Forging a Majority: The Formation of the Republican Party in Pittsburgh, 1848–1860* (New Haven, 1969); Robert D. Ilisevich, "The Formation of the Republican Party in Erie and Crawford Counties, 1846–1856," *Journal of Erie Studies* 2 (1973): 1–16; Irvin D. Solomon, "The Grass Roots Appearance of a National Party: The Formation of the Republican Party in Erie, Pennsylvania, 1852–1856," *Western Pennsylvania Historical Magazine* 66 (1983): 209–22.

38. *New York Daily Tribune,* Nov. 28, 1855; *Public Ledger,* Dec. 3, 1855.

39. *Cong. Globe,* 34th Cong., 1st sess., p. 39. The *Richmond Enquirer* of Dec. 21, 1855, was blunt: "No man is recognized as a member of the Democratic Party who votes against Colonel Richardson."

40. *Cong. Globe,* 34th Cong., 1st sess., p. 45.

41. Ibid., 34th Cong., 1st sess., p. 12. For discussion of balloting, see Fred H. Harrington, "The First Northern Victory," *Journal of Southern History* 5 (1939): 186–205.

42. *Cong. Globe,* 34th Cong., 1st sess., p. 218. Grow later claimed that he had been reelected to do the talking for the Republican side.

43. Ibid., 34th Cong., 1st sess., pp. 33–39, 92–93, 262; *Erie Weekly Observer,* Dec. 15, 1855; *Lewisburg* (Pennsylvania) *Chronicle,* Dec. 21, 1855.

44. David L. Anderson, "Anson Burlingame: Reformer and Diplomat," *Civil War History* 25 (1979): 293–308.

45. Samuel Smith of Tennessee referred to those who voted for Banks as "Black Republicans." He supposed they were called that because they wanted to equalize the two races. Grow said that the term when used by southerners applied to all free-soilers.

46. Schuyler Colfax to Alfred Wheeler, Apr. 9, 1856, Colfax Papers.

47. Schuyler Colfax, "Anson Burlingame," (South Bend) *St. Joseph Valley Register,* Apr. 28, 1870. In a series of letters, E. B. Morgan discussed the determination of the steering group to stick with Banks once he had been decided upon. It had become a "matter of honor," Morgan wrote. Like Grow, he had switched to Banks on the twenty-eighth ballot (Temple R. Hollcroft, ed., "A Congressman's Letters on the Speaker Election in the Thirty-fourth Congress," *Mississippi Valley Historical Review* 43 [1956]: 444–58).

48. *New York Daily Tribune,* Dec. 13, 1855.

49. *Lewisburg Chronicle,* Dec. 21, 1855.

50. Quoted in *Richmond Enquirer,* Dec. 21, 1855.

51. *Cong. Globe,* 34th Cong., 1st sess., p. 228.

52. Ibid., 34th Cong., 1st sess., p. 218.

53. The Democrats did everything to stave off the plurality resolution (John Dick to David Dick, Feb. 8, 1856, in John Dick Papers, Crawford County Historical Society, Meadville, Pa.).

54. *New York Daily Tribune,* Dec. 17, 1855.

55. Quoted in the *Charleston Mercury,* Feb. 11, 1856.

56. *Independent Republican,* Jan. 17, 1856; *Montrose Democrat,* Feb. 6, 14, 1856; *Tioga Eagle,* Feb. 7, 1856.

57. For example, see Michael F. Holt, *The Political Crisis of the 1850's* (New York, 1978).

58. Editors of the *Chicago Daily Tribune* to Nathaniel Banks, Feb. 20, 1856, in Nathaniel Banks Papers, Library of Congress.

7. *Leader of the Opposition*

1. *New York Weekly Tribune,* July 5, 1856.

2. *Charleston Mercury,* Feb. 18, 1856.

3. *Richmond Enquirer,* Feb. 8, 1856.

4. Ibid., Jan. 22, 1856.

5. *New York Daily Tribune,* Feb. 13, 1856.

6. Richardson, ed., *Messages and Papers,* 7:2885–93.

7. *Cong. Globe,* 34th Cong., 1st sess., p. 353.

8. This address of March 5 is in ibid., 34th Cong., 1st sess., Appendix, pp. 145–49. Grow had voted against the reading of the president's message.

9. Ibid., 34th Cong., 1st sess., p. 639.

10. *Pittsburgh Gazette,* Feb. 22, 23, 25, 1856; *New York Daily Tribune,* Feb. 29, Mar. 12, 1856.

11. *Montrose Democrat,* Feb. 14, Mar. 6, 1856.

12. *Independent Republican,* Apr. 10, 1856.

13. *Cambria Tribune* (Johnstown, Pa.), May 28, 1856.

14. *Charleston Mercury,* July 25, 1856. Lawrence Keitt of South Carolina was accused of encouraging, if not aiding, Brooks in the affair.

15. *Cong. Globe,* 34th Cong., 1st sess., pp. 1367, 1628, 1641.

16. Giddings to daughter, May 28, 1856, in Giddings-Julian Papers, Library of Congress. Earlier, John Brown had written to Giddings to see if Congress intended to do anything with the Kansas issue, "Will Congress suffer us to be driven to such dire extremities?" (Brown to Giddings, Feb. 20, 1856, in Giddings Papers, OHS).

17. *Charleston Mercury,* July 2, 1856.

18. *Cong. Globe,* 34th Cong., 1st sess., p. 1443. For debate on the Oregon bill, see pp. 1443–56.

19. Ibid., 34th Cong., 1st sess., Appendix, pp. 723–29.

20. *New York Weekly Tribune,* July 5, 1856.

21. Grow's remarks are printed in *Cong. Globe,* 34th Cong., 1st sess., Appendix, pp. 718–22.

22. Ibid., 34th Cong., 1st sess., pp. 1486, 1491. For the lengthy discussion that followed, see pp. 1513–23, 1540–41.

23. Ibid., 34th Cong., 1st sess., p. 1541. Thirteen southerners who had initially voted against the bill did not participate in the July 3 balloting.

24. *Charleston Mercury,* July 9, 1856.

25. *Cong. Globe,* 34th Cong., 1st sess., p. 1574.

26. Ibid., 34th Cong., 1st sess., p. 1817.

27. Ibid., 34th Cong., 1st sess., pp. 1790–91.

28. Ibid., 34th Cong., 2nd sess., p. 83.

29. Ibid., 34th Cong., 1st sess., pp. 1925–26. Grow's committee continued not to recommend appropriations for Kansas. In its report of Feb. 4, 1857, the committee urged that monies not be appropriated for public buildings in Kansas because it had been unable to obtain any information from departments on how the money already appropriated had been spent (U.S. Congress, House of Representatives, Committee on Territories, 34th Congress, Papers, Record Group 233, National Archives).

30. Allan G. Bogue, "Some Dimensions of Power in the Thirty-seventh Senate," in *The Dimensions of Quantitative Research in History,* ed. William Aydedotte, Allan G. Bogue, Robert W. Fogel (Princeton, N.J., 1972), pp. 285–318.

8. *Holding the Line on Kansas*

1. Philip S. Klein, *President James Buchanan: A Biography* (University Park, Pa., 1962), p. 259.

2. *Cong. Globe,* 34th Cong., 3rd sess., Appendix, p. 106.

3. George V. Larrabee, "Galusha A. Grow as I Remember Him," in *The Montrose Independent,* Dec. 14, 1928.

4. Ibid.; *Independent Republican,* Sept. 25, 1856.

5. *Montrose Democrat,* Sept. 25, 1856.

6. *Bradford Reporter,* June 21, 1856. Grow's brother, Frederick, was politically active in Carbondale and was named to the Republican State Committee. Several years earlier, when the Grow brothers were still in the Democratic party, they had worked together to support Charles R. Buckalew to the U.S. Senate (Galusha Grow to Charles R. Buckalew, July 10, 1853, and F. P. Grow to Buckalew, Sept. 26, 29, 1853, in Charles R. Buckalew Papers, Library of Congress).

7. *Montrose Democrat,* June 12, 1856.

8. Galusha A. Grow, "Curtin and Pennsylvania at the Beginning of the War," in *Andrew Gregg Curtin: His Life and Services,* ed. William Egle (Philadelphia, 1895), pp. 473–84.

9. Wilmot to unnamed associate, July 24, 1856, Wilmot Papers.

10. *Independent Republican,* Aug. 28, 1856.

11. *Cong. Globe,* 34th Cong., 1st sess., p. 1817. Grow had agreed to go along with the Dunn bill since it called for the release of the free-state prisoners in Kansas, thus destroying the validity of the Kansas legislature, and restored the Missouri Compromise. Republicans supported the bill while southerners voted against it.

12. *Montrose Democrat,* Oct. 9, 1856.

13. Thaddeus Stevens to McPherson, Aug. 24, 1856, in McPherson Papers.

14. *Bradford Reporter,* Nov. 27, 1856.

15. McClure, *Old Time Notes,* 1:264.

16. *Charleston Mercury,* Aug. 25, 1856.

17. *Cong. Globe,* 34th Cong., 3rd sess., Appendix, p. 109.

18. *The National Era* (Washington, D.C.), Dec. 4, 1856.

19. *Cong. Globe,* 34th Cong., 3rd sess., pp. 3–5.

20. Ibid., 34th Cong., 3rd sess., pp. 6, 17–18.

21. Ibid., 34th Cong., 3rd sess., p. 69.

22. Richardson, *Messages and Papers,* 7:2930–50.

23. *Cong. Globe,* 34th Cong., 3rd sess., Appendix, pp. 87–91, 118–19.

24. Robert Toombs to Thomas W. Thomas, Feb. 5, 1857, in *The Correspondence of Robert Toombs, Alexander H. Stephens and Howell Cobb,* in *Annual Report of the American Historical Association,* ed. U. B. Phillips (Washington, D.C., 1911), 2:394.

25. *Cong. Globe,* 34th Cong., 3rd sess., Appendix, pp. 85–87.

26. Richardson, *Messages and Papers,* 7:2954.

27. *Reports of Committees of the House of Representatives,* 34th Cong., 3rd sess., I, Report Number 173, Washington, 1857; *Cong. Globe,* 34th Cong., 3rd sess., p. 523.

28. *Cong. Globe,* 34th Cong., 3rd sess., p. 733.

29. *New York Weekly Tribune,* Feb. 28, 1857.

30. *Cong. Globe,* 34th Cong., 3rd sess., pp. 517–18.

31. Ibid., 34th Cong., 3rd sess., p. 518.

32. Ibid., 34th Cong., 3rd sess., p. 519.

33. Ibid., 34th Cong., 3rd sess., p. 607.

34. Ibid., 34th Cong., 3rd sess., pp. 275–77.

35. *New York Weekly Tribune,* Feb. 28, 1857. Grow's enemies back home could not wait to attack him for objecting to the report. The editor of the *Montrose Democrat* remarked: "Mr. Grow's zeal in behalf of the nigger is only outstripped by his sympathy for his bribed associates" (Oct. 1, 1857).

36. *Cong. Globe,* 34th Cong., 3rd sess., pp. 761, 766–71.

37. Ibid., 34th Cong., 3rd sess., pp. 762, 768, 893.

38. Ibid., 34th Cong., 3rd sess., p. 773.

39. Presumably the deaths of John C. Montgomery of Pennsylvania and John Quitman of Mississippi were the result of food poisoning at the hotel. Two explanations at the time suggested that the illness was due to poisoned rats contaminating the drinking water or sewer gas working its way into the hotel.

40. *Cong. Globe,* 34th Cong., 3rd sess., p. 589.

41. Ibid., 34th Cong., 3rd sess., p. 970.

42. Richardson, *Messages and Papers,* 7:2961–67.

9. *"First Blow for Freedom"*

1. Grow to Buckalew, July 10, 1853, in Buckalew Papers.

2. *Bradford Reporter,* July 23, 1857.

3. *Montrose Democrat,* Mar. 12, 1857.

4. *Independent Republican,* Apr. 23, 1857. The editor charged John P. Sanderson with starting the lie against Grow and using his pro-Buchanan paper, the *Philadelphia Daily News,* to spread the falsehood.

5. *Montrose Democrat,* Apr. 9, 1857.

6. Nathaniel Banks to Hannibal Hamlin, Nov. 18, 1857, in Hannibal Hamlin Papers, Library of Congress.

7. *Cong. Globe,* 35th Cong., 1st sess., pp. 1–2.

8. Richardson, *Messages and Papers,* 7:2967–94.

9. *Cong. Globe,* 35th Cong., 1st sess., pp. 14–18.

10. Stephens to voters of Eighth Congressional District of Georgia, Aug. 14, 1857, in Phillips, *Correspondence of Toombs, Stephens and Cobb,* 2:409–20.

11. *Charleston Mercury,* Jan. 12, 1858.

12. Elbert B. Smith, *The Presidency of James Buchanan* (Lawrence, Kans., 1975), p. 46.

13. C. H. Ray to Lyman Trumbull, Dec. 18, 1857, in Lyman Trumbull Papers, Library of Congress.

14. *South Bend Register,* Dec. 17, 1857, quoted in Smith, *Schuyler Colfax,* pp. 90–91.

15. For remarks of both Stephens and Grow, see *Cong. Globe,* 35th Cong., 1st sess., pp. 198–200.

16. *House Journal,* 35th Cong., 1st sess., pp. 424–25.

17. *Cong. Globe,* 35th Cong., 1st sess., pp. 887–88.

18. Ibid., 35th Cong., 1st sess., pp. 135–36, 181.

19. Ibid., 35th Cong., 1st sess., p. 324.

20. Quoted in Hibbard, *Public Land Policies,* p. 360.

21. *Cong. Globe,* 35th Cong., 1st sess., pp. 143–45.

22. Ibid., 35th Cong., 1st sess., p. 146.

23. Richardson, *Messages and Papers,* 7:3002–12. According to Klein, the president did not defer to threats from the southern extremists on Lecompton. He intended to enforce the letter of the law in Kansas (Klein, *Buchanan,* p. 308). Republicans believed from the start that Buchanan stood behind the Lecompton convention, its constitution, as well as the extremists who opposed the idea of submission (*National Era,* Dec. 17, 1857).

24. *Cong. Globe,* 35th Cong., 1st sess., p. 541.

25. Ibid., 35th Cong., 1st sess., p. 596.

26. There are numerous accounts of the affray. An adequate treatment can be found in the *New York Times,* Feb. 8, 1858, as well as in Ben Perley Poore, *Perley's Reminiscences of Sixty Years in the National Metropolis* (Philadelphia, 1886), 1:532–36.

27. *Erie Weekly Observer,* Feb. 13, 1858.

28. Quoted in the *Bradford Reporter,* Feb. 18, 1858.

29. *Southern Fire-Eater,* quoted in *Tioga County Agitator,* Feb. 18, 1858.

30. *Cong. Globe,* 35th Cong., 1st sess., pp. 622–23. Keitt remarked, "If any blow was directed at me, I am not conscious of it. I am at least utterly unconscious of having received any." This comment was explained to Grow as being intended to satisfy the code that required a challenge from a man if he acknowledged receiving a blow (DuBois and Mathews, *Grow,* pp. 176–77).

31. *Cong. Globe,* 35th Cong., 1st sess., pp. 622–23.

32. *New York Daily Tribune,* Feb. 11, 1858.

33. *Cong. Globe,* 35th Cong., 1st sess., p. 1075.

34. Ibid., 35th Cong., 1st sess., pp. 1103–10.

35. Ibid., 35th Cong., 1st sess., pp. 1264–65.

36. Buchanan to James W. Denver, Mar. 27, 1858, in *Works,* ed. Moore, 10: 200–02.

37. *Cong. Globe,* 35th Cong., 1st sess., pp. 1334–35.

38. *New York Daily Tribune,* Mar. 31, 1858.

39. *Cong. Globe,* 35th Cong., 1st sess., p. 1437. The Republicans believed that the only way to defeat the administration on Lecompton was to support Montgomery's amendment, which, they knew, would be rejected by the Senate (Hans L. Trefousse, *The Radical Republicans; Lincoln's Vanguard for Racial Justice* [New York, 1968], p. 119).

40. *Charleston Mercury,* Apr. 2, 1858.

41. *Cong. Globe,* 35th Cong., 1st sess., p. 1590.

42. Ibid., 35th Cong., 1st sess., p. 1857.

43. Ibid., 35th Cong., 1st sess., pp. 1880–81. Northern Democrats hoped that their compromise plan in the English bill would assure that Kansas would come in later as a free state. Buchanan favored the plan as a way to permit a vote in Kansas, but not on the resubmission of Lecompton.

44. Ibid., 35th Cong., 1st sess., pp. 1905–06. Annoyed and exhausted, the fiery Giddings exclaimed that he understood that every Douglas Democrat had pledged to stand united with the Republicans. Some of the Republicans shouted their approval. Giddings then fainted and had to be helped from the hall.

45. Grow to Charles Robinson, May 2, 1858, in Charles Robinson Papers, Kansas State Historical Society.

46. Alexander, *Sectional Stress,* pp. 97–98, 248–52.

10. *"Free Homes for Free Men"*

1. Quoted in the *Erie Weekly Observer,* Aug. 21, 1858.

2. Richardson, *Messages and Papers,* 7:3028–60.

3. *Cong. Globe,* 35th Cong., 2nd sess., pp. 612–13.

4. Ibid., 35th Cong., 2nd sess., pp. 726–27. The bill appears on p. 726.

5. *Daily Pittsburgh Dispatch,* Feb. 4, 1859.

6. See *Daily National Intelligencer* for the month of February 1859.

7. *Cong. Globe,* 35th Cong., 2nd sess., p. 1076.

8. Ibid.

9. Ibid., 35th Cong., 2nd sess., pp. 1326, 1432–33. For subsequent debate on the homestead bill, see pp. 1351–63.

10. Ibid., 35th Cong., 2nd sess., p. 1007. Only two Republicans voted against Grow's appeal.

11. Ibid., 35th Cong., 2nd sess., p. 944.

12. Ibid., 35th Cong., 2nd sess., p. 979.

13. Ibid., 35th Cong., 2nd sess., pp. 1666–67.

14. Richardson, *Messages and Papers,* 7:3083–3107.

15. *Tioga County Agitator,* Oct. 6, 1859; Stephenson, *Public Lands,* p. 222.

16. John Hutchins to Joshua Giddings, Nov. 20, 1858, in Giddings Papers, OHS.

17. J. H. Smith to Alexander Stephens, Dec. 10, 1859, in Alexander Stephens Papers, Library of Congress.

18. Martin Crawford to Alexander Stephens, Dec. 22, 1859, in Stephens Papers.

19. John Jones to Alexander Stephens, Dec. 12, 1859, in Stephens Papers.

20. Thaddeus Stevens to Joshua Giddings, Nov. 4, 1858, in Giddings Papers, OHS; H. W. Hoffman to John Covode, Nov. 15, 1859, in John Covode Papers, Historical Society of Western Pennsylvania; James Harvey to John Sherman, Oct. 31, 1859, in John Sherman Papers, Library of Congress.

21. J. W. Jones to Sherman, Nov. 7, 1859; William Mihaffey to Sherman, Nov. 14, 1859; Henry Cook to Sherman, Nov. 17, 1859, all in Sherman Papers.

22. Andrew Larner to Sherman, Mar. 12, 1859; Henry Cook to Sherman, Nov. 17, 1859, both in Sherman Papers.

23. *Cong. Globe,* 36th Cong., 1st sess., pp. 2–3; John Sherman, *Recollections of Forty Years in the House, Senate and Cabinet* (New York, 1895), 1:169. There had to be some pressure on Grow to withdraw from the speakership contest to make it easier for John Forney to become clerk of the House. Forney's friends did not support Grow, and if Grow had won, it is questionable that Forney would have been elected clerk. Republicans conceded that Forney was needed to bring anti-Lecomptonites to the side of the Republicans in their bid to organize the House. Grow's friends objected to Forney, who, in their opinion, would use his official position to support Douglas should he be the Charleston nominee (*New York Times,* Dec. 4, 1859; *Tioga County Agitator,* Dec. 15, 1859).

24. *New York Herald,* quoted in *The Weekly Press,* Feb. 11, 1860.

25. The speech delivered on Feb. 29, 1860, is printed in *Cong. Globe,* 36th Cong., 1st sess., Appendix, pp. 127–31.

26. Ibid., 36th Cong., 1st sess., p. 1115. The vote given is 115–65, though 66 nays are listed.

27. DuBois and Mathews, *Grow,* pp. 233–34.

28. *Cong. Globe,* 36th Cong., 1st sess., pp. 244–45.

29. A. R. Newsome, ed., "Letters of Lawrence O'Bryan Branch, 1856–1860," *North Carolina Historical Review* 10 (1933): 72.

30. *New York Times,* Jan. 2, 1860. Apparently Grow had arranged a plan to keep a rendezvous with Branch, somewhere near Silver Spring, Maryland, but his hackman failed to keep the secret; thus the arrest.

31. Quoted in *Southern Editorials on Secession,* ed. Dwight L. Dumond (New York, 1931), p. 59.

32. *Cong. Globe,* 36th Cong., 1st sess., pp. 1297, 1508.

33. For debate on homestead bill, see ibid., 36th Cong., 1st sess., pp. 1555–56, 1649–50, 1750–53, 1998–99, 2042–43.

34. *New York Daily Tribune,* Mar. 19, 1860.

35. *The Weekly Press,* Apr. 7, 1860.

36. *Cong. Globe,* 36th Cong., 1st sess., pp. 2462, 2477–78, 2813, 2846.

37. Ibid., 36th Cong., 1st sess., pp. 2988, 3179.

38. Ibid., 36th Cong., 1st sess., pp. 3159, 3179.

39. Quoted in the *Daily Pittsburgh Gazette,* June 25, 1860.

40. Richardson, *Messages and Papers,* 7:2965.

41. Ibid., 7:3139–45.

42. *Cong. Globe,* 36th Cong., 1st sess., pp. 3267–72.

43. Quoted in Stephenson, *Public Lands,* p. 216.

44. June 29, 1860. Also, see Stanton L. Davis, *Pennsylvania Politics* (Cleveland, 1935), pp. 48–49.

45. *New York Daily Tribune,* June 30, 1860.

46. *Cong. Globe,* 36th Cong., 1st sess., pp. 2252–53.

11. Triumph and Defeat

1. Reinhard H. Luthin, *The First Lincoln Campaign* (Cambridge, Mass., 1944), pp. 186–87.

2. Samuel Colver to John Covode, Dec. 14, 1859, in Covode Papers.

3. Grow to Horace Greeley, Sept. 13, 1860, in Horace Greeley Papers, New York Public Library.

4. *Bradford Reporter,* Oct. 18, 1860.

5. McClure, *Old Time Notes,* 1:435.

6. Going, *David Wilmot,* p. 547.

7. Grow to Abraham Lincoln, Jan. 18, 1861, in Abraham Lincoln Papers, Library of Congress.

8. McClure, *Old Time Notes,* 1:453.

9. *Cong. Globe,* 36th Cong., 2nd sess., pp. 2–3.

10. Ibid., 36th Cong., 2nd sess., p. 39.

11. Ibid., 36th Cong., 2nd sess., pp. 14–16, 23.

12. *Bradford Reporter,* Jan. 17, 1861.

13. *Cong. Globe,* 36th Cong., 2nd sess., pp. 1259, 1284–85, 1375.

14. *New York Herald,* Dec. 7, 1860.

15. Quoted in *Bradford Reporter,* Feb. 2, 1860.

16. Blaine, *Twenty Years,* 1:270.

17. *Cong. Globe,* 36th Cong., 2nd sess., pp. 484–87.

18. Tarbell Papers. Ida Tarbell makes reference to this interesting incident in her *Life of Lincoln* (New York, 1895), 2:20–21. An early biography of Houston by Marquis James, *The Raven: A Biography of Sam Houston* (Indianapolis, 1929), also refers to the mission of Giddings. In *Lincoln and His Party in the Secession Crisis* (New Haven, Conn., 1942), David Potter rejects the story on the basis that James is the *only* authority and was misinformed. M. K. Wisehart and Llerena Friend, recent biographers of Houston, have agreed that there was a George Giddings who made a secret mission for Lincoln. None of Houston's biographers mentions Grow in this connection.

19. Grow, "Curtin and Pennsylvania," pp. 473–84.

20. *The Weekly Press,* June 29, 1861.

21. Hamlin to his wife, July 4, 1861, in Hamlin Papers.

22. *Cong. Globe,* 37th Cong., 1st sess., p. 5.

23. *Pennsylvania Daily Telegraph* (Harrisburg), July 2, 1861.

24. Smith, *Schuyler Colfax,* p. 156.

25. Frank L. Klement, *The Limits of Dissent* (Lexington, Ky., 1963), p. 74.

26. McClure, *Old Time Notes,* 1:453.

27. Gideon Welles, *Diary of Gideon Welles* (New York, 1911), 1:482.

28. Salmon Chase to Lincoln, July 19, 1861, in Lincoln Papers.

29. Jean H. Baker, "A Loyal Opposition: Northern Democrats in the Thirty-seventh Congress," *Civil War History* 25 (1979): 139-55.

30. Quoted in Hubert B. Fuller, *The Speakers of the House* (Boston, 1909), p. 151.

31. *Cong. Globe,* 37th Cong., 1st sess., p. 197.

32. DuBois and Mathews, *Grow,* pp. 250, 263-64, 267.

33. Butler to Grow, Sept. 3, 1861, in Benjamin F. Butler, *Private and Official Correspondence of General Benjamin F. Butler* (Norwood, Mass., 1917), 1:237-38.

34. *New York Times,* Dec. 6, 7, 1861.

35. Erwin S. Bradley, *Simon Cameron, Lincoln's Secretary of War* (Philadelphia, 1966), p. 176.

36. DuBois and Mathews, *Grow,* pp. 264-65.

37. Letter is in ibid., pp. 243-44.

38. *Cong. Globe,* 37th Cong., 2nd sess., pp. 909-10.

39. Ibid., 37th Cong., 2nd sess., p. 1035.

40. Ibid., 37th Cong., 2nd sess., p. 1951.

41. John Hay and John G. Nicolay, eds., *Abraham Lincoln, Complete Works* (New York, 1894) 1:637.

42. Letter of May 16, 1862, in *Bradford Reporter,* May 29, 1862.

43. The act is printed in the *Cong. Globe,* 37th Cong., 2nd sess., Appendix, p. 352.

44. Leonard P. Curry, *Blueprint for Modern America; Nonmilitary Legislation of the First Civil War Congress* (Nashville, 1968), pp. 248-49.

45. *Cong. Globe,* 37th Cong., 3rd sess., pp. 830-31, 1010.

46. *House Journal of the Commonwealth of Pennsylvania,* 1862, pp. 814-15; *Journal of the Senate of the Commonwealth of Pennsylvania,* 1862, p. 382.

47. *The Luzerne Union* (Wilkes-Barre), Sept. 10, OCT. 15, 1862.

48. McClure, *Old Time Notes,* 1:557.

49. *Montrose Democrat,* Sept. 16, 1862.

50. Oct. 1, 3, 9, 1862. The peace movement was strong in Luzerne and the immigrant workers were among its supporters. See Arnold M. Shankman, *The Pennsylvania Antiwar Movement, 1861-1865* (Cranbury, N.J., 1980).

51. *Montrose Democrat,* Oct. 7, 14, 1862.

52. Ibid., Oct. 28, 1862.

53. Unpublished essay on Grow, Hempstead papers.

54. *Montrose Democrat,* Nov. 25, 1862.

55. *Bradford Reporter,* Apr. 9, 1863. It was to appease the demands of the slave oligarchy, he wrote, that the present Democratic party abandoned the principles of the old party. "The old Democracy was in favor of preserving the Territories as homes for free men; the modern Democracy would fill them with slaves."

56. *Tioga County Agitator,* quoted in *Bradford Reporter,* Nov. 6, 1862.

57. Joel H. Silbey, *A Respectable Minority: The Democratic Party in the Civil War Era 1860–1868* (New York, 1977), pp. 48–61; T. Harry Williams, *Lincoln and the Radicals* (Madison, Wis., 1969), pp. 230–62.

58. DuBois and Mathews, *Grow,* pp. 270–73.

12. The Search for a Constituency

1. Writing to Elihu Washburne on Aug. 27, 1867, Grow explained that for nearly two years he had been "rolling around in the lumber woods and about oil wells." Elihu Washburne Papers, Library of Congress.

2. For general coverage of Pennsylvania politics from 1866 to 1872, see Erwin Stanley Bradley, *The Triumph of Militant Republicanism: A Study of Pennsylvania and Presidential Elections* (Philadelphia, 1964); Frank B. Evans. *Pennsylvania Politics, 1872–1877: A Study in Political Leadership* (Harrisburg, Pa., 1966); James A. Kehl, *Boss Rule in the Guilded Age: Matt Quay of Pennsylvania* (Pittsburgh, Pa., 1981).

3. *Crawford Democrat,* Jan. 26, 1867.

4. *Tioga County Agitator,* June 12, 1867.

5. Erwin S. Bradley, "Post-Bellum Politics in Pennsylvania, 1866–1872," Ph.D. diss., Pennsylvania State University, 1952, p. 146.

6. Bradley, *Simon Cameron,* p. 284.

7. Grow to John Covode, Oct. 17, 1867, in Covode Papers.

8. *Titusville Morning Herald,* June 27, 1867. Next to the northern counties, Grow was probably most popular in the oil region of the state.

9. *Harrisburg Patriot and Union,* Feb. 1, 1868.

10. Of the three candidates before the national convention, Fenton had to be the weakest. See letters of N. Ewing to John Covode, Feb. 27, 1868; John Hayes to Covode, May 1868, both in Covode Papers.

11. *Tioga County Agitator,* Feb. 26, 1868. The editor quotes the *Joliet* (Illinois) *Republican,* which speculated that Grant and Grow would be a tough combination.

12. *Public Ledger,* Mar. 13, 1868.

13. McClure, *Old Time Notes,* 2:218.

14. The *Tioga County Agitator,* Mar. 25, 1868, referred to the selection of Curtin by the "*Signores Blitz*" as a "flagrant usurpation of popular prerogatives."

15. Quoted in *Crawford Democrat,* Apr. 4, 1868.

16. *Harrisburg Patriot and Union,* Mar. 13, 1868.

17. One opposition paper accused Grow of saber rattling by warning the voters that should they support the Democratic ticket of Seymour and Blair they would begin another Civil War; *Harrisburg Morning Patriot,* Sept. 1, 1868.

18. *Conneautville Record and Courier,* June 4, 1868.

19. E. O. Goodrich to Cameron, Dec. 23, 1868; H. Cobb to Cameron, Oct. 22, Dec. 18, 1868; G. C. Harbison to Cameron, Dec. 19, 1868; H. C. Johnson to Cameron, July 31, Aug. 20, 1868, all in Simon Cameron Papers, Library of Congress.

20. McClure, *Old Time Notes,* 2:226.

21. Carl Schurz, *Speeches, Correspondence, and Political Papers,* ed. Frederick Bancroft (New York, 1913), 2:361–62.

22. For a political biography of McClure, see William H. Russell, "A Biography of Alexander K. McClure," Ph.D. diss., University of Wisconsin, 1953. John Forney believed that, at the time of the Liberal Republican movement, no one better understood public men and offices than McClure (*Anecdotes of Public Men* [New York, 1873], p. 326).

23. *Pittsburgh Daily Gazette,* Apr. 22, 1872.

24. Henry Watterson, *Marse Henry* (New York, 1919), 1:249–50.

25. George W. Julian, *Political Recollections* (Chicago, 1884), p. 337.

26. Alexander McClure, *Our Presidents and How We Make Them* (New York, 1900), pp. 230–31.

27. McClure, *Old Time Notes,* 2:334.

28. *Crawford Journal,* July 18, 1872.

29. Published in the *Pittsburgh Daily Post,* Aug. 16, 1872.

30. *Venango Spectator,* Nov. 25, 1880.

31. *The Nation,* Aug. 15, 1872.

32. *Harper's Weekly,* Aug. 3, 1872.

33. *Pittsburgh Daily Gazette,* July 19, 1872.

34. McClure, *Old Time Notes,* 2:348–49.

13. The Warrior Returns

1. Evans, *Pennsylvania Politics,* pp. 249–51.

2. Quoted in *Crawford Journal,* Oct. 23, 1875.

3. *Montrose Democrat,* Feb. 2, 1876.

4. Quoted in ibid., Aug. 23, 1876.

5. Ibid., Sept. 6, 1876.

6. For the Grow-Hawley feud, see ibid., Aug. 23, Sept. 6, 1876.

7. Ibid., Sept. 27, 1876.

8. Quoted in *New York Times,* Mar. 24, 1878.

9. Ibid.

10. Printed in *Crawford Journal,* Feb. 14, 1878.

11. Ibid., Jan. 24, Feb. 28, Apr. 11, 1878.

12. *Scranton Republican,* Apr. 5, 1878.

13. *New York Times,* Mar. 24, 1878.

14. *Pittsburgh Telegraph,* May 16, 1878.

15. Full text in *Crawford Journal,* Aug. 22, 1878.

16. *Montrose Democrat,* Aug. 21, 1878.

17. William Evarts to Grow, Aug. 6, 1879; Grow to Evarts, Aug. 8, 1879, both in Grow Papers. It was also rumored that Grow might be offered the English mission.

18. Full text in *Crawford Journal,* July 31, 1879.

19. He claimed he had fifty-eight instructed for him (interview with Grow, *Philadelphia Press,* quoted in *Crawford Journal,* Nov. 18, 1880). Grow placed consider-

able importance on the election of state lawmakers. During the campaign, he had assured Garfield that, despite Cameron's chairmanship of the party's national committee, state Republicans would work together to win the election and secure the next state legislature (Grow to Garfield, June 30, 1880, James Garfield Papers, Library of Congress).

20. *Venango Spectator,* Nov. 11, 18, 1880.

21. *Bradford Era,* Nov. 15, 1880; *Pittsburgh Daily Post,* Dec. 25, 1880; *Venango Spectator,* Nov. 25, 1880.

22. Quoted in *Crawford Journal,* Dec. 23, 1880.

23. *Pittsburgh Evening Chronicle,* Dec. 31, 1880. According to this paper, more than 1,500 manufacturers and professional citizens endorsed Oliver's candidacy — one of the strongest popular approvals ever given to a candidate from Allegheny County. For additional biographical information, see Henry Oliver Evans, *Iron Pioneer: Henry W. Oliver* (New York, 1942).

24. *Venango Spectator,* Sept. 2, 1880.

25. *Pittsburgh Commercial Gazette,* Jan. 1, 1881.

26. *Daily Post,* Jan. 3, 1881; *Venango Spectator,* Jan. 6, 1881.

27. *The Advertiser* (Mansfield, Pa.), Feb. 16, 1881.

28. *Daily City News* (New Castle, Pa.), Jan. 6, 8, 1881; *The Western Press* (Mercer, Pa.), Jan. 7, 1881.

29. *Pittsburgh Evening Telegraph,* Jan. 14, 1881.

30. *Public Ledger,* Jan. 14, 1881.

31. *Meadville Daily Tribune,* Jan. 17, 1881.

32. Kehl, *Boss Rule,* p. 51. Others also wrote to Garfield, suggesting that he appoint Pennsylvanians including Grow to his cabinet. Charles Maples to Garfield, Jan. 31, 1881; W. H. Mason to Garfield, Dec. 22, 1880; J. M. Scovill to Garfield, Jan. 31, 1881, all in Garfield Papers.

33. A. B. Farouker to Cameron, Jan. 18, 1881, Cameron Papers.

34. *Titusville Weekly Herald,* Jan. 20, 1881.

35. *New York Times,* Jan. 18, 1881; *Harrisburg Daily Patriot,* Jan. 19, 1881.

36. The make-up of the legislature was as follows: 154 Republicans, 92 Democrats, 2 National Greenbacks, 1 Greenback Democrat, 1 Fusion (*Smull's Legislative Handbook* [1881], pp. 674, 686).

37. *New York Times,* Jan. 25, 1881.

38. *Daily Patriot,* Feb. 11, 1881.

39. Ibid., Feb. 10, 1881.

40. Ibid.

41. *Crawford Journal,* Mar. 4, 1881. Writing to Beaver on Aug. 21, 1882, Henry Caton commented that Mitchell was not considered an independent in Tioga, but only a compromise candidate (Caton to Beaver, James Addams Beaver Papers, Pennsylvania State University). S. A. Davenport of Erie believed that Beaver would have been nominated had it not been for the ambitious Wolfe (Davenport to Beaver, May 10, 1882, in Beaver Papers).

42. Quoted in *Crawford Journal,* Feb. 25, 1881.

43. Ibid., Mar. 4, 1881.

14. Congressman-at-Large: The Last Hurrah

1. *Daily Patriot,* Apr. 15, 1884; *Erie Morning Dispatch,* Apr. 15, 1884.

2. *Daily Patriot,* Apr. 14, 17, 1884. For a number of years Grow had been interested in coal mines in the vicinity of East Brady, Clarion County. The Brady's Bend Mining Company opened the first mine in 1878, just above the town, under the direction of Grow. The Hardscrabble mines were owned and operated by Grow and Hartwell.

3. Ibid., Apr. 29, 1884.

4. Grow to Washburne, May 17, 1884, in Alexander G. Washburn Autograph Collection, Massachusetts Historical Society.

5. Quoted in the *Daily Patriot,* June 6, 1884.

6. McClure, *Old Time Notes,* 2:588. Grow claimed that the organization did not promptly decide to crush his candidacy because at the time of Lilly's death, Quay was fishing in Florida (DuBois and Mathews, *Grow,* p. 279).

7. A good write-up of the Republican state convention appears in the *Tri-Weekly Journal* (Susquehanna, Pa.), Jan. 4, 1894.

8. *Meadville Daily Republican,* Jan. 4, 1894. Other leading newspapers that endorsed Grow included the *Harrisburg Telegraph, Scranton Republican,* and the *Pittsburgh Gazette.*

9. *Pittsburgh Times,* quoted in *Meadville Messenger,* May 31, 1894.

10. *Montrose Democrat,* Dec. 15, 1893; Jan. 19, 1894.

11. *Smull's Legislative Handbook* (1895), pp. 425–26.

12. *Congressional Record,* 52nd Cong., 1st sess., p. 505.

13. Ibid., 53rd Cong., 2nd sess., pp. 2705–2706.

14. Ibid., 53rd Cong., 2nd sess., pp. 5932–38, 7714.

15. With other Republicans, Grow voted against the amended bill. For a thorough discussion of the Democratic tariff of 1894, see Edward Stanwood, *American Tariff Controversies in the Nineteenth Century* (New York, 1903), 2:296–359.

16. *Cong. Record,* 53rd Cong., 3rd sess., p. 1515.

17. *Smull's Legislative Handbook* (1895), pp. 435–36. After his victory in 1898, Grow boasted to his good friend DuBois that his next term would complete a stretch of fifty years in Congress — a record he did not think would ever be broken (Grow to DuBois, Dec. 3, 1898, in Grow Papers).

18. *Cong. Record,* 54th Cong., 2nd sess., pp. 29–31.

19. Ibid., 57th Cong., 2nd sess., pp. 201–203.

20. *Washington Post,* cited in *Crawford Journal,* Jan. 23, 1896.

21. *Cong. Record,* 55th Cong., 2nd sess., p. 3439.

22. Ibid., 55th Cong., 2nd sess., p. 4734.

23. Ibid., 57th Cong., 1st sess., pp. 5580–82. In his remarks, Grow spoke disparagingly of a class of cruel Asiatics who have always engaged in barbarities in time of war. These "barbarous elements," he contended, did not exist anywhere outside Asian civilization. Being in favor of "Asia for the Asians," he approved of Chinese exclusion and American immigration laws that kept out Asians. Interviewed by Ida Tarbell in 1898, Grow exclaimed that he did not fear that America could not

govern the Philippines. "They are not so bad as the Indians and they can't be worse than the Negroes" (Tarbell Papers).

24. *Cong. Record,* 57th Cong., 1st sess., pp. 240–42.

25. Cited in *Crawford Journal,* Mar. 12, 1903.

26. Quoted in DuBois and Mathews, *Grow,* p. 281.

27. A number of newspapers covered this story. See *New York Times,* Apr. 11, 1907; *Montrose Democrat,* Apr. 11, 18, May 9, 1907; *Independent Republican* (Montrose, Pa.), May 17, 1907; *New York American,* Oct. 17, 1909.

28. The securities held by Grow consisted of railroad bonds, including those of the Houston and Texas Central and the Albany and Susquehanna. In scribbled notes Grow describes the events as they occurred from day to day (manuscript in Grow Papers).

29. DuBois tells his story in the *Independent Republican,* May 17, 1907, and the *Montrose Democrat,* May 23, 1907.

30. Relevant documents to this case are in the Grow Papers.

Bibliography

Archival Collections

GOVERNMENT DOCUMENTS

United States Congress. House of Representatives. Committee on Territories. 34th Congress. Papers. Record Group 233, National Archives, Washington, D.C.

MANUSCRIPTS

Diary of Charles F. Adams. Massachusetts Historical Society, Boston.
Nathaniel Banks MSS. Library of Congress.
James Addams Beaver MSS. Pennsylvania State University Library, University Park.
William Bigler MSS. Historical Society of Pennsylvania, Philadelphia.
James Buchanan MSS. Library of Congress.
Charles R. Buckalew MSS. Library of Congress.
Simon Cameron MSS. Library of Congress.
Schuyler Colfax MSS. Library of Congress.
John Covode MSS. Library of Congress.
———. Library and Archives, Historical Society of Western Pennsylvania, Pittsburgh.
John Dick MSS. Crawford County Historical Society, Meadville, Pa.
James Garfield, MSS. Library of Congress.
Joshua Giddings MSS. Ohio Historical Society, Columbus.
Joshua Giddings–George Julian MSS. Library of Congress.
Simon Gratz Collection. Historical Society of Pennsylvania, Philadelphia.
Horace Greeley MSS. New York Public Library.
Galusha A. Grow MSS. Susquehanna County Historical Society, Montrose, Pa.
———. A few items in Amherst College Archives, Amherst, Mass.
Hannibal Hamlin MSS. Library of Congress.

Ernest Hempstead MSS. Crawford County Historical Society, Meadville, Pa.

Andrew Johnson MSS. Library of Congress.

Abraham Lincoln MSS. Library of Congress.

Edward McPherson MSS. Library of Congress.

Charles Robinson MSS. Manuscripts Department, Kansas State Historical Society, Topeka.

John Sherman MSS. Library of Congress.

Alexander Stephens MSS. Library of Congress.

Thaddeus Stevens MSS. Library of Congress.

Ida Tarbell MSS. Special Collections, Pelletier Library, Allegheny College, Meadville, Pa.

Lyman Trumbull MSS. Library of Congress.

Alexander G. Washburn Autograph Collection, Elihu Washburne MSS. Massachusetts Historical Society.

Elihu Washburne MSS. Library of Congress.

David Wilmot MSS. Bradford County Historical Society, Towanda, Pa.

Legislative Records and Handbooks

UNITED STATES

American State Papers: Public Lands
Annals of the Congress of the United States, 1789–1824
Congressional Globe
Congressional Record
Journal of House of Representatives

PENNSYLVANIA

Journal of the House of Representatives
Journal of the Senate
Laws of the General Assembly of the Commonwealth of Pennsylvania
Smull's Legislative Handbook

Newspapers

The newspapers, including microfilm reproductions, are located in the Library of Congress, Pennsylvania State Library, Carnegie Library of Pittsburgh, University of Pittsburgh Library, and the Crawford County Historical Society.

PENNSYLVANIA

Bradford *Era*
Brookville *Jefferson Star*

Conneautville   *Conneautville Courier*
                Record and Courier
Erie   *Erie Weekly Observer*
       Erie Morning Dispatch
Franklin   *Venango Spectator*
Greensburg   *The Pennsylvania Argus*
Harrisburg   *Daily Patriot*
             Democratic Union
             Keystone
             Morning Patriot
             Patriot and Union
             Pennsylvania Daily Telegraph
Johnstown   *Cambria Tribune*
Lewisburg   *Lewisburg Chronicle*
Linesville   *The Linesville Herald*
Mansfield   *The Advertiser*
Meadville   *Crawford Democrat*
            Crawford Journal
            Meadville Daily Republican
            Meadville Messenger
            The Spirit of the Age
Mercer   *The Western Press*
Montrose   *Independent Republican*
           Montrose Democrat
           Northern Democrat
           The Susquehanna Register
New Castle   *City News*
Philadelphia   *Public Ledger*
               Public Ledger and Daily Transcript
Pittsburgh   *Commercial Gazette*
             Daily Pittsburgh Gazette
             Daily Post
             Evening Chronicle
             Pittsburgh Daily Gazette and Advertiser
             Pittsburgh Telegraph
Susquehanna   *Tri-Weekly Journal*
Towanda   *Bradford Reporter*
Wellsboro   *The Tioga Eagle*
            Tioga County Agitator
Wilkes-Barre   *Luzerne Democrat*
               The Luzerne Union

OTHER STATES

Baltimore   *The Sun*
Boston   *The Liberator*
Charleston, S.C.   *Charleston Mercury*

Jackson, Miss.   *Mississippi Palladium*
New York   *Champion of Freedom*
          New York American
          New York Daily Times
          New York Daily Tribune
          New York Times
          New York Weekly Tribune
Richmond, Va.   *Richmond Enquirer*
Washington, D.C.   *Daily National Intelligencer*
          The National Era
          Washington Union
Wilmington, N.C.   *Daily Journal*

Books

Alexander, Thomas B. *Sectional Stress and Party Strength: A Study of Roll-Call Voting Patterns in the United States House of Representatives, 1836–1860*. Nashville, 1967.

Benedict, Michael L. *A Compromise of Principle: Congressional Republicans and Reconstruction, 1863–1869*. New York, 1974.

Benton, Thomas Hart. *Thirty Years View*. 2 vols. New York, 1854.

Blaine, James C. *Twenty Years of Congress*. 2 vols. Norwich, 1884–1886.

Blue, Frederick J. *The Free Soilers: Third Party Politics, 1848–54*. Urbana, Ill. 1973.

Bogue, Allan G. "Some Dimensions of Power in the Thirty-Seventh Senate." In *The Dimensions of Quantitative Research in History*, ed. William Aydedotte, Allan G. Bogue, Robert William Fogel. Princeton, N.J. 1972.

Bradley, Erwin Stanley. "Post-Bellum Politics in Pennsylvania, 1866–1872," Ph.D. diss., Pennsylvania State University, 1952.

———. *The Triumph of Militant Republicanism: A Study of Pennsylvania and Presidential Politics*. Philadelphia, 1964.

———. *Simon Cameron, Lincoln's Secretary of War*. Philadelphia, 1966.

Buchanan, James. *Works of James Buchanan*. Ed. John B. Moore, 12 vols. New York, 1960.

Butler, Benjamin F. *Private and Official Correspondence of General Benjamin F. Butler*. Ed. Jesse A. Marshall. 5 vols. Norwood, Mass., 1917.

Calhoun, John C. *The Works of John C. Calhoun*. Ed. Richard L. Cralle. 6 vols. New York, 1854.

Chase, Salmon. *Diary and Correspondence of Salmon P. Chase,* in *Annual Report of the American Historical Association*. 2 vols. Washington, D.C., 1902.

Coleman, John F. *The Disruption of the Pennsylvania Democracy, 1848–1860*. Harrisburg, 1975.

Crippen, Lee F. *Simon Cameron, Ante-Bellum Years*. Oxford, Ohio, 1942.

Curry, Leonard P. *Blueprint for Modern America: Nonmilitary Legislation of the First Civil War Congress*. Nashville, 1968.

Davis, Stanton L. "Pennsylvania Politics, 1860–1863," Ph.D. diss., Western Reserve University, 1935.

DeVoto, Bernard. *The Year of Decision, 1846.* Boston, 1942.

Dick, Everett. *The Lure of the Land.* Lincoln, 1970.

Douglas, Stephen A. *The Letters of Stephen A. Douglas.* Ed. Robert W. Johannsen. Urbana, Ill., 1961.

Douglass, Frederick. *The Life and Writings of Frederick Douglass.* Ed. Philip S. Foner. New York, 1950.

DuBois, James T., and Mathews, Gertrude S. *Galusha A. Grow, Father of the Homestead Act.* New York, 1917.

Dumond, Dwight L., ed. *Southern Editorials on Secession.* New York, 1931.

Egle, William, ed. *Andrew Gregg Curtin: His Life and Services.* Philadelphia, 1895.

Eiselen, Malcolm R. *The Rise of Pennsylvania Protectionism.* Philadelphia, 1932.

Evans, Frank B. *Pennsylvania Politics, 1872–1877: A Study in Political Leadership.* Harrisburg, Pa., 1966.

Evans, Henry Oliver, *Iron Pioneer: Henry W. Oliver.* New York, 1942.

Fitzhugh, George. *Sociology for the South.* Richmond, Va., 1854.

Foner, Eric. *Free Soil, Free Labor, Free Men.* New York, 1970.

Forney, John. *Anecdotes of Public Men.* New York, 1873.

Fuller, Hubert B. *The Speakers of the House.* Boston, 1909.

Giddings, Joshua. *History of the Rebellion: Its Authors and Causes.* New York, 1864.

Going, Charles Buxton. *David Wilmot, Free-Soiler: A Biography of the Great Advocate of the Wilmot Proviso.* New York, 1924.

Hibbard, Benjamin H. *A History of the Public Land Policies.* New York, 1924.

Holt, Michael F. *Forging a Majority: The Formation of the Republican Party in Pittsburgh, 1848–1860.* New Haven, Conn., 1969.

————. *The Political Crisis of the 1850s.* New York, 1978.

Isley, Jeter A. *Horace Greeley and the Republican Party, 1853–1861.* Princeton, N.J., 1947.

Jenkins, John S. *The Life of Silas Wright.* Alburn, N.Y., 1847.

Johannsen, Robert W. *Stephen A. Douglas.* New York, 1973.

Johnson, Ludwell H. *Division and Reunion: America 1848–1877.* New York, 1978.

Julian, George W. *Political Recollections.* Chicago, 1884.

Kehl, James. *Boss Rule in the Gilded Age: Matt Quay of Pennsylvania.* Pittsburgh, Pa., 1981.

Klein, Philip S. *President James Buchanan: A Biography.* University Park, Pa., 1962.

Klement, Frank L. *The Limits of Dissent: Clement L. Vallandigham and the Civil War.* Lexington, Mass., 1970.

Korngold, Ralph. *Thaddeus Stevens.* New York, 1955.

Lincoln, Abraham. *Abraham Lincoln, Complete Works.* Ed. John Hay and John Nicolay. 2 vols. New York, 1894.

Luthin, Reinhard H. *The First Lincoln Campaign.* Cambridge, Mass. 1944.

McClure, Alexander K. *Old Time Notes of Pennsylvania*. 2 vols. Philadelphia, 1905.

———. *Our Presidents and How We Make Them*. New York, 1900.

Mohr, James C., ed. *Radical Republicans in the North: State Politics during Reconstruction*. Baltimore, 1976.

Morrison, Chaplain. *Democratic Politics and Sectionalism*. Chapel Hill, N.C., 1967.

Myers, C. Maxwell. "The Rise of the Republican Party in Pennsylvania, 1854–1860," Ph.D. diss., University of Pittsburgh, 1940.

Nevins, Allan. *Ordeal of the Union*. 2 vols. New York, 1947.

Nichols, Roy F. *The Democratic Machine, 1850–1854*. New York, 1923.

———. *Franklin Pierce, Young Hickory of the Granite Hills*. Philadelphia, 1931.

———. *The Disruption of American Democracy*. New York, 1948.

Polk, James. *The Diary of James K. Polk*. Ed. M. M. Quaife. 4 vols. Chicago, 1910.

Poore, Benjamin Perley. *Perley's Reminiscences of Sixty Years in the National Metropolis*. 2 vols. Philadelphia, 1886.

Potter, David M. *Lincoln and His Party in the Secession Crisis*. New Haven, 1942.

———. *The South and the Sectional Conflict*. Baton Rouge, 1968.

———. *The Impending Crisis, 1848–1861*. New York, 1976.

Rayback, Joseph G. *Free Soil, The Election of 1848*. Lexington, Mass., 1970.

Richardson, James D., ed. *A Compilation of the Messages and Papers of the Presidents*. 20 vols. New York, 1897–1917.

Robbins, Roy M. *Our Landed Heritage*. Princeton, N.J., 1942.

Rozwenc, Edwin C., ed. *The Causes of the American Civil War*. Lexington, Mass., 1972.

Russell, William H. "A Biography of Alexander K. McClure," Ph.D. diss., University of Wisconsin, 1953.

Schurz, Carl. *Speeches, Correspondence, and Political Papers*. Ed. Frederick Bancroft. New York, 1913.

Sellers, Charles. *James K. Polk, Continentalist, 1843–1846*. Princeton, N.J., 1966.

Sewell, Richard H. *John P. Hale and the Politics of Abolition*. Cambridge, Mass., 1965.

Shankman, Arnold M. *The Pennsylvania Antiwar Movement, 1861–1865*. Cranbury, N.J., 1980.

Sherman, John. *Recollections of Forty Years in the House, Senate and Cabinet*. 2 vols. New York, 1895.

Silbey, Joel H. *The Shrine of Party: Congressional Voting Behavior, 1841–1852*. Pittsburgh, 1967.

———. *A Respectable Minority: The Democratic Party in the Civil War Era, 1860–1868*. New York, 1977.

Smith, Elbert B. *The Presidency of James Buchanan*. Lawrence, Kans., 1975.

Smith, Willard H. *Schuyler Colfax*. Indianapolis, 1952.

Spencer, Donald. *Louis Kossuth and Young America: A Study of Sectionalism and Foreign Policy, 1848–1852*. Columbia, Mo., 1977.

Stampp, Kenneth M. *The Imperiled Union.* New York, 1980.

Stanwood, Edward. *American Tariff Controversies in the Nineteenth Century.* New York, 1903.

Stephens, Alexander. *A Constitutional View of the Late War between the States.* Philadelphia, 1870.

Stephenson, George M. *The Political History of the Public Lands, 1840–1862.* Boston, 1917.

Toombs, Robert. *The Correspondence of Robert Toombs, Alexander H. Stephens, and Howell Cobb,* in *Annual Report of the American Historical Association for the Year 1911,* ed. U. B. Phillips. 2 vols. Washington, D.C., 1913.

Trefousse, Hans L. *The Radical Republicans: Lincoln's Vanguard for Racial Justice.* New York, 1968.

Watterson, Henry. *Marse Henry.* New York, 1919.

Welles, Gideon. *Diary of Gideon Welles.* Intro. John T. Morse. 3 vols. New York, 1911.

Williams, Harry T. *Lincoln and the Radicals.* Madison, Wis., 1969.

Selected Articles

Anderson, David L. "Anson Burlingame: Reformer and Diplomat." *Civil War History* 25 (1979): 293–308.

Baker, Jean H. "A Loyal Opposition: Northern Democrats in the Thirty-seventh Congress." *Civil War History* 25 (1979): 139–55.

Curry, Leonard. "Congressional Democrats, 1861–1863." *Civil War History* 12 (1966): 213–29.

Dodd, William E. "The Fight for the Northwest, 1860." *American Historical Review* 16 (1911): 774–88.

Foner, Eric. "The Wilmot Proviso Revisited." *Journal of American History* 56 (1969): 262–79.

―――――. "The Causes of the Civil War: Recent Interpretations and New Directions." *Civil War History* 20 (1974): 197–214.

Gates, Paul W. "The Homestead Law in an Incongruous Land System." *American Historical Review* 41 (1936): 652–81.

―――――. "Western Opposition to the Agricultural College Act." *Indiana Magazine of History* 37 (1941): 103–36.

Harrington, Fred H. "The First Northern Victory." *Journal of Southern History* 5 (1939): 186–205.

Holt, Michael. "The Politics of Impatience: The Origins of Know Nothingism." *Journal of American History* 55 (1973): 309–31.

Ilisevich, Robert D. "The Formation of the Republican Party in Erie and Crawford Counties, 1846–1856." *Journal of Erie Studies* 2 (1973): 309–31.

Marshall, Schuyler. "The Free Democratic Convention of 1852." *Pennsylvania History* 12 (1955): 146–67.

Maxey, Edwin. "Galusha A. Grow, Father of the Homestead Bill." *Overland Monthly* 52 (1908): 75.

Montgomery, David. "Radical Republicanism in Pennsylvania, 1866–1873." *Pennsylvania Magazine of History and Biography* 85 (1961): 439–57.

Newsome, A. R., ed., "Letters of Lawrence O'Bryan Branch, 1856–1860." *North Carolina Historical Review* 10 (1933): 44–79.

Nichols, Roy F. "The Kansas–Nebraska Act: A Century of Historiography." *Mississippi Valley Historical Review* 43 (1956): 187–212.

Osofsky, Gilbert. "Abolitionists, Irish Immigrants, and the Dilemmas of Romantic Nationalism." *American Historical Review* 80 (1975): 889–912.

Perkins, Howard C. "A Neglected Phase of the Movement for Southern Unity, 1847–1852." *Journal of Southern History* 12 (1946): 153–203.

Shannon, Fred A. "The Homestead Act and the Labor Surplus." *American Historical Review* 41 (1936): 637–51.

Solomon, Irwin D. "The Grass Roots Appearance of a National Party: The Formation of the Republican Party in Erie, Pennsylvania, 1852–1856." *Western Pennsylvania Historical Magazine* 66 (1983): 209–22.

Wakelyn, Jon L. "Party Issues and Political Strategy of the Charleston Taylor Democrats of 1848." *South Carolina Historical Magazine* 73 (1972): 72–86.

Wilson, Rufus R. "Personal Recollections of Honorable Galusha A. Grow." *Saturday Evening Post,* Jan. 19, Mar. 2, 1901.

Index